Practicing Forensic Criminology

Practicing Forensic Criminology

Kevin Fox Gotham

Daniel Bruce Kennedy

ACADEMIC PRESS

An imprint of Elsevier

Academic Press is an imprint of Elsevier
125 London Wall, London EC2Y 5AS, United Kingdom
525 B Street, Suite 1650, San Diego, CA 92101, United States
50 Hampshire Street, 5th Floor, Cambridge, MA 02139, United States
The Boulevard, Langford Lane, Kidlington, Oxford OX5 1GB, United Kingdom

Notices
Knowledge and best practice in this field are constantly changing. As new research and experience broaden our understanding, changes in research methods, professional practices, or medical treatment may become necessary.

Practitioners and researchers must always rely on their own experience and knowledge in evaluating and using any information, methods, compounds, or experiments described herein. In using such information or methods they should be mindful of their own safety and the safety of others, including parties for whom they have a professional responsibility.

To the fullest extent of the law, neither the Publisher nor the authors, contributors, or editors, assume any liability for any injury and/or damage to persons or property as a matter of products liability, negligence or otherwise, or from any use or operation of any methods, products, instructions, or ideas contained in the material herein.

Library of Congress Cataloging-in-Publication Data
A catalog record for this book is available from the Library of Congress

British Library Cataloguing-in-Publication Data
A catalogue record for this book is available from the British Library

ISBN 978-0-12-815595-0

For information on all Academic Press publications
visit our website at https://www.elsevier.com/books-and-journals

Publisher: Stacy Masucci
Acquisition Editor: Elizabeth Brown
Editorial Project Manager: Leticia M. Lima
Project Manager: Anitha Sivaraj
Cover Designer: Christian J. Bilbow

Typeset by SPi Global, India

Working together
to grow libraries in
developing countries

www.elsevier.com • www.bookaid.org

Contents

Acknowledgments

Writing this book has been a rewarding experience, not least because of the chance to engage the work of many excellent forensic social scientists, researchers, and scholars. Many of them appear in the following pages in the citations and the references, as they played an influential role in the development of our ideas. We owe a great deal of thanks to several people who helped make this book possible through their support, encouragement, and comments at various stages. We would first like to thank the staff of the Howard-Tilton Memorial Library and the Law Library at Tulane University for their help in locating court records and assisting with data collection and analysis. During the course of writing and research, we benefited from the support of the Carol Lavin Bernick Faculty Grant program at Tulane University. We thank the Tulane University Institutional Review Board (IRB) for reviewing our materials and determining that our research does not constitute "human subjects research" as defined by federal regulations (IRB Reference #:2018-1404). As such, IRB approval was not required. To protect the confidentiality of people and places, we have either avoided using names or employed pseudonyms.

Special thanks are due to individuals whose goodwill and assistance helped sustain us on the hard work of writing this book. First, we would like to thank the people who commented on the proposal for the book: Stephen Morewitz, Dennis Savard, and Thomas Kelley. The feedback and comments these reviewers shared were particularly helpful to us in honing our ideas and sharpening our insights. We owe them an immense debt of gratitude. We also like to thank Madeline Jascha, Jose Batalla, Jonathan Campi, Megan Faust, and Hannah Sansone for their copy editing assistance. At Elsevier Press, Anitha Sivaraj, Elizabeth Brown, Andrea Gallego Ortiz, and Letícia Melo Garcia de Lima provided invaluable guidance and suggestions at different stages of the editorial process: many thanks for the advice and for the opportunity to work with such an awesome and dedicated group of people.

Finally, we would like to thank our families. Kevin would like to thank his wife Adele and daughters Audrey and Alex. During the time this book was written, Adele patiently endured alternating bouts of writer's block and furious work and, as always, her love is endless inspiration. Thank you to Audrey and Alex for welcome interruption, rejuvenating distraction, and constant joy and humor. Without the aid and support of family, the job of writing this book would have been more difficult.

Dan has much to be thankful for in this life, particularly his wife Shirley and daughters, Kelley and Katie. Kelley and Jason blessed him with grandson Connor and granddaughter Skylar. Katie and Tony blessed him with grandsons Aidan, Blake, and Chase. Dan also wishes to express his appreciation to Terry Myers for his friendship and advice over the years and to Tom Hupp, Chuck Bartley, Dennis Savard, Erika St. Angelo Rohde, and Cecil Scott for their camaraderie, forensic insights, and technical assistance during our many years of casework together. Finally, Jay Meehan is gratefully acknowledged for creating the criminal justice program at Oakland University which has been Dan's academic home for the past several years.

INTRODUCTION TO THE PRACTICE OF FORENSIC CRIMINOLOGY

1

INTRODUCTION

The word forensic comes from the Latin term, *forensis*, which means "forum," the place where citizens and leaders conducted trials and held political debates in ancient Roman times. In modern times, researchers and practitioners have applied the term forensic to a corpus of knowledge useful to the courts in the resolution of conflicts within a legal context. In some academic centers, *forensic studies* have come to mean the art or study of argumentative discourse, while other disciplines emphasize the legal and judicial aspects of forensics. *Forensic science* is the application of the scientific method to criminal and civil laws as governed by the legal standards of admissible evidence and criminal procedure (Iacono et al., 2002; Osterburg and Ward, 2010). Forensic science encompasses varied forms of scientific knowledge and evidence used by the courts to solve crimes and adjudicate legal disputes. Some researchers conflate forensic science with criminalistics—the analysis and testing of physical evidence in a crime lab for the purpose of crime detection (DeForest et al., 1983; Gilbert, 1986; Saferstein, 2001). Others draw a firm distinction between the two and argue that criminalistics is a loose collection of nonscience forensic techniques (Saks and Faigman, 2008). Over the last several decades, forensic science has become a major agent of interdisciplinarity, a field that is constantly expanding to include many additional areas of specialization and expertise used by the courts to solve crimes and adjudicate legal disputes (James and Nordby, 2003, p. xvi). Today, forensic science crosses numerous disciplinary fields and now includes the burgeoning subfields of forensic engineering, forensic cybertechnology, forensic economics, forensic photography, forensic radiology, forensic accounting, forensic anthropology, forensic psychology, and forensic sociology, among others.

Interest in the interactions of crime, criminology, and forensic science has experienced a virtual explosion in recent years. Books by Petherick and colleagues (2010) and Williams (2014) provide broad overviews of topics related to the subject matter of theoretical and applied criminology, forensic casework and investigation, and the law. Savard and Kennedy (2017) note that criminological theories, methods, and analytical techniques are not discipline specific but cross many different social science fields including sociology, psychology, and anthropology. Turvey and Petherick (2010, p. 3) define forensic criminology as "the scientific study of crime and criminals for the purpose of addressing investigative and legal questions." This generalist definition encompasses applied aspects of criminal investigation, forensic mental health, and forensic science (crime reconstruction and criminalistics). A major assumption is that forensic criminology is a science concerned with the analysis of crime and criminality with the intent and purpose to assist with "investigations, administrative inquiries, legal proceedings or providing expert findings or testimony" (p. xxi). Williams (2014, p. 9) defines forensic criminology as "the applied use of scientific and criminological research and analytical techniques for the purposes of addressing proactive and reactive investigative work, and for aiding legal cases and issues." Williams' definition has the same elements as outlined by Turvey and Petherick and includes four core areas: scientific research and techniques, criminological research, proactive and reactive investigative work, and legal issues. Williams prefers a broad definition since "[c]riminology does not simply deal with crime and horrific acts of behaviour against human beings; it also has to deal with a broad gamut of social problems"—from poverty and inequality, discrimination, substance misuse, violence, and mental illness.

In our book, we draw on examples from actual court cases and expert witness reports and testimony to demonstrate the different roles forensic criminologists can play in the courts. We detail the uses of criminological theories, methodologies, data analytic techniques, and literature reviews in the applied setting of civil law and the courts. We show how expert witnesses can apply their research and testifying skills to assist judges and juries in rendering legal decisions. The term "expert witness" has a specific meaning in legal proceedings. An expert witness is a person accepted by the judge or hearing officer as being qualified to make judgments and offer conclusions in the area of her or his expertise. The expert witness plays an important role in the U.S. system of jurisprudence. Courts may rely on expert witness investigations and testimony in civil and criminal cases to explain scientific matters and provide their opinions to jurors and judges to interpret the facts of a case. Standards of admissibility for expert testimony vary depending on state and federal rules of procedure and evidence. Expert witnesses must have knowledge, skill, experience, training, or education to assist the judge and jury in understanding the evidence and facts of a case. We draw from real life expert witness investigations to describe the rich and varied experience of forensic criminology in the courts and illustrate how criminology can reach beyond the academy to influence legal proceedings. In doing so, we seek to strengthen the scientific foundation of applied criminological research and improve the quality of forensic social scientific research in the legal system.

If we view criminology as the scientific study of the etiology, patterns, and control of crime, then when this type of information becomes useful to the courts, we are then describing forensic criminology. For us, the scope of forensic criminology includes the application of criminological knowledge before the courts which includes the scientific study of lawmaking, criminal violations of the law, and societal reactions to the breaking of law. At the same time, we draw a firm distinction between forensic criminology and criminalistics which is a loose collection of nonscience forensic techniques and practices such as fingerprint analysis, handwriting analysis, document examination, pattern recognition, eyewitness analysis, arson analysis, and trace evidence. In addition, the main object of analysis for the forensic criminologist is neither the offender nor the victim per se but the criminal event. Scholars tend to divide theories of crime into those theories that seek to explain the development of criminal offenders and those that seek to explain the development of criminal events. Theories of and research on offenders have been dominant in the development of criminology (Clarke, 1980; for an overview, see Wilcox and Cullen, 2018). Most research on crime and crime prevention has been focused on why certain types of people commit crime and what we can do about them.

In contrast, the forensic criminologist uses criminological theory to organize data collection and analysis toward the specific goal of understanding the causes of the criminal event. Thus, any analysis and explanation of how and why a crime happens will need to account where and when it happens. The analytical focus on how and why criminal events occur at particular places is not unique or specific to forensic criminology. What is unique to forensic criminology is the application of scientific knowledge and evidence to address research questions about crime events for legal purposes. Also of concern is whether a criminal event could have been prevented and if so how. We will explore these issues throughout the book.

GOALS AND OBJECTIVES

Our book has three basic goals. Our first goal is to introduce readers to the significance and impact of forensic social science investigations in the legal system. Forensic criminology books by Williams and Petherick and colleagues are important because of the broad and interdisciplinary perspectives they bring to the study of the interactions of forensic science and crime. A major contribution of our book is to build on the foundational value of these books by drawing on specific examples of social science investigations in the forensic realms of premises liability, administrative negligence, workplace violence, wrongful conviction litigation, and litigation involving police and corrections facilities. Our chapters include excerpts from actual forensic investigations and expert witness reports, in-depth discussions of the methodological and analytical bases of these investigations, and important lessons learned from actual litigation cases. By engaging and analyzing expert witness reports, we aim to describe the nature and role of expert forensic testimony and the impact of criminological theory and methods in the U.S. legal system. The expert witness reports we analyze reveal how forensic criminologists can carry out basic and practice-oriented research, conduct evaluations, assist in policy analysis, and prepare and provide expert testimony before the courts.

Our second goal is to demonstrate the usefulness of forensic criminology as a research tool that can reveal novel relational dynamics among crime events and the larger socio-spatial context. In the preface to *Forensic Criminology*, Turvey and Petherick (2010, p. xx) advocate for a criminology that is a "forensic behavioral science," a perspective that focuses on the actions, choices, psychology, and personality of criminals to answer investigative and legal questions. While our social science perspective has obvious intersections with this psychological-oriented position, our forensic work is informed by theoretical and empirical research in environmental criminology, routine activities theory, situational crime prevention approaches, crime prevention through environment design (CPTED), situational opportunity perspectives, crime pattern theory, and place management theory (Atlas, 2013; Brantingham and Brantingham, 1981; Cohen and Felson, 1979; Roncek and Maier, 1991; Sherman, 1995; Sherman et al., 1989; Clarke, 1983; Cozens and Love, 2015; Wilcox and Cullen, 2018). While diverse in their topics and investigative orientations, many of the expert witness reports we draw on examine criminal behavior as significantly influenced by the nature of the immediate environment in which it occurs. This environmental perspective assumes that individual action and behavior including crime events result from a person-situation interaction. The environment is not just a passive backdrop for crime but plays a central role in providing opportunities for crime, constraining criminal actions, and initiating a criminal event and shaping its course and consequences.

Our third goal is to advance the development of a "translational criminology"—that is, the translation of knowledge from criminological theory and research to forensic practice—as an expedient to forming robust interactive relationships among criminological social scientists and policy makers. Proponents of translational criminology have lamented the rigid institutional and cultural barriers between basic and applied research and have called for creating a dynamic interface between research and practice (Coble and Scott, 2017; Henning and Stewart, 2015; Stevenson et al., 2013). This interactive process involves the work of scientists in the discovery of new tools/ideas for use in the field and the evaluation of their impact. In turn, practitioners can offer novel observations from the field that stimulate basic investigations and catalyze public policy reform. At the nexus of science and practice is the knowledge creation process. To achieve our goal of a translational criminology, we describe the different roles and activities of the practicing forensic criminologist in the legal system with an eye toward improving the translation of forensic knowledge, theory, and methods into policy and practice. The translation of knowledge from research to policy and practice is a varied, dynamic, and sequential process in criminal justice. As we see it, practicing forensic criminology can be a vehicle for translating otherwise abstract and academic criminological theories into concrete applications in the legal realm as well as fostering greater interest among students to begin thinking forensically.

In short, we demonstrate through empirical examples—for example, expert witness investigations and testimony—how forensic work can be an effective mechanism for transferring research knowledge to influence public policy reform. That is, we provide examples of how actual forensic criminological research can provide both knowledge and opinions to the courts that can, in turn, lead to policy reforms that benefit communities and society. Relatedly, we illustrate, using actual case studies, the value of substantive knowledge a forensic criminologist can offer judge, jury, and attorneys in deciding cases. We believe criminological theories, knowledge, and methods can help judges and juries render their decisions more efficiently and can also help lawyers craft their arguments more tightly and persuasively, secure in the knowledge there is foundation in the social sciences for many of their arguments. In order to render such a service, however, the forensic criminologist needs to understand his or her role in the civil litigation process, the major case law that controls it, and the rules governing the admissibility of expert testimony. Although a forensic criminologist will testify in only a small percentage of cases, given that most cases will settle out of court, he or she must be prepared to enter the courtroom should such testimony be required.

ROLES OF THE PRACTICING FORENSIC CRIMINOLOGIST IN THE U.S. COURT SYSTEM

Forensic criminologists should be familiar with the basic rules, processes, and procedures involved in the civil litigation process. Forensic criminologists do not need to know as much about litigation as lawyers. But forensic criminologists should know some of the basic features of civil law to assist the courts and the legal system.

LEGAL BACKDROP AND THE CIVIL LITIGATION PROCESS

We differentiate between *criminal forensic criminology* which focuses on crime and guilt within the system of criminal law and *civil forensic criminology* which focuses on tort and liability within the system of civil law. Criminal law broadly refers to federal and state laws that make certain behaviors illegal and punishable by imprisonment and/or fines. In criminal cases, a person accused of a crime is generally charged in a formal accusation called an indictment (for felonies or serious crimes) or complaint (for misdemeanors). The government prosecutes the accused offender and the victim is not a party to the action. When a court determines that an individual committed a crime, that person will receive a sentence. The sentence may be an order to pay a monetary penalty (a fine and/or restitution to the victim), imprisonment, or supervision in the community (by a court employee called a U.S. probation officer if a federal crime), or some combination of these three things.

Criminal forensic criminologists typically work within the criminal justice system to address evidence that will help identify and predict psychological, sociological, and economic characteristics that may lead people to commit crimes. Police and courts might use a criminal forensic criminologist to reconstruct the crime and analyze physical evidence such as blood, DNA, fingerprints, and other evidence. The criminal forensic criminologist might also use various laboratory techniques to collect and test data from the crime scene. In addition to the investigation of criminal cases, forensic criminologists may be tasked by prosecutors or defense attorneys to provide testimony or submit written reports related to particular aspects of a criminal case. They also can testify during the sentencing process to explain the circumstances in which someone participated in a crime. Other criminal forensic criminologists may offer criminal profiles, testify as to the validity of confessions, or assist investigators seeking search warrants by attesting to the manner in which certain criminal types gather and hoard contraband. Depending on the type of criminal case, the efforts of a criminal forensic criminologist may be differentially constrained by evidentiary and procedural matters and the trial judge's interpretation of the applicable law.

In our book, we focus on the roles the practicing forensic criminologist can play within the system of civil law. While criminal cases involve an action that is considered to be harmful to society as a whole, civil cases usually involve private disputes between persons or organizations. While many people understand that they may be able to take legal action if they are injured due to the negligent or reckless actions of another person, they often do not know what exactly a "tort" is and how it applies to civil law. A tort is a legal claim in the form of a lawsuit. A tort can be for almost any type of injury to the person, including psychological and physical damage. Specifically, a "tort" is a civil wrong, as opposed to a criminal wrong that one person commits against another. A person who suffers injury caused by someone else may be able to pursue compensation from the person (or persons) responsible through a civil lawsuit. To prevail in a civil lawsuit involving a personal injury, the plaintiff—a person who brings a case against another in a court of law—typically must demonstrate that he or she was harmed by the defendant's breach of some duty. The defendant can be an individual, company, or institution sued or accused in a court of law.

In order to prove a personal injury case in court, the plaintiff's attorneys will typically need to show that the four essential elements of a tort are present: (1) duty (of which foreseeability of harm is an integral element), (2) breach of duty (failure to act reasonably or to follow a recognized standard of care), (3) causation (whether proximate cause or cause-in-fact), and (4) injury. Box 1.1 describes these four elements. In other words, the victim of the wrong (the plaintiff) makes a claim (the complaint) against the perpetrator of the wrong (the defendant) for the wrong allegedly committed by the defendant. This claim is for compensation for the harm that the victim suffered. The viability of this claim requires the plaintiff to demonstrate that the defendant breached a legal duty that was owed by the defendant to the plaintiff. In short, in civil court, personal injury claims are disputes between private parties with the plaintiff attempting to gain compensation for a loss that was caused by the actions of the defendant.

There are two types of causation. First, "cause-in-fact" concerns the question whether a cause-and-effect relationship between the defendant's wrong and the plaintiff's harm exists. Cause-in-fact refers to the actual cause of an injury. One test for cause-in-fact is the "but for" test: but for the action or

---

BOX 1.1 UNITED STATES CIVIL COURT AND THE FOUR BASIC TORT ELEMENTS

A civil case begins when a person or entity (such as a corporation or the government), called the plaintiff, claims that another person or entity (the defendant) has failed to carry out a legal duty owed to the plaintiff. Both the plaintiff and the defendant are also referred to as "parties" or "litigants." The plaintiff may ask the court to tell the defendant to fulfill the duty, or make compensation for the harm done, or both. Legal duties include respecting rights established under the Constitution or under federal or state law. Civil suits are brought in both state and federal courts. An example of a civil case in a state court would be if a citizen (including a corporation) sued another citizen for not living up to a contract.

In a personal injury case, the four basic elements of a tort include:
1. *Duty*. Demonstrating that the defendant had a duty to observe or protect the safety of the plaintiff
2. *Breach of Duty*. The defendant breached that duty and endangered the health and safety of the plaintiff
3. *Causation*. The plaintiff suffered injury in some form. There are two types of causation:
   * *Cause-in-fact*. A plaintiff must prove that the defendant's actions caused the plaintiff's injury.
   * *Proximate causation* relates to the scope of a defendant's responsibility in a negligence case. A defendant in a negligence case is only responsible for those harms that the defendant could have foreseen through his or her actions.
4. *Injury*. The plaintiff's injuries were caused by the negligence of the defendant. A plaintiff in a negligence case must prove a legally recognized harm, usually in the form of physical injury to a person or to property. It is not enough that the defendant failed to exercise reasonable care. The failure to exercise reasonable care must result in actual damages to a person to whom the defendant owed a duty of care.

---

failure to act, the harm to the plaintiff would not have happened. This test suggests the existence of an actual, factual link between the defendant's breach of duty and the plaintiff's resulting harm or damage. The concept of cause-in-fact is centrally important in a lawsuit because the plaintiff must demonstrate a relationship between the breach of duty and the harm, such that the harm would not have occurred but for the actions of the defendant. Another common test is the "substantial factor" test. If several causes could have caused the harm, then any cause that was a substantial factor is held to be liable.

The second issue, "proximate cause," assumes the existence of actual causation and addresses whether the relationship between the wrong and harm was sufficiently close in time and space, for example, whether the causal link was proximate rather than distant and remote. In most torts cases, proximate cause is a question of foreseeability. If the particular injury that resulted was a foreseeable consequence of the defendant's conduct, then proximate cause exists. Courts typically address four key questions: first, was the injury foreseeable and, second, was the *type* of harm foreseeable? In most cases, a defendant will be held liable for all the direct consequences of her or his actions as long as some part of the harm is foreseeable. Also, the defendant may be liable even if the injury that occurred was unlikely, as long as a reasonable person would have taken steps to prevent that kind of injury from occurring. Third, was the *manner* of harm foreseeable? Usually, if the plaintiff's injury is the type that might be reasonably foreseen, then the way in which the injury occurred does not have to be foreseeable. Finally, was the *extent* of the harm foreseeable? The defendant will be liable even if the injury is much more severe than she or he would have expected.

Expert witnesses can be critical to any successful litigation and they should understand the various steps in the litigation process. Each party in a lawsuit files initial papers, known as *pleadings*. The pleadings explain each party's side of the dispute. Litigation begins when the plaintiff files a complaint with the court and formally delivers a copy to the defendant. The complaint describes what the defendant did (or failed to do) that caused harm to the plaintiff and the legal basis for holding the defendant responsible for that harm. The defendant is given a specific amount of time to file an answer to the complaint. The answer provides the defendant's side of the dispute. The defendant may also file counterclaims against the plaintiff, alleging that the plaintiff has harmed the defendant and should be held liable for that harm. In some instances, a party may request that the other party clarify or correct deficiencies in its factual allegations or legal theories, or may ask the court to dismiss part or all of the suit. Parties may amend complaints or amended answers. Once the parties have completed the complaint, answer, and any reply, the issues for resolution by the court have been defined.

Discovery is the method by which parties gather relevant information from each other or from third parties. Attorneys will assess the merits of claims and defenses based on research of the law, document review and evaluation, and interviews and meetings with expert witnesses. Attorneys for the plaintiff and defense may need one or more experts to testify about the connection between the defendant's conduct and the loss suffered by the plaintiff, or the existence and amount of the plaintiff's damages. Expert witnesses work closely with retaining counsel to prepare the case. In the discovery phase of a case, the attorneys ask each other and third parties for information about the facts and issues of the case. Attorneys will gather information formally through written questions (known as "interrogatories"), requests for copies of documents, and requests for admission (which ask a party to admit or deny statements of fact).

Another key method of obtaining information is to conduct "depositions," in which witnesses are questioned under oath by retaining and opposing counsel and the witnesses' answers are recorded by a court reporter. Attorneys use depositions to learn more about the facts of a case and question and interrogate expert witnesses about their investigations and reports of findings and opinions. In particular, attorneys will question the expert as to his or her assignment, qualifications, documents reviewed, research and investigation, and opinions. Attorneys may also use depositions at trial to show inconsistencies in an expert witness's methodology and findings, or question the witness's credibility.

Before trial, the attorneys for the plaintiffs and defense may use motions to ask the court to rule or act. Motions usually pertain to law or facts in the case, but sometimes they seek clarification or resolution of procedural disputes between the parties. Some motions, such as a motion for summary judgment, which asks the court to dismiss part or all of a plaintiff's case or a defendant's defense, dispose of issues without trial. A summary judgment is a judgment entered by a court for one party and against another party that resolves a lawsuit before there is a trial. The party making the motion marshals evidence in its favor, compares it to the other side's evidence, and argues that there are no issues of fact that should go before a trial. Other motions might ask the court to order a party to produce documents or to exclude all or some of the expert witness's investigative report from trial.

In Chapter 2, we elaborate on the standards for the admissibility of expert testimony as outlined by the U.S. Supreme Court. As we stress throughout our book, expert witnesses must be familiar with the Federal Rule of Evidence 702 which is the standard for the admissibility of expert testimony. This standard requires that the expert demonstrate that she or he is qualified to testify as an expert, that she or he will assist the fact finder (judge and jury) in making a determination, that she or he has employed a reliable methodology by reviewing all relevant facts and identifying applicable industry standards, and that she or he has applied the methodology to the specific facts of the case. We discuss these points in Chapter 2.

A *trial* consists of jury selection, opening statement, plaintiff's case presentation, defendant's case presentation, plaintiff's rebuttal case, closing argument, jury instructions, jury deliberations, verdict, and judgment. In a jury trial, both parties question potential jurors during a selection process known as "voir dire." Once the trial begins, each party presents its outline of the case in an opening statement. Then, both sides present their evidence and call witnesses to testify. The plaintiff goes first since she or he is making claims against the defendant. The plaintiff's attorney will begin with direct examination, asking the questions for which the expert witness was called to testify. Next, the opposing party or parties conduct a cross-examination, which is limited in scope to the subject matter of the direct examination and to issues affecting the credibility of the witness or the testimony. Sometimes, the plaintiff is allowed to present additional evidence, called rebuttal evidence, after the defendant has finished presenting its case. The court may, at its discretion, ask questions of an expert witness by any party to the litigation, if it determines that the testimony is required to understand the facts of the case. Once all the testimony and evidence has been offered, each side will make a closing argument. In a jury trial, the judge gives instructions to the jury regarding the applicable law and the evidence that may be considered. The jury deliberates to reach a verdict. Unlike a criminal trial, where the jury must reach a unanimous decision to convict a defendant, the jury in a civil trial often need not decide to find in favor of one side or the other. In a bench trial, the judge considers all the evidence and makes a decision.

Following trial, a party dissatisfied with the result may *appeal* the decision and request a higher court to review the trial court proceedings. The parties present their arguments in briefs, which are submitted to the appellate court along with the record of evidence from the trial court. The appellate court will review the trial record only for prejudicial legal error, not factual error. This means that the appellate court will decide whether the trial judge (who decided the legal issues) made any erroneous decisions that affected the outcome of the jury verdict or court judgment. Errors can include allowing or excluding evidence, giving the jury improper instructions, or deciding a motion to dismiss or for summary judgment. Such a judgment may be issued on the merits of an entire case or on discrete issues in that case. An appellate court may make one of three rulings regarding the trial court's judgment—it may affirm, reverse, or reverse and remand for a new trial. The appellate court announces its decision in a document called an opinion. The appellate court will affirm the verdict if it finds that there was no error in the trial court proceeding. If there was an error, however, the appellate court can reverse the verdict or order the trial court to conduct a new trial.

HETEROGENEITY OF ROLES AND TASKS OF FORENSIC CRIMINOLOGISTS

A forensic criminologist may serve as a consulting expert whose main purpose is to act as a resource for plaintiff or defense attorneys, but the identity of a consulting expert need not be disclosed to opposing counsel. Some experts may be appointed by a judge to advise the court, but this practice is found more often in Europe than the United States. Such an expert can advise as to liability issues, standards of care, and causation and can help plan the discovery process. Consulting experts can also provide background on opposing experts and their likely arguments. Testifying expert witnesses do all of the above but are also expected to provide written reports, give deposition testimony, and testify at trial. As we describe in more detail in Chapter 3, a forensic criminologist who specializes in negligent security may be expected to opine on questions of crime foreseeability and standards of care considering this foreseeability. The causal relationship between any alleged breach of standards and the damages suffered by a plaintiff may also be addressed by the forensic criminologist. These three areas of input correspond directly to three of the four basic elements of a tort noted before. Because issues in tort litigation may involve the failure of a landholder or employer to protect against criminal behavior or may involve the actions of police, corrections, and security personnel, the insights provided by the forensic criminologist in the form of expert investigative reports and testimony can be of crucial assistance to judicial and jury decision-making.

Forensic criminologists play multiple roles in the court system. They perform scientific research related to lawmaking, criminal events, and societal reactions to crime; provide assessments of different types of evidence at a crime scene; and present data, weigh evidence, and give impartial opinions to the courts. Thornton and Voigt (1988, p. 114) argue that "the roles of the criminologist in the applied setting are essentially the same as for criminologists in academic settings" and include the roles of: (1) *reviewer* that can synthesize, summarize, and assess data and scholarship; (2) *educator* that has teaching skills and can impart knowledge; (3) *researcher* that can employ the scientific method to conduct a thorough and objective investigation; and (4) *reformer* that can use research results to suggest ways of improving social life or formulating policies. For Thornton and Voigt (1988, p. 114) "[w]hat differentiates applied criminologists from academic criminologists are not roles but the setting or context where they work."

Over the decades, forensic criminologists have made numerous contributions to legal matters before the courts. Many researchers have studied and analyzed how forensic social science principles, theories, and methods have been used in a variety of areas such as personal injury, child custody, and employment. There are many examples of the different ways forensic criminologists have applied criminological methods and theories in the service of the courts and legal system. Forensic criminologists can assist attorneys and law firms by conducting thorough and detailed investigations. They can also construct juror questionnaires and interview protocols for the voir dire process by designing case-specific juror profiles. They can also assist attorneys in developing strategies for deposition. They can also observe trials and provide feedback to retaining counsel during trials (Morewitz and Goldstein, 2014).

As consultants, forensic criminologists may also play an evidential role and assist an attorney in understanding the evidence of the other side's expert or in devising a line of cross-examination designed to show flaws in that expert's evidence, reasoning, or methods. In litigation, forensic criminologists can assist in the evaluation of police use-of-force practices, pursuits, custody suicide, and premises security practices (Alpert and Dunham, 1990; Fyfe, 1988; Kennedy, 2006; Kennedy and Homant, 1988). Finally, forensic criminologists can testify in cases involving state police agencies, municipal police departments, and county sheriffs' departments. Their testimony can involve explaining to jurors the appropriate standards of care for the use of deadly force, vehicle pursuits, emergency psychiatric evaluations, prisoner health care, and prevention of prisoner suicide, among other issues. They can also evaluate lawsuits concerning premises liability for negligent security in the private sector involving properties both in the United States and overseas. Box 1.2 shows the different types of criminology as practiced in the United States.

Many forensic psychologists use criminological theories and methods to provide evaluations of criminal responsibility. These forensic evaluations can include, for example, insanity and mental state issues relevant to culpability, including negation of *mens rea*, provocation and passion, extreme mental or emotional disturbance, voluntary and involuntary intoxication, imperfect self-defense, and duress. Using psychological methods and theories, a forensic criminologist can provide assessments of psychopathy, child sexual abuse, violence risk, and evaluations of parents and children in cases of disputed custody (Delisi, 2016; Gould and Martindale, 2013; Hart and Storey, 2013); evaluate emotional damages in tort cases (Foote and Lareau, 2013); provide evaluations of people who allege emotional harm stemming from alleged discrimination and harassment (Baker et al., 2013); assess a sex offender's

---

BOX 1.2 VARIETIES OF CRIMINOLOGY

Academic Criminology—scientific study of crime, including its causes, consequences, trends, and patterns of development. The analytical focus is on the nature of offenders, victims, and crime events. As an intellectual domain, academic criminology comprises contributions from multiple academic disciplines, including psychology, biology, anthropology, law, and, especially, sociology. Academic criminology is mainly practiced by sociologists, criminologists, psychologists, and other social scientists employed in universities.

    Applied Criminology—application of criminological theories, methods, and data to address criminological problems. A major goal is to assist law enforcement in crime prevention. Applied criminology is practiced by academic criminologists and other nonacademic criminologists employed by law enforcement, nonprofit organizations, public agencies, and private firms.

    Forensic Criminology—application of criminological theories, methods, data, and research to legal matters before the courts. Forensic criminologists carry out social science research to assist criminal courts in the determination of guilt and punishment, and civil courts through litigation. The expectation is criminological research and knowledge will be used in court, as opposed (or in addition) to being published in an academic, scholarly journal. Forensic criminology is practiced by academic and nonacademic social scientists and criminologists.

---

mental state and risk for recidivism (Witt and Conroy, 2013); and assess the competence of a defendant to stand trial (Stafford and Sellbom, 2013). While much forensic psychology practice involves evaluation of litigants whose mental states are at issue in legal proceedings, forensic criminologists may also be involved in the legal arena in nonclinical and nonassessment capacities. These capacities can include identifying and assisting in the selection of potential experts, reviewing the work of experts retained by opposing counsel, and assisting the retaining attorney in developing cross-examination strategies and questions (for an overview, see Otto and Weiner, 2013).

Likewise, a variety of sociological methods and theories are useful to forensic criminologists to help examine, for example, the impact of psychopathy on different types of crime (Delisi, 2016); the dynamics of child abuse and violence against women (Connolly et al., 2006); investigate gang-involved criminality and violence (Taylor-Austin, 2014); and identify the predictors of crime foreseeability (Kennedy, 2014; Voigt and Thornton, 1996). In addition, sociological perspectives have been used by forensic criminologists to conduct change-of-venue research (Richardson et al., 1987), establish emotional damages (Mulkey, 2009), advise on ongoing trial tactics (Moore and Friedman, 1993), measure the potential damage done to a politician's career as a result of an arrest and prosecution record (Hirsch and Quartaroli, 2011), and assist jurors in understanding "specific intent" criminal action based on social science theories and scholarship (Peyrot and Burns, 2001). Other classical works by Anderson and Winfree (1987) and recent research (Burns, 2008) address the intersection of law and science in the constitution of expert evidence.

Stephen Morewitz and Alan Goldstein's *Handbook of Forensic Sociology and Psychology* (Morewitz and Goldstein, 2014) offers a detailed and comprehensive road map of the impact of social science on a variety of civil and criminal issues. Contributors offer insights into the usefulness of sociological evidence in suicide litigation, product liability litigation, medical malpractice, drug-associated litigation, child custody evaluations, human factors-related litigation, forensic evaluations of child abuse, and toxic tort lawsuits; the application of criminological knowledge to issues before the courts (Kennedy, 2014); the importance of preemployment screening and enforcement of workplace conduction expectations in presenting workplace violence (Sugahara and Sugahara, 2014); the role of mitigating factors in cases of violent crime (Forsyth, 2017, 2014); sources of failure and detection in interrogation-induced false confession (Davis and Leo, 2014); target selection by criminal groups and gangs (Erickson and Erickson, 2014), the role of a gang expert in court (Taylor-Austin, 2014), and the impact of gender analysis in military court-martials (Caldwell, 2014).

CRIMINALISTICS AND FORENSIC CRIMINOLOGY

Forensic criminologists are not criminalists. Criminalists practice criminalistics, which is a field of forensic investigation that emphasizes individualization and pattern matching, for example, the effort to associate a crime scene mark or object with its source. Criminalistics involves the comparison of fingerprints, handwriting, bitemarks, voiceprints, toolmarks, firearms, tire prints, shoe prints, and so on. The goal of criminalistics investigation is to link a latent fingerprint, a writing, a bitemark, a bullet, or similar objects to the one and only finger, writer, teeth, gun, or other specific object that made the markings. The objective of forensic identification science is individualization, "[t]he process of placing an object in a category which consists of a single, solitary unit. Individualization implies uniqueness" (Thornton and Peterson, 2008, p. 71). The crime scene investigation techniques of individualization and pattern matching are popular within the forensic fields of fire, arson and explosives, gunshot residue, comparative bullet lead analysis, and aspects of forensic pathology. While many forensic criminologists have a basic understanding of criminalistics they seldom develop such a mastery as to consider themselves experts in its practice.

There are four major differences between forensic criminologists and criminalists.

First, forensic criminologists conduct thorough, objective, and detailed investigations using the scientific method. They use social science techniques to make observations, formulate hypotheses, gather data to test hypotheses, and develop theories and explanations of crime events. In contrast, the subfields and investigative techniques of criminalistics have come under heated criticism in recent years with critics stigmatizing them as "nonscience" approaches (Saks and Faigman, 2008, p. 168). According to an oft-cited National Research Council (NRC) (2009) report, in nonscience forensic disciplines, "forensic science professionals have yet to establish either the validity of their approach or the accuracy of their conclusions, and the courts have been utterly ineffective in addressing this problem" (p. 109). The NRC report found that "no forensic method has been rigorously shown to have the capacity to consistently, and with a high degree of certainty, demonstrate a connection between evidence and a specific individual or source" (p. 7). "The simple reality," as noted by the NRC, "is that the interpretation of forensic evidence is not always based on scientific studies to determine its validity" (pp. 7, 8). Saks and Faigman (2008) point out that criminalistics investigators rarely use the scientific method in their research or submit their findings for peer review.

Second, forensic criminological research is theoretically driven with explanations of crime events tied directly to theoretically derived propositions. A criminological theory is a set of two or more propositions in which concepts—terms that we use to classify and categorize knowledge about the social world—refer to social phenomena that researchers assume to be causally related. While not all criminologists may accept this definition verbatim, many criminologists share the sentiments this definition of theory expresses. A theory describes the relationship between component concepts and propositions depict relationships in a causal fashion. A theory's scope conditions include the time and place within which the phenomenon (crime event) supposedly occurred. A theory's units of analysis may be the actual crime event, individuals (e.g., offenders, victims, place managers), complex organizations, small groups, laws, sociolegal regulations, and so on. Individualization and pattern matching do not address questions of causality or explain how and why questions about social phenomena. For social scientists and criminologists, theories must be capable of being put into proposition form if they are to qualify under a scientific definition of acceptable social science criminological theory.

Third, a forensic criminologist uses case evidence materials and criminological theories to develop statements about relationships among observable phenomena (e.g., the crime event and related contextual factors). In so doing, the forensic criminologist may apply different levels of analysis and deductive and inductive reasoning to understand the etiology of a crime event. Deduction is a form of reasoning that moves from the general to the specific, a top-down approach to understanding evidence. Inductive reasoning moves from specific observations to broader generalizations and theories, a bottom-up approach. In deductive reasoning, a criminologist might begin with a preexisting theory about a topic of interest in the legal case. She or he would then review the literature and develop more specific descriptions of crime phenomena that she or he can apply to the case and then evaluate using case-specific data and evidence. The process then narrows down even further when the investigator evaluates particular theoretical statements with specific observable data to confirm or disconfirm the original theories. In inductive reasoning, the forensic criminologist begins with specific observations and measures to detect patterns and regularities. She or he then formulates tentative statements that can be explored, and finally she or he ends up developing some general conclusions or theories about the crime event. Importantly, most forensic criminological research involves using both inductive and deductive reasoning processes in an investigation (for an overview of the use of inductive and deductive reasoning in forensic criminology, see Petherick and Ferguson, 2017).

Fourth, researchers and investigative journalists have drawn attention to the unsupported assumptions, exaggerated claims, and fraud that sometimes affect the subfields of criminalistics. Cole (2009, 2008a, b) suggests that the rules of practice that formed the basis for the authority and credibility of latent fingerprint examination (LFPE) during the 20th century have proven to be vulnerable to a contemporary resurgence of interest in establishing the scientific foundations of forensic evidence. As researchers have noted, the findings of criminalistics experts have been particularly vulnerable to cognitive and contextual bias. Dror and colleagues (2006) found that it is possible to alter identification decisions on the same fingerprint solely by presenting it in a different context (see also Dror and Charlton, 2006).

Turvey (2013) has documented a number of cases in which criminalists in criminal cases have deliberately offered fraudulent evidence to the courts. In 2015, the Justice Department and FBI formally acknowledged that nearly every examiner in an elite FBI forensic unit gave flawed testimony in almost all trials in which they offered evidence against criminal defendants over more than a two-decade period before 2000. According to the *Washington Post*, "[o]f 28 examiners with the FBI Laboratory's microscopic hair comparison unit, 26 overstated forensic matches in ways that favored prosecutors in more than 95 percent of the 268 trials reviewed so far." The errors were uncovered in a three-year review by the National Association of Criminal Defense Lawyers and the Innocence Project. Over the years, investigations by the *Wall Street Journal* (1999), *PBS Frontline* (2012), and the *Washington Post* (2017) have exposed the forensic certification organization American College of Forensic Examiners Institute (ACFEI) as bogus purveyors of junk science in the business of fabricating inauthentic certifications such as "forensic consultant," "forensic professional technologist," and "certified medical investigator." In 2014, the members of the American Board of Forensic Accounting, the advisory board behind the ACFEI's Certified Forensic Accountant credential, unanimously resigned amid questions about the legitimacy of the credential and the organization behind it

(Cohn, 2014). Given the accusations of fraud and deception, academics and legal practitioners are adopting a more critical attitude toward criminalistics, the way criminalistics evidence is introduced at trial, and the role pattern matching and individualization techniques play in convictions or acquittals once admitted. De facto deference to the weight ascribed to forensic evidence in the courtroom or indeed to the opinions of experts is becoming less common than in the past.

Finally, we can understand the problems and limitations of criminalistics by recognizing that the research culture in criminalistics is underdeveloped and lacks clear strategies for standard setting; managing accreditation and testing processes; and developing and implementing rulemaking, oversight, and sanctioning processes (Giannelli, 2017). The investigative techniques of individualization and pattern matching used in criminalistics often fail to meet recognized legal standards for scientific reliability including peer review and conscientious evaluation. Forensic examiners that employ pattern matching and individualization typically work in a law enforcement environment that is geared toward prosecuting criminal suspects, a concern that may be at odds with and even hostile toward the scientific method. Over the decades, forensic practices have been developed by law enforcement to assist in criminal investigations. Crime labs are often housed in police departments, staffed by police officials. Scholars and researchers suggest that these connections to police and prosecutors may compromise the independence of criminalists and could create frequent opportunities to inject biases into the investigation process (National Research Council, 2009).

In contrast, the research culture in forensic criminology is founded upon the scientific method and has strong and long-standing ties to the broader field of criminology and related social sciences—anthropology, economics, geography, psychology, and sociology—through national research and teaching communities, government funders, and professional organizations. Unlike the field of criminalistics, the forensic criminologist's close connections to the social science disciplines mean that the research process is designed to follow quality control procedures to identify mistakes, fraud, and bias. In U.S. universities, graduate students in the social sciences are usually introduced to a series of training tools in their courses and research activities including conflicts of interest—personal, professional, and financial; policies regarding human subjects; mentor/mentee responsibilities and relationships; collaborative research including collaborations with industry; peer review; data acquisition management; research misconduct and policies for handling misconduct; responsible authorship and publication; the scientist as a responsible member of society; contemporary ethical issues in research; and the environmental and societal impacts of scientific research. These research training tools can provide guidance to the forensic criminologist in determining how well her or his specific plans for responsible conduct of research compare with the best practices accumulated over the past decades by the research training community.

PLACE, TIME, AND ENVIRONMENTAL CRIMINOLOGY

The theoretical foundations of forensic criminology draw inspiration from environmental criminology—the criminality of place—which is centrally concerned with the interaction of crime events and the immediate socio-spatial context in which they occur (Weisburd et al., 2016). That is, criminal actions, behaviors, and crime events do not happen at random but are significantly influenced by social and environmental factors. According to Brantingham and Brantingham (1981, 1991, p. 2), "environmental criminology argues that criminal events must be understood as confluences of offenders, victims or criminal targets, and laws in specific settings at particular times and places."

Environmental criminologists, therefore, ask questions about where and when crimes occur; the physical and social characteristics of crime sites; the routines and movements that bring the offender and target together at the crime site; the perceptual processes that lead offenders to select particular sites to commit crimes; the spatial patterning in laws and the ways in which legal rules create crime sites; and the spatial distribution of targets and offenders in urban, suburban, and rural settings. Environmental criminologists recognize that criminal behaviors are dependent upon situational factors and crime is patterned according to the location of criminogenic environments. "Crime will be concentrated around crime opportunities and other environmental features that facilitate criminal activity" (Wortley and Townsley, 2017, p. 2). The purpose of crime analysis is to identify these crime opportunities and environmental facilitative factors and explain how they interact to enable crime events to happen at particular places and times.

The focus on the spatial location of crime events rather than crime rates or trends represents a shift in both the locus of explanation and the unit of analysis for criminological research. Crime is an event, something that happens. A criminal is an individual who violates a law. "Explaining why people behave one way or another is not the same as explaining why a particular event happens at a particular time or in a particular place" (Benson and Simpson, 2015, p. 95). Crime and criminals are conceptually separate and analytically distinct. Moreover, without an opportunity, there cannot be a crime event. Thus, to understand why a particular crime happens at a particular time and place, it is necessary to pay attention not only to the person who commits the crime but to the surrounding social and environmental situation in which the crime event and offender are located.

Scholars recognize that criminal opportunities and environmental inducements are important causes of all crime (Felson, 2002; Stark, 1987; for recent overviews, see Natarajan, 2017; Wilcox and Cullen, 2018). In the past few decades, the study of crime has increasingly focused on the situational and ecological factors that create or facilitate opportunities for crime. Opportunities shape and constrain individual choices to commit a crime or not. Opportunities can provide incentives and motivations to offend. Rational choice theory views offenders as rational actors who make purposive decisions about engaging in crime (Cornish and Clarke, 2014; Newman and Clarke, 2016). These decisions can be considered rational in as much as the offender seeks to benefit in some way from the contemplated behavior. Crime will occur when the perceived benefits outweigh the perceived costs. An implicit assumption in rational choice theory is that criminals can be pragmatic and utilitarian. They can make rational choices and purposeful decisions about crime targets in order to maximize their gain and minimize expected costs. Decisions to commit crime, according to rational choice theory, are based on rational considerations of choice, calculation, effort, provocations, and excuses (Clarke and Felson, 1993). Rational choice involves the way persons reach a decision to engage in behavior (or refrain) and assumes that persons can and do choose between alternative courses of action, including whether or not to commit a crime (Cornish and Clarke, 2014).

Offender theories examine how people come to be criminal offenders and the circumstances under which they desist from offending. Offenders may be highly motivated but unless they create a crime event there is nothing to explain. Eck and Weisburd (1995, p. 10) note that "[s]o even if we had a good explanation for the development of offenders, we would still need a good explanation for criminal events. Specifically, we would want a theory that could tell us why certain targets are selected by offenders—why some targets are attractive and others are repellent. What are the impediments to offending that are presented to offenders, and how are they overcome?" Environmental criminologists acknowledge that many criminals may be highly motivated to commit particular crimes. Nevertheless, the main analytical and explanatory problem for environmental criminologists is to understand how potential offenders select specific targets and what factors enter into the thinking of the potential criminal before the decision to commit a crime occurs.

For the forensic criminologist, environmental criminology provides a set of conceptual tools with which to evaluate the foreseeability of crime occurring at a particular place. Routine activities theory asserts that a crime event is foreseeable when motivated offenders and suitable targets come together in time and place in the absence of capable guardians (Cohen and Felson, 1979). Capable guardians can be anything that either physically prevents the offender from getting to the target or that can cause the offender to decide it is too risky to attack the target. Fig. 1.1 presents a diagram on the major components of routine activities theory. Routine activities theory has had a considerable impact on the field of forensic criminology since it compactly articulates the necessary elements that must converge for a crime event to happen.

Since the 1980s, many criminologists have used routine activities theory to explain a broad range of crime events, including violence (Sampson, 1987), property crimes (Massey et al., 1989; Lynch and Cantor, 1992; Wilcox et al., 2007, 2003b), sexual assault (Schwartz and Pitts, 1995), and stalking (Mustaine and Tewksbury, 1998).

In recent years, scholars have elaborated on routine activities theory and proposed additional elements to address where, how, and why questions concerning crime events (for an overview, see Andresen and Farrell, 2015). Tillyer and Eck (2011) propose six elements: targets/victims, guardians, places, place managers, offenders, and handlers. Guardians protect targets from being victimized, place managers supervise specific places, and handlers control potential offenders (Eck and Madensen, 2015). Eck has subdivided the concept of capable guardians into three categories—target, place, or offender—based on whom or what they are supervising. This more comprehensive version of routine activities theory has been depicted as a double triangle by Eck (2003) (see Fig. 1.2). The inner triangle represents the necessary elements for a crime to occur: a motivated offender and suitable target must come together at an accessible place. The outer triangle represents the potential controllers who must be absent or ineffective for a crime to occur.

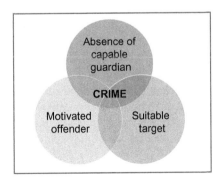

FIG. 1.1

Routine activities theory.

Source: Cohen, L.E., Felson, M., 1979. Social change and crime rate trends: a routine activity approach. Am. Sociol. Rev. 44(4), 588–608.

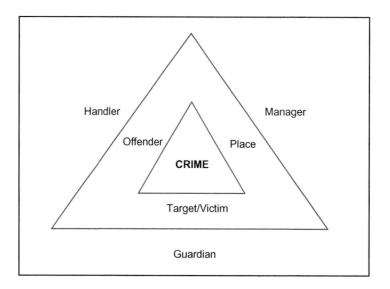

FIG. 1.2

The crime event triangle.

Source: Eck, J. E., 2003. Police problems: the complexity of problem theory, research and evaluation. In: J. Knutsson (Ed.), Problem-Oriented Policing: From Innovation to Mainstream. Monsey, NY: Criminal Justice Press, pp. 79–113.

To assess the foreseeability of crime events at particular locations, criminologists have used concepts such as crime generators/enablers, crime attractors (or more generally crime magnets), crime detractors, crime facilitators, and crime precipitators. Table 1.1 provides a basic summary of these concepts. Crime generators are places to which large numbers of people are attracted for reasons unrelated to criminal motivation (Brantingham and Brantingham, 1995). Sports stadiums, shopping malls, bus stations, nightclubs, festivals, transportation hubs, and bars and taverns can provide large numbers of opportunities for offenders and targets to come together in time and place with the outcome being crime or disorder. The large number of crimes is due principally to the large number of place users and targets. Crime attractors are places affording many criminal opportunities that are well known to offenders (Cui and Walsh, 2015; Malleson and Andresen, 2016). People with criminal motivation are drawn to such places. In the short run, offenders may come from outside the area, but over longer time periods, and under some circumstances, offenders may relocate to these areas. Crime facilitators or enablers occur when there is little regulation of behavior at places and rules of conduct are absent or are not enforced. Crime enablers can occur with the erosion of guardianship and handling and where management practices encourage crime to occur (Clarke and Eck, 2005). Crime precipitators are situational factors that can prompt, permit, provoke, or pressure individuals to perform criminal behavior.

Social scientists have documented the crime generating and crime attractive features of certain properties and land uses. Properties close to bars (Roncek and Maier, 1991), public housing (Roncek et al., 1981), and schools (Roncek and Lobosco, 1983) can be more vulnerable to crime, particularly if these areas have a history of criminal attack. Studies of "hot spots" find that areas characterized by a large concentration of motivated offenders and suitable targets but lacking capable guardians have a high concentration of crime (e.g., Roncek and Maier, 1991; Sherman et al., 1989).

Table 1.1 Crime Places and Crime Opportunities

Crime Places	Crime Opportunities	Examples
Crime generators	Places with high numbers of crime events because of many targets. Places attract large numbers of people for noncriminal purposes; activities at a particular location pull masses of people toward them who do not necessarily have any predetermined motivations to offend	Sports stadiums, festivals, shopping malls, bus stations, nightclubs, festivals, transportation hubs, bars
Crime attractors	Places affording many criminal opportunities that are well known to offenders	Blighted and abandoned housing and businesses; seedy bars, drug markets, and red-light districts where offenders come to fence stolen goods, sell or obtain drugs, or pimp for prostitutes
Crime detractors	Places that discourage offenders and offending	Sites with good natural surveillance, strong cohesive communities
Crime facilitators/ enablers	Places that foster the capability of offenders or assist them in circumventing existing crime prevention measures. They can be physical (e.g., firearms), social (e.g., gangs and organized criminal networks), or chemical (e.g., alcohol/drugs)	Unsupervised public areas such as parking lots, playgrounds, school grounds, where crimes can occur unobserved, where there is little regulation of behavior, or there is an absence of capable guardians
Crime precipitators	Situations that can prompt, pressure, permit, or provoke individuals to commit crimes	Employees are more likely to steal from the company if they observe superiors doing it; uncollected newspapers may prompt a burglary; offenders may blame others for their criminal actions; lack of public toilets may encourage public urination; crowding and loud noise may intensify aggression and offending

Adapted from Brantingham, P., Brantingham, P., 1995. Criminality of place. Eur. J. Crim. Pol. Res. 3(3), 5–26; Clarke, R.V., Eck, J.E., 2005. Crime Analysis for Problem Solvers in 60 Small Steps. Office of Community Oriented Policing Services, U.S. Department of Justice, Washington, DC; Kinney, J.B., Brantingham, P.L., Wuschke, K., Kirk, M.G., Brantingham, P.J. 2008. Crime attractors, generators and detractors: Land use and urban crime opportunities. Built Environ. 34(1), 62–74; Cozens, P., Love, T., 2015. A review and current status of crime prevention through environmental design (CPTED). J. Plan. Lit. 30(4), 393–412.

Wilcox and colleagues (2003a) have developed the concept of "criminal opportunity contexts" to address the circumstances in which motivated offenders and suitable targets converge in time and space in the absence of capable guardians. Eck and colleagues (2007, p. 226) coined the concept "risky facilities" to refer to spatial concentrations of crime in which "for any group of similar facilities (e.g., taverns, parking lots, or bus shelters), a small proportion of the group accounts for the majority of crime experienced by the entire group." Risky facilities might show up as hot spots on a city's crime map and can include schools, transportation depots, and bars and taverns. While some hot spots improve on their own and new ones may appear, research suggests that crime concentrations are relatively stable over long periods (Weisburd et al., 2004).

Over the decades, a substantial body of research has documented the positive relationship between neighborhood conditions and criminal offending generally (Bursik and Grasmick, 1993; Sampson,

1985; Sampson et al., 1997; Shaw and Mckay, 1942). Decades of research has shown that neighborhoods characterized by high density, intense poverty, mixed use, transience, and dilapidation tend to attract and/or generate criminal behavior (for a paradigmatic statement, see Stark, 1987). The foreseeability of a criminal event may be established or refuted to the extent that a landholder defendant was aware of these conditions, particularly if supported by census or other socioeconomic data (and given the correlation between crime and unemployment, poverty, etc.). Bursik Jr. and Grasmick (1993) argue that poverty, high residential mobility, racial or ethnic heterogeneity, and high population density contribute to community or social disorder and lead to poor neighborhood controls, including poor supervision and surveillance by the residents and a low willingness to intervene to prevent crime and disorder. Sampson and colleagues (1997) argue that a low degree of "collective efficacy" in a neighborhood—for example, a low degree of informal social control and an unwillingness of neighbors to intervene on behalf of the "common good"—is a major causal factor in high crime rates (for recent assessments, see Armstrong et al., 2015; Collins et al., 2017; Hipp, 2016).

For proponents of social disorganization theory, ecological characteristics of neighborhoods influence the degree of social disorganization in the community. This is because certain characteristics can impede the development of social ties that promote the ability to solve common problems, including crime. Ecological characteristics of greatest interest to social disorganization researchers include poverty, joblessness, population mobility or turnover, racial composition, and family disruption, among others. Although community characteristics such as poverty or residential instability are related to crime, these factors themselves do not directly cause crime. Rather, according to the theory, ecological characteristics are related to crime only indirectly through various neighborhood processes such as informal social control. As such, poverty, residential instability, and other ecological characteristics are important in as much as they affect the mediating processes of social disorganization (Kubrin and Wo, 2016; Kubrin and Weitzer, 2003).

The oft-cited work on "broken windows" theory links disorder and incivility within a community to subsequent occurrences of crime (Wilson and Kelling, 1982). Disorder, incivility, and neighborhood disinvestment may yield more crime not only because they tend to attract offenders, but also because they can lead to withdrawal and detachment from community residents who might otherwise operate as an important social control function (Sampson et al., 1997; Skogan, 1990). Weak local social bonds, lowered community attachment, anonymity, and reduced capacity for surveillance and guardianship impede social controls. According to Sampson (1987, p. 109): "[r]esidents in areas characterized by family disorganization, mobility, and building density are less able to perform guardianship activities, less likely to report general deviance to authorities, to intervene in public disturbances, and to assume responsibility for supervision of youth activities; the result is that deviance is tolerated and public norms of social control are not effective."

What unites the various concepts and theories discussed before is that they embrace an opportunity perspective on crime: socio-spatial conditions can provide disincentives, barriers, or opportunities for crime. "Opportunity" is a central concept that explains how individuals make decisions based on choices within constraints and according to their desires and beliefs. Rather than consider crime as the result of psychological characteristics of offenders or outcomes of a few people with high motivations and propensities to offend, opportunity perspectives focus on proximal situations: people choose whether to offend given the incentives and constraints that they face. Opportunity makes the crime. That is, a person cannot engage in a criminal event unless she or he has an opportunity to do so. In all cases, the immediate situation matters in generating the crime event. As Eck and Eck (2012,

p. 284) note: "[if] people who offend have stable propensities, they cannot act on them unless there is an opportunity to do so. If people have unstable propensities to offend, proximal circumstances not only provide opportunities but also can trigger offending by providing temptations. In either case, the immediate situation matters."

As we point out in the chapters ahead, forensic criminologists can use and apply the theoretical assumptions of environmental criminology to determine whether particular places have a high propensity, risk, or foreseeability of crime. As we will demonstrate, environmental criminology can provide the conceptual tools with which to evaluate the foreseeability of crime occurring at a given location. At the very core of scholarly research efforts in environmental criminology is an attempt to explain *why* criminals commit crimes *where* they commit them. To the extent that expert witnesses know why certain sites may be selected over others as crime targets, they will be better equipped to assess whether particular crime events are foreseeable. As will become evident in the following chapters, the degree to which a crime event is foreseeable is a key element in the determination of premises liability for negligent security.

PLAN OF THE BOOK

In the chapters that follow, we examine the ways in which forensic criminologists can use social science methods and theories to determine adjudicative or case-specific facts and provide general contextual information to assist the courts in determining the facts of a case. In Chapter 2, we discuss the interactions of law and science in expert testimony; the rules regarding the legal admissibility of exert testimony; and emphasize the merits of candor, objectivity, and ethics in forensic investigation.

In Chapter 3, we explore in detail the concepts of foreseeability, breach of duty, and causation as they relate to premises liability for negligent security. Premises liability for negligent security has been a fast growth area of tort litigation in the United States and is becoming an emerging basis of civil liability worldwide. Negligent security is a theory of premises liability law that victims of crime assert against owners and occupiers of land for failing to prevent foreseeable and avoidable attacks from occurring. As we show, underlying all arguments advanced by plaintiff and defense is the understanding that, generally speaking, the defendant had a duty to act as a reasonable person would act under similar circumstances. We discuss the historical development of premises security litigation, the four tests of foreseeability which are routinely applied in common law jurisdictions, breach of duty (failure to act reasonably or to follow a recognized standard of care), and causation (whether proximate cause or cause-in-fact). In all premises liability cases, the expert witness must also be aware of a property's history, all security related policies and procedures, relevant industry standards, and the legal process as well.

In Chapters 4 through 7, we draw on examples from the burgeoning litigation on premises liability for negligent security to examine the roles sociologists and criminologists play as experts in establishing or refuting the elements of tort that control a case as it moves through the litigation process. We discuss how an effective expert addresses different theoretical levels of explanation that are most appropriate for juries to understand. In these chapters, we draw on premises liability litigation in high-risk places including parking lots, apartments, hotels/motels, shopping centers, and entertainment venues (e.g., casinos, bars, and nightclubs). We address four basic issues: first, how the forensic criminologist uses past cases and social science and criminological theory to demonstrate foreseeability; second, how the forensic criminologist establishes the reasonableness of the extant security measures to determine whether the defendant breached appropriate standards of care; third, how the forensic criminologist may determine whether any such breach of duty was a proximate cause and cause-in-fact of injuries suffered by the plaintiff; and fourth, how the forensic criminologist can use scientific evidence and investigation to assess damages and assign monetary compensation to victims injured by liable others. An overarching concern for any reputable social scientist would also include broader policy implications of the sociological/criminological testimony placed in evidence as well as overall case outcomes.

In Chapter 8, we examine litigation surrounding administrative negligence which includes negligent hiring, negligent retention, negligent training, negligent assignment, negligent entrustment, negligent supervision, negligent failure to direct, among other areas. We discuss the notion of vicarious liability through the doctrine of respondeat superior. In personal injury and similar torts cases, "respondeat superior" is a rule of law stating that the employer of a negligent defendant is also responsible for the defendant's actions. Respondeat superior is a type of vicarious liability, which allows a third party to be held liable for a defendant's negligence in some cases, even if the third party was not there when the injury occurred and did not cause the injury or make it worse. An employer can be held liable for administrative negligence if it can be shown through a preponderance of the evidence that the employer negligently hired, trained, supervised, assigned, entrusted, or retained an errant employee. We address how forensic criminologists can advise attorneys on liability issues, standards of care, causation, and assist with the discovery process.

In Chapter 9, we discuss litigation involving workplace violence. According to the Occupational Safety and Health Administration (OSHA), more than two million workers become victims of workplace violence each year. Assaults on workers occur on company premises, at off-site job locations, while making deliveries, and during other business-related activities. Litigation involving workplace violence is complex and complicated with a variety of different types of crimes, victims, and forms of violence. We discuss the four types of workplace violence, the limitations of workman's compensation as a remedy for crime victims, different forms of employer liability, and the variety of roles that forensic criminologists can play in workplace violence litigation. Forensic criminologists can assess the relative degree of foreseeability, evaluate the reasonableness of employer security and safety measures and actions, and opine on whether any breach of duty was a proximate cause and cause-in-fact of injuries or death suffered by the victim. Finally, we consider the evolving nature of terrorist threats and mass casualty events and explain their potential impact on foreseeability approaches, standards of care, and liability judgments.

In Chapter 10, we examine the major sources of debate and controversy surrounding wrongful conviction litigation. We identify the common causes of wrongful convictions and discuss how courts and attorneys can draw on criminological scholarship to explain the actions of investigators, prosecutors, and the police in their decision to bring a case forward and prosecute it. Scholars have begun to sort out the problems in criminal justice systems that create wrongful convictions. Police practices related to eyewitness misidentifications and false confessions have drawn the most criticism, along with questionable forensic evidence and shoddy laboratory practices. Others have criticized judicial doctrines that tolerate law enforcement errors. Still others focus on prosecutors who supervise and litigate the cases that end in wrongful convictions, engaging in what is called "wrongful conviction practice." We engage these points and draw on expert witness testimony to address the different impacts forensic criminologists can have on the nature and outcomes of this burgeoning area of litigation.

In Chapter 11, we address three high litigation risks associated with police and correctional operations: (1) detainee suicide, (2) allegations of deliberate indifference to the medical needs of mentally ill and emotionally disturbed persons, and (3) use of force in law enforcement actions. We first discuss a case of detainee suicide and describe how a forensic criminologist would investigate and gather evidence in such a case. Next, we examine a case involving allegations of violations of constitutional rights and violations of federal and state law for injuries a young woman incurred after she was released from police custody. Finally, we analyze two cases of police use of force, a critical topic in civil liability. In the first case, we examine the response of a police officer to a late-night traffic stop. We address issues relating to fundamental attribution error, perceptions of the dangers of traffic stops, the nature of early morning/weekend traffic stops, police officer fatalities, and the "use-of-force" continuum. In the second case, we examine a police officer's decision to use force during an arrest in a poor, high crime neighborhood. Our goal is to show how a forensic criminologist would investigate the intersection of police officer actions, situational constraints, and the totality of circumstances in an encounter with an offender.

In the final chapter, we elaborate on the issues raised in previous chapters, point to long-standing litigation trends and the emergence of new forms of litigation, and provide advice and suggestions to students on cultivating a forensic criminological skill-set or repertoire. We hope that academics, students, professionals, and practitioners reading this book will develop an appreciation for the field of forensic criminology as a whole, recognizing its uniqueness, its complexity, and the need for specialized training and knowledge. In addition, each chapter serves as a reference source on a specific forensic topic and reveals the current state of research.

CRIMINOLOGY ON TRIAL: SCIENCE, LAW, AND THE ADMISSIBILITY OF EXPERT TESTIMONY

INTRODUCTION

In this chapter, we address three important aspects of the practice of forensic criminology that are central to the production and reception of social science knowledge in the courts.

First, we discuss the interactions of law and science in expert testimony, paying close attention to debates over conceptions of the two institutions as cultural opposites. While practical tensions undoubtedly exist between law and science, we argue that forensic criminological work and trial procedure are broadly congruent with the values and methods of scientific inquiry.

Second, we discuss the general legal rules that govern expert testimony, including the Federal Rules of Evidence, and statutes and case law that determine who can be qualified as an expert and how that occurs. Here we address how expert testimony is bound up with norms and rules concerning the skill, experience, training, or education of expert witnesses. We discuss the case law guiding admissibility of expert testimony as found in *Frye v. United States* (1923), *Daubert v. Merrell Dow Pharmaceuticals, Inc.* (1993), *General Electric Co. v. Joiner* (1997), and *Kumho Tire Co. v. Carmichael* (1999).

Third, we then consider the importance of candor, objectivity, and ethics in expert testimony. The integrity of the legal system is based on the honesty of all participants. Deceit and fraudulence can have very negative systemic consequences: "If a significant number of ... people violated the trust upon which our interactions are based, our court system ... would be swamped into immobility," as noted by Alan Greenspan, Chairman of the Federal Reserve Board, in a commencement address at Harvard College in 1999. Honesty and integrity in research and investigation increase trust, build reputation, promote loyalty, and ensure dispute resolution. Objectivity is an ethical principle that one follows to avoid bias and deception in data collection, data analysis, and expert testimony. Trust, objectivity, and duty to follow ethical principles in research are the foundation of expert witness work.

Over the decades, litigation has been an essential tool for addressing social problems, promoting sociolegal reform, and transforming social institutions and public policy. From Louis Brandeis's brief in *Muller v. Oregon* (208 U.S. 412 (1908)) to Mamie and Kenneth Clark's doll studies in *Brown v. Board of Education* (347 U.S. 483 (1954)) to Gary Gates's studies of same-sex couples in *Obergefell v. Hodges* (135 S. Ct. 2071 (2015), courts have frequently relied on social science research to guide their decision-making and provide empirical support for rulings. Similarly, with regard to criminal law, research on the reliability of eyewitness identifications has affected the admissibility of such evidence at trial and influenced how the police conduct lineups and other identification procedures

Practicing Forensic Criminology. https://doi.org/10.1016/B978-0-12-815595-0.00002-X
© 2019 Elsevier Inc. All rights reserved.

(Loftus et al., 2013). Moreover, research on polygraphs, police-induced false confessions, forensic interviews of child witnesses, racial bias in capital cases, and juror comprehension of jury instructions has also affected judge and jury decision-making and impacted the law in various ways and to varying degrees (Cicchini and White, 2017, 2015; Leo, 2017; Greene and Heilbrun, 2014; Domanico et al., 2012).

Social science theories, methods, and evidence have been frequently cited in judicial opinions that have overturned established legal precedent (for an overview, see Monahan and Walker, 2014). The landmark *Shelley v. Kraemer* (1948) U.S. Supreme Court decision ruled that courts could not enforce explicitly racially restrictive covenants on homes thus undermining the ability of real estate agents to maintain racial residential segregation through deed restrictions. *Shelley v. Kraemer* portended a major shift in the acceptability of social science evidence on the linkages among housing segregation and racial inequalities (Gotham, 2000, 2014). In 1954, the *Brown v. Board of Education of Topeka* (347 US 483) U.S. Supreme Court decision overturned segregation in public school education and thus outlawed the "separate but equal" principle espoused in *Plessy v. Ferguson*. We can view *Brown* as the paragon case in which the Supreme Court found racial segregation to be harmful due to novel understandings about the negative psychological housing impacts of segregated schooling (Rublin, 2011). Social scientists Kenneth Clark and Mamie Clark played a major role in the famous *Brown* case by conducting studies showing the negative effects of discrimination and segregation on child development (Clark and Clark, 1947).

In short, forensic criminologists need to be aware of the significance of case outcomes to public policy since litigation can have far-reaching societal impacts and can profoundly affect the lives of litigants. As expert witnesses, forensic criminologists can assess evidence in a personal injury case; evaluate damages done to a person's reputation by an arrest and subsequent prosecution; address a plaintiff's claim that a company engaged in unequal treatment on the basis of race, gender, or age; or refute such claims and offer alternative explanations for unequal treatment in the workplace (Bielby and Coukos, 2007; Fiske et al., 1991; Hirsch and Quartaroli, 2011). In discussing forensic psychological evaluations in civil proceedings, Otto and Goldstein (2013, p. 7) make the following observation regarding the stakes involved in civil proceedings: "Litigants in civil proceedings can receive financial awards, important personal rights can be restricted or removed in guardianship and related proceedings—including the right to manage one's finances and make health-care decisions, the right to parent or visit one's children can be removed or limited in dependency or family court proceedings, and persons' liberty can be restricted via different involuntary hospitalization proceedings." Because law is deeply implicated in our economic, political, and social institutions, pursuit of social change invariably involves an engagement with law via litigation and expert witness investigation and testimony.

ADVERSARY AND ALLY: INTERACTIONS OF LAW AND SCIENCE IN EXPERT TESTIMONY

The work of forensic criminologists—for example, expert witnesses at trial—is different from the work of academic criminologists. Whereas academic criminologists work in a classroom, forensic criminologists provide expert testimony in courtroom, a conflictual setting that operates as a forum in which contending groups and interests struggle to produce sociolegal knowledge.

The legal process is organized confrontation, a structure that locks attorneys into an adversarial relationship in which plaintiffs and defendants each propose different accounts of the behavior and action of the accused. Each side may call one or more expert witnesses who will testify regarding the ways various theories can be applied to the facts of the case. Each side will challenge and contest the opposing theory, seek to refute it, and attempt to marshal evidence in support of its own theory. Criminological theories map directly onto legal doctrines of duty (of which foreseeability is an integral element), breach of duty (failure to act reasonably or to follow a recognized standard of care), and causation (whether proximate cause or cause-in-fact). These doctrines, in turn, provide explicit criteria for judging the theories and their application. Thus the courtroom becomes a battleground of theories, a forum of theoretical competition in which each side attempts to establish its position over the others and competes to prevail as the correct explanation of the events. Attorneys will question their own witnesses to elicit supporting testimony. They will also cross-examine opposing expert witnesses in an effort to obtain disconfirming expert testimony. In short, when a social scientist becomes an expert witness he or she faces a rugged and torturous challenge to his or her status as an expert and to the relevancy of the expertise.[1]

Over the decades, much discussion and debate has focused on the so-called conflictual and competitive relationship of law and science and the differences among forensic research and academic research (Burns, 2008; Jasanoff, 2009; Monahan and Walker, 2014; Peyrot and Burns, 2001; Smith, 2004). The adversarial nature of a trial addresses law and science as divergent institutions with antagonistic and competing camps of knowledge, values, and goals (Edmond and Mercer, 2004; Edmond, 2007). Haack (2009) argues that there are "deep tensions" between the goals and values of the scientific enterprise and the culture of the law. These tensions include the investigative character of science versus the adversarial culture of our legal system, the scientific search for general principles versus the legal focus on particular cases, the openness of science to new evidence versus the concern of the law for prompt and final resolutions, the scientific push for innovation versus the legal system's concern for precedent, and science's problem-oriented and pragmatic approach versus the legal system's reliance on formal rules and procedures.

In their discussion of wrongful conviction litigation, Leo and Gould (2009) contrast the different methodological orientations of legal scholarship and criminological and social science research. Criminological and social scientific methods tend to accept the multifactorial and complex nature of causation in legal cases and seek generalizable knowledge. Legal scholarship, in contrast, tends to embrace a narrative methodology focused on the presentation of idiosyncratic stories with the goal of particularizing knowledge. As Leo and Gould (2009, p. 14) argue:

> Unlike the social and physical sciences, legal scholarship is premised on doctrinal, not empirical, research. Although there has been a move of late to bring empirical skills to legal scholarship, neither quantitative nor qualitative methods are endemic to legal study, nor would a typical law professor be expected to acquire a facility with these methods. The typical path to the law professoriate is either through legal practice or a series of status markers based on one's performance as a law student (good grades and law review, leading to a prestigious judicial clerkship and an impressive first job). By contrast, scholars in the social sciences receive substantial methodological training and undergo an extensive apprenticeship while in graduate school to become proficient empirical researchers.

---

[1]For scholarship that addresses expert roles, role conflict, and role strain, see Anderson and Winfree (1987); Jenkins and Kroll-Smith (1996); Thornton and Voigt (1988).

There are important differences between the quest for truth in the courtroom and the quest for truth in science. "Scientific conclusions are subject to perpetual revision. Law, on the other hand, must resolve disputes finally and quickly," as noted by the U.S. Supreme Court.[2] According to an oft-cited report from the National Research Council (NRC) (2009, p. 12), the adversarial process relating to the admission and exclusion of scientific evidence is "not suited to the task of finding 'scientific truth.'" Judges and lawyers "generally lack the scientific expertise necessary to comprehend and evaluate forensic evidence." Moreover, trial judges who are normally sitting alone must decide evidentiary issues in the context of opposing experts. Typically, trial judges do not have the benefit of judicial colleagues or other avenues of rigorous review and evaluation that exist outside the court system. In addition, trial judges often have little time to familiarize themselves with the research, scholarship, and methods necessary to evaluate contending points of view. Some scholars have claimed that some judges are biased and make use of social science evidence only when it is supportive of a ruling a judge wants to make. Sometimes courts have ignored, dismissed, or misrepresented the findings of social science research (Cicchini and White, 2017). According to Costanzo and Krauss (2010, pp. 24–25):

> Intellectually, judges know little about empirical research and are unable (or perhaps unwilling) to make sense of it ... But the resistance is not only intellectual. There are also personal reasons ... Judges tend to be self-confident ... and protective of their prestige and power. When confronted with empirical research, they are likely to feel that they do not need help from social scientists ... [T]hey may view social science as undermining their power.

Another component of the adversary system is the default strategy of attorneys to neutralize the impact of science on legal decision-making or, ideally, to keep it out of legal proceedings altogether. To quote Jasanoff (1992, p. 348), the adversarial nature of litigation "is particularly conducive to the deconstruction of scientific facts, since it provides both the incentive (winning the lawsuit) and the formal means (cross-examination) for challenging the contingencies in the opponents' scientific arguments." Field (2010) suggests that there is a basic tension between attorneys and expert witnesses since each considers themselves to be an "expert." The "bottom line," as Field puts it, "is that lawyers do not like other experts on their turf and do not understand the specialist material which experts normally deliver in report form" (p. 544). As a result, lawyers will "argue against the need to call experts in the first place, challenge the expertise of individual witnesses, call their own experts with contrary views, and attempt to discredit the experts in the witness box by any means which does not involve actually engaging those experts in their own specialist area" (p. 544).

In discussing the relationship among law and expert witnesses, Dawid and colleagues (2014, p. 381) contend that there is "a yawning disconnect between how the law defines expert proof and the ability of science validly to supply such proof." Science typically wishes to infer "the effects of causes" (EoC), through experiments and observational studies, but legal fact finders want answers to "the causes of effects" (CoE). Legal fact finders cannot reasonably infer from general data alone that a particular effect is attributable to a known cause, yet they are ultimately charged with exactly this responsibility— of determining at some level of certainty what caused a particular effect. Dawid and colleagues note that applied science "which encompasses all of the science that the law cares about" (p. 381) is limited

---

[2]*Daubert v. Merrell Dow Pharmaceuticals, Inc.*, 509 U.S. 596–97 (Supreme Court 1995).

by the methods, both research and statistical, that are available to it in particular contexts. "The law, in contrast, constructs legal doctrines, either with utter disregard for what scientists might be able to say about the facts relevant to those doctrines or in light of a folk understanding of the science that might bear on those relevant facts" (p. 381).

Dawid and colleagues subscribe to a long-standing view that law and science "are entirely separate institutions," with distinctive and contrasting objects of concern and approaches to identifying what is important to examine (p. 382). As they put it,

> From the scientist's standpoint, law very often suggests hypotheses of interest or permits the application of hypotheses to new and salient contexts. From the law's standpoint, science very often supplies the brute facts integral to legal decision-making or policy formation or creates new matters that legal doctrine must address. In short, when law and science intersect, the two institutions continue to maintain their separate methods and objectives, with each eyeing the other for its own purposes. The law and science intersection can only be described from each of their relative perspectives (p. 382).

A central problem in the courtroom use of science is how best to reason from group data to an individual case. Whereas social scientists usually orient their research tasks to focus on phenomena at the group level, trial courts typically seek knowledge and evidence to solve cases at the individual level. That is, social scientists tend to seek knowledge that is generalizable while courts seek knowledge that is particularizing. In describing the gap between conventional scientific practice and ordinary trial practice, Faigman and colleagues (2014) argue for an analytical process they designate as "G2i" that involves reasoning from group data to decisions about individuals. All applied science and all expert evidence represent G2i issues. As Faigman and colleagues (2014, p. 420) describe:

> Experts testify to such matters as the conditions likely to lead to false confessions, the indicia of schizophrenia, factors that contribute to eyewitness misidentification, the cancer-causing properties of benzene, and thousands more. These are all general-population-based-statements about the empirical world. They are the "G" of G2i and represent the ordinary perspective of most research and most expertise. However, in the courtroom, the operative questions pertain to the particular case at hand, the "I" of G2i: Did the suspect falsely confess? Does the defendant have schizophrenia? Was the witness's eyewitness identification accurate? Did benzene cause the plaintiffs leukemia? … In terms of scientific inference, reasoning from the group to an individual case presents considerable challenges and, simply put, is rarely a focus of the basic scientific enterprise. In the courtroom, it is the enterprise.

Not all researchers and scholars agree with the assumption that law and science represent estranged institutions that are frequently in tension or conflict with one another. While it is true that attorneys will be successful at times in excluding scientific evidence from criminal and civil trials, the legal system does not have a universal antipathy toward science *en masse*. According to Roberts (2013, p. 50), "[t]he long history of legal reliance on scientific expertise and its central role in contemporary criminal investigations, prosecutions and trials flatly contradicts any suggestion of a criminal justice process or legal establishment with a pathological cultural resistance to science."

We argue that forensic criminological work and trial procedure are broadly congruent with the values and methods of scientific inquiry. We are skeptical of claims that dichotomize and reify distinctions between law and science as wholly adversarial, opposing, and contradictory. While there are adversarial elements across and within both institutions, there are also important convergences, similarities, and synergies. That is, the scientific research process for forensic criminologists in court shares many of the same features with the research process in academia. First, both science and law are the product of institutionalized decision-making that involves contest, dispute, and struggle. In both institutions, decision-making and evidentiary processes rely on formal rules of conduct, norms of research integrity, and ethical codes.

Second, both involve scrutinizing theoretical assumptions, empirical data, and methodological procedures to assess how we come to know what we know and under what conditions. Contestation and conflict are not peculiar to the courts and legal system per se. Rather, the application of the scientific method in forensic criminology reveals truth seeking to be a pragmatic quest for answers to the case at hand.

Third, there is a close relationship between judicial procedure and modern science since both pursue truth through open inquiry, vigorous testing by rivals, and objective reporting of results. As Roberts (2013, p. 54) notes, "the guiding thought animating adversarial legal process is that the best way of finding the truth ... is to allow the parties to collect their own evidence, marshal their own arguments, and battle it out between themselves in the presence of an impartial factfinder who will then render a verdict on the basis of the information adduced in evidence and tested in the course of the trial." These points dovetail with Cole's (2013) assertion that the legal system's putative adversarialism is analogous to the academy's tradition and culture of organized skepticism and peer review—features in Merton's (1973) idealized model of scientific practice, in which demonstrable evidence becomes the hallmark of empirical reality.

Fourth, the products and outcomes of the research process in the academic sector and in the court system depend on effective partnerships that are founded on norms of cooperation, empathy, and reciprocity. Effective partnerships between lawyers and forensic scientists are indispensable for exchanging information, communicating rules and procedures, and integrating scientific evidence into civil court proceedings. According to Roberts (2013, p. 49), "effective communication in the production of forensic science evidence is built on mutual respect, trust and understanding." A sense of empathy is the common bond that unites each professional participant in criminal proceedings. Each participant must be able to understand the respective roles, values, and objectives of the other. Scientific and legal fact-finding is a collective activity that is undergirded by institutionally approved research protocols and shared assumptions about evidence, proof, research inquiry, and ethics of research conduct. Fact-finding in civil trials is regulated by rules of admissibility tailored to juridical ends. Partnerships provide the social support for rules of conduct governing research activities including the collection and analysis of data and the evaluation of evidence. For attorneys and scientists, effective partnerships can help each group understand the legal, ethical, and social dimensions of science-based challenges in the courts. Partnerships can also help demonstrate how the application of scientific knowledge and technical skills can address legal issues before the courts.

In the adversarial context of the courtroom, the professional expertise of the academic criminologist is put to the test in ways unique to the legal process. The research work, evaluations, and investigative findings of forensic criminologists are highly scrutinized by attorneys, juries, and judges given the seriousness of the issues under litigation and the gravity of the stakes. In any courtroom setting, opposing attorneys may challenge the expert witness to the extent of his or her expertise, stigmatize an expert's research as bogus or irrelevant, and attack the credibility of the expert through cross-examination. Indeed, academic criminologists at trial are no longer the taken-for-granted experts that they typically are in the classroom. Instead, they face aggressive challenges to their expertise and objectivity, especially from lawyers whose job it is to limit their expert testimony and discredit their opinions. Criminologists and other social scientists who seek to do research in this context will do well to recognize its unique characteristics (for overviews, see Bates and Frank, 2010; Saks and Faigman, 2005; Brodsky, 2012; Brodsky and Gutheil, 2015; Wise, 2005).

Ultimately, the forensic criminologist is a guest of the courtroom and while he or she "may rule the lab or the classroom, the courtroom is ruled by judges and lawyers" (Kennedy, 2010, p. xvi). Forensic scientists conduct investigations and prepare evidence but judges and lawyers control the use and application of that evidence in court. Burns (2008, p. 108) reinforces these important points, stressing the different filters that govern the scrutiny of experts in the context of the courtroom:

> Expert witnesses must have and establish certain minimum qualifications and meet particular legal requirements before being permitted to offer their opinions at trial. In their own scientific communities, physical and social scientists are held to standards of accuracy and rigor in research and theory development. But in the courtroom, the proffered expert's credentials and opinions are also scrutinized and filtered through legal standards of evidence, admissibility, substantive law, and trial procedure, much of which is accomplished through the interactional practices of direct and cross examination.

In short, forensic criminologists must hone their skills and be prepared to have their research expertise, methods, opinions, and professional status exposed to intense examination and scrutiny by attorneys, judges, and juries. Before venturing into this precarious arena, social scientists need to be familiar with the rules and requirements they must meet in order to become an expert witness. That is, they must be knowledgeable about specific statutes, case law, rules of evidence, and have experience in conducting forensic investigations and assessments. They must also understand the standards of admissibility for expert testimony. As we discuss, although practical tensions undeniably exist between the institutions of law and science, these tensions are plausible once we understand the major components of civil law trial procedure, including evidentiary rules of admissibility, trial by jury, adversarial fact-finding, cross-examination, and the ethical duties of expert witnesses.

RULES REGARDING THE LEGAL ADMISSIBILITY OF EXPERT TESTIMONY

Before agreeing to serve as an expert witness, a forensic criminologist should know the general legal rules that govern expert testimony, including the Federal Rules of Evidence, statutes and case law that determine who can be qualified as an expert and how that occurs. Expert witnesses should be familiar with the law surrounding the admissibility of expert testimony and the limitations placed on experts when testifying. Statutory and evidentiary rules govern the qualification of an individual as an expert witness in court. The Federal Rules of Evidence—FRE Rule 702 provides basic background credentials for an expert, stating that an expert must be qualified by "knowledge, skill, experience, training, or education."[3] FRE 702 authorizes a judge to admit expert testimony into evidence if it assists the trier

---

[3]Federal Rules of Evidence. Article VII. Opinions and Expert Testimony. Rule 702. Testimony by Expert Witnesses. Available from: https://www.law.cornell.edu/rules/fre/rule_702 (Accessed 7 July 2017).

BOX 2.1 RULE 702. TESTIMONY BY EXPERT WITNESSES

A witness who is qualified as an expert by knowledge, skill, experience, training, or education may testify in the form of an opinion or otherwise if:

(a) the expert's scientific, technical, or other specialized knowledge will help the trier of fact to understand the evidence or to determine a fact in issue;

(b) the testimony is based on sufficient facts or data;

(c) the testimony is the product of reliable principles and methods; and

(d) the expert has reliably applied the principles and methods to the facts of the case.

Source: Cornell Law School. Legal Information Institute. Federal Rules of Evidence. Article VII. Opinions and Expert Testimony. Rule 702. Testimony by Expert Witnesses. https://www.law.cornell.edu/rules/fre/rule_702 (Accessed 8 August 2017).

---

of fact to "understand the evidence or to determine a fact in issue." Rule 702 establishes the rules for legal admission of expert testimony and specifies the role of the expert witness in the courts. The "trier of fact" is the judge and jury. If the expert's opinion is not based upon a reliable methodology, then it may not assist the trier of fact and the judge may exclude it. In general, in order for expert evidence to be admitted, it must be relevant, necessary, and given by a properly qualified expert. See Box 2.1 for a description of Rule 702.

Courts have long struggled to develop a set of rules and guidelines regarding the admissibility of expert evidence. "The task is easily framed," according to Saks and Faigman (2005, p. 106), "[h]ow is a judge to determine which kinds of opinions from which areas of asserted expertise are dependable enough to be permitted at trial?" Courts face a dilemma. They need experts and specialists to assist them in understanding the facts of a case. Courts also need assistance in "making decisions on issues about which they by definition know far less than the expert, yet for that very same reason courts are in a poor position to assess the expertise." Thus the "history of rules and procedures for screening expert witnesses represents successive responses to that dilemma" (p. 106).

While judges have been evaluating expert evidence for centuries, it was not until 1923 that the U.S. Supreme Court enunciated a test in *Frye v. United States* 293 F. 1013 (1923), a District of Columbia Court of Appeals decision on the admissibility of evidence from an early version of the polygraph. In *Frye*, the court established a general acceptance test for scientific testimony:

> Just when a scientific principle or discovery crosses the line between the experimental and demonstrable stages is difficult to define. Somewhere in this twilight zone the evidential force of the principle must be recognized, and while courts will go a long way in admitting expert testimony deduced from a well recognized scientific principle or discovery, the thing from which the deduction is made must be sufficiently established to have gained general acceptance in the particular field in which it belongs (p. 1014).

In *Frye*, the court held that expert testimony is admissible if the underlying scientific principles applied by the expert to the case have gained general acceptance within the relevant scientific community. The *Frye* test or *Frye* standard set the bar for the admissibility of expert testimony by requiring that experts demonstrate their expertise through education or experience. *Frye* also required that experts show through peer-reviewed literature and/or other scientific forums that their methods and theories are generally accepted in the scientific community. The overall purpose of the *Frye* decision was to prevent the admission of invalid data or evidence based on untested scientific principles that would bias and influence the court to reach an unfounded conclusion (Fradella et al., 2003). In short, *Frye* divided the admissibility of expert evidence into two categories: the credentials of the expert and the body of scientific knowledge the expert presents in the proceedings of a court case. Importantly, the *Frye* test became the major standard for one notion of the proper criterion for the admissibility of scientific evidence: the general acceptance of particular expertise within its scientific field.

SETTING THE STANDARDS FOR EXPERT TESTIMONY: THE SIGNIFICANCE OF THE DAUBERT TRILOGY

In the 1990s, the U.S. Supreme Court revisited the issue of the admissibility of expert testimony in three different cases: *Daubert v. Merrell Dow Pharmaceuticals, Inc.* 509 U.S. 579 (1993), *General Electric Co. v. Joiner* 522 U.S. 136 (1997), and *Kumho Tire Co., Ltd. v. Carmichael* 526 U.S. 137 (1999). Collectively, these three cases are known as the Daubert trilogy. See Box 2.2 for a short description of these court cases pertaining to admissibility.

In *Daubert*, the Supreme Court charged trial judges with the responsibility of acting as gatekeepers to allow or exclude expert testimony. The *Daubert* case arose when the parents of two children with limb reduction birth defects sued the manufacturer of the drug Bendectin, alleging that the children's birth defects had been caused by the mother's prenatal ingestion of the prescription drug to combat morning sickness. The District Court granted respondent summary judgment based on an expert's affidavit concluding, upon reviewing the extensive published scientific literature on the subject, that maternal use of Bendectin had not been shown to be a risk factor for human birth defects.[4] The court

---

BOX 2.2 KEY U.S. SUPREME COURT RULINGS ON THE ADMISSIBILITY OF EXPERT TESTIMONY

Daubert v. Merrell Dow Pharmaceuticals, 509 U.S. 579 (1993) ruling established the gatekeeping role of judges to exclude unreliable expert testimony. The U.S. Supreme Court held that the judge determines if evidence can be entered into a trial. Admissibility is determined by: (1) whether the theory or technique can be tested, (2) whether the theory or technique has been subject to peer review, (3) the known or potential rate of error of the technique or theory, and (4) whether the technique or theory has been generally accepted in the scientific community. The Court in *Daubert* declared that the focus must be solely on principles and methodology, not the conclusions that they generate.

General Electric Co. v. Joiner, 522 U.S. 136 (1997) affirmed the role of judges as gatekeepers to ensure expert testimony is both relevant and reliable to be admissible. The decision also required judges to have a deeper understanding of the scientific issues in order to determine if an expert's methodology and data support the conclusions.

Kumho Tire Co. v Carmichael, 526 U.S. 137 (1999) required that courts evaluate all scientific and experience-based expert evidence by the same admissibility criteria. The *Kumho* ruling clarified that the judge's gatekeeping function applies to all expert testimony, thereby eliminating the task of having to differentiate between scientific and nonscientific evidence.

---

[4]Summary judgment is a judgment entered by a court for one party and against another party summarily dismissing the case without a full trial. Such a judgment may be issued on the merits of an entire case or on discrete issues in that case. "Summary judgment procedure is a method for promptly disposing of actions in which there is no genuine issue as to any material fact" (Cornell Law School. Federal Rules of Civil Procedure; Title VII. Judgement. Rule 56. Summary Judgment. Available from: https://www.law.cornell.edu/rules/frcp/rule_56 (Accessed 24 July 2018)).

determined that the plaintiffs' evidence in the case did not meet the *Frye* "general acceptance" standard for the admission of expert testimony. The Court of Appeals agreed and affirmed. The U.S. Supreme Court decided to review and granted certiorari—an order by which a higher court reviews a decision of a lower court—to determine the appropriate standard for admission of expert testimony. The Court also established a nonexclusive checklist for trial courts to use in evaluating the reliability of expert testimony (see Box 2.2). Under *Daubert*, the basis of expert evidence must comprise information that is based on scientifically valid reasoning, is reliable, and was obtained through sound scientific methods (for overviews, see Solomon and Hackett, 1996; Jasanoff, 2002; Edmond and Mercer, 2013).

In *General Electric v. Joiner* (1997), the U.S. Supreme Court affirmed the role of judges as gate-keepers to the admissibility of expert testimony. The case concerned whether the "abuse of discretion" standard is the correct standard an appellate court should apply in reviewing a trial court's decision to admit or exclude expert testimony. Abuse of discretion refers to a standard of review used by appellate courts to review decisions of lower courts. A judgment will be termed an abuse of discretion if the adjudicator has failed to exercise sound, reasonable, and legal decision-making skills. The U.S. Supreme Court held that appellate courts must review trial court admission decisions under *Daubert* deferentially and that an expert must demonstrate how his or her conclusions are derived from a reliable methodology rooted in the scientific method. The Supreme Court also underscored the importance of judicial gatekeeping by insulating the trial judge's admissibility determinations from appellate review.

The case arose in 1992 when Robert Joiner sued General Electric Co. in Georgia state court, alleging that his small cell lung cancer was caused by workplace exposure to chemical "PCBs" and their derivatives, including polychlorinated dibenzofurans (furans) and polychlorinated dibenzodioxins (dioxins). Attorneys for Joiner provided the District Court with expert witnesses' depositions that testified that PCBs, furans, and dioxins promote cancer. The court granted General Electric summary judgment, reasoning that there was no genuine issue as to whether Joiner had been exposed to furans and dioxins and that his experts' testimony had failed to show that there was a link between exposure to PCBs and small cell lung cancer. In reversing, the Court of Appeals held that the District Court erred in excluding the testimony of Joiner's expert witnesses. In 1997, the U.S. Supreme Court ruled that abuse of discretion, the standard ordinarily applicable to review of evidentiary rulings, is the proper standard by which to review a district court's decision to admit or exclude expert scientific evidence. Additionally, the Court held that the proper application of the correct standard of review indicates that the District Court did not err in excluding the expert testimony at issue.[5]

Finally, *Kumho Tire Co. v. Carmichael* (1999) ruled that *Daubert*'s evidentiary reliability requirement applies to all fields of expert evidence, not only to science. In 1993, the right rear tire of a minivan driven by Patrick Carmichael blew out and the vehicle overturned. One passenger died in the accident and several others were severely injured. Subsequently, the Carmichaels sued the Kumho Tire Company and others, claiming that the tire was defective. A significant part of the Carmichaels' case turned on the testimony of Dennis Carlson, Jr., an expert in tire failure analysis. Carlson intended to testify to support the Carmichaels' conclusion that a defect in the tire's manufacture or design caused the blow out. To support this conclusion, Carlson used a methodology that was partly disputed. Attorneys for Kumho moved to exclude Carlson's testimony on the ground that his methodology failed to satisfy

---

[5]*General Electric Company* v. *Joiner*. Oyez, Available from: https://www.oyez.org/cases/1997/96-188. Accessed 25 July 2017.

Federal Rule of Evidence 702. The Federal District Court granted the motion, excluded Carlson's testimony, and entered summary judgment for Kumho. The court found that Carlson's methodology was insufficiently reliable. In reversing, the Court of Appeals concluded that a federal trial judge's "gatekeeping" obligation under the Federal Rules of Evidence was limited to scientific context, and not Carlson's testimony, which the court characterized as skill-based or experience-based. In 1999, the U.S. Supreme Court ruled that a federal trial judge's "gatekeeping" obligation, under the Federal Rules of Evidence, applies not only to "scientific" testimony but to all expert testimony.[6]

LESSONS OF THE DAUBERT TRILOGY

The Daubert trilogy of cases offers four lessons for forensic criminologists. First, taken together, the Daubert trilogy of cases places the admissibility of expert evidence and testimony in the trial judge. That is, *Daubert* requires judges to evaluate whether the research methods and theories used by the expert witness are reliable. To quote Saks and Faigman (2005, p. 110), "Under *Frye*, judges did not need to understand research methodology because it was sufficient to inquire into the conclusions of professionals in the pertinent fields. *Daubert* mandates that judges query which methods support the scientific opinions that experts seek to offer as testimony, and this requires that they understand those methods and data." As Dawid and colleagues (2014, p. 371) put it, the "basic distinction between *Frye* and *Daubert* is one of perspective. *Frye* requires judges to ask the respective fields from which the science comes whether it is 'generally accepted,' while *Daubert* puts the onus on judges to inspect the scientific foundation for the proffered testimony."

Second, the four *Daubert* factors (See Box 2.2) reflect the everyday operation and conduct of scientific investigation. These factors are the suggested standards for lower courts to use to admit good science, exclude "junk science," and prevent unqualified experts from testifying based on irrelevant information. That said, the four-factor test of *Daubert* is a set of suggested criteria courts can use to evaluate ostensibly scientific evidence. It is not strict and rigid but flexible and accommodating. No one criterion or codified set of criteria would be necessary to assess the validity of every kind of science much less every kind of expertise. As noted in the Advisory Committee Notes to the 2000 Amendments to Rule 702: "no single factor is necessarily dispositive of the reliability of a particular expert's testimony."[7] The ruling of *Daubert*, as made clear in *Kumho*, applies to all expert testimony and obligates trial courts to determine whether the basis for proffered expert testimony is reliable and valid. Importantly, the four *Daubert* factors offer guidance regarding a large proportion of experts, particularly those from professional fields in which quantitative empirical methods are the norm of investigation. But other *Daubert* factors, such as error rates, for example, have no meaning in qualitative methods or inductive forms of theorizing that are popular in the humanities and social sciences. Moreover, as noted by Justice Blackmun, the author of the majority opinion in *Daubert*,

---

[6]*Kumho Tire Company, Ltd.* v. *Carmichael*. Oyez, Available from: https://www.oyez.org/cases/1998/97-1709. Accessed 25 July 2017.

[7]*See, e.g., Heller v. Shaw Industries, Inc.*, 167 F.3d 146, 155 3d Cir. (1999) ("not only must each stage of the expert's testimony be reliable, but each stage must be evaluated practically and flexibly without bright-line exclusionary (or inclusionary) rules."); *Daubert v. Merrell Dow Pharmaceuticals, Inc.*, 43 F.3d 1311, 1317, n.5 9th Cir. (1995) (noting that some expert disciplines "have the courtroom as a principal theatre of operations" and as to these disciplines "the fact that the expert has developed an expertise principally for purposes of litigation will obviously not be a substantial consideration").

"[p]ublication (which is but one element of peer review) is not a sine qua non of admissibility; it does not necessarily correlate with reliability" (Edmond, 2007, p. 860).

Importantly, the U.S. Supreme Court recognized the diversity of forms of scientific investigation and expert testimony and noted that trial judges should apply *Daubert* factors flexibly. Moreover, the Court in *Kumho* did not attempt to offer a universal set of criteria for evaluating experts for whom some or all of the *Daubert* criteria might not be decisive or sufficient. "Auto mechanics, historians, accountants, clinical medical doctors, and scores of others have traditionally testified but would not be able to meet one or more *Daubert* criteria" (Saks and Faigman, 2005, p. 113). Clearly, the U.S. Supreme Court and the Federal Rules of Evidence suggest that courts could permit many experts from these fields and others to testify. At the same time, trial judges are empowered to determine if the bases for the opinions experts intend to offer are sufficiently valid to admit. *Kumho* makes clear that what matters is not merely the field of expertise, but the expert's specific proposition. The trial judge is to assess reliability based on "the nature of the issue, the expert's particular expertise, and the subject of the testimony."[8]

Third, in addition to the four *Daubert* factors listed in Box 2.2, courts before and after *Daubert* have found other factors relevant in determining whether expert testimony is sufficiently reliable to be considered by the trier of fact. These factors include: (1) whether experts are "proposing to testify about matters growing naturally and directly out of research they have conducted independent of the litigation, or whether they have developed their opinions expressly for purposes of testifying";[9] (2) whether the expert has unjustifiably extrapolated from an accepted premise to an unfounded conclusion;[10] (3) whether the expert has adequately accounted for obvious alternative explanations;[11] (4) whether the expert "is being as careful as [he or she] would be in … regular professional work outside … paid litigation consulting."[12] As Justice Stephen Breyer made clear in *Kumho*, the objective of *Daubert* gatekeeping "is to make certain that an expert … employs in the courtroom the same level of intellectual rigor that characterizes the practice of an expert in the relevant field."[13] (5) Whether the field of expertise claimed by the expert is known to reach reliable results for the type of opinion the expert would give.[14]

The U.S. Supreme Court in *Daubert* declared that the evaluation of the admissibility of expert testimony "must be solely on principles and methodology, not on the conclusions they generate" (509 U.S. at 595). Yet as the Court later recognized, "conclusions and methodology are not entirely distinct from

---

[8]*Kumho Tire*, 526 U.S. at 151, 119 S. Ct. 1167 (1999).

[9]*Daubert v. Merrell Dow Pharmaceuticals, Inc.*, 43 F.3d 1311, 1317 9th Cir. (1995).

[10]*See General Elec. Co. v. Joiner*, 522 U.S. 136, 146 (1997) (noting that in some cases a trial court "may conclude that there is simply too great an analytical gap between the data and the opinion proffered").

[11]*Claar v. Burlington N.R.R.*, 29 F.3d 499 9th Cir. (1994) (testimony excluded where the expert failed to consider other obvious causes for the plaintiff's condition). Compare *Ambrosini v. Labarraque*, 101 F.3d 129 D.C.Cir. (1996) (the possibility of some un-eliminated causes presents a question of weight, so long as the most obvious causes have been considered and reasonably ruled out by the expert).

[12]*Sheehan v. Daily Racing Form, Inc.*, 104 F.3d 940, 942 7th Cir. (1997).

[13]*Kumho Tire Co. v. Carmichael*, 119 S.Ct. 1167, 1176 (1999).

[14]*Kumho Tire Co. v. Carmichael*, 119 S.Ct. 1167, 1175 (1999) (*Daubert's* general acceptance factor does not "help show that an expert's testimony is reliable where the discipline itself lacks reliability, as, for example, do theories grounded in any so-called generally accepted principles of astrology or necromancy"); *Moore v. Ashland Chemical, Inc.*, 151 F.3d 269 5th Cir. (1998) (en banc) (clinical doctor was properly precluded from testifying to the toxicological cause of the plaintiff's respiratory problem, where the opinion was not sufficiently grounded in scientific methodology); *Sterling v. Velsicol Chem. Corp.*, 855 F.2d 1188 (6th Cir. 1988) (rejecting testimony based on "clinical ecology" as unfounded and unreliable).

one another."[15] The trial court scrutinizes not only the principles and methods used by the expert, but also whether he or she properly applies those principles and methods to the facts of the case. Under the Daubert trilogy of cases, the task for the "court in deciding whether an expert's opinion is reliable is not to determine whether it is correct, but rather to determine whether it rests upon a reliable foundation, as opposed to, say, unsupported speculation."[16] Dvoskin and Guy (2008) argue that *Daubert* encourages courts to ask two questions of experts: "Why should we believe you?" and "Why should we care?" The first speaks to the credibility, reliability, and validity of experts' opinions while the second question speaks to the relevance of the opinions to be offered to the specific questions raised in the case. Rule 702 simply requires that: (1) the expert be qualified, (2) the testimony address a subject matter on which the fact finder can be assisted by an expert, (3) the testimony be reliable, and (4) the testimony "fit" the facts of the case. Importantly, opposing counsel can challenge qualifications, reliability, and relevance separately. Nevertheless, courts have found that despite the tendency of these elements of admissibility to overlap, each of these elements of expert evidence "are distinct concepts that courts and litigants must take care not to conflate."[17]

Fourth, the trilogy of cases requires an expert to demonstrate by a preponderance of the evidence that his or her methods and opinions are reliable. Preponderance of evidence refers to the relevant degree of certainty or standard of persuasion to establish claims and defenses. A preponderance of evidence is evidence that is more credible, convincing, reasonable, and probable than evidence offered in opposition to it. These sources of support or foundation include the expert's training, experience, special expertise, literature review, reliability of the method(s), and applicability of research and methods to help explain to the trier the facts of the immediate case. As noted by Greenberg (2003, p. 237), "[t]o be a preponderance, the weight of evidence for one side must outweigh the evidence for the other." Preponderance does not simply mean the number of witnesses, documents, or simple arguments and facts in favor of one side. Rather, preponderance means that the "overall composite balance of which side's argument, opinion, and information is likely to be correct or is more persuasive."

Over the decades, the *Daubert* standard has gradually replaced the *Frye* test by which the courts evaluate expert evidence in many jurisdictions. As of 2017, only nine states still followed *Frye*, three states used both *Frye* and *Daubert*, and the rest of the states had adopted the *Daubert* standard (Morgenstern, 2017). Saks and Faigman (2005, p. 118) note that one "unmistakable impact" of *Daubert* "has been the production of many hundreds of scholarly articles on the admissibility of expert testimony … concerning the meaning and role of the Daubert trilogy and their application by lower courts." Through 2005, "the federal courts alone have recently averaged about 500 decisions per year on *Daubert*-related issues. Many of those decisions involved *Daubert* hearings at which scrutiny was given to proffers of expert evidence, many of which, before *Daubert*, entered court with little if any scrutiny." Over the last decade, researchers and scholars have continued to debate what standards of admissibility should apply to expert testimony, the impact of the Daubert trilogy of decisions on the nature and role of expert testimony, and whether *Daubert* has conferred excessive power on judges to be gatekeepers of

---

[15]*General Electric. Co. v. Joiner*, 522 U.S. 136, 146 (1997).

[16]See, e.g., In re Scrap Metal Antitrust Litigation, 527 F.3d 517 6th Cir. (2008). Quoted material appears in Dunitz, Jonathan M. 2013. *"Daubert* in the realm of financial damages experts." *Insights.* Autumn, 2011. Available from: www.willamette.com.

[17]*Quiet Technology DC-8 v. Hurel-Dubois UK Ltd.*, 326 F.3d 1333, 1341 (11th Cir. 2003).

BOX 2.3 RULE 26. DUTY TO DISCLOSE; GENERAL PROVISIONS GOVERNING DISCOVERY

(2) Disclosure of Expert Testimony. (B) Witnesses Who Must Provide a Written Report. Unless otherwise stipulated or ordered by the court, this disclosure must be accompanied by a written report—prepared and signed by the witness—if the witness is one retained or specially employed to provide expert testimony in the case or one whose duties as the party's employee regularly involve giving expert testimony. The report must contain:

(i) a complete statement of all opinions the witness will express and the basis and reasons for them;

(ii) the facts or data considered by the witness in forming them;

(iii) any exhibits that will be used to summarize or support them;

(iv) the witness's qualifications, including a list of all publications authored in the previous 10 years;

(v) a list of all other cases in which, during the previous 4 years, the witness testified as an expert at trial or by deposition; and

(vi) a statement of the compensation to be paid for the study and testimony in the case.

Source: The Federal Rules of Civil Procedure (FRCP) are published in the official U.S. Code in the appendix to Title 28, Judiciary and Judicial Procedure. This portion (26(a)(2)(B)) discusses the expert's report. For the complete rule, visit http://www.law.cornell.edu/rules/frcp/. Source: Cornell University Law School. https://www.law.cornell.edu/rules/frcp/rule_26 (Accessed 28 July 2017).

---

expert evidence.[18] These debates will no doubt continue and forensic criminologists will need to take into account patterns of judicial decision-making that could affect the admissibility of expert testimony.

Finally, no discussion of admissibility of expert evidence would be complete without specifying the criteria for expert reports. Box 2.3 provides an overview of the Federal Rules of Evidence-Rule 26. The box lists guidelines to the discovery process and flow of information between the expert and the client-attorney. Rule 26 provides the basic requirements, from the federal court's perspective, for the expert's written report. In addition to the components specified in Rule 26, the report should include a list of the specific issues the retaining attorney has asked the expert to address. Importantly, the expert witness report should contain a detailed and thorough description of methods, data sources, and analytical techniques used in the research and investigation. The report should also include a bibliography. In addition to the requirements listed in Box 2.3, experts are required to compose a list of all professional publications upon which they have relied with complete bibliographic information. Experts should also provide a list of all other cases that they have testified in during the previous 4 years. Rule 26 also requires an accurate statement of the compensation to be paid for the investigation and testimony in the case. This statement should include the following: a copy of a current fee schedule or engagement letter for the specific case; and/or a case-specific invoice for the fees, expenses, and estimates of time for future work.

CANDOR, OBJECTIVITY, AND ETHICS IN EXPERT TESTIMONY

Whether on the stand at trial or seated in the witness chair during deposition, the forensic criminologist must understand his or her role in the civil court system. The fundamental purpose of the expert is to assist the trier of fact, be it judge or jury, in deciding the issues of a given case by providing technical

---

[18]The impact of *Frye* and the *Dauberg* trilogy of cases on the admissibility of social science evidence in general is discussed in Buchman (2007); Edmond and Mercer (2004); Edmond (2007); Saks and Faigman (2005); Faigman and Monahan (2005); Mark (1999); Smith (2004); Tenopyr (1999); Jenkins and Kroll-Smith (1996); Field (2010); Wise (2005).

opinions on subject matter considered to be beyond the realm of common knowledge. In so doing, the forensic criminologist is to "present findings and opinions in a fair and objective manner, to not engage in nor participate in a partisan distortion or misrepresentation of evidence, and generally to provide services in an objective manner" and in a way consistent with the highest standards of their profession (Greenberg, 2003, p. 235). Civil courts expect to hear from competent experts who will provide testimony that is both relevant and reliable and who will bring to the stand the same judiciousness they would apply in the laboratory, the classroom, or at a presentation to their colleagues. Thus every forensic criminologist should consider whether his or her investigations and contributions would meet the expectations expressed in the Daubert trilogy of cases.

Scholars have debated the meaning and importance of objectivity for decades. As in the past, there remains much controversy over the goals and outcomes of objectivity. Being objective requires a researcher to be precise, unbiased, open, honest, and receptive to criticism. All social sciences aspire to the goal of objectivity, which is a frame of mind so that personal prejudices, preferences, or predilections of the researchers do not contaminate the processes of data collection and data analysis. Federal guidelines require universities to develop and implement an "objectivity in research policy" in order to be eligible to receive sponsored research. Regulations from the National Institutes of Health (NIH), National Science Foundation (NSF), and the Department of Health and Human Services (HHS) establish standards and procedures to be followed by institutions that apply for research funding to ensure that the design, conduct, and reporting of research "will not be biased by any conflicting financial interest of those investigators responsible for the research."[19] Like all scientific investigations, expert witness investigations and testimony should be free from deception, prejudices, and ideological biases. Objectivity suggests that the design, conduct, and reporting of research will be based on the ethical principles of fairness and transparency. These ethical principles are important to protect the credibility and integrity of the research process.

We believe it is important for the forensic criminologist to "clearly limit himself or herself to the role of expert rather than advocate" and "avoid the pitfalls of advocacy research and emotive statistics" (Kennedy, 2010, p. xvi). The forensic criminologist is an impartial party, a fair-minded expert who renders an opinion based on the facts presented in a legal case. Taylor-Austin (2014, p. 109) reminds us that "[t]he role of the expert is to remain neutral, review the facts presented by the prosecution and defense, and render their expert opinion based on those facts." Importantly, the expert witness does not advocate or work for the plaintiff or the defense. Rather, the expert "renders an unbiased opinion based on [his or her] education, knowledge, skill, experience, and understanding of scholarly resources." Forensic social scientists are not at trial to act as partisans and argue a position as advocates for retaining counsel. An expert is paid for his or her time and expertise, not the conclusions. The forensic criminologist most accurately represents the state of criminological knowledge and applies criminological methods and theories to understand the results of the forensic examination in question. He or she is to render an opinion as a dispassionate teacher.

Moreover, ideologically oriented opinions and emotionally driven testimony are not likely to be admitted under Rule 702 if opinions and testimony cannot assist the trier of fact to understand the

---

[19]National Institutes of Health (NIH). 1995. *Objectivity in Research NIH Guide*, 24(25), July 14, 1995. This document was published in the Federal Register of July 11, 1995 with an effective date of October 1, 1995. The National Science Foundation has published a similar policy in the same issue of the Federal Register. The requirements are almost identical.

evidence and facts. The judge's decision on the admissibility of expert evidence, quite appropriately, will thus center on the expert's credibility and the relevance of his or her opinions to the question before the court. Burns (2008, p. 108) summarizes the role of the judge in admitting expert evidence:

> Significantly, it is the judge who makes the final decision on the admissibility of scientific evidence when that evidence is disputed or an objection is raised by the other side. A proper objection to expert testimony can result in an admissibility hearing to determine what scientific evidence the jury will be permitted (or not permitted) to hear at trial. During admissibility hearings, challenges are regularly made by the opposing side to the qualifications and expertise of the purported expert and/or to the scientific basis of his or her testimony. The adversary commonly characterizes the "science" in question as not widely accepted by others in the relevant field, as provisional knowledge claims at best, and/or as scientifically flawed in its assumptions, procedures, or conclusions … Many times, the adversary argues that the testimony amounts to "junk science" … and it is left up to the judge to sort things out and make a ruling.

If the testimony of forensic criminological experts is not based on the principles of competence, relevance, balance, and candor, it is unlikely to be trustworthy and it is probably not going to be beneficial to the courts. The expert must be stringently honest about his or her credentials and publications because they will be carefully checked by opposing counsel. Dvoskin and Guy (2008, p. 208) argue that expert testimony is a "simple process": "By simply answering questions honestly, telling the court what we know, how we know it, and what we do not know, we will not only abide by our legal oath to be truthful, but also will maintain the credibility that is ultimately the only asset for which we get paid."

In short, forensic criminologists should embrace the holy trinity of credibility: expertise, trustworthiness, and relevance. Expertise refers to the formal aspects of experience and training, such as academic and clinical training, positions held, and professional accolades received. Trustworthiness addresses the degree of confidence that the trier of fact places in the expert and his or her motivations, opinions, and testimony. Relevance addresses the fit between the forensic investigation and the facts of the case that concern the plaintiffs and defendants. Importantly, although credibility is achieved through years of education, experience, and preparation, it can be easily destroyed if an expert is caught in a lie. Experts should cross-examine themselves prior to giving testimony and frequently ask themselves the same question that they will likely be asked at trial: "How do I know that?" (i.e., credibility) and "Why should anyone care?" (i.e., relevance).

CONCLUSIONS: AS CRIMINOLOGY MEETS THE FORENSIC REALM

As we conclude this chapter, we wish to state that a forensic criminologist's investigation and testimony should have five basic elements or components. First, expert investigation and testimony should produce case-specific evidence derived from social science principles. Second, expert investigations should be thorough and relevant to assist the trier of fact to understand the evidence or to determine a fact in a case. Third, expert investigation and testimony should reflect mainstream disciplinary knowledge and draw on extant scholarship to develop case-specific opinions and evidence. Fourth, in their expert witness reports and testimony at deposition and trial, forensic criminologists should develop explanations that begin with middle-range theories and evolve toward substantive theories or ad hoc explanations of the etiology of the criminal event and the relationship of the event to the larger socio-spatial context (Blaikie, 2000; Bourgeois, 1979; Merton, 1968). In the work of Robert Merton, middle-range theory starts its theorizing with delimited aspects of social phenomena rather than with a broad, abstract entity such as society or social system. Theories of the middle-range are firmly backed up by observed data and have a limited conceptual range. Neither judges nor attorneys will be impressed with the jargon of grand theory. Moreover, highly abstract theorizing in which the formal organization and arrangement of concepts takes priority over understanding the facts of a case will be received quite lukewarmly in the lawyer's office and will mystify and confuse the jury.

Fifth, forensic criminologists should write their reports for lay audiences and minimize the use of complex and complicated scientific language. We recognize that this can be a challenge. A scientist's specialized knowledge can sometimes be a hindrance to effective communication with a lay audience. Successful lay communication requires that the expert anticipate the audience's (e.g., jury's) knowledge or perspective on the subject. One strategy to enhance communication to a lay audience is to present the findings and conclusions first, answering why and how questions, and then communicate more detailed background information later.

Forensic criminologists should best approach juries in a manner appropriate for an introductory social science course rather than as one might teach a graduate seminar for aspiring academic sociologists and criminologists. Experts must beware of being caught up in highly technical lingo or statistical elaboration lest they lose the attention of jurors and judges alike. In short, an effective witness will act as an educator rather than a lecturer. As Dvoskin and Guy (2008, p. 209) put it,

> Experts by definition are well-educated people, but the effective expert will not try to put this on display. In short, be humble and be simple. Most experts want the jury to realize how smart the expert is; but the most effective experts want the jury to realize how smart the jury is. This means explaining one's opinion, and the inferences and evidence on which they are based, clearly and in English. The expert who educates the trier of fact is able to convince instead of impress. If the judge or jury truly understands and agrees with the evidence and logic that form the basis of the inferences and opinions, then the expert will have excelled. "Blowing them away" with complicated verbiage and sophisticated theories just encourages juries to dismiss an expert's input.

Finally, we wish to express to the reader that, as a general principle, the law expects forensic criminologists and other expert witnesses to be staunch supporters and promoters for their methodology. The forensic criminologist's role is to present evidence relevant to his or her expertise and not to champion for a given verdict. These points are entirely consistent not only with the rules and standards of admissibility of expert testimony, but also with the methods of scientific inquiry.

PREMISES LIABILITY FOR NEGLIGENT SECURITY LITIGATION

3

INTRODUCTION

This chapter examines the concepts of foreseeability, breach of duty, and causation as they relate to premises liability for negligent security litigation. A premises liability for negligent security lawsuit is a claim for damages in civil court on behalf of a crime victim against the owner or controller of the premises where the crime event occurred (Kaminsky, 2008, p. 3). The injury in a negligent security case may arise out of robbery, rape, assault, carjacking, kidnapping, or battery. If someone dies or is killed due to the negligence or misconduct of a premises owner or manager, the victim's family or survivors may sue for "wrongful death." These types of lawsuits seek compensation for the survivors' loss, such as lost wages from the deceased, lost companionship, and funeral expenses. The victim of the crime (or survivors) usually asserts that owners of the premises failed to prevent foreseeable and avoidable attacks from happening. Negligent security assumes that appropriate security measures could have prevented the crime or at least made it less likely to happen. That is, the landlord's failure to provide adequate security to protect people from crime events at the premises was the cause of the victim's injuries. Even though the landlord did not actually commit the crime, the crime victim will claim that the landlord should be held liable for it and compensate the crime victim for his or her injuries.

A basic scenario for cases involving property owner responsibility for criminal acts that occur on the premises is as follows:

> A business invites members of the public to come onto its property. Jane Doe, a member of the public, legitimately enters the property. For jurisdictions that keep track of such designations, she would be an "invitee." While on the property, Ms. Doe is attacked and injured. Her assailant either flees or is caught and convicted. Regardless of whether the attacker remains at large or in jail, Ms. Doe sues the property owner on a theory of premises liability. She would argue that the property owner should have known that there was a likelihood of an attack and should have taken steps to prevent it. The courts will decide whether the property owner owes a duty to the plaintiff and is liable for her injuries based on the *foreseeability* of the attack (quoted from La Fetra, 2006, pp. 409–10, emphasis in original).

In this example, the duty to provide security is related to the foreseeability of crime. That is, the more foreseeable the crime, the greater the duty to provide security. Concerning cause-in-fact, Ms. Doe might argue that "but for" the business owner's negligence, the attack would not have occurred, or that this negligence was a substantial factor contributing to the injury. As for proximate cause, she must

41

show that the business owner possessed or should have possessed knowledge concerning the possibility of danger to customers on the property or that the injury was a natural and direct consequence of conditions there. The property owner may have ignored complaints about past violent incidents, undesirable loiterers, and poor lighting. Several muggings may have taken place on and/or near the property in recent months. Finally, there must be actual damages to Ms. Doe for which she might claim compensation.

Over the decades, courts have imposed a legal duty on landlords and business owners to exercise reasonable care to prevent foreseeable criminal acts from occurring on their premises (for an overview, see Kaminsky, 2008). Insofar as the merchant controls the particular space for business purposes, the courts will generally hold the merchant responsible for taking reasonable precautions for protecting the customer from foreseeable harms, including the criminal acts of third parties (Zinober, 2015). The rationale underlying the courts' imposition of legal duty upon business owners is that individuals should be relatively safe in their apartments, schools, shopping areas, restaurants, entertainment venues, and workplaces. For example, a customer attacked in a store's restroom or car park may sue the business owner or manager. A hotel guest sexually assaulted in her room by a nighttime intruder may have a cause of action against hotel management. Students at a university, visitors to a corporate headquarters, and tenants of an apartment complex are increasingly looking to the courts to order compensation from the owners and managers of the premises where they were injured (Adolf, 2012; Kennedy, 2013; Michael and Ellis, 2003; Savard and Kennedy, 2014; Walby, 2014). In these kinds of cases, the plaintiff must prove that the defendant owed him/her a duty to protect against reasonably foreseeable criminal acts. The plaintiff also must prove that his or her injuries were caused by the defendant's breach of duty.

Prior the 1970s, premises liability for negligent security lawsuits were rare and large verdicts and settlements were uncommon (Moore, 1984; Purcell, 2010). According to Kaminsky (2008, p. ix), "[a]s recent as the mid-1980s, personal injury actions against landlords for crimes committed within their buildings were virtually unheard of. Yet today, these high-exposure cases constitute a large percentage of caseloads of most state courts located in urban areas." A 2003 survey of businesses conducted by the Institute of Management and Administration (2004) reported that one out of every five organizations faced a security-related lawsuit in 2003, and nearly one in two large companies (30,000 employees or more) suffered the same fate (see also Kennedy 2006, p. 120). Kaminsky (2008, p. 5) suggests that "premises security lawsuits are among the fastest growing segment of personal injury lawsuits … Moreover, owners of residential property are not alone in being targeted as defendants in premises security cases. Claims against hospitals, colleges, day care centers, and especially shopping malls are increasing dramatically."

Over the last several decades, multimillion-dollar settlements and jury verdicts against owners and landlords have become commonplace (Bates, 2004; de Treville, 2004). An oft-cited study conducted by Liability Consultants suggested that the average reported verdict against a landlord in favor of an assault victim was over $1 million. Of the reported cases from 1992 to 2001 studied by Liability Consultants, 40% of the awards or settlements were amounts less than $250,000; 16% were between $250,000 and $500,000; 13% were in the $500,001 to $1 million range; and another 13% fell in the $1 to $2 million category. Ten percent of plaintiffs received $2 to $5 million, and 8% obtained more than $5 million (Anderson, 2002).

Other data suggests that there have been millions of dollars in punitive and compensatory damages awarded to plaintiffs by juries. In 2011, a $4,255,280 jury verdict was rendered in favor of a plaintiff who was shot outside Boomers!, a children's entertainment and fun park in Dania Beach, FL. Juries have awarded damages of $1.7 million to a plaintiff after a fatal stabbing at a nightclub; $1.6 million to a plaintiff who was raped at a mobile home park; $68,318.14 verdict to patron assaulted at a bar; and $8,010,000 to the estate of a man shot and killed in a parking lot while walking to his vehicle.[1] In May 2018, a jury in Georgia handed down a $1 billion verdict against a security company after an apartment complex guard was convicted of raping a 14-year-old girl (Brumback, 2018; Victor, 2018). These reported cases are only the tip of the iceberg, however. Far more cases go unreported because they are resolved by settlement between the parties before trial, and these settlements can often involve amounts exceeding a million dollars.

In this chapter, we describe how forensic criminologists can be crucial in premises liability cases based on negligent security. We first discuss the various political, cultural, and social factors underlying the historical development of negligent security litigation. We then describe the four tests for assessing crime foreseeability: imminent danger/harm test, prior similar incidents test, totality of circumstances test, and the balancing test. Next, we discuss breach of duty, standards of care, and the two elements of causation: cause-in-fact and proximate causation. Finally, we describe the notion of abstract negligence and show how a forensic criminologist can use different criminological theories and perspectives to evaluate crime foreseeability and address causation in the analysis of crime events.

As we point out, in any forensic investigation, the forensic criminologist must use a scientific methodology in compliance with *Daubert* and Federal Rule of Evidence 702 ("Rule 702").[2] Expert testimony may be a product of the conscientious application of data collection procedures and the use and application of observational and descriptive research to the facts of the case (Mitchell et al., 2010, p. 1109). An expert's report should be detailed and contain opinions, bases for opinions, and materials relied upon. The report should not provide conclusory allegations of negligence. Instead, using the scientific method, the expert should consider such things as the type of business, level of security on the premises, crime demographics, the location of the premises, and crime foreseeability. Importantly, the forensic criminologist must apply these concepts to the facts of the specific case to form opinions. Of course, the forensic criminologist should use his or her education, training, and experience to develop case-specific opinions. In addition, the forensic expert can assist counsel in pointing out faulty opposing arguments, preparing witnesses, and marshaling affirmative defenses.

ESTABLISHING A DUTY OF CARE: THE HISTORICAL DEVELOPMENT OF NEGLIGENT SECURITY LITIGATION

The historical development of premises liability for negligent security litigation has been fraught with struggles and conflicts over issues related to meanings and definitions of duty, foreseeability, causation, and assessment of damages. Prior to 1960, appellate court decisions affirming a civil judgment in favor of a crime victim against a defendant who did not commit the crime were rare. Courts typically held that the defendant owed no duty to protect the victim from criminal attack. Courts also held that a criminal act severed any proximate causal link between the alleged negligence of the defendant and the

---

[1]These and other cases are reported in LexisNexis Litigation Resource Community Staff. June 11, 2012. "Inadequate Security Cases Involving Third-Party Crimes Yield Favorable Results." https://www.lexisnexis.com/legalnewsroom/litigation/b/jverdicts/archive/2012/10/19/inadequate-security-cases-involving-third-party-crimes-yield-favorable-results.aspx (Accessed 20 September 2017).
[2]Bates and Frank (2010) and Keller (2004) provide information and overviews of the impact of *Frye*, *Daubert*, and *Kumho* on premises security admissibility considerations.

harm. In general, courts considered criminal attacks to be events that people and institutions could not anticipate and, as such, declined to hold third parties liable. In *Weihert v. Piccione*, a restaurant owner was not held liable for failing to provide necessary protection in his restaurant to the plaintiffs, who were patrons in the eatery, from an assault and battery upon them by another customer. The court held that "failure to have provided 'guards' or 'bouncers' in the establishment did not constitute causal negligence, for the reason that had such been provided, it cannot be assumed that they would have prevented the assault which occurred instantly and without warning."[3]

For decades, courts applied this general no-duty stance to landlords, landowners, and property managers. Before the 1970s, a landlord was not considered liable to tenants for injuries caused by the criminal acts of third persons, regardless of the inadequacy of the security measures provided by the landlord. Generally, courts refused to impose a duty to protect others from criminal acts because of an unwillingness to treat security deficiencies as the proximate cause of a tenant's criminally induced injuries. The prevailing public sentiment was that "imposing a security obligation on landlords would be unfair, either because of the difficulty of defining with clarity a standard of care for landlords to follow or because of the fact that landlords, who already pay taxes to support police, would be burdened with additional crime-prevention expenses" (Moore, 1984, p. 17). Related, many courts and government officials held the belief that the imposition of any security responsibility should be left up to the prerogative and discretion of legislatures and not businesses themselves (see Yelnosky, 1986, pp. 883, 889).

Through the 1960s, states struggled over whether to impose a duty on businesses to provide guests with security and protection from reasonably foreseeable criminal assaults. In 1965, section 344 of the American Law Institute's *Restatement (Second) of Torts* recognized a general duty owed by businesses to ensure a reasonable degree of safety and security for visitors. According to this section,

> A possessor of land who holds it open to the public for entry for his business purposes is subject to liability to members of the public while they are upon the land for such a purpose, for physical harm caused by the accidental, negligent, or intentionally harmful acts of third persons or animals, and by failure of the possessor to exercise reasonable care to (a) discover that such acts are being done or are likely to be done, or (b) give a warning adequate to enable the visitors to avoid the harm, or otherwise to protect them against it.

Furthermore, comment (f) to section 344 spoke directly to the business possessor's duty to police the premises:

> Since the possessor is not the insurer of the visitor's safety, he is ordinarily under no duty to exercise any care until he knows or has reason to know that the acts of the third person are occurring, or are about to occur. He may, however, know or have reason to know, from past experience, that there is a likelihood of conduct on the part of third persons in general which is likely to endanger the safety of the visitor, even though he has no reason to expect it on the part of any particular individual. If the place or the character of his business, or his past experience, is such that he should reasonably anticipate careless or criminal conduct on the part of third persons, either generally or at some particular time, he may be under a duty to take precautions against it, and to provide a reasonably sufficient number of servants to afford a reasonable protection.

---

[3]*Weihert v. Piccione*, 273 Wis. 457, 78 N.W.2d 757, 78 N.W. 757 (1956).

Several social, economic, and legal factors converged during the 1960s and 1970s to catalyze a transformation in cultural attitudes toward premises security litigation and landlord–tenant relations. First, the passage of Great Society legislation and the rise of many social movements including the anti-Vietnam war movement, the women's movement, the gay rights movement, the environmental movement, and the civil rights movement helped set in motion a broad shift in American social and political culture and public policy. Through protest and agitation, these social movements heightened the politicization of other protest groups during the 1960s and 1970s, including combative groups of housing activists committed to fair housing and the adoption of an implied warranty of habitability, a warranty implied by law in residential leases that the premises are fit and habitable for living (Mostafa, 2006, p. 979). In 1977, the American Law Institute (1977) approved and issued the Restatement of the Law Second, Property, which comprehensively set forth landlord-tenant law, including the implied warranty of habitability. The Restatement represented the legal establishment's full embrace of this shift in responsibility for an apartment's livability from tenants to landlords. Today, the District of Columbia and every state except Arkansas have recognized the implied warranty of habitability through legislation or case law (Brower, 2010).

Second, the civil rights movement, anti-Vietnam war movement, women's movement, consumer's movement, and fair housing movement operated in tandem to reinforce and bolster the victims' rights movement, a fledgling grassroots coalition that emphasized the rights of individuals to seek justice and compensation for criminal harm. Central to the victims' rights movement was the promotion of legislation that would guarantee substantive rights for victims and provide procedural mechanisms to enforce those rights. Also important was the emphasis on victim restitution and victim compensation, the provision of educational resources and legal assistance, and the establishment of the country's first hotlines and shelters for victims of crime. As a result of political mobilization, victims' rights advocates were successful in creating several powerful organizations to champion victims' interests and concerns. These organizations included the National Crime Victim Law Institute (NCVLI), National Alliance of Victims' Rights Attorneys (NAVRA), National Organization for Victim Assistance (NOVA), the National Center for Victims of Crime, and Respect Inspire Support Empower (RISE), a nongovernment organization advocating for a bill of rights for sexual assault victims. Through legal advocacy, training and education, direct services to victims, and public policy work, these organizations were successful in getting legislation passed including the Victims of Crime Act of 1984 (codified as 42 U.S.C. §§ 10601–10604 (2006)) which enumerated the rights afforded to victims in federal criminal cases (for overviews, see Beloof, 2005; Carrington and Rapp, 1991; Spalek, 2016; Wallace and Roberson, 1998). Over the decades, many states have created crime victim compensation programs to mitigate the financial burdens thrust upon crime victims. These programs provide funds to cover victim medical expenses, lost work time, and property loss and damage (Adams and Osborne, 2001; Roland, 1989).

A third major impetus for the rise of premises security litigation was a series of court cases during the 1970s that ruled landlords had a duty to take steps to protect tenants from foreseeable criminal acts committed by third parties. In the 1970 case of *Kline v. 1500 Massachusetts Avenue Apartment Corporation*, Sarah Kline, a tenant, sued her landlord for injuries she sustained from being assaulted and robbed in the common hallway of the apartment complex. She moved into an apartment owned by 1500 Massachusetts Avenue Apartment Corporation in October 1959. At the time, the three entrances to the apartments and the adjoining garage area were patrolled by security guards. However, by 1966, decreases in funding and guard shortages resulted in the entrances being unprotected. Larcenies, robberies, and violent crimes began increasing against the tenants of the apartment building. On November

17, 1966, Kline was assaulted and robbed in the common area outside her apartment. Two months earlier another woman had been assaulted and robbed in the same area. Kline sued the apartment corporation claiming it had a duty to take reasonable measures to protect tenants from foreseeable criminal assaults and violence. The district court held there was no duty, and Kline appealed. The appeals court ruled the landlord had a duty to take steps to protect Kline since only the landlord had sufficient control of the premises to do so. The court also ruled that "the most analogous relationship to that of the modern day urban apartment house dweller is not that of a landlord and tenant, but that of innkeeper and guest."[4] In short, the duty of care the courts impose on innkeepers also applied to the landlord and, therefore, the landlord–tenant contract required the landlord to provide those protective measures that are within its reasonable capacity.

In *Garzilli v. Howard Johnson's Motor Lodges, Inc.,* the internationally known recording artist, Connie Francis Garzilli, sued Howard Johnson's for an assault and rape she suffered in 1974 while in her motel room. The sliding glass doors in the motel room gave the false appearance of being securely locked, but an intruder could easily open the faulty latches from the outside. The property manager had known the locks were defective but had not yet provided for secondary locking devices. The notoriety of the Connie Francis case came because of her star status and because the jury initially awarded her an unprecedented $2,650,000 in total damages after finding that the motel's failure to provide reasonable security measures was the proximate cause of the beating and rape. At the time, the recovery in *Garzilli* was the largest judgment ever awarded where a jury held a third party liable for a sexual assault that had occurred on the premises (Palmer, 1989). The *Garzilli* case was a "watershed event" in the history of negligent security litigation, according to Addicott (2017, pp. 862–863):

> *Garzilli* greatly expanded the legal obligations owed to tenants in terms of "reasonableness"; which, in turn, expanded the level of care now owed to prevent such foreseeable criminal harm … Now viewed through the new prism of the Connie Francis case, if premises owners did not institute greater level of reasonable precautions to protect guests on their property from the foreseeable criminal acts of third parties, they could face huge monetary punishments.

The convergence of the *Kline* and *Garzilli* cases, the rise of the implied warranty of habitability, and the growth in social consciousness about victims' rights all emboldened crime victims to pursue redress through the civil courts. Buell (1995, pp. 58, 59) identified the *Garzilli* case as the "mother if not grandmother" of all premises security cases since it launched a tidal wave of litigation against owners and operators of business establishments, not just hotels. In the wake of *Garzilli*, according to Addicott (2017, p. 863), "scores of civil actions were filed across the nation not only by victims assaulted at hotels or motels, but also at shopping malls, movie theatres, restaurants, bars, public parks." Bublick's (2006) study of sexual assault cases found that the number of civil cases brought by sexual assault victims increased dramatically in the 30 years after the *Garzilli* case and that the "vast majority" of cases at the appellate level involved at least some claims against a third-party defendant. This shift toward suing third parties has been so prominent that Bublick described it as "an evolution in the very nature of the litigation itself" (p. 61). Research by Bazyler (1979), Homant and Kennedy (1997), Rooney (1995), Chock and Kondo (1989), and Ciaccio (1993) document the increasing frequency of

---

[4]*Kline v. 1500 Massachusetts Avenue Apartment Corp.*, 439 F.2d 477 116 D.C. Cir. (1970).

negligent security litigation in the 1980s and later. Today, all states now recognize that business possessors owe, under circumstances that vary from state to state, a duty to protect their customers from the criminal acts of third parties. Courts may hold property owners legally liable should an assailant harm a customer, client, tenant, guest, or other category of visitor while on the property (Kaminsky, 2008; Dain and Brennan Jr, 2003; Kennedy, 2014; Kennedy and Hupp, 1998; Mostafa, 2006).

FORESEEABILITY APPROACHES TO NEGLIGENT SECURITY CLAIMS

In a premises liability for negligent security case, the plaintiff must establish by a preponderance of the evidence that (1) the defendant owed the plaintiff a duty to protect him/her from harm generally or harm from criminal assault; (2) the defendant breached this legal duty by failing to act as the duty required; (3) the defendant's breach of duty was the cause-in-fact and a proximate cause of injuries sustained by the victim of the assault; (4) the plaintiff suffered harm or injury. The concept of harm translates to financial damages a court awards to a plaintiff. There will be no liability where the defendant owed no duty of care to the victim under the facts of the case; the defendant exercised reasonable care in discharging any duty to the victim; and the defendant's actions or lack of actions did not proximately cause the victim's injury.

Special relationships, such as those involving an innkeeper-guest, landlord-tenant, common carrier-passenger, hotel-guest, employer-employee, convenience store employee-customer, and school-student relationships, may give rise to a duty to protect the guest, tenant, passenger, employee, student, customer, or visitor (Zinober, 2015, pp. 290–291). These special relationships dictate that the legal duty of the owner or controller of the premises is limited to protecting against only those criminal acts that are reasonably foreseeable. Judges apply the law of a particular jurisdiction to establish the existence of a special relationship.

Attorneys, judges, and juries may rely on the analyses of trained forensic criminologists to assess and determine the foreseeability of a harm given a specific set of facts. In premises liability cases, foreseeability is a factor in the analysis of (1) whether the property owner had a duty to the injured person, and (2) whether the alleged failures of the property owner to provide adequate protection caused the injury. Importantly, without foreseeability, there is no duty to provide security. Conventional premises liability for negligent security cases will fail in the absence of foreseeability. To establish that a crime was foreseeable to a defendant, the plaintiff must show that the defendant knew or should have known that a crime was reasonably likely to occur (Kaminsky, 2008). As one attorney notes, "[w]ithout proof that the crime was foreseeable to the property owner or controller, a court will have no choice but to enter a directed verdict on behalf of the defendant" (Zinober, 2015, p. 315).

Duty and foreseeability, however, are malleable and flexible concepts. The same criminal attack may be reasonably foreseeable under one set of circumstances but a remote possibility under another situation. Foreseeability is a critical issue in negligent security cases because it is an element of both duty and causation (La Fetra, 2006, pp. 409–410). Definitions of the legal concept of foreseeability vary by state and each jurisdiction will sometimes provide more than one designation based on its own case law (Jacobs, 2006, p. 54). In its tenth edition, Black's Law Dictionary defines foreseeability as "a reasonable or likely consequence of an act" (Black et al., 2009). Most jurisdictions use variations of this definition such as "reasonably likely to occur," "reasonable cause to anticipate," or "appreciable chance."

To prove foreseeability, plaintiffs typically must show that the defendant had actual or constructive prior notice of the type of harm in question. *Actual notice* refers to past criminal conduct in the general area or on the specific site. Actual notice is important to forensic criminologists because past events tend to be reliable predictors or forecasters of future events. To determine whether crime is likely to happen in the future, a forensic criminologist examines what has happened in the past, particularly immediate past, and investigates whether there is evidence that the business owner was aware or should have been aware of the danger. *Constructive notice* may occur independently of actual notice to suggest that a certain level of crime is reasonably foreseeable. Here the forensic criminologist would examine whether "there was sufficient information available that a reasonably prudent person would have been aware of the danger" (Homant and Kennedy, 1997, p. 5).

When determining whether a premises owner had actual or constructive knowledge that an atmosphere of violence existed, the forensic criminologist should investigate (1) the overall pattern of criminal activity prior to event in question that occurred in the general vicinity of defendant's business premises, and (2) the frequency of criminal activity on premises. The challenge for the defense counsel in negligent security cases is to "limit the breadth of evidence that plaintiff may present related to foreseeability" (Dain and Brennan Jr, 2003, p. 85). If the plaintiff is unable to offer any evidence of notice to the landlord, then the defense could be in a position to make a request for summary judgment and thereby end the litigation. In contrast, attorneys for the plaintiff may try to expand the scope of what is relevant to the issue of foreseeability.

To provide guidelines on how to apply foreseeability to the fact pattern of a case, many jurisdictions embrace particular "tests" of foreseeability. While a definition of foreseeability is useful in orienting the forensic criminologist to the concept, a test of foreseeability suggests which analytical steps a court is likely to follow to determine whether a certain crime was foreseeable, and thus whether there exists a duty to protect. For analytic purposes, a forensic criminologist should consider foreseeability as a continuous rather than a discrete variable and evaluate foreseeability on a continuum from not foreseeable to highly foreseeable (Petherick et al., 2010, pp. 246–247; Voigt and Thornton, 1996).

In general, courts use four basic tests of foreseeability in premises liability for negligent security cases. These tests include the imminent harm test, prior similar incidents test, totality of circumstances test, and the balancing test. See Box 3.1 for a description of these tests. A few jurisdictions do not impose any duty on a business owner to protect patrons from third-party criminal assault, absent a "special relationship" between the business owner and patron. Some jurisdictions, such as Alabama, follow a restrictive approach that imposes liability only in exceptional circumstances. At the other end, the broadest exposure of defendants to liability comes in those jurisdictions that follow the "totality of circumstances" approach, for example, Arizona and Massachusetts. Other jurisdictions follow either a "known aggressor/imminent danger" approach, for example, Alaska and Oregon, or a "prior similar incidents" approach, for example, Texas and Washington. Remaining jurisdictions follow other approaches that are analytical hybrids of the previous approaches or follow the "balancing test," for example, Louisiana, Tennessee, and North Carolina, among other states. In short, not all courts follow the same test in defining and measuring foreseeability. Thus, the forensic criminologist must be familiar with past case law, legal precedent, and the controlling cases in a particular jurisdiction.

BOX 3.1 FOUR TESTS OF FORESEEABILITY

(1) *Specific Imminent Harm Test*. According to this test, a landowner does not owe a duty to protect patrons from the violent acts of third parties unless she or he is aware of specific imminent harm about to affect them. Most courts reject the "specific imminent" harm test as too restrictive in limiting the duty of business owners to their invitees. **Major Cases**: *Burns v. Johnson*, 458 S.E. 2d 448 (Va. 1995); *Dudas v. Glenwood Golf Club, Inc.*, 540 S.E.2d 129 (2001); *Neagele v. Dollen*, 63 N.W.2d 165 (Neb. 1954); *Bailey v. Bruno's Inc.*, 561 So.2d 509, 510–511 (Ala. 1990); *McDonald v. PKT, Inc.*, 628 N.W. 2d (Mich. 2001); *Willonon v. Walmart Stores, Inc.*, 957 F.Supp 1074 (E.D. Ark 1997); *Taboada v. Daly Seven, Inc.*, 271 Va. 313, 626 S.E.2d 428 (2006); *Delta Tau Delta v. Johnson*, 712 N.E.2d 968, 973 (Ind.1999).

(2) *Prior Similar Incidents Test*. In order to establish foreseeability requiring a landowner to take precautions against third-party crime, the plaintiff must establish a past history of similar criminal conduct on or near the premises. Legal scholars and researchers have criticized the "similar incidents test" because of the variability of what kind of crimes and how many crimes are necessary to trigger a duty. **Major Cases**: *Laverdorf v. Supermarket General Corp.* 657 N.Y.S.2d 732 (N.Y. App. Div. 1997); *Wood v. Centermark Properties, Inc.* 984 S.W.2d 517, 523 (Mo. App. 1998); *L.A.C. V. Ward Parkway Shopping Center Co., L.P.*, 75 S.W.3d 247, 258 (Mo. 2002); *Boren v. Worthen National Bank of Arkansas*, 921 S.W.2d 934 (Ark. 1996); *Timberwalk Apartments, Partners, Inc., et al. v. Cain* (972 S.W.2d 749 Tex. 1998); *Trammell Crow Cent. Texas, Ltd. v. Gutierrez*, 267 S.W.3d 9 (Tex. 2008).

(3) *Totality of Circumstances Test*. This test looks to a host of factors such as the nature, condition and location of the land, the level of crime in the surrounding area, and any other factors that may alert the landowner to the likelihood of crime. Some courts have rejected the "totality of circumstances" test as being too broad and open-ended. **Major Cases**: *Isaacs v. Huntington Memorial Hospital* 211 Cal.Rptr. 356, 695 P.2d at 659; *Reitz v. May Co. Dept. Stores*, 583 N.E. 2d 1071, 1074 (Ohio Ct. App. 1990); *Maguire v. Hilton Hotels Corp.* 899 P.2d 393, 400 (Haw. 1993); *Whittaker v. Saraceno*, 635 N.E. 2d 1185, 1188 (Mass. 1999); *District of Columbia v. Doe,*524 A.2d 30, 33 (D.C.1987); *Seibert v. Vic Regnier Builders, Inc.*, 253 Kan. 540, 856 P.2d 1332, 1339 (1993); *Doud v. Las Vegas Hilton Corp.*, 109 Nev. 1096, 864 P.2d 796, 802 (1993); *Clohesy v. Food Circus Supermarkets, Inc.*, 149 N.J. 496, 694 A.2d 1017, 1023–1024 (1997); *Reitz v. May Co. Dept. Stores*, 66 Ohio App.3d 188, 583 N.E.2d 1071, 1074 (1990).

(4) *The Balancing Test*. This test seeks to address the interests of both business proprietors and their customers by balancing the foreseeability of harm against the burden of imposing a duty to protect against criminal acts of third persons. **Major Cases**: *Ann M. v. Pacific Plaza Shopping Center*, 863 P.2d 207, 215 (Cal. 1993); *McClung v. Delta Square Ltd. Partnership*, 937 S.W.2d 891 (Tenn. 1996); *Posecai v. Walmart Stores, Inc.* 753 So.2d 762, 767–768 (La. 1999); *Bass v. Gopal, Inc.* 716 S.E. 2d 940 (S.C. 2011).

Source: Kennedy, D.B., 2006. Forensic Security and the Law. In: Gill, M. (Ed.), Handbook of Security. Palgrave Macmillan, New York, pp. 118–45; Kennedy, D., Sakis, J., 2008. From crime to tort: criminal acts, civil liability and the behavioral science. In: Canter, D., Zukauskiene, R. (Eds.), Psychology and Law. Ashgate Publishing, Aldershot, UK, pp. 119–142; Twerski, A., Shane, J., 2018. Bringing the science of policing to liability for third-party crime at shopping malls. Marquette Law Rev. 101 (3), 775–802.

IMMINENT DANGER/HARM TEST

The imminent danger approach posits that a property owner is generally not liable to protect visitors or keep tenants safe from third-party criminal activities unless there is a reason to know that an assailant was aggressive or prone to violence. The imminent danger approach to foreseeability is one of the older tests that tends to be stricter and more rigid than the other tests. Essentially, this test requires the plaintiff to show that a landlord was aware that a specific individual was acting in a manner to pose a clear and present danger to the safety of an identifiable target. Courts in some states ask whether a landholder knew or should have known from situational cues that a particular crime was about to happen (Jacobs, 2006, p. 54). Here, the level of the duty depends on whether a crime is imminent. Without imminence, courts will generally find that the landowner or property manager owes no duty to protect visitors from criminal acts of third parties.

Only a few states follow this "known aggressor/imminent danger" approach. In Alaska, a district court held that the owner of a bar where a fight broke out was not liable in the absence of sufficient evidence that the assailant was a violent, quarrelsome patron.[5] In Arkansas, a business owner or proprietor owes a duty to provide reasonable protection to patrons "only where the owner or its agent was aware of the danger presented by a particular individual or failed to exercise proper care after an assault has commenced."[6] In a case cited by Jacobs (2006, p. 54), a plaintiff was forced into a hotel room where she was robbed and assaulted. The hotel was in close proximity to a high-crime area, and there were previous occurrences of violence at that property. Nevertheless, the court found no duty to protect because the defendant could not have reasonably anticipated the harm's occurrence.[7] The general rule in Virginia is that there is no common law duty for an owner or occupier of land either to warn or to protect an invitee on her or his property from the criminal act of a third party.[8] Overall, Young (2014) and Rajan and colleagues (2015, p. 57) note that the "known aggressor/imminent danger" approach is an outlier. Few courts are willing to hold that a criminal act is foreseeable only if the landlord had knowledge that a third-party assault was imminent. Accordingly, the majority of states have adopted one of the remaining three tests of foreseeability.

PRIOR SIMILAR INCIDENTS: HISTORY IS MORE IMPORTANT THAN IMMINENCE

The prior similar incidents approach focuses on the similarity of past criminal events at or near the premises to establish foreseeability and thus determine whether a property owner is liable for negligent security. A plaintiff must show that these past incidents are sufficiently similar, numerous, and geographically and temporally proximate to the premises to provide adequate notice to a reasonable individual that a violent crime may occur. That is, the foreseeability of a crime event will be primarily based on whether there were prior, similar crimes in the same location that the owner or possessor knew or should have known about. In the absence of prior similar incidents, a property owner is not obligated to anticipate the criminal activities of third persons.[9]

Courts often raise the question as to how "similar" the prior criminal conduct must be to prove relevant. Zinober (2015, pp. 316–319) suggests that Florida courts "seem to be split on the subject" and Young (2014, p. 21) argues that "these issues remain unsettled" in California. Referring to Wisconsin cases, Purcell (2010) contends that "most courts demand that the prior crimes and the subject crime be an 'apples to apples' comparison" for prior criminal activity to establish a reasonable foreseeability with respect to a specific crime. In other words, prior criminal assaults on the defendant's property make another assault "reasonably foreseeable." In contrast, several incidents of nonviolence (e.g., property vandalism) on the defendant's premises do not make a violent crime at that same location foreseeable.

Most courts require a "substantial similarity" between the prior criminal activity and the particular crime in question. That is, the foreseeability of future criminal acts may be established by evidence of

---

[5]*Hedrick v. Fraternal Order of Fishermen of Alaska* (13 Alaska 652, 103 F. Supp. 582 (Terr. Alaska 1952)).

[6]*Boren v. Worthen Nat. Bank of Arkansas*, 324 Ark. 416, 921 S.W.2d 934, 940 (1996).

[7]*Rosen v. Red Roof Inns Inc.* 950 F Supp. 156 (E.D. Va. 1997).

[8]*Taboada v. Daly Seven*, Inc., 271 Va. 313, 626 S.E.2d 428 (2006).

[9]*Isaacs v. Huntington Meml. Hosp.*, 695 P.2d 653, 658 Cal. (1985) (quoting *Wingard v. Safeway Stores, Inc.*, 176 Cal. Rptr. 320, 324 Cal. App. 3d Dist. (1981)); La Fetra (2006), p. 412.

prior criminal acts of a "substantially similar" nature to those at issue, such that "a reasonable person would take ordinary precautions to protect his or her customers ... against the risk posed by that type of activity."[10] Importantly, "substantially similar" does not mean identical. That is, courts do not usually require proof of prior identical acts to warrant finding a duty to protect. Quoting La Fetra (2006, p. 419), "[t]he sheer difficulty of weighing various types of criminal activity to determine foreseeability is one reason why the question is deemed a matter of law for the court to decide, rather than left to more unpredictable juries." Related, courts that use prior criminal activity to determine foreseeability and, hence, liability will address whether or not the prior crimes resembled closely enough the criminal activity generating the claimed injury. As one Texas court pointed out:

> Although criminal conduct is difficult to compartmentalize, some lines can be drawn. For instance, we have held that reports of vandalism, theft, and neighborhood disturbances are not enough to make a stabbing death foreseeable. Similarly, although the repeated occurrences of theft, vandalism, and simple assaults at the [defendant's premises] signal that future property crimes are possible, they do not suggest the likelihood of murder.[11]

Rajan and colleagues (2015, p. 56) argue, citing New York cases, that "there is no requirement that previous criminal activity be of the same kind as that which a plaintiff experienced. Rather, the criminal conduct need only be reasonably predictable based on prior occurrences of the same or similar criminal activity at a location sufficiently proximate to the subject location, and it need not occur at the subject location." In an oft-cited 2002 case involving the rape of a 12-year-old girl in a shopping mall in Kansas City, the Missouri Supreme Court found that "[f]oreseeability does not require identical crimes and identical locations."[12] What is required is that prior incident be sufficient to attract the landowner's attention to a dangerous condition which resulted in the litigated incident.[13]

The Texas Case of *Timberwalk Apartments, Partners, Inc., et al. v. Cain* offers a comprehensive and exhaustive framework for assessing foreseeability by considering the most relevant and applicable aspects of prior similar incidents. The court in that case decided that fact finders must consider five

---

[10]*Martin v. Six Flags Over Georgia* II, LP, 801 SE 2d 24—Ga: Supreme Court (2017); *Sturbridge Partners, Inc.*, 267 Ga. at 786, 482 S.E.2d 339; *Lau's Corp., Inc. v. Haskins*, 405 SE 2d 474 477 Ga: Supreme Court (1991): "Many circumstances may require a landowner to warn the invitee of latent dangers." See, e.g., *Knowles v. La Rue*, 102 Ga.App. 350, 116 S.E.2d 248 (1960); *Ward v. Veterans of Foreign Wars Post 2588*, 109 Ga.App. 563, 136 S.E.2d 481 (1964); *Sutton v. Sutton*, 145 Ga. App. 22, 243 S.E.2d 310 (1978). An establishment's location in a high crime area may also support the finding of a duty on the part of the landowner to guard against criminal attacks. "Certainly, a high crime rate in a particular area may increase the risk of harm to patrons so that a prudent owner will take security precautions" as noted in *Lau's Corp., Inc. v. Haskins*, 405 SE 2d 474–477 Ga: Supreme Court (1991). That said, courts have been reluctant to require owners to post signs warning of a generalized risk of crime. See, for example, *Woodall v. Rivermont Apartments Ltd. Partnership*, 239 Ga.App. 36, 40–41, 520 S. E.2d 741 (1999). Evidence that the landowner had knowledge of a volatile situation brewing on the premises can establish foreseeability as well. See, for example, *Good Ol' Days Downtown, Inc. v. Yancey*, 209 Ga.App. 696, 697 (2), 434 S.E.2d 740 (1993) (summary judgment improper where bar owner's employees witnessed escalation of hostile behavior for more than five minutes prior to assault on patron).

[11]*Trammell Crow Cent. Texas, Ltd. v. Gutierrez*, 267 S.W.3d 9 (Tex. 2008).

[12]*Lac v. Ward Parkway Shopping Center Co.*, 75 S.W.3d 247 259 (Mo. 2002).

[13]*Agnes Scott College, Inc. v. Clark*, 273 Ga. App. 619, 616 S.E.2d 468, 200 Ed. Law Rep. 888 (2005), cert. denied (Sept. 19, 2005); *Sturbridge Partners, Ltd. v. Walker* (267 Ga. 785 (1997)).

factors to determine whether criminal conduct was foreseeable: proximity, recency, frequency, similarity, and publicity. That is, "courts should consider whether any criminal conduct previously occurred on or near the property, how recently it occurred, how often it occurred, how similar the conduct was to the conduct on the property, and what publicity was given the occurrences to indicate that the landowner knew or should have known about them."[14] Importantly, these factors—proximity, recency, frequency, similarity, and publicity—must be considered *together* in determining whether criminal conduct was foreseeable. As the Texas Supreme Court ruled in the *Timberwalk* case:

> Thus, the frequency of previous crimes necessary to show foreseeability lessens as the similarity of the previous crimes to the incident at issue increases. The frequent occurrence of property crimes in the vicinity is not as indicative of foreseeability as the less frequent occurrence of personal crimes on the landowner's property itself. The court must weigh the evidence using all the factors.[15]

Generally, courts are more likely to find a crime "reasonably foreseeable" if prior criminal activity has occurred on the premises of the defendant and within relatively close proximity to the crime at issue.[16] However, courts have struggled with issues of geographic and temporal proximity of crime, and no "hard and fast" rules exist to determine whether a particular geographic or temporal relationship between the defendant and prior criminal activity satisfies the "reasonably foreseeable" standard. Some courts have held that the prior criminal activity must have actually occurred on the same premises to be relevant.[17] Other courts have allowed evidence of prior criminal activity within an area "sufficiently proximate" to the premises.[18] As discussed by Purcell (2010, p. 10), the definition of "sufficiently proximate" can include anything from the parking lot immediately adjacent to the defendant's premises to a neighboring property. The judge typically has the discretion to set the geographic boundaries of the prior crime evidence that the court will consider in determining "reasonable foreseeability."

A related concern is the appropriate period of time for which courts should evaluate prior similar incidents. The trial judge sets the time limitations on prior criminal acts that the court can consider in its evaluation of "reasonable foreseeability." According to Purcell (2010), no consistent time frame exists. Courts have allowed evidence of prior crimes going as far back as 10 years to establish "reasonable foreseeability." Some courts have limited the admissibility of prior criminal activity to one year before the crime event in question.[19] While a forensic criminologist working for the plaintiffs may wish to

---

[14]*Timberwalk Apartments, Partners, Inc. v. Cain*, 972 SW 2d 757 (Tex. 1998).

[15]*Timberwalk Apartments, Partners, Inc. v. Cain*, 972 S.W.2d 759 (Tex. 1998).

[16]See, for example, *Romero v. Giant Stop-N-Go of New Mexico, Inc.*, 146 N.M. 520, 212 P.3d 408 (2009) (holding that evidence of prior robberies, theft, physical altercations, domestic violence, harassment, narcotics and suspicious persons at same location did not make targeted and deliberate shooting of plaintiff's decedents foreseeable). Courts have held that the prior acts must have happened in the vicinity of the location where the act at issue occurred before that act can be deemed foreseeable. See *Sigmund v. Starwood Urban Inv.*, 475 F.Supp.2d 36, 46 D.C. (2007) (looking at a five-block radius around area of the attack and concluding that sudden and unexpected attack was not foreseeable).

[17]See, for example, *Rivers v. Hagner Management Corp.*, 959 A.2d 110 Md. App. (2008).

[18]See, for example, *Novikova v. Greenbriar Owners Corp.*, 694 N.Y.S.2d 445 (1999).

[19]Some courts have held that the prior acts must have happened relatively recently, *Dwiggins v. Morgan Jewelers*, 811 P.2d 182, 183 Utah (1991) (one robbery 5 years earlier insufficient to make subsequent robbery foreseeable), and with some degree of frequency. See *Dudas v. Glenwood Golf Club, Inc.*, 261 Va. 133, 140, 540 S.E.2d 129 (2001) (two robberies within the month preceding the attack on plaintiff was not enough for foreseeability because there was no imminent danger).

extend the number of years back in time upon which to assess foreseeability, defense experts generally prefer that courts consider a much shorter time period. The International Association of Professional Security Consultants (IAPSC) and the *General Security Risk Assessment* Guideline published by the ASIS International (formerly the American Society for Industrial Security) (ASIS, 2003, p. 12) suggest 3–5 years prior to the date of the incident as a relevant time frame. Many courts consider a two- to three-year prior history to be a relevant time frame to assess crime foreseeability. Generally, the closer in time prior crime is to the subject crime, the more likely it will support a crime foreseeability argument.

TOTALITY OF CIRCUMSTANCES TEST

Critics of the prior similar incidents test argue that the test implies that a landlord or premises controller is entitled to one free assault before the failure to take appropriate security measures subjects him or her to the risk of civil liability (Gerson and Schwartz, 2002). Foreseeability under the prior similar incidents test requires only that the general risk of attack, not the sequence of events that produced the criminal event, be anticipated by the business. Critics have argued that the prior similar incidents rule is "contrary to public policy" because "the first victim always loses, while subsequent victims are permitted recovery. Such a result is not only unfair but is inimical to the important policy of compensating injured parties."[20] Esper and Keating (2006, p. 320) argue that the prior similar incidents rule "means that a landowner has no duty to protect against a crime, however likely it may be, until one such crime has actually occurred." The impact of the rule "creates an incentive for landowners to disregard the safety of their patrons and take an unjustifiably low level of precaution." As between the first and the second victim, the injustice of the rule is clear: "it sacrifices the safety of the first victim to no good end. Why should one person suffer a rape which might have been avoided at reasonable cost just because no one has yet been raped?" (p. 320; see also Steiner, 2006, pp. 134, 148, 155, 165, 166).

In response to the limitations of the prior similar incidents rule, several states have adopted a "totality of circumstances" test for determining when a fact finder can deem criminal acts of third parties sufficiently foreseeable to impose liability on landowners. Jurisdictions that embrace this test do not require the existence of prior similar incidents to conclude that a given crime was foreseeable. Rather, courts will consider all relevant factual circumstances, "including the nature, condition, and location of the land, as well as prior similar incidents, to determine whether a criminal act was foreseeable." Therefore "[t]he lack of prior similar incidents will not preclude a claim where the landowner knew or should have known that the criminal act was foreseeable."[21]

This test, most notably articulated in the famous California case *Isaacs v. Huntington Memorial Hospital Inc.*, suggests that other factors, including whether the crime event occurred in a "high crime" area, in a dimly lit parking lot with no security, and in a place of many incidents of harassment, can be important in determining crime foreseeability.[22] A plaintiff may introduce evidence of foreseeability that would generally not be admissible in a jurisdiction using a prior similar incidents rule. Such evidence can include the crime rates in surrounding neighborhoods, environmental characteristics which may or may not make the premises an attraction to criminals, and the appropriateness of any security measures (e.g., cameras, guards, and lighting) that a business owner has adopted.

---

[20]*Isaacs v. Huntington Memorial Hospital*, 695 P.2d 653, 658 Cal. (1985).
[21]*Delta Tau Delta v. Johnson*, 712 N.E.2d 968, 972, 973 (Ind.1999).
[22]*Isaacs v. Huntington Memorial Hospital*, 695 P.2d 653, 658 Cal. (1985).

Generally, violent crimes are foreseeable if the property has been the site of other prior violent crimes, including robbery, assault, burglary, arson, abduction, murder, and rape. Other issues include the architectural design of the landlord's premises; the character of the business itself; the character of neighboring businesses and the surrounding neighborhood; and all prior crimes, violent and nonviolent, on or near the premises. In short, a crime is foreseeable under the "totality of the circumstances" test if a reasonable person would be able to identify the presence of one or more social–environmental factors commonly associated with crime. Courts would consider all the circumstances surrounding an event, including the nature, condition, and location of the land, the nature of human behavior regularly occurring on the property, as well as prior similar incidents, if any.

BALANCING TEST

Over the years, courts have struggled over foreseeability issues related to whether the imminent harm test is too limited, whether the prior similar incidents test can unfairly relieve landowners of liability (as the first victim is concerned), and whether the totality of circumstances test implies too broad a standard of foreseeability. In response to criticisms of the other tests of foreseeability, courts have developed a fourth test, the balancing test, which measures "the foreseeability of harm against the burden of imposing a duty to protect against the criminal acts of third persons."[23] Accordingly, the foreseeability of the crime risk on the defendant's property and the level of crime risk will determine the existence and the extent of the defendant's duty. The greater the foreseeability of the harm, the greater the duty of care that will be imposed on the business. "A very high degree of foreseeability is required to give rise to a duty to post security guards, but a lower degree of foreseeability may support a duty to implement lesser security measures such as using surveillance cameras, installing improved lighting or fencing, or trimming shrubbery."[24] Correspondingly, a business owner should not be expected to take new security precautions unless the security need is convincingly established, often through the occurrence of prior similar incidents. In *McClung v. Delta Square Ltd. Partnership*, the Tennessee Supreme Court wrote,

> In determining the duty that exists, the foreseeability of harm and the gravity of harm must be *balanced* against the commensurate burden imposed on the business to protect against that harm. In cases in which there is a high degree of foreseeability of harm and the probable harm is great, the burden imposed upon defendant may be substantial. Alternatively, in cases in which a lesser degree of foreseeability is present or the potential harm is slight, less onerous burdens may be imposed.[25]

The California Supreme Court first articulated the balancing test in *Ann M. v. Pacific Plaza Shopping Center*, a case that arose out of a civil complaint filed by Ann M. after an assailant raped her at her place of employment. At issue was whether the shopping center was negligent for failing to institute security patrols in the common areas of the shopping center. In rejecting the totality of circumstances test, the California Supreme Court went on to define the scope of a landlord's duty as follows:

---

[23]*Posecai v. Wal-Mart Stores, Inc.*, 752 So. 2d 767 - La: Supreme Court (1999).
[24]*Posecai v. Wal-Mart Stores, Inc.*, 768 So. 2d 762 - La: Supreme Court (1999).
[25]*McClung v. Delta Square Ltd. Partnership*, 937 S.W.2d 891, 901–902 Tenn. (1996), emphasis added.

[T]he scope of the duty is determined in part by balancing the foreseeability of the harm against the burden of the duty to be imposed ... In cases where the burden of preventing future harm is great, a high degree of foreseeability may be required ... On the other hand, in cases where there are strong policy reasons for preventing the harm, or the harm can be prevented by simple means, a lesser degree of foreseeability may be required.[26]

Early versions of the balancing test were guided by Judge Learned Hand in *U.S. v. Carroll Towing* (1947): "if the burden of security is less than the probability of attack multiplied by the seriousness of the potential injury, the landlord will be liable. If, on the other hand, the burden outweighs the probability times the harm, there is no negligence." In *McCall v. Wilder*, the Tennessee Supreme Court observed that "[a] risk is unreasonable and gives rise to a duty to act with due care if the foreseeable probability and gravity of harm posed by defendant's conduct outweigh the burden upon defendant to engage in alternative conduct that would have prevented the harm."[27] As the Louisiana Supreme Court has put it,

[A] balancing test is the best method for determining when business owners owe a duty to provide security for their patrons. The economic and social impact of requiring businesses to provide security on their premises is an important factor. Security is a significant monetary expense for any business and further increases the cost of doing business in high crime areas that are already economically depressed. Moreover, businesses are generally not responsible for the endemic crime that plagues our communities, a societal problem that even our law enforcement and other government agencies have been unable to solve. At the same time, business owners are in the best position to appreciate the crime risks that are posed on their premises and to take reasonable precautions to counteract those risks.[28]

Kennedy (2006, p. 128) identifies three issues that constitute the core of current balancing tests: (1) the level of crime foreseeability, (2) the likelihood a given combination of security measures will prevent future harm, and (3) the burden of taking such precautions.

BREACH OF DUTY AND STANDARDS OF CARE

After considering the issue of duty to protect and the question of foreseeability, a forensic criminologist will consider whether a business owner defendant breached or violated the duty. A forensic criminologist will conduct an analysis of the breach of the duty of care by examining the presence or absence of "adequate security" at the premises. In a negligent security case, the plaintiff may allege that the defendant's security (in)actions were negligent and in violation of the appropriate standard of care. Here, forensic criminologists should research any standards promulgated by various professional associations, the defendant's own policies, community practices, and learned treatises. Most industries

---

[26]*Ann M. v. Pacific Plaza Shopping Center*, 6 Cal. 4th 666, 676–679, 25 Cal. Rptr. 2d 137, 863 P.2d 207 (1994).
[27]*McCall v. Wilder*, 913 S.W.2d at 150, 153 Tenn. (1995).
[28]*Posecai v. Wal-Mart Stores, Inc.*, 768 So. 2d 762—La: Supreme Court (1999).

sponsor or support professional or trade associations whose purpose is to advance members' interests. For example, the American Hotel and Lodging Association (AHLA) serves the hospitality industry. The International Council of Shopping Centers (ICSC) serves retailers and developers of varying sizes. The National Apartment Association (NAA) and the Institute of Real Estate Management (IREM) represent the interests of property managers of varying sizes. The National Association of Realtors (NAR) represents realtors, residential and commercial brokers, salespeople, property managers, appraisers, counselors, and others engaged in the real estate industry.

The forensic criminologist can begin by researching the appropriate standards of care for the relevant professional or trade organization. ASIS International is the organization for security professionals worldwide. ASIS International publishes standards on Chief Security Officer—An Organizational Model (CSO), Investigations (INV), Risk Assessment (RA), Security Management Standard: Physical Asset Protection (PAP), Supply Chain Risk Management: A Compilation of Best Practices (SCRM), and Workplace Violence Prevention and Intervention Standard (WPVI). ASIS International also publishes a "Private Security Service Providers Services" with standards dealing with quality of service, risk management, and protection of human rights in areas around the world where the rule of law has been weakened due to conflicts or natural disasters. ASIS International also publishes a "Resilience Series" with standards that address the risks of disruptive events and resilience management. Trade groups such as the British Security Industry Association and the United States Security Industry Association (SIA) represent security equipment manufacturers and service providers. Other specialty associations are concerned with security in specific institutional settings. The International Association for Healthcare Security and Safety and the International Association of Campus Law Enforcement Administrators are two such examples.

Other associations that provide specialized products may also offer standards or guidelines. For example, the National Association of Security Companies represents the interests of contract and proprietary security officer providers in all settings. The Illuminating Engineering Society of North America (IESNA) publishes comprehensive lighting standards. The National Parking Association and the Institutional and Municipal Parking Congress are two trade organizations whose members are knowledgeable of appropriate parking practices. Organizations such as the American Society for Testing and Materials (ASTM), the American National Standards Institute (ANSI), and Underwriters Laboratories (UL) are active in setting standards for security equipment.

Table 3.1 presents a listing of different types of standards that courts have used and followed over the years. A standard is a set of criteria, guidelines, and best practices that can be used to enhance the quality and reliability of products, services, or processes (ASIS International, 2012a, *Security Management*, Chapter 3). Many of the organizations listed in Table 3.1 publish materials and guidelines that provide checklists and standards to evaluate the adequacy of a security program.

Security industry standards may address a product, service, or process. Regulations may require compliance with a standard. Table 3.2 provides a list of various types of security industry standards, benefits of standards, and a list of the major committees and associations that promulgate security standards. According to the ASIS International, there are more than 100 active standards relating to a broad range of security concerns, as of 2018.

A forensic criminologist's analysis of the "breach of duty" should typically focus on the steps taken by the defendant to protect the plaintiff from, or warn the plaintiff about, the possibility of criminal activity. Purcell (2010, p. 13) lays out several issues frequently explored in security cases to determine breach of duty. These issues include the adequacy of door and window locks, adequacy of the lighting

Table 3.1 Types of Standards

Type of Standards	Sources of Standards	Description	Examples
National Consensus Standards	Standards set by neutral, consensus-setting organizations; organizations follow formal procedures in formulating standards	Standards set forth by industry-recommended best practices	American Society for Testing Materials (ASTM) International, American National Standards Institute (ANSI), Underwriters Laboratories of Canada, ASIS International, National Fire Protection Association (NFPA); National Association of Realtors (NAR); Illuminating Engineering Society of North America (IESNA); National Parking Association
Community Standards	Standards commonly found in a particular geographical area; or practices preferred by a particular industry	Courts may ask to assess reasonableness of a company's security practices by comparing these practices to those of other companies in the same geographical area	Security practices would be reasonable to the extent that numerous companies follow that practice (e.g., key controlled guestrooms in hotels; patrol of exterior parking lots at enclosed malls; similarity of infant safety and security practices at maternity wards; criminal background checks for new hires)
Self-Imposed Standards	Standards organizations have set for themselves by inclusion in their own internal policies and procedures/training manuals	A company will implement security measures which it deems reasonable. Thus, should a company violate its own policies, procedures, and practices, it may be acting negligently	Statements of principles and values which companies aspire to abide by when accepting a contract from a client, including codes of conduct to ensure they adhere to other standards (e.g., proof of patrol by security personnel or by camera that is logged to demonstrate compliance to self-imposed standards)
Mandatory Standards	Legally mandated standards by state and local governments; administrative codes	In some jurisdictions, negligence per se may apply where legally required security measures have not been implemented.	Lighting levels for municipal car parks, security officer staffing at shopping malls, the number of clerks on duty at convenience stores by time of day, ventilation window locks for rental property windows, alcohol server training in certain states, pub doorman licensing, preassignment security officer training, and the installation of secondary door and window-locking devices

Continued

Table 3.1 Types of Standards—cont'd

Type of Standards	Sources of Standards	Description	Examples
Learned Treatises	Judges' references to expert testimony	Expert witness reports that comply with Rule 26 of the Federal Rules of Civil Procedure	Where an established expert has provided substantial evidence in a security-related case, his or her testimony on reasonable security measures can play a significant role in a judge's formulation of case law and, in effect, become a standard in that particular jurisdiction

Source: Kennedy (2006, pp. 129–133).

Table 3.2 Security Industry Standards

Benefits, Associations, Organizations	Basic, Product, Design, Process, Specification, Code, Management Systems, Conformity Assessment, and Personal Certification
Benefits of Standards	• Officially organizes best practices and processes • Shares lessons learned • Provides tools to "consistently" assess threats, risks, vulnerabilities, criticalities, and impacts • Defines measurement methods (benchmarks, testing) • Documents equipment performance requirements to ensure effectiveness and safety • Establishes design requirements for devices, systems, and infrastructure to withstand threats • Define effective (consistent) methods for identification of individuals • Enhance cross-jurisdictional information sharing and interoperability • Provide for consistency of services
Associations and Organizations	• ASIS International Standards • ASTM International (formerly the American Society for Testing and Materials) • National Fire Protection Association (NFPA) (Several security standards—premises security and installation of electronic premises security systems) • American National Standards Institute (ANSI) • Deutsches Institut für Normung (Germany) • Japanese Industrial Standards Committee • International Organization for Standardization, ISO (world's largest standards developer—159 member countries)

Source: ASIS International, 2012a. Security Management; Legal Issues; Security Officer Operations; and Crisis Management. Protection of Assets (POA). Dennis Shepp. October 2017. "Certified Protection Professional (CPP) Certification Examination Review."

conditions, existence of video surveillance, presence of a security guard, existence of an intercom system, measures taken to adequately screen visitors or eject unruly visitors, and the existence of placards or signs warning about criminal activity. Related, Hewitt (2004, p. 2) suggests that plaintiffs may be able to establish breach of duty by showing how the property owner failed to follow industry standards for security at comparable commercial properties. Professional bodies, such as ASIS International, the American National Standards Institute, and the Illuminating Engineering Society of North America, promulgate industry standards for security. Landlords may be accused of violating industry standards by:

- failing to perform criminal background checks on employees, particularly those who might have a direct impact on the security of the property, its tenants, or its invitees.
- failing to properly screen new tenants, especially when other tenants have relied on such screening to enhance their security.
- failing to inform tenants about security problems or criminal activities on or near the property.
- failing to establish or follow security policies and procedures.
- failing to seek the advice of law enforcement or independent consultants.
- failing to provide or enhance patrols by security guards or other personnel such as the property manager.
- failing to continually review lighting, fencing, entrances and exits, lock and barrier systems (both manmade and natural), identification systems, and closed-circuit TVs and other monitoring and alarm devices.
- engaging in misleading advertising that overstates security measures.

A forensic criminologist can obtain security surveys of the property conducted in-house or by a security company, any reports or reviews of reports by the owner or property manager, and all the company's policies and procedures, in order to compare this information to industry standards. Harris (2002, p. 2) suggests that the forensic expert should check to see if the property owner maintained written operating and security policies and procedures. "When a defendant adopts a policies-and-procedures manual, it has, in effect, set standards." Use fact-witness depositions to determine whether personnel at the premises adhered to these policies. If employees' practices do not meet the minimum standards set by the manual, they may have breached the standard of care. In the absence of published standards, the question becomes did the landholder act reasonably in light of the circumstances.

Attorneys, scholars, and the courts often disagree over the appropriate standards of care in different industries and much debate surrounds the efficacy of different security measures employed to protect invitees and deter offenders. Criminologists have raised concerns about relationships among crime prevention and social costs related to different forms of public area surveillance. In recent years, CCTV, improved street lighting, and the other major forms of public area surveillance have been the subject of several reviews to assess their unique as well as comparative effectiveness in preventing crime. For example, Clarke (2008) and Welsh and Farrington (2008) reviewed the effects of improved street lighting on crime. Ratcliffe (2006) and Welsh and Farrington (2009, 2014) reviewed the effects of public area CCTV on crime. Eck (2006) assessed the effectiveness of place managers and security guards, and Welsh and colleagues (2010) reviewed the effectiveness of place managers, security guards, and defensible space. Most of these reviews draw conclusions based on the highest-quality evaluation studies (i.e., experimental and rigorous quasi-experimental designs).

Drawing on this research, Welsh and colleagues (2015) conclude that CCTV is effective primarily in car parks, improved street lighting is somewhat effective in city and town centers and residential/public housing communities, and the defensible space practice of street closures or barricades can be effective in inner-city neighborhoods.

Importantly, public area surveillance measures such as CCTV, improved lighting, security guards, place managers, and defensible space (e.g., street closures) are not panaceas in reducing crime. The evidence suggests that their crime prevention effectiveness varies by time and place. That is, these crime prevention tools appear to be more effective in some areas and less effective in other areas. Researchers and scholars have suggested that CCTV and improved street lighting can be more effective in reducing property (and vehicle) crimes than in reducing violent crimes. Street closure or barricade schemes can be effective in reducing both property and violent crimes. The weight of the evidence suggests that security guards may be effective as a crime control strategy when stationed in car parks and targeted at vehicle crimes. Whether security guards are effective at preventing crime in other circumstances and other premises remains to be seen. The effectiveness of place managers—people who perform a surveillance function by means of employment (bus drivers, parking lot attendants, train conductors, etc.)—in preventing crime is unknown. As Welsh and colleagues (2015, p. 116) conclude, "[t]hese less-than-conclusive statements about the effectiveness of security guards and place managers have everything to do with the small number of high-quality evaluations that have been carried out on these measures."

Industry leaders and security professionals have long recognized the challenge of creating and applying universally consistent standards of protection across the diverse business types, land uses, and property forms in the United States. On the one hand, many industry leaders and security professionals would prefer a set of transparent and across-the-board standards that could be easily applied in all situations and at all places (Bates, 2007). On the other hand, properties are unique in their land-use configurations, crime risks, and security threats. An apartment building located in a dilapidated low-income neighborhood in the inner city may face different crime risks and security threats than another apartment located in a gated complex in an affluent suburb. Much research has revealed that foreclosures attract criminal activity, and with each percentage point increase in the rate of foreclosures, the rate of violent crime in the same area rises by more than 2% (Immergluck, 2006; Ellen et al., 2013). Thus, not all security measures will fit all business types and land uses. Each individual property will have unique security requirements.

In short, a forensic criminologist will face two major tasks concerning breach of duty in a negligent security case. First, she or he will have to investigate and determine what behavior should reasonably have been expected on the part of the defendant based on the foreseeability of the attack. Related, the forensic criminologist can research various standards promulgated by professional associations, defendant's own policies, community practices, and learned treatises to evaluate whether the defendant followed the appropriate standard of care in the discharge of her or his duty to maintain a safe and secure premises. The second task is to determine whether the defendant violated any standards of care. In some cases, both plaintiff and defendant may agree on the appropriate standard of care. But they may disagree on whether the defendant actually breached the standard of care. Importantly, as we discuss below, a defendant will not become liable for negligence unless the plaintiff can show by a preponderance of evidence that the failure to act reasonably was causally related to the injuries sustained.

CAUSATION: CAUSE-IN-FACT AND PROXIMATE CAUSATION

Even if a crime at a property was foreseeable and there was breach of a standard of care, plaintiffs in civil litigation must still prove by a preponderance of evidence that the breach caused harm to the plaintiffs. As we noted in Chapter 1, the U.S. legal system defines causation in two ways: cause-in-fact and proximate causation. Cause-in-fact refers to the actual cause of an injury. One test of actual cause is the "but for" test which asks "but for the failure to implement a reasonable security program, would the plaintiff have been injured?" Here the plaintiff must prove that she or he would not have been injured but for the defendant's breach of its duty of care. A second test is the "substantial factor" test which asks "was the failure to implement a reasonable security program a substantial factor in the plaintiff's injury or loss?" In short, cause-in-fact means that the intentional criminal act is the cause of the injury or harm.

Proximate causality implies that a defendant's breach of security contributed to the criminal act. The most common test of proximate cause in the United States is foreseeability. It determines if the harm resulting from an action could reasonably have been predicted. As we discussed earlier, in premises liability cases, foreseeability is a factor in the analysis of whether the property owner owed a duty to the injured person. But foreseeability is also a factor in the investigation of whether the alleged failures of the property owner to provide adequate protection caused the injury.[29] As discussed by La Fetra (2006, p. 410), *duty-foreseeability* cases "center on the question of whether the property owner should have provided security measures that would have reduced the probability of a certain type of criminal attack." In addition, *causation-foreseeability* cases focus on "whether the property owners' adoption of the duty-required security measures would have prevented the actual attack that precipitated the lawsuit."

A plaintiff might argue that enhanced security features of a property could have deterred the crime. To address this question, a forensic criminologist could draw on rational choice theory to argue that the place and time of the crime is important for understanding the cause of the crime since offenders will select targets using means-ends calculation, for example, what is the most efficient means to accomplish a goal (crime) (Cornish and Clarke, 2014). The point being that crime is more likely to occur if the perceived gains outweigh the perceived losses. Routine activities theory would suggest that reasonably rational offenders, while engaging in their routine activities, will assess the crime-committing potential of places without guardians and managers (Cohen and Felson, 1979). Crime pattern theory suggests that the interactions of offenders with their physical and social environments influence offenders' choices of targets (Brantingham and Brantingham, 1995). What unites all three of these criminological theories is the assumption that "crime is a choice, and offenders choose to commit crime in much the

---

[29]The absence of prior similar incidents does not mean that the business owes no duty to protect its customers against third-party criminal acts. In *Pinsonneault v. Merchants & Farmers Bank & Trust Co.*, 816 So.2d 270, 277–278 La. (2002), a bank customer had been murdered at the bank's night deposit box and the customer's parents sued the bank for wrongful death. The court determined that the bank did not have "a duty to employ heightened security measures for the protection of patrons of its night depository" because there had been no similar prior incidents. The bank was located in a comparatively low crime area for its district, and there was a low statistical likelihood that night deposit crimes would occur (*Id.* at 276–277). However, the court still determined that the bank "had a duty to implement reasonable security measures" because the bank's written security plan "clearly envision[ed] the recognition of a duty by [the bank] to implement reasonable security measures for the protection of its customers" (*Id.* at 278). The steps the bank had taken to implement this plan, "providing lighting at its night time depository, erecting fencing along vulnerable perimeters, and setting up a schedule for the installation of modern surveillance cameras at each of its branches" also supported the court's conclusion (*Id.* 278).

same way that we choose to execute any type of behavior" (Sidebottom and Wortley, 2016, p. 164). Criminologists understand the criminal decision-making process in terms of the perceived risks and benefits associated with a particular behavior at a particular time in a particular environment.

The previous points draw our attention to the importance of understanding the processes of target selection and the decision to commit a crime at a specific time and place. Environmental criminologists acknowledge that many criminals may have socially deprived backgrounds and/or pathological personalities. Yet, a fundamental assumption of environmental criminology is that the disposition to commit crime is variable and contingent. It can change from time to time depending on the situation, circumstance, and activity. There is generally very little facility site managers and security specialists can do about the broader social–psychological causes of crime. The problem for environmental criminologists is to understand how criminals select specific targets and what factors enter the thinking of the potential criminal before the decision to commit a crime happens.

As noted before, rational choice theory assumes that many criminals will make fairly "rational" choices about crime targets. Therefore, security professionals and practitioners may be able to apply "situational" crime prevention strategies to specific places in an effort to deter the criminal act from occurring. This approach to understanding and preventing criminal behavior, termed "situational crime prevention" has a long history and research tradition in both the United States and Great Britain. Table 3.3 presents Clarke's classification of 25 situational prevention techniques arranged into five principal categories of action within an overarching rational choice theory. The classification assumes that offenders choose to commit specific crimes for the benefits they bring. These techniques are outlined in the table.

Proximate causation requires the plaintiff to show a close connection between the assault and the business owner's failure to exercise reasonable care. Presenting this argument is always a challenge because the harm inflicted upon a victim is the result of an intentional act of the criminal. In such a case, the landlord, landowner, or property manager is being accused of negligence and could be held liable for the injury even though that person did not commit the crime. Realizing this basic challenge, business owners and operators will defend themselves by arguing that their own actions or inactions did

Table 3.3 25 Techniques of Situational Crime Prevention				
Increase the Effort	Increase the Risk	Reduce the Rewards	Reduce Provocations	Remove Excuses
Harden targets	Extend guardianship	Conceal targets	Reduce frustrations and stresses	Set rules
Control access to facilities	Assist natural surveillance	Remove targets	Avoid disputes	Post instructions
Screen exits	Reduce anonymity	Identity property	Reduce emotional arousal	Alert conscience
Deflect offenders	Utilize place managers	Disrupt markets	Neutralize peer pressure	Assist compliance
Control tools/ weapons	Strengthen formal surveillance	Deny benefits	Discourage imitation	Control drugs and alcohol

Source: Cornish, D.B., Clarke, R.V., 2003. Opportunities, precipitators, and criminal decisions: a reply to Wortley's critique of situational crime prevention. Crime Prev. Stud. 16, 41–96.

not cause the victim's injuries. Business owners frequently attempt to focus responsibility for the criminal act and therefore place the causes of the victim's injuries on the criminal, the person who committed the crime itself, or the victim's own activities. However, the law does not require crime victims to prove that their injuries were solely caused by the business owner's actions or inactions. "Plaintiffs are merely required to show that business owner's failure to provide protection was *a* proximate cause, *not the sole proximate cause* of the harm" (Kennedy and Sakis, 2008, p. 123, emphasis in original). "To be sure, the test is not whether proper security measures would have absolutely prevented an attack, but whether it was more likely than not that the attack would have been prevented absent the business owner's negligence" (p. 123; Kaminsky, 2008, p. 10; Zinober, 2015, p. 323).

Importantly, a forensic criminologist's evaluation of causation is intertwined with the evaluation of the foreseeability of the crime event. That is, the crime must have been reasonably foreseeable at the time for the victim to establish the necessary proximate causal link between the negligent conduct of the defendant and the injury-causing crime. Foreseeability exists if the property owner should have expected or anticipated the crime event.[30] "If the property has a history of violent crime, the possessor is assumed to know this and must protect invitees from that danger. The possessor's failure to protect the invitee is the proximate cause of the harm" (Leighton, 2000, p. 1). Purcell (2010) contends that attorneys for the plaintiff must present facts that "show *more* than the conduct creates an *opportunity* to commit crime" (p. 15). The facts must show that the defendant committed negligent acts and that he or she "*knew or should have known* that, because of his acts, the crime (or one like it) might occur" (p. 15, emphasis in original). Generally, the more random, sudden, and disastrous the criminal violence, the more likely that a court will find the criminal act unforeseeable, thereby severing any proximate cause link. According to the State of California Court of Appeal, Sixth District:

> [T]he predicate of any duty to prevent criminal conduct is its foreseeability. Property owners have no duty to prevent unexpected and random crimes ... [A] duty to take affirmative action to control the wrongful acts of a third party will be imposed only where such conduct can be reasonably anticipated ... This phrasing reaffirms a passage in the Restatement Second of Torts that a duty arises "[i]f the place or character of his [or her] business, or his [or her] past experience, is such that he [or she] should reasonably anticipate careless or criminal conduct on the part of third persons" ... "Reasonable anticipation" is another description of foreseeability.[31]

Over the years, forensic security experts have expounded on the concept of "abstract negligence" which refers to a plaintiff's critique of a defendant's security measures with reference to abstract standards espoused by a security expert. Abstract negligence implies that a property owner's security measures were inadequate—for example, insufficient numbers of security guards—but without specific evidence

---

[30]In Louisiana, the United States Court of Appeals, Fifth Circuit, rejected a district court's ruling of summary judgment for Dollar Tree for negligent security arguing that the plaintiff's alleged facts might show that the Dollar Tree store was aware of a foreseeable risk of violent crime to its customers. These facts include: (1) the store's practice of escorting or watching female employees to their cars at night, (2) the store's practice of either escorting customers to their car or providing an escort even if unasked, (3) the assistant manager's requests to install security cameras, (4) whether or not the store ever employed security personnel, and (5) a prior armed robbery. *Simpson v. Dollar Tree Stores, Inc.*, No. 17-30282. Summary Calendar 5th Cir. (September 28, 2017).

[31]*Nicole M. v. Sears, Roebuck and Co.*, 90 Cal. Rptr. 2d 922, 76 Cal. App. 4th 1238 Ct. App. (1999).

to show what security measures could have prevented the victim's injuries. The California Supreme Court describes "abstract negligence" as follows:

> Where ... there is evidence that the assault could have occurred even in the absence of the landlord's negligence, proof of causation cannot be based on mere speculation, conjecture and inferences drawn from other inferences to reach a conclusion unsupported by any real evidence or on an expert's opinion based on inferences, speculation and conjecture.[32]

As Kennedy (2006, p. 133) elaborates,

> Plaintiff security experts will often criticize multiple aspects of a defendant's security program even if these aspects of the program were totally unrelated to the criminal attack. For example, an expert might criticize a landlord's key control or access control program even though an attacker entered upon the property legally as an invited guest. A security officer's training history may be criticized even though his actions at the scene of an incident were completely appropriate. A defendant landlord's failure to repair a garage security gate cannot be the legal cause of an assault if there is no evidence a perpetrator actually entered through the open gate. Without proving the critical element of causation, of course, the plaintiff cannot make his or her case.

A long history of court cases shows that a security expert's attempt to apply subjective and speculative notions of adequate security to criticize a defendant's security measures will not be sufficient to establish a causal nexus between breach of duty and the resulting injuries.[33] The security expert "must do more than simply critique a defendant's security measures or compare them to some abstract standard espoused by the plaintiff's security expert."[34] The plaintiff must prove a causal connection between the lack of reasonable security measures and the plaintiff's harm. Twerski and Shane (2018) argue that what is needed are data-driven standards for adequate security. In their discussion of the premises security in Mississippi, Wilkins and Latimer (2014, p. 9) maintain that that an expert witness should conduct a thorough investigation that entails "a physical walk around and inspection of the property, relevant pleadings, Calls-for-Service for the property and vicinity, depositions, documents produced by the defendants in discovery, and the defendant's designation of expert witnesses." Experts can also review and rely on industry standards (see Table 3.1) and examine whether violations of industry standards show evidence of negligence.

Insufficient proof of causation can be a major problem and challenge for plaintiffs. In conducting an investigation, a forensic criminologist is not required to establish causation with absolute certainty. Instead, the forensic criminologist must show that the defendant's conduct was a "substantial factor" in the criminal act that brought harm to the victim. It is not enough for the plaintiff to show that the defendant owed a duty and breached that duty. The plaintiff must show that the breach of duty was the proximate cause of the injury or harm.

---

[32]*Saelzler v. Advanced Group* 400, 23 P.3d 1143, 1147 Cal. (2001).

[33]*Nobel v. Los Angeles Dodgers*, 214 Cal. Rptr. 395, 398 Cal. App. (1985); *Nola M. v. University of Southern California*, 20 Cal. Rptr. 2d 97, 109 Cal. App. (1993).

[34]*Noble v. Los Angeles Dodgers*, Inc., supra, 168 Cal.App.3d at pages 916–917, 214 Cal.Rptr. 395 (1993).

CONCLUSION

The historical development of premises liability for negligent security litigation reflects changing political and legal conflicts and struggles over meanings and definitions of duty, breach of duty, causation, and assessment of damages. Today, the duty to protect against third-party crimes is a doctrinal reality. Courts and public policy agree that individuals should be relatively safe in their apartments, schools, shopping areas, restaurants, entertainment venues, and workplaces. Over the decades, the imposition of a legal duty upon business owners to prevent foreseeable and avoidable criminal attacks from occurring has come to encompass a plethora of public issues related to public safety, crime victim compensation, and financial burdens landowners may face to protect against the threat of crime. Apartment owners have been sued for not hiring security guards; banks have been sued for faulty alarm systems; construction engineers have been sued for failing to secure construction sites; hotels have been sued for allowing unsupervised access to swimming pools; lawyers have even been sued for failing to properly prosecute negligent security claims; and security companies have been sued for failing to follow proper security procedures, not abiding by acceptable standards of care, inadequate supervision of security staff, and improper training of security staff. As noted by Blake and Bradley (1999), Landoll and Landoll (2016), and Vellani (2007), security risk assessment and prevention are big business. Governments and the private sector pay huge amounts of money on risk assessment techniques, implementing and assessing security measures, and undertaking cost–benefit analyses concerning the incorporation of new security measures.

As we point out in subsequent chapters, forensic criminologists can be indispensable to premises security investigations since they can use their expert knowledge of criminological methods and theories of criminal behavior to explain the linkages among motivated offenders, suitable targets, and capable guardians in the etiology of a criminal event. Negligent security cases present major challenges for defense and plaintiff trial lawyers. A successful case requires proof that the defendant owed the plaintiff a duty of care, that the defendant breached that duty, and that the breach was a proximate cause of the damage. The failure to meet each proof requirement ends the case. The plaintiff must prove that the defendant should not only have been put on notice that the crime was foreseeable but should have taken reasonable steps to prevent the crime from occurring. Then, the plaintiff must convince the jury that those measures more likely than not would have prevented the crime.

In short, to be an expert witness in a negligent security case, a forensic criminologist must become familiar with tort law and master operational meanings of foreseeability, standards of care, and legal causation. These three issues cross social science disciplines including criminology, sociology, psychology, and psychiatry, among other fields. In the increasing litigious business environment, forensic criminologists' skills in research design and understanding of criminal behavior, security systems, and legal principles can make them essential assets to plaintiffs and defendants, attorneys, and corporate leadership. Indeed, many cases require the contributions of forensic criminologists and security experts if they are to be prosecuted and defended properly.

APARTMENT SECURITY I: MEASURING AND ANALYZING CRIME FORESEEABILITY

4

INTRODUCTION

In this chapter and the next chapter, we draw on expert witness reports to illustrate the ways in which a forensic criminologist can use social science methods and criminological theories to evaluate the major elements of a negligent security case involving multifamily housing. We address the issues of foreseeability (as part of the duty element of a tort), standards of care in the context of apartment building security (whether there was a breach of duty), and whether any negligence by apartment management substantially contributed to the criminal act (proximate causation). This chapter focuses specifically on the evaluation of crime foreseeability while the next chapter addresses standards of care and causation.

For us, environmental criminological theories such as rational choice theory, crime prevention through environmental design (CPTED), crime pattern theory, and the techniques of situational crime prevention (SCP) (all described later) can be useful for explaining the genesis of a crime event, assessing the foreseeability of the crime in question, and evaluating the causal factors responsible for the crime. According to rational choice theory, offenders are active decision makers who use environmental cues to evaluate risks and rewards about committing a crime (Clarke and Cornish, 2001; Cornish and Clarke, 2014). As such, the theory focuses on the decision-making process of the offender.

CPTED is a set of principles that suggests environmental design factors can have a deterrent effect on crime. Properties designed with security and crime prevention in mind will consider the layout of the property, lighting, access points, sight lines, and other factors, with the purpose of creating a space where the offender feels more vulnerable to detection. Early conceptions of CPTED identified principles of territoriality, surveillance, image management, access control, legitimate activity support, and target hardening as physical design features that could be effective in reducing the incidence and fear of crime. More recent conceptions have emphasized social dimensions in what is known as second-generation CPTED. This conception emphasizes the social characteristics of the community, social cohesion, and "collective efficacy" (Sampson et al., 1997). Second-generation CPTED uses risk assessments, socioeconomic and demographic profiling, as well as active community participation (Cozens et al., 2005).

Fig. 4.1 illustrates the concepts of CPTED. The figure suggests that CPTED concepts may not be successful in reducing or preventing crime if a neighborhood is not cohesive, lacks collective efficacy, and neighbors are wary of each other and unwilling to act against crime (Merry, 1981; Lab, 2007, pp. 64–65, 74; Morenoff et al., 2001; Sampson et al., 1997). As Cozens and Love (2015, p. 92) have

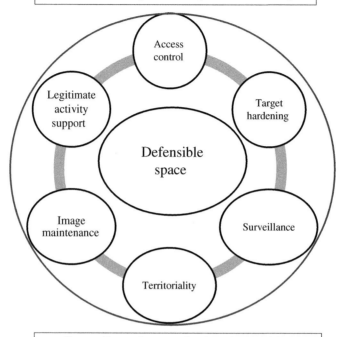

FIG. 4.1

A dynamic integrated model for crime prevention through environmental design (CPTED) principles.

Source: Cozens, P., Love, T., 2015. A review and current status of crime prevention through environmental design (CPTED). J. Plan. Lit. 30(4), 4.

argued, "given the complexity of crime, and its dependence on many aspects of the socio-cultural milieu, taking into account the social dimension should always be part of the CPTED process."

Fig. 4.1 links to Newman's notion of Defensible Space by encouraging researchers, urban planners, and CPTED practitioners to consider the potential criminogenic capacity of the surrounding environment. Box 4.1 lists the four elements of Defensible Space. According to Newman (1973, 1995, 1996), the four elements of Defensible Space can work together to promote a sense of ownership, community, and responsibility in residents to secure and maintain a safe, productive, and well-maintained neighborhood. Newman (1973, p. 2) argued that the built environment can act to encourage criminal activities and therefore the incorporation of Defensible Space elements can be a "means for restructuring the residential environments of our cities so they can [be] livable and controlled not by police, but a

---

BOX 4.1 ELEMENTS OF DEFENSIBLE SPACE

Defensible Space is made up of four design elements, which act individually and in combination to help create a safer urban environment:

Territoriality: the capacity of the built form to create perceived areas of proprietary concern by clearly defining ownership of space using both symbolic and real barriers.

Surveillance: the capacity of the built form to provide opportunities for surveillance for residents and others using the building configuration and the design and placement of windows and building entrances.

Image and milieu: the capacity of design and management of the built form to influence the perception of space, promoting clean, well-maintained, and well-ordered places.

Geographical juxtaposition (environment): the capacity of the surrounding spaces to influence the security of adjacent areas and vice versa.

Source: Newman, O., 1973. Defensible Space: Crime Prevention Through Urban Design. Macmillan, New York, NY.

---

community of people sharing a common terrain." More recently, Cozens and Love (2015) maintain that researchers and scholars can incorporate the elements of CPTED and Defensible Space to investigate the criminogenic aspects of a community via the analysis of the routine activities of the area and the potential location of crime generators, crime attractors, crime detractors, crime facilitators, and crime precipitators.

As we noted in the previous chapter, Situational Crime Prevention (SCP) is another variant of environmental criminology that emphasizes the reduction or elimination of opportunities for crime using various techniques that increase the effort, increase the risks, reduce the rewards, reduce provocations, and remove the excuses (Clarke, 1980; Cornish and Clarke, 2003). Proponents of SCP suggest that these techniques can be used in different situations to prevent crime (Cullen and Agnew, 2006). Erecting physical barriers to make access to a crime target difficult can increase the effort of committing a crime. Instituting surveillance can increase the risks of being caught and thereby raise the chance of an offender being seen by someone who is likely to take action (Clarke, 1980, p. 142). In other words, whether a person chooses to commit crime or not will be influenced by situational factors that are context specific (Cornish and Clarke, 2003). Two other variants of environmental criminology—crime pattern theory and routine activities theory (mentioned in Chapter 1)—stress the importance of place and locational opportunities in the generation of crime events.

Overall, the theoretical variants of environmental criminology are mutually supportive and can contribute to understanding the relationship between crime and multifamily housing. Criminologists can use each theory to investigate the place ("where") and time ("when") of crime in order to explain why and how the crime happened. In addition to theorizing and examining the spatiotemporal dynamics of crime, these theories also focus on the criminogenic impact of environmental design and the ecological patterns in crime (e.g., Jeffery, 1971; Newman, 1973; Poyner, 1983; Van Soomeren, 1989; Rondeau et al., 2005; Brantingham and Brantingham, 1984; Wikstrom, 1985; Felson, 2006). Each theory suggests that the socio-spatial organization and physical environment of multifamily housing developments can give off powerful behavior cues that can either motivate offenders to commit crimes or deter them from engaging in a criminal act. Social and physical cues—lack of natural surveillance, absence of place managers, and prominent crime targets—can suggest to potential offenders that the risks are low and the rewards could be high for committing an opportunistic crime (Kinney et al., 2008; Andresen and Farrell, 2015; Piquero, 2015).

The sociotemporal activities taking place in and around an apartment complex can operate either as a crime attractor, crime generator, or crime detractor. Different land uses can have different concentrations of social activities. Different routine activity nodes—for example, school locations, shopping areas, public transit stations, entertainment districts, apartments, and so on—may have special characteristics that can pull in people with high levels of criminal motivation and histories of repeat offending. Such special activity nodes can become crime attractors. Crime generators are places that are easily accessible to the public. They may become hot spots of crime when the presence of large groups of people creates occasions for crime. Typical examples are parks, parking lots, bars, and commercial land uses in which their function makes them well suited for motivated offenders to find attractive and weakly guarded victims or targets (Blair et al., 2017; Brantingham and Brantingham, 1995). Crime detractors are locations that discourage offending and repel offenders. Examples can include a "stable business, the presence of middle-aged women, mixes of activities or easy natural surveillance" (Tilly 2013, p. 66).

Analyzing and explaining the spatiotemporal dynamics of crime in a particular geographical area means that we should understand crime as having much in common with other, routine and nondeviant, forms of human activity. As noted by Kinney and colleagues (2008, p. 62), "[p]eople in general, offenders included, move about from one activity to another, gaining knowledge of some parts of the city and remaining relatively ignorant of others. Crimes tend to follow the routine pushes and pulls of activities across an urban environment." Unlike traditional criminological theories that focus on explaining why an offender commits a crime, environmental criminologists search for crime patterns and explain these patterns in terms of opportunity structures and influences within the built environment. Rational choice theory, CPTED, and situational crime prevention theory are highly relevant to studying crimes that occur in a residential apartment building, a potentially criminogenic environment that can be heavily influenced by opportunity structures. In short, we stress the central importance of theoretically informed empirical research to assess the major determinants of criminal acts. The challenge is to understand and explain why a particular crime occurred at a particular place and at a particular time to a particular victim. An understanding of crime events cannot be attained without careful attention to the application of criminological methods to assess the relationship between crime and place.

A forensic criminologist might find it useful to employ "social fact" studies which Walker and Monahan (1988) refer to as the use of social scientific principles and methods to develop opinions about the parties, practices, or behaviors involved in a lawsuit (see also Mitchell et al., 2010). With "social fact" studies, a forensic criminologist applies scientific principles and methods to case-specific data in the "same way that the expert would use scientific principles and methods to analyze data outside the litigation context." Social fact studies, if properly conceived to shed light on the issues in dispute in a particular case, should generate useful information that the fact finder would otherwise lack. Forensic social scientists should be explicit about data sources and metrics, report the exact steps and procedures used in the data collection process, and disclose the analytical scheme applied to the data.

The field of apartment security litigation is vast and complex with many examples of premises security cases involving a diversity of criminal acts, victims, and offenders. The field is ever-changing and has changed dramatically over the decades (Kaminsky, 2008; Blake and Bradley, 1999; Kennedy, 2014, 2013, 2006). Apartment security litigation defies blanket generalizations and cases cannot be easily classified or categorized. Laws and foreseeability tests vary by jurisdiction and each case must be judged on its own merits with an understanding that properties, victims, and offenders are unique in their own ways. In some states, premises security law is in a state of flux as case law continues to evolve and develop in a variety of new and multifaceted directions. Thus, our coverage of the litigation in the field is partial, selective, and necessarily incomplete. One goal in this chapter and the next chapter is to provide the reader with a broad overview of several delimited areas of security litigation involving multifamily housing. A related goal is to orient the reader to the latest forensic criminological theories and research that provide the framework and context for understanding the historical evolution of apartment security litigation.

HOME, SECURITY, AND MULTIFAMILY HOUSING

The historical development of apartment security litigation in the United States is much more than a history of lawsuits pertaining to physical shelter, real estate, and multifamily housing. Rather, apartment security litigation expresses the interplay of meanings of security, property, and home. As the famous poet Robert Frost once remarked, "home is the place where, when you have to go there, they have to let you in" (Jackson, 1985, p. 73). As Frost recognized, housing is not just a dwelling and a place to live; it is a symbol of personal worth, social status, and security. Unlike the premises of a bar, tavern, restaurant, hotel, or other commercial land use, the home is residential land use that expresses deep and personal meanings connected to refuge, haven, and retreat from the impersonality of the outside world. Home is the foci for identity, familial relations, and community sentiment all of which are bound up with notions of safety and security.

The maxim that a "man's house is his castle" is one of the oldest and most deeply rooted principles in Anglo-American jurisprudence. This common law castle doctrine, also known as castle law or defense of habitation law, suggests that a person's legally occupied dwelling is a place in which that person is free to defend himself/herself against an intruder. The castle law doctrine has historically permitted self-governance of the home separate from other political institutions and governments. Related to this doctrine, dwellers have historically viewed their home as "the castle" where they have dignity, self-esteem, and autonomy from other mundane and routine activities that are interwoven into their lives.[1]

For a large number of the U.S. population—more than 111 million people—an apartment is their home. As of 2016, 35% of the U.S. population resided in renter-occupied households (see Table 4.1). That is, one out of three Americans rents and one out of three renters lives in an apartment. America's renter households live in a wide variety of housing types, from single-family houses and townhomes to garden apartments and high-rises (Fuller, 2013). Because of demographic shifts, economic challenges, and changing consumer preferences, renter households continue to grow as a larger portion of the overall housing picture. Almost 3.8 million new renter households were formed between 2005 and 2010, growing their ranks from 33.7 million to 37.4 million renter households, according to the U.S. Census Bureau.[2]

Living in an apartment can offer benefits and advantages to residents that homeowners living in single-family homes do not enjoy. In some apartment complexes, renters may have access to a suite

---

[1] *Weeks v. United States*, 232 U.S. 383, 390 (1914) (discussing the influence of the castle doctrine on the U.S. Supreme Court).
[2] U.S. Census Bureau, 2006 Housing Vacancy Survey, Table 9: Estimates of the Total Housing Inventory; U.S. Census Bureau, 2011 Housing Vacancy Survey, Table 11: Estimates of the Total Housing Inventory. Previous-year totals from each table were used to account for stock adjustments. See Fuller (2013).

Table 4.1 U.S. Households: Renters and Owners

Type of Household	Households	Percent of U.S. Total (%)	Residents	Percent of U.S. Total (%)
Renter-occupied	43,837,496	37	111,054,354	35
Owner-occupied	75,022,569	63	203,993,282	65
Total	118,860,065	100	315,047,636	100

Source: 2016 American Community Survey, 1-Year Estimates, US Census Bureau. Updated 9/2017. Table appears in National Multi-Family Housing Council. Quick Facts: Resident Demographics. http://www.nmhc.org/Content. aspx?id=4708 (Accessed 4 December 2017).

of services from on-site fitness and business centers to package collection to trash removal and 24-hour video surveillance and security guards. Apartment communities also offer many conveniences. Many are located close to job centers and in urban areas, and many are located in walkable neighborhoods surrounded by restaurants, theaters, and shops. Indeed, the close proximity to employment opportunities as well as cultural, entertainment, and retail amenities is a major selling point for many landlords. In trumpeting the competitive advantages of apartments, Fuller (2013) contends that renting an apartment can provide financial flexibility and mobility that can, in turn, allow people to more easily pursue new opportunities including a new job or living in a new neighborhood.

The benefits and advantages of apartment living can also invite security challenges for owners and tenants. Decades of criminological research have recognized that an apartment complex is often a community of strangers. Apartments tend to have high turnover which can lead to an absence of capable guardians or "eyes on the street" to monitor and surveil the comings and goings of residents and others (Rand, 1983, p. 5; Rand, 1984). Residents are often transient and thus less likely to know one another. Visitors and delivery persons come and go at different hours and community watch groups can be more difficult to create and sustain because many residents are not permanent. For many residents, especially young, single adults, an apartment is their first home. Because millions of young women reside in large apartment complexes, predatory attacks and sexual assaults are not infrequent. Security is one of the foremost problems facing apartment community owners, particularly in lower income neighborhoods, because apartments with lax security measures can attract criminals. The combination of all of these factors in certain properties can provide fertile ground for litigation involving premises liability for negligent security (Kennedy and Hupp, 1998; Wayne and DeHart, 1998; Kaminsky, 2008; Sorrells, 2016).

A negligence tort can arise when a landlord fails to take appropriate security measures to provide tenants reasonable protection against foreseeable criminal attacks. As we have discussed in previous chapters, in order to prove a tort, a plaintiff must establish that (1) the defendant owed a duty to provide reasonable security, (2) the defendant breached the duty to provide reasonable security, (3) this breach of duty was the cause-in-fact and proximate cause of the plaintiff's (4) injury. Proximate causation requires the victim of an assault to show a close connection between the assault and the business owner's failure to exercise reasonable case. Generally, the plaintiff must prove all four elements of a tort to a civil jury who will decide whether a defendant is liable based on a "preponderance of the evidence."

Apartment negligent security cases are heterogeneous and fall into several different types and categories. Rape and assault incidents generally take place within the dwelling unit itself, but a substantial number occur within the common areas of the building and on the grounds themselves. Locks, guard issues, and lighting can be major points of contention (Kennedy and Hupp, 1998). Many cases focus on the actions and inactions of security personnel, who may not have been properly trained, or who took inappropriate action in a violent crime situation. Plaintiffs may accuse security guards and security companies of lax supervision and thereby argue that supervision was inadequate at the apartment complex. Plaintiffs may focus on the apartment's and security companies' policies and procedures to argue that the landlord or landowner did not have security policies and procedures in place or the security personnel did not follow those procedures (Leighton, 2009). Other cases may focus on lighting issues, which may have been inadequate at the start or poorly maintained after installation. Other cases may be concerned with security equipment, including access control, locking mechanisms, and closed circuit television. Still other cases may focus on perimeter control and limiting access to a property through fencing, landscaping, or other means (Ford, 2011).

Many security experts are familiar with these security issues and with tort elements but not all of them are trained to use criminological theory and research methods to analyze the individual and social structural causes of crime, assess the degree of crime foreseeability, and explain the role of time and place in the constitution of a crime event. Specialized training in social science methods is needed to adequately evaluate the validity and reliability of crime data, interrogate evidence systematically, and address disconfirming evidence forthrightly. Many forensic criminologists have a repertoire of skills to assist the courts in resolving legal matters. These skills can include, among others, the ability to identify sources of data and information applicable to a particular sociolegal problem, capacity to understand and synthesize large quantities of data, proficiency to design sophisticated research projects, and competence to sort and evaluate data.

APARTMENT SECURITY AND CRIME FORESEEABILITY

Evaluating the foreseeability of a criminal attack is extremely important in any premises liability case because the level of foreseeability dictates the standard of care applicable to the security measures which should be in place at a given property (Pastor, 2007, pp. 3–32). A landlord's duty to protect tenants has evolved over time and can arise in several ways. First, local ordinances or regulations can impose specific legal obligations on landlords or define the duties of landlords to their tenants. In some jurisdictions, city ordinance requires landlords to provide certain security measures such as guards.

Second, the property owner can assume a duty to protect the victim of an assault based upon a special relationship arising out of law. Here, courts may apply general negligence standards to establish a duty deemed either inherent to the landlord-tenant relationship or resulting from factors weighted to special circumstances. As Glesner (1992, p. 689) puts it, the "landlord's control of the common premises or the landlord's voluntary assumption of a duty to provide security serves as the basis for the landlord's duty." "[W]hen the owner has control over the property in question," according to Zinober (2015, p. 290), she or he "assumes a duty of reasonable care to the victim of the assault, commensurate with the legal status of the visitor."

Forensic criminologists should familiarize themselves with the controlling case law in a jurisdiction so that they can plan and organize their research procedures for gathering evidence of crime foreseeability. For example, does the jurisdiction adhere to the prior similar acts test for the issue of foreseeability or does the jurisdiction follow the totality of circumstances test? If the jurisdiction follows the prior similar acts test, is it sufficient that there were prior crimes committed in the neighborhood or does the jurisdiction require evidence of prior crimes committed in the specific apartment building? For the prior similar acts test, a forensic criminologist may consider multiple crime-related sources—incident reports, calls for service, and police narrative reports—for the premises and nearby properties. A forensic criminologist can provide relevant, comparative data from the local, state, and national level, if needed and applicable to the case. If the case is in a jurisdiction that follows the totality of circumstances test, a forensic criminologist should consider prior similar acts and examine the location and land use of a property to assess the degree of foreseeability of crime at the given property. Overall, the forensic criminologist can organize her or his investigation to address three initial questions: (1) Is there evidence of prior crimes within the building or the surrounding neighborhood? (2) Is there evidence that the apartment is in a high crime neighborhood? and (3) Is there evidence that the condition of the premises attracts criminal activity?

Engagement with criminological theories can guide the collection and analysis of crime data. One key insight of routine activities theory (Cohen and Felson, 1979) is that a criminal event requires a convergence in space and time of a likely offender (someone motivated to commit crime), a suitable target (someone or something that the likely offender is attracted to offend against), and the absence of capable guardians (persons who are able and empowered to protect the target and deter offenders). Moreover, this convergence is not haphazard but is explicable in terms of the everyday activities that people engage in as they travel through the city. Residential burglary clusters in residences near major roads or shopping areas where few people are home during the day (Cromwell et al., 1991; Wiles and Costello, 2000). Assaults at residential land uses concentrate in the residential areas close to the commercial land uses. Environmental criminologists have long reported that offenders, as a general rule, do not venture very far from their home or relatively familiar areas in order to commit crimes. According to the principle of least effort (Zipf, 1949), offenders will prefer shorter trips over longer trips. Therefore, a particular area is more likely to experience crime if it is located nearby an offender's home (Bernasco and Block, 2011, p. 36). So-called journey-to-crime research confirms this prediction (Snook, 2004). An offender's familiarity with the territory and socio-spatial context facilitates both crime site targeting and avoidance of apprehension. As Kinney and colleagues (2008, pp. 63–64) elaborate:

> For occasional offenders, crimes occur when tempting opportunities are discovered in the course of routine, legitimate daily activity. For persistent offenders, the search for criminal opportunities and the commission of crime can become a routine activity. In either case, the offender's target search starts from some known location such as home, a friend's home, a local pub or a shopping area … In both cases, the pattern of offending is located close to major activity nodes: home and a few major destination points.

These criminological insights have four important implications for the assessment of crime foreseeability. First, criminological research intimates that crime will concentrate where the routine movements of targets and offenders overlap. Second, criminologists suggest that the source of these movements can be legitimate activities unrelated to crime. Third, spatial and temporal variations in crime rates can be explained by examining fluctuations in the supply and movement of offenders, victims, and guardians as a function of their everyday routine activities (Sidebottom and Wortley, 2016, p. 162). Fourth, the degree of security or capable guardianship at various places and times at which targets and offenders intersect will explain, in part, the distribution or variation of crime.

NATURE OF THE NEIGHBORHOOD: FORESEEABILITY OF CRIME BY PLACE

One of the most important factors in premises liability/security cases is the profile of the socio-spatial environment of the criminal act (Calder and Sipes, 1992; Voigt and Thornton, 1996). Socioeconomic and demographic factors may suggest the likelihood or not of a convergence of suitable targets, motivated offenders, and lack of capable guardians. The socio-spatial environment is the context within which to evaluate crime foreseeability because spatial-temporal factors can suggest opportunities for motivated offenders to victimize targets at particular properties. Meta-analytic studies have shown that disadvantaged neighborhoods are significantly associated with crime (Ellis et al., 2009, pp. 36–37; Hsieh and Pugh, 1993; Pratt and Cullen, 2005). Disadvantaged neighborhoods are characterized by high levels of poverty, low levels of home ownership or vehicle ownership, frequent residential turnover, meager and few business and cultural amenities, high levels of physical disorder and environmental decay (e.g., graffiti, dilapidated and burnt buildings, abandoned vehicles and appliances, trash and litter), and high levels of social disorder (e.g., open and flagrant drug sales and drug use, prostitution, and unemployed persons loitering) (Sampson et al., 1997).

Over the decades, numerous studies have shown that neighborhoods with higher poverty rates tend to have higher rates of violent crime (Hipp, 2007; Sampson, 2012). According to a Department of Housing and Urban Development (HUD) summary of research on the relationship between housing, community development, and crime:

[C]rime is concentrated in disadvantaged neighborhoods. Research shows that living in a disadvantaged neighborhood can increase the risk of a youth or adult engaging in criminal activity, even after controlling for individual sociodemographic characteristics. In other words, the prevalence of crime in these areas is explained in some measure by neighborhood disadvantage itself. This finding results in part from disparities in the physical environment. Older, deteriorating housing stock, for example, increases exposure to lead-based paint, which has been linked to aggressive and antisocial behavior that sometimes results in criminal acts. Physical blight, as evident in dilapidated housing, is also associated with increased criminal activity. Signs of physical disorder are a signal to criminals that residents are not invested in a neighborhood and are therefore less likely to report crimes. Similarly, research shows that vacant properties, which often deteriorate in physical quality and leave fewer "eyes on the street," contribute to increased crime, including assault and arson. Other mechanisms that potentially influence criminal behavior in a neighborhood context include peer groups; social interactions; the quality of schools, police, and other social goods; and the design of the built environment (Department of Housing and Urban Development (HUD), 2016, pp. 3–4).

Table 4.2 presents a general overview of the major noncrime factors that may be relevant in the analysis of crime foreseeability. The table is neither exhaustive nor comprehensive in the listing of noncriminal

Table 4.2 Relevant Noncrime Data to Consider in the Assessment of Crime Foreseeability

Socioeconomic and Demographic Data	Land Use, Housing, and Commercial Activity	Neighborhood Characteristics and Physical Attributes
Poverty rate	Percentage of nonresidential land uses	Physical disorder indicators: the number of incidents of illegal dumping, litter, graffiti, overgrown weeds, inoperable cars on the street, junk storage, exterior abatement, substandard housing, and minor property damage
Unemployment rate	Foreclosures and vacancies (residential and commercial)	
Median family income	Household density	
Resident income distribution	Residential stability	Unsupervised groups of teenagers
Percentage of female-headed households	Number and location of low-income housing units	Street connectivity, transportation availability and infrastructure, pedestrian and cycling infrastructure (presence, condition, and maintenance of sidewalks, bike lanes, cross walks, street lights, traffic lights)
Children under 18	Homeless and transient population	
Education Achievement	Evictions	
	Pawn brokers, check-cashing stores, drug treatment centers, halfway houses, homeless shelters, beer establishments, and liquor stores	Transportation nodes and arteries: subway stations, bus stops, and expressway off ramps

Sources: Andresen, M.A., 2005. Crime measures and the spatial analysis of criminal activity, Br. J. Criminol. 462, 258–285; Blair, L., Wilcox, P., Eck, J., 2017. Facilities, opportunity, and crime: an exploratory analysis of places in two urban neighborhoods. Crime Prevent. Commu. Saf. 191, 61–81; Block, R.L., Block, C.R., 1995. Space, place and crime: hot spot areas and hot places of liquor-related crime. Crime Place 4, 145–184; Bordua, D., 1958. Juvenile delinquency and "Anomie": an attempt at replication. Soc. Probl. 6, 230–38; Brantingham, P.L., Brantingham, P.J., 1993. Nodes, paths, and edges: considerations on the complexity of crime and the physical environment, J. Environ. Psychol. 13, 3–28; Chilton, R., 1964. Continuities in delinquency area research: a comparison of studies for Baltimore, Detroit, and Indianapolis. Am. Sociol. Rev. 29, 71–83; Groff, E.R., Lockwood, B., 2014. Criminogenic facilities and crime across street segments in Philadelphia: uncovering evidence about the spatial extent of facility influence. J. Res. Crime Delinq. 51(3), 277–314.; Kurtz, E. M., Koons, B. A., Taylor, R. B., 1998. Land use, physical deterioration, resident-based control, and calls for service on urban streetblocks. Justice Q. 15, 121–149; Lander, B., 1954. Towards an Understanding of Juvenile Delinquency. Columbia University Press, New York, NY; Loukaitou-Sideris, A., 1999. Hot spots of bus stop crime: the importance of environmental attributes. J. Am. Plan. Assoc., 65(4), 395–411; McCord, E.S., Ratcliffe, J.H., Garcia, R.M., Taylor, R.B., 2007. Nonresidential crime attractors and generators elevate perceived neighborhood crime and incivilities. J. Res. Crime Delinq. 44(3), 295–320; Newton, A.D., Partridge, H., Gill, A., 2014. In and around: identifying predictors of theft within and near to major mass underground transit systems. Secur. J. 27(2), 132–146; Rhodes, W., Conly, C., 1981 Crime and mobility: an empirical study. In Brantingham, P.J. and Brantingham, P.L. (Eds.), Environmental Criminology. Sage, Beverly Hills, CA; Roncek, D., Faggiani, D., 1985. High schools and crime. Sociol. Q. 26 (4), 491–505; Roncek, D., Lobosco, A., 1983. The effect of high schools on crime in their neighborhoods. Soc. Sci. Q. 64(3), 598–613; Sampson, R.J., Lauritsen, J.L., 1990. Deviant lifestyles, proximity to crime, and the offender-victim link in personal violence. J. Res. Crime Delinq. 27(2), 110–139.; Sampson, R.J., Raudenbush, S.W., Earls, F., 1997. Neighborhoods and violent crime: a multilevel study of collective efficacy. Science 277 (5328), 918–924; Sampson, R. J., Morenoff, J. D., Gannon-Rowley, T., 2002. Assessing "Neighborhood Effects": social processes and new directions in research. Annu. Rev. Sociol. 28, 443–78; Sampson, R., Raudenbush, S., 1999. Systematic social observations of public spaces: a new look at disorder in urban neighborhoods. Am. J. Sociol. 105 (3), 603–51; Sampson, R., Raudenbush, S., 2004. Seeing disorder: neighborhood stigma and the social construction of "Broken Windows" Soc. Psychol. Q. 67 (4), 319–42; Shaw, C.R., McKay, H., 1942. Juvenile Delinquency in Urban Areas. University of Chicago Press, Chicago, IL; South, S.J., Messner, S.F., 2000. Crime and demography: multiple linkages, reciprocal relations. Annu. Rev. Sociol. 26(1), 83–106; Stark, R., 1987. Deviant places: a theory of the ecology of crime. Criminology 25(4), 893–910.; Taylor, R. B., Koons, B. A., Kurtz, E. M., Greene, J. R., Perkins, D. D., 1995. Street blocks with more nonresidential land use have more physical deterioration: evidence from Baltimore and Philadelphia. Urban Aff. Rev. 31(1), 120–136; Voigt, L., Thornton, W., 1996. Sociology and negligent security: premises liability and crime prediction. In Jenkins, P. and Kroll-Smith, S. (Eds.), Witnessing for Sociology: Sociology in Court, pp.167–193. Praeger, Westport, MA, pp. 183–184; Weisburd, D., Groff, E.R., Yang, S.M., 2014. Understanding and controlling hot spots of crime: the importance of formal and informal social controls. Prev. Sci. 15(1), 31–43.

activities that are associated with criminal activities. Elevated risks for crime victimization are often found near certain schools (Roncek and Lobosco, 1983; Roncek and Faggiani, 1985) and fast food restaurants (Brantingham and Brantingham, 1981) due to the youthfulness of the individuals often using these locations. Other high-risk crime spots may be near bars (Roncek and Bell, 1981), parks, and bus terminals. In the former, there is a clear possibility of alcohol abuse while the latter two may attract a lower income clientele, transients, and those intent on victimizing them (Gabor, 1981). Shopping centers may be crime magnets due to spatial convenience of location, teenage loitering, and the multiple opportunities for shoplifting and assault on female shoppers (Brantingham et al., 1990; Engstad, 1975). Likewise, apartments near roller skating rinks, discount jewelry stores, liquor stores, and probation/parole offices may be at risk for criminal events.

A forensic criminologist should be careful not to rely exclusively on noncrime data and census tract level data as listed in Table 4.2 to make bold predictions and sweeping generalizations about crime foreseeability. There are two reasons for collating other sources of data with noncrime data in the analysis of crime foreseeability at a particular site. First, population, demographic, and socioeconomic data as collected by the U.S. Census Bureau are not crime data. The primary purpose of census tracts is to provide a stable set of geographic units for the presentation of statistical data. Census tracts generally have a population size between 1200 and 8000 people, with an average size of 4000 people (U.S. Census Bureau, 2017). Second, the data listed in Table 4.2 are not site-specific data and therefore do not indicate an actual crime incidence or crime rate at a specific property. The data sources in Table 4.2 are correlates of crime incidents based on group data.

COLLECTING AND ANALYZING CRIME DATA

To assess the criminogenic nature of the neighborhood, a forensic criminologist should also examine the criminal history of the property and the surrounding area. To do so, she or he should collect past law enforcement records summarized by category and location of the criminal event. There are three major national sources of crime data in the United States: Federal Bureau of Investigation's (FBI) Uniform Crime Reports (UCR) which reports data on crime counts, crime rates, and arrests; the National Crime Victimization Survey which tracks self-reported victimizations of crime; and the National Vital Statistics System which has data on deaths including homicides.

NATIONAL LAW ENFORCEMENT RECORDS

Each year, the Federal Bureau of Investigation (FBI) publishes the Uniform Crime Reports which consists, in part, of a detailed analysis of eight major crime categories covering jurisdictions of various sizes in the United States. The UCR Program collects statistics on the number of offenses known to law enforcement. In the traditional Summary Reporting System (SRS), there are eight crimes, or Part I offenses (murder and nonnegligent homicide, forcible rape), robbery, aggravated assault, burglary, motor vehicle theft, larceny-theft, and arson) to be reported to the UCR Program. The FBI collects information on these offenses because they are serious crimes, they occur with regularity in all areas of the country, and they are likely to be reported to police. While there are limitations with the UCR, the UCR data are the most comprehensive and consistently collected data on crime in the United States.

In most cases, analysis of UCR data is the first step, and additional in-depth analysis of crime in local areas is required to understand the nature and context of crime problems.

In recent years, the FBI has been moving from the UCR system's summary-based measurement of crime to incident-based measures via the National Incident-Based Reporting System (NIBRS). While the UCR is an aggregate system that includes the total number of crimes, NIBRS collects details on each single crime incident—as well as on separate offenses within the same incident—including information on victims, known offenders, relationships between victims and offenders, arrestees, and property involved in crimes. Unlike data reported through the UCR Program's traditional Summary Reporting System (SRS)—an aggregate monthly tally of crimes—NIBRS provides circumstances and context for crimes including specific location and time of day. Plans are for the UCR Program's traditional Summary Reporting System (SRS) to be phased out and transition to a NIBRS-only data collection by January 1, 2021 (Federal Bureau of Investigation (FBI), 2018b).

To measure the crime rate, a forensic criminologist can compute the volume of offenses experienced against the population of the area which results in a certain number of crimes occurring in that area. Within this information, a forensic criminologist can compare crime across scales, for example, neighborhood, intersection, or city. Whenever comparing crimes between two cities, however, the researcher must take the fact that city A may have more assaults than city B simply because there are more people in city A. To control for disparate population size, a forensic criminologist normally determines the crime rate per 100,000 people. The simple formula which divides the number of crimes by the number of people and multiplies by 100,000 will allow a forensic criminologist to compare crime rates across cities.

There are two issues that a forensic criminologist should be aware of when determining crime rates. First, using residential census data, many more people may be in any given town on a daily basis because they go there to work. Second, the unit of analysis can vary across locales. When comparing burglary rates between cities, for example, it may be appropriate to use number of dwelling units rather than the population in the denominator (Boggs, 1965; Harries, 1990). That is, when comparing burglary and other nonviolent crimes across cities, it may be more appropriate for a forensic criminologist to differentiate between crime density (crimes per land area) and victimization risk (crimes per target).

LOCAL LAW ENFORCEMENT RECORDS

In many cases of negligent security, forensic criminologists will be more interested in within-city comparisons than across-city comparisons in order to assess crime foreseeability. Some cities will provide crime maps so that viewers can see reported criminal activity. Some cities may also provide annual UCR crime data from the local police department going back a certain number of years. Forensic criminologists may also request records of local police department calls for service at the site and the immediate vicinity. The calls for service data received should include the offense number, date of call, time of call, address of caller, and how the call was initially coded by law enforcement (e.g., murder, assault, trespassing, etc.).

An important question for the forensic criminologist is the appropriate time period to gather and analyze crime data. As we noted in the last chapter, the General Security Risk Assessment Guideline published by the ASIS International (ASIS, 2003, p. 12) suggests 3-5 years prior to the date of the incident as a relevant time frame. The International Association of Professional Security Consultants' (IAPSC) (2014) threat assessment methodology also recommends a 3-5 year time frame prior to evaluate relevant crimes. That said, many courts will consider a 2-3 year prior history as the relevant and appropriate time to evaluate prior similar criminal acts. Not surprisingly, plaintiff expert witnesses may want to extend the number of years back while defense experts may prefer to consider a much shorter period. Time limitations on prior similar acts are most likely to be decided during in limine motions preceding trial (Kennedy, 2006, p. 125). In addition, the forensic criminologist should use both demographic and population figures and crime data to determine any unique features and attributes about the time, date, and place of the criminal event, as well as victim descriptions by age, gender, and race/ethnic status. The forensic criminologist should consult with retaining counsel to formulate requests to local law enforcement for access to local crime records. Requests for crime data can include a formal public records request, a Freedom of Information Act (FOIA) request, or a subpoena.

There is no standard, universally agreed upon definition of foreseeability. Scholars and courts may define "reasonable foreseeability" as probable, possible, and/or predictable. Some legal scholars and experts have used phrases such as "appreciable change" or "reasonably likely to occur." Courts avoid quantifying the concept of foreseeability given the elastic nature of the concept. Sherman and colleagues (1989) contrasted absolute foreseeability—asking how likely it is that a crime (or type of crime) will occur to any victim at some particular place over some indefinite time period, with relative foreseeability—the statistical probability of some particular crime occurring in a particular location. Jacobs (2005) has argued that foreseeability has two dimensions: theoretical and realistic. Theoretical foreseeability refers to "the *possibility* that a given criminal incident will occur irrespective of time" (pp. 19–20, emphasis in original). In contrast, realistic foreseeability refers to "the *probability* that an incident will occur at a specific place over a specific time period" (p. 20, emphasis in original). According to Jacobs, "realistic foreseeability is a much more precise and meaningful concept" because it is "determined through a rate" (p. 20).

The importance of calculating crime rates for a site or area is emphasized by Voigt and Thornton (1996) and Vellani (2010, p. 32). Crime rates provide context to crime levels and numbers of crimes in an area. Crime rates allow one to compare crime across different geographical areas and at various facilities. Crime rates also allow the researcher to speak of "low" or "high" crime areas. By computing the crime rate, a forensic criminologist is able to make apples-to-apples comparisons of properties of similar design and operations in the same city, to similar businesses in the area, and to larger geographic areas such as the city in which the property is situated.

These points imply that foreseeability does not have a definite and precise character that a forensic criminologist can easily quantify and measure. Rather, foreseeability is a legal construct the courts use to determine whether landlords and other businesses have a legal duty to protect tenants and invitees from foreseeable criminal acts. Moreover, foreseeability is not based on an absolute certainty. It is a consideration of the likelihood that a criminal event may occur in the future based on historical data at the site; the history of criminal events at similar sites; the nature of the neighborhood, immediate vicinity, and overall geographical location; and other situational factors that may affect crime foreseeability.

Two other points are worth mentioning with respect to the analysis of local crime data to establish foreseeability. First, a forensic criminologist may draw on the five Timberwalk factors mentioned in Chapter 3 to determine whether a criminal event was foreseeable: proximity, recency, frequency, similarity, and publicity. Second, a forensic criminologist may want to use *hot spot analysis* to identify where crimes occur on or around a particular property. Hot spots are geographical areas where a substantial amount of crime occurs (Sherman et al., 1989). Hot spot analysis is concerned with where the crime occurred rather than who committed the crime. "Hot spot analysis identifies small places in which the occurrence of crime is so frequent that it is highly predictable" (Vellani, 2010, p. 41). Hot spot analysis assumes that repeat criminal events will happen in the future at the same place. Hot spots have higher risk and a higher number of crimes when compared to other similarly sized areas

(Wortley, 2017). Hot spots are an example of the Pareto principle that holds that a small number of contributors to a phenomenon typically account for a disproportionately large amount of that phenomenon. Over the decades, criminologists have mapped hot spots for a wide range of crime and disorder, including burglary (Johnson and Bowers, 2004b), street robbery (Ratcliffe, 2010), cash-in-transit robbery (Hepenstal and Johnson, 2010), alcohol-related violence (Block and Block, 1995), terrorist insurgency (Braithwaite and Johnson, 2012), and maritime piracy (Marchione and Johnson, 2013).

ADDITIONAL SOURCES

Some forensic social scientists, including Voigt and Thornton (1996) have used interviews with residents to develop a general sense of the past criminal threat to a neighborhood. A forensic criminologist can conduct interviews of neighborhood residents to determine their views and perceptions of crime in the neighborhood and thereby evaluate the criminogenic nature of the area. When evaluating crime foreseeability at an apartment complex, Edenhofer (1998) suggests that any interview should focus on the knowledge of prior criminal activity, prior security-related complaints to the property manager, and security measures in place before and at the time of the incident in question.

While neighborhood residents and tenants can often add a qualitative dimension not generally found in police annual reports, forensic criminologists should be cautious in interpreting these subjective impressions of the denizens. For example, women and the elderly may fear crime more than men and younger people, even though women and the elderly are less likely to be victims (Fox et al., 2009; Toseland, 1982). People who watch television news regularly may fear crime more than those who do not (Research and Forecasts, 1980). People new to a neighborhood or who are not socially integrated into it tend to fear crime more than long-term residents (Donnelly, 1988). One often underestimates crime in one's own block or neighborhood and overestimates crime in another, on top of the fact that fear of crime, in general, often exceeds actual victimization rates, at least in some neighborhoods (Donnelly, 1988; Lewis and Salem, 1986). Nevertheless, much information can be gleaned from surveys of local residents, and they should not be discounted as an important source of information.

A forensic criminologist may also consider interviewing the landlord, property manager, and officials of the security company. The interviews can probe their knowledge of the criminal event, awareness and understanding of the security protocol, and any changes in security since the incident occurred. Interviews can reveal the names of security personnel, the names of any service or company that has provided security, the names and addresses of former tenants, and any security inadequacies. Professional property management officials will often keep a record of security incidents occurring on their property. Apartment complex managers, for example, often serve as a repository of tenant complaints. Thus, a forensic criminologist may use these complaints as baseline data to evaluate whether security conditions are improving or getting worse. The point of all of this, of course, is that a forensic criminologist has a variety of qualitative data sources with which to develop the profile of a property. Voigt and Thornton (1996, p. 174) argue that interviews can provide detailed information to supplement other data gathered as part of the crime analysis.

Often, the experts must conduct interviews and develop other supplemental information using standard social science methodologies. For instance, if an official incident report appears incomplete or somehow confusing, the expert may attempt to check out certain details of facts by going on location and interviewing individuals in residence or businesses where the incident took place. The expert may also conduct interviews to confirm or refute certain perceptions of dangerousness ("fear of crime") or opinions regarding the adequacy of security on the premises. If this information is intended to be used as evidence in court, all the rigors of the scientific method come into play.

A forensic criminologist can also access newspaper articles to determine if the criminal event was reported in the media. Newspaper articles may contain relevant information about the property owner, landlord, management company, security company, criminal, and other parties involved. Using newspaper articles, a forensic criminologist may be able to ascertain whether the neighborhood has experienced a crime spree or a recent increase in particular crimes. Articles may feature quotes from property managers about prior crimes. That said, a forensic criminologist should be careful and not rely exclusively on media reports as a measure of crime foreseeability. Some courts have argued that actual notice cannot be satisfied by "media reports of crime in a region, city, or neighborhood, or by evidence that persons in the area subjectively believe that crime is more prevalent there than in other areas."[3]

OTHER CONSIDERATIONS

A forensic criminologist should be cautious of relying on the Crimecast CAP Index, a crime index consisting of a computer modeled crime score for an area. Crimecast scores represent the probability that a crime will be committed in a given location, relative to national averages. Scores range from 0 to 2000, with the average score being 100. Crimecast scores were initially created for three different crimes against persons (homicide, sexual assault, assault). The CAP Index is supposedly based on these overall crimes against persons. The Crimecast scores are modeled by combining criminology data (national and local police reports, client loss reports, offender surveys, and victim surveys) and demographic data (education, economic, population mobility, housing data, and population data).

Details of the methods and algorithms used to create the Crimecast scores are proprietary and not in the public domain. That is, the methods used to construct CAP Index reports are unknown. Consequently, one cannot determine the validity and reliability of the CAP Index. Therefore, there is no way to verify if the scores reported in the CAP Index reports are appropriate when trying to determine a property's risk for crime or to evaluate the appropriate level of security to respond to such threats.

In consideration of the *Daubert* factors discussed in previous chapters, the limitations of the CAP Index can provide powerful ammunition to opposing counsel to challenge the methodology of the security expert in a negligent security litigation case. In initiating a *Daubert* challenge, opposing counsel could argue the following before a court:

1. the security expert could not offer any evidence that the methodology of the CAP Index had been subject to peer review or publication;
2. the security expert acknowledged that the methodology of the CAP Index had not been tested;

---

[3]Certification from The United States Court of Appeals For Ninth Circuit in *McKown v. Simon Property Group, Inc.,* Wash: Supreme Court 2015. See also Gilliam and Iyengar (2000) reporting that crime accounts for more than 75 percent of all news coverage in certain cities and that viewers' attitudes about crime vary depending on the race of the alleged perpetrators.

3. the methodology did not have a known error rate; and

4. the security expert could not identify any evidence suggesting that the CAP Index methodology was generally accepted by a relevant professional community (e.g., academic criminologists).

As the previous points illustrate, a *Daubert* challenge could disqualify a security expert that used the CAP Index to evaluate crime foreseeability. Using an unpublished methodology that has not been subjected to peer review, the Crimecast CAP Index purports to depict the crime risks surrounding particular locations. But the methodology cannot tell us when a crime occurred, where it occurred, or how it occurred at a specific property. In addition, the accuracy rate for the CAP Index is not known because the methodology is not published or publicly accessible.

A forensic criminologist should not rely on one data source such as police "calls for service" at a property as the sole source of evidence of crime foreseeability. Call data can be ambiguous since the call represents the location where a complaint was made, which may or may not be the site of the criminal event. Moreover, some courts have argued that call data do not amount to actual crimes on the subject property (Boba, 2009, pp. 85–86; Wilkins and Latimer, 2014). Call data may be possible crimes and they may not actually describe or report what actually happened. Calls for service may be officer generated and not the result of citizens' calls.

That said, calls for service can serve as a measure of police activity and can be an important factor in understanding the criminal history of the property and surrounding socio-spatial environment, provided that call data are corroborated with other data sources. Sherman and colleagues (1989) study of call data in Minneapolis found strong evidence that previous calls to police were predictive of future calls. According to Vellani (2010, p. 29), "the location and precise nature of the calls can be verified and reliability enhanced when CFS [calls for service] are used in conjunction with offense reports."

As part of the overall methodology for evaluating the criminogenic nature of the neighborhood in which the criminal event occurred, a forensic criminologist can review calls for service to find out how many residents reported incidents on the premises and in the immediate vicinity. These calls for service will also show when and where those incidents occurred and their similarity or other relationship to the actual criminal event. After examining the calls for service, a forensic criminologist can obtain actual narrative police incident reports which provide more detail than calls for service. From a plaintiff's perspective, one attorney suggests the importance of close examination of every police report from the premises:

> Familiarity with crimes that occurred on the property is fundamental. Do not rely on crime statistics or grids. Read every police report from the property, going back at least three years from your client's assault. What may appear to be a simple property crime can yield the greatest notice and foreseeability witnesses. For example, a police report showing theft of a cell phone from a vehicle may appear trivial and unrelated on its face. However, the victim of that property crime often will have reported it to management and felt violated by that intrusion, especially if it happened more than once. The best witness regarding notice of on-premises crimes may be a robbery victim who constantly complained to management (Marlow, 2013, p. 3).

Actual narrative police incident reports are the "gold standard" for proper analysis of crime foreseeability at a given property (Vellani, 2001, p. 29). The International Association of Professional Security Consultants (www.iapsc.org) and the ASIS International (2003), *General Security Risk Assessment Guideline,* both endorse the use of narrative police incident reports to evaluate crime risk.

The takeaway here is that a forensic criminologist can use several different methodologies and data sources to assess the level of crime foreseeability in a given location. Calder and Sipes (1992, p. 75) suggest that the expert "bring to the attention of the court a reasonable triangulation of crime statistics that estimate the probability of particular types of crime at particular locations." Triangulation refers to using more than one particular method or data source when doing criminological research in order to get richer, fuller data and/or to help confirm the results of the research. The basic idea is to collect two or more types of data more or less simultaneously (concurrent design) so that the investigator can cross-check and confirm the accuracy of the data sources. Triangulation encompasses a dual strategy to increase the validity of research results and increase the scope, depth, and consistency in forensic criminological investigations.

CASE EXAMPLE: SHOOTING IN PARKING LOT IN OFF-CAMPUS APARTMENT COMPLEX

Negligent security claims can arise in a variety of different contexts. Quoting Ford (2011, p. 8), "[i]t is often said that the three most important words in real estate are location, location, location. The same is true in a negligent security claim. The location in which a criminal act occurs will have an impact on the exposure that a landowner faces, as well as the potential award. Not surprisingly, the most common location in which a criminal act occurs giving rise to a claim of negligent security is a parking lot." As noted by Kennedy (2014, 1993), parking areas vary in level of crime foreseeability, and their criminogenic nature will depend on their location, history, characteristics of facility users, and the real or perceived efficacy of security measures.

A forensic criminologist can use the heuristic device of "critical intensity zones" (Angel, 1968) to explain victimization in parking lots and the concepts of *prospect*, *refuge*, and *escape* to explain crime in parking structures. Critical intensity is that tipping point where there are enough potential victims in a parking lot to attract predators but not enough potential targets or witnesses to deter these predators. Prospect refers to the limited surveillance capacity available to a pedestrian in a parking area. Refuge refers to multiple criminal hiding places in a garage and fewer escape routes feasibly open to a potential victim (Kennedy, 1993).

The following case concerns the shooting death of a young man in a parking lot of an apartment complex that serves two nearby college campuses. The young man was a student living at the property when he was killed under disputed circumstances. The assailants claim the man approached them in the parking lot of the residential property in order to sell them marijuana. A neighbor and property employee disputed this version of the events based on what she personally saw and her disbelief that the young man would have solicited these strangers. Experts do not resolve factual disputes involving witness credibility, so the forensic analysis considers crime foreseeability with regard to security issues in the apartment industry. According to the forensic criminological report:

A major subfield of criminology is known as environmental criminology, which deals with the impact of one's social and physical environment on the decision to commit and the manner of commission of a crime [citation to Kennedy, 1990]. A related concept is Crime Prevention Through Environmental Design (CPTED) which focuses on the relationship of the built environment to criminal behavior [citation to Crowe, 1991]. As I will explain below, I believe a criminogenic environment existed at [the apartment complex] and that this environment contributed to the death of [the young man]. Furthermore, it appears that a number of reasonable residential security measures were not in place at this property.

The apartment complex was populated by young people attracted there by curb appeal and college residence hall principles (e.g., private room, common areas in unit, Community Assistants to act almost as Resident Assistants, etc.), thus implying one might find the same secure living at [the apartments] as one might find at, say, [the university dormitories]. This was not the case.

Based on testimony, crime incident reports, and a review of police calls-for-service (CFS), this apartment complex seemed somewhat "out of control" as many underage and barely of age young people engaged in excessive drinking, partying, drug sales and consumption, and off-lease squatting in various units. Thus, testimony given by [a resident leader] at the apartments describes rampant underage drinking, loitering, and drug sales. [The] mother of one of the perpetrators describes [the apartment complex] as a dangerous place because of guns, drugs, and inadequate security. A statement from [a] student resident … attests to rampant drug use, undependable security, and out-of-control partying. [This student] was also the victim of an armed home invasion robbery at [the apartment complex], a not unexpected occurrence where cocaine transactions take place [citation to Goldstein, 1985]. The relationship between alcohol and violence has long been established [citation to Quigley and Leonard, 2004/2005].

[One student] claimed in a statement she was afraid to live at [the apartments] and reported there is a lot of crime and drug abuse at the complex. In deposition testimony given by [a] Deputy Sheriff [of the local sheriff's office], the deputy comes right out and says that [the apartment complex] is itself a high-crime area [citation to deposition of deputy sheriff].

This testimony is further buttressed by law enforcement and complex management records. There were approximately 1,292 police "calls for service" (CFS) during the three years prior to the murder of [the young man]. Although there are many problems with criminological reliance on CFS alone, CFS will still serve as a measure of police activity and, in this case, the CFS data further support [the] deputy sheriff's impressions of [the apartment complex]. I also reviewed sheriff's reports of assault with a weapon, home invasion, batteries, carjacking, and robbery. Records kept by [the apartment complex's] own management office ("concern forms") shows roommates reporting robbery, burglary, drug use, theft, gunshots, and the brandishing of knives.

That conditions had devolved to such a state could not have surprised property management. In terms of criminal behavior, young people between the ages of 15–24 are the prime source for violent behavior [citations to Ellis et al., 2009, pp. 17–20; Hazan, 1998]. When youth and substance abuse are mixed together, particularly without adequate supervision, even college communities can experience serious behavioral problems [citation to Seaman, 2006]. Based on testimony I have reviewed so far, this property also experienced the presence of many "hangers on" or nonstudents who felt comfortable just "crashing" at [the apartment complex], paying no rent at all. Thus, with no accountability for their behavior, such squatters could certainly contribute to the general "anything goes" atmosphere which would encourage young men to believe they could just walk around a property and commit robberies, and get away with it. I therefore conclude that a crime of violence was reasonably foreseeable at [the apartment complex] due to both prior acts of violence and the totality of the circumstances.

The previous points draw our attention to how certain socio-spatial characteristics—absence of capable guardians, presence of suitable targets, and lack of informal social controls—can affect the type and incidence of criminal events. In opportunity theories of crime, motivated offenders are assumed to increase the risk of crime (Cohen and Felson, 1979). A key indicator of motivated offenders is high-risk juveniles (see Baumer et al., 1998; Bernasco and Nieuwbeerta, 2005; Bursik and Grasmick, 1993). Weisburd and colleagues (2014, p. 40) point out that various indicators of physical disorder especially the presence of unsupervised juveniles "more than doubles the odds" of a particular area being a crime hot spot. Situational opportunities and social characteristics of places strongly distinguish chronic crime hot spots from areas with little crime. In the case above, the presence of unsupervised youth created opportunities for crime and provided fertile ground for the formation of a criminogenic environment.

Moreover, the analysis suggests a low level of informal social control or collective efficacy in the apartment complex. Sampson and colleagues (1997, p. 919) coined the concept collective efficacy of communities to refer to the "willingness [of residents] to intervene for the common good." The concept emphasizes the mechanisms by which a community can prevent crime through enhanced informal rather than formal controls. Sampson and colleagues point out that the sources of the differential ability of communities to regulate their residents are reflected in structural characteristics such as poverty and residential mobility, or the ability of neighborhoods to restrain unruly juveniles. The case of the apartment complex discussed before suggests that the inability to restrain unruly juveniles combined with an absence of capable guardians can foster the growth of crime opportunities.

CASE EXAMPLE: APARTMENT ASSAULT AND THE PRESENTATION OF FORENSIC CRIMINOLOGICAL EVIDENCE

We use the following excerpts from an actual case of negligent security to illustrate how a forensic criminologist may undertake an analysis of foreseeability with an application of the totality of circumstances test. The case involves a 2009 stabbing of a woman (Jamie Ryan, a pseudonym) and her infant son while they were home in their apartment located at Hellen Patrick Apartments (a pseudonym). Mrs. Ryan's husband had recently left the apartment to take his daughter to school when the offender, Willie Martin (a pseudonym), gained entry to the unit. Mrs. Ryan and her baby were attacked during what appears to have been a robbery, wherein Willie Martin made off with several thousand dollars after committing murder and assault. The following excerpts are from an analysis of foreseeability and security negligence in the case.

[Hellen Patrick Apartments] enjoys a prime location in the […] City downtown area. Land values are relatively high due to proximity and ease of travel to [the metropolitan area] and due to availability to scenic views along the […] River. [Hellen Patrick Apartments] is located in census tract [0083], the inhabitants of which enjoy an income which is 39 percent higher than the median household income for all […] City residents [$75,833 versus $55,826]. Census data for the area within a half mile radius of [Hellen Patrick Apartments] reveal a median household income of $99,020 compared to the [State] median of $68,981 and a U.S. median household income of $51,425. Indeed, the [Hellen Patrick] neighborhood of […] City compares favorably with other neighborhoods, enjoys higher rents, and benefits from residents who occupy more lucrative occupational positions when compared to residents in other locations. Neighborhoods with incomes like this are not associated with street crime or stranger-on-stranger predatory violent crime.

Of course, even in the best of neighborhoods, inappropriate land use can become a magnet for crime. Some properties can be crime generators, such as sports stadiums and shopping centers, in that the sheer numbers of people they draw will inevitably include some bad actors. Other properties are crime attractors in that they draw potential criminals by the very nature of the activities at their locations. Examples would include open air drug markets, red light districts, and "fighting bars" or dives. [Hellen Patrick Apartments] is a strictly residential property with no pattern of such pernicious activities. It is best described as "crime neutral" as it is in an upscale neighborhood surrounded by businesses, offices, and retail establishments. [Hellen Patrick Apartments] is located in the East District of the […] City Police Department, a district consistently reporting fewer crimes in its geographical area than in the city's other three comparably populated police districts.

As we noted in the previous chapter, it may not be necessary for there to have been prior similar crimes for the crime in question to have been deemed foreseeable.[4] Chamallas (2011, p. 1376) refers to two Georgia cases, *Sturbridge Partners, Ltd. v. Walker*, 482 S.E.2d 339, 341 (Ga. 1997) where the court held that burglaries of vacant apartments were enough to make rape of the tenant foreseeable; and *Walker v. Aderhold Props., Inc.*, 694 S.E.2d 119, 122 (Ga. Ct. App. 2010) in which the court held that prior burglaries were enough to put the landlord on notice that rape could foreseeably occur. In *Czerwinski v. Sunrise Point Condominium*, 540 So.2d 199 (Fla. App. 1989), a Florida appellate court held that a landlord could be held liable for a third party's sexual assault on a tenant where the landlord was aware of two violent crimes and nine burglaries that had occurred in the same apartment complex during the five years preceding the attack on the tenant.

The following excerpt illustrates the steps a forensic criminologist may take to assess the foreseeability of a criminal event.

Because the "totality of circumstances" test of foreseeability tends to include within it an analysis of prior similar criminal acts on the premises, I undertook a survey of prior crimes at [Hellen Patrick Apartments] dating back three years. Following the criminological insight displayed by the Texas Supreme Court, analysts often consider whether prior crimes on a property could be compared to the case at bar in terms of proximity, recency, frequency, similarity, and publicity. As will be illustrated below, under none of these factors would the crimes against Mrs. [Ryan] and her son be foreseeable based on past history. Furthermore, none of the people who saw Mr. [Willie Martin] that morning discerned that he posed an "imminent danger" to anyone. Even Mr. Ryan did not consider Willie Martin to be a threat based on his behavior or appearance. In fact, Mr. Ryan rode downstairs in the elevator with Martin and apparently saw no reason to alter his plan to walk his daughter to school.

---

[4]*Jacqueline S. v. City of New York*, 81 N.Y.2d 288, 598 N.Y.S.2d 160 (1993); *Tambriz v. P.G.K. Luncheonette, Inc.*, 124 A. D.3d 626, 2 N.Y.S.3d 150 (2d Dep't 2015); *Haire v. Bonelli*, 107 A.D.3d 1204, 967 N.Y.S.2d 475 (3d Dep't), appeal denied, 22 N.Y.3d 852, 975 N.Y.S.2d 734 (2013).

Importantly, a forensic criminologist must be able to organize the crime data and information in such a way that is understandable to a lay audience, for example, a jury. If the testimony of an expert witness is not understandable and useful to the untrained layman juror, it will either be excluded by the trial court judge as a waste of time or ignored by the jury. For the research and testimony to be useful to the courts, expert testimony should be clear, concise, and coherent. A forensic criminologist should define any scientific terms, explain the meanings of the criminological theories, and clearly describe less commonly used lay terms—such as offenders, targets, criminology, criminogenic, and so on. Charts, models, diagrams, and visual materials can be important in presenting data and evidence. As one judge has put it, "[a]lthough juries should not be talked down to, they should also not be burdened with information that is not necessary. The expert is acting as a teacher to the jury and the judge—the students" (Weinstein, 1999, p. 356).

In the following excerpts, we illustrate the presentation of crime data and statistics in an understandable way to a fact finder. Here the findings of a forensic investigation and testimony are understandable, reliable, and to the point. The opinions are backed by objective tests.

> With regard to the overall criminal history at [Hellen Patrick Apartments], I formally requested from the […] City Police Department all official narrative crime reports involving violence for the property for the years 2006–2009. In response to a subpoena, I was provided with thirteen written incident reports dealing with assaultive crime; one for 2009; four for 2008; five for 2007, and three for 2006. Of these thirteen reports, nine involved people who knew each other and scuffled or became violent with one another. Of the thirteen reports, six involved what I believe to be simple batteries, which would not even be reportable to the FBI as a Part I crime. For statistical analysis purposes, however, I have treated them all as felonies even though these six were not.

> Among a building population of 900 residents, as reported by management, the violent crime rate for [Hellen Patrick Apartments] was as follows:
> 2006   333 per 100,000
> 2007   556 per 100,000
> 2008   444 per 100,000
> 2009   111 per 100,000 (not counting Ryan)
> For comparison purposes, the violent crime rate for […] City in 2008 was 944 per 100,000. For [a nearby city], it was 951 per 100,000 and for the U.S. as a whole, the rate was 455 per 100,000. Thus, the [Hellen Patrick] community suffered significantly less violent crime than the local community and less than other comparison jurisdictions as well. I also remind you that a true comparison of violent felonies only (the FBI UCR reports only "aggravated assault") would cut the [Hellen Patrick Apartments] crime rate by almost 50 percent, thus again illustrating my opinion that this apartment building was a relatively safe and secure residential facility. In other words, based on an analysis of prior crimes of violence reportable as Part I crimes to the FBI, the brutal murder of Mrs. Ryan was not reasonably foreseeable.

The previous points illustrate the importance of analyzing and presenting crime statistics in a clear and logical manner. Quantitative data and statistics can be challenging for lay people and juries to grasp. Moreover, some people might be suspicious of complex figures and view the presenter of such information as dubious and untrustworthy. Therefore, when presenting the facts, a forensic criminologist must present data and information in a way that will help judges and jurors understand the facts of the case.

CONCLUSIONS

Lawsuits alleging negligent apartment security are complex and multidimensional. They involve issues relating to duty, breach of duty, causation, and damages. The basic concept in a negligent security lawsuit is that an apartment owner or manager has a legal duty to make sure the property is reasonably safe, secure, and does not present an attractive opportunity for criminal activity. That is, property owners generally have a duty to provide "reasonable care" for people legally on the premises and to protect them from "foreseeable" criminal events.

Negligent security law pertaining to apartments is diverse and multifarious. There are no books that list a code of security measures for landlords. According to Dain and Brennan (2003, p. 74), "[l]iability is premised on a series of considerations or elements that a jury gets to weigh, and juries may weigh those considerations or elements differently in each case." The absence of clear rules or standards governing what level of security is reasonable makes apparent the need for careful and detailed forensic criminological investigation. How landlords and landowners manage security and safety on the apartment premises may have an effect on the risks of crime at the location. The individual or corporation exercising control over a property must take steps to prevent reasonably foreseeable criminal events from occurring. Failure to do so may expose the property owner to litigation and she or he may be sued under tort law (or contract law) for negligence and assessed compensatory, exemplary, or punitive damages.

Our forensic criminological approach to investigating negligent security matters in rental housing is informed by theoretical perspectives that emphasize the immediate situational crime opportunities presented by particular places. These theoretical perspectives include routine activities theory (Cohen and Felson, 1979), situational crime prevention (Cornish and Clarke, 2003), and crime pattern theory (Brantingham and Brantingham, 1993) all of which place great emphasis on the specific opportunities offered by specific places and situations. In addition, rational choice perspectives stress that crime will occur when the perceived benefits outweigh the perceived costs. The implication is that criminal events will increase in particular places if criminal opportunities increase. A related implication is that the socio-spatial environment can make crime an unattractive option from the perspective of the decision maker. Moreover, situational factors can interact with socio-spatial conditions to actively precipitate criminal behavior and thereby create a criminogenic environment. Crime events can result from a combination of contextual criminogenic elements of the crime scene and the specific actions of criminogenic individuals.

Over the decades, courts have struggled over whether the character or place of a business can be a consideration in evaluating the foreseeability of a criminal act. Some courts address whether the "place" of a business within a high crime urban area justifies imposing a duty on the business to protect others from third-party criminal acts. In particular, Michigan and Washington have rejected the idea that location of a premises in an urban area with a high incidence of crime favors imposing a duty. According to the Washington State Supreme Court, "[w]e have recognized that mere statistical evidence, such as a higher crime rate in a particular city or neighborhood, or a higher crime rate among similar businesses nationwide or statewide, is insufficient to support the imposition of a duty."[5] In *McNeal v. Henry,* the Michigan Court of Appeals held,

> Some of our big cities have more than their share of destructive and violent persons, young and old, who roam through downtown department stores and other small retail businesses stealing and physically abusing legitimate patrons. … We fear that to hold businessmen liable for the clearly unforeseeable third-party torts and crimes incident to these activities would eventually drive them out of business.[6]

Related, in *Stafford v. Church's Fried Chicken, Inc.,* a Michigan District Court rejected a plaintiff's argument that since the restaurant where a criminal assault occurred was in a high crime area, the business knew security was necessary to protect the patrons. The court ruled that requiring the business to provide police protection against criminal third parties may drive businesses out of those neighborhoods.[7]

Foreseeability is an elastic term that is subject to much challenge and contestation. In addition, the various tests of foreseeability—for example, imminent harm, prior similar acts, totality of circumstances, and balancing test—vary from state to state and are constantly being questioned and redefined by the courts. In premises liability cases, foreseeability is a factor in the analysis of whether the apartment owner owed a duty to the injured person and whether the property owner's actions or inactions to provide adequate security caused the injury. That is, foreseeability encompasses both the duty and proximate causation elements of a negligence lawsuit. As we point out in the next chapter, breach of duty may be a failure to prevent reasonably foreseeable crime, but litigants generally have to locate the breach against a set of existing security standards or other measures of reasonableness. Ultimately, allegations of negligent security not only depend on foreseeability but also on "adequacy of security" and a determination of whether or not the lack of adequate security caused injury or death to the victim of a criminal act.

---

[5]Certification from The United States Court of Appeals for Ninth Circuit in *McKown v. Simon Property Group, Inc.*, Wash: Supreme Court 2015. See also *Kim v. Budget Rent A Car Sys.*, 143 Wn.2d 190, 199, 15 P.3d 1283 (2001), noting that "this court has rejected utilization of high crime rates as a basis for imposing a tort duty"; See also *Hutchins,* 116 Wn.2d at 236. "[I]f the premises are located in an area where criminal assaults often occur, imposition of a duty could result in the departure of businesses from urban core areas—an undesirable result."
[6]*McNeal v. Henry* 82 Mich. App. 88, 90 n.1, 266 N.W.2d 469 (1978).
[7]*Stafford v. Church's Fried Chicken, Inc.* 629 F. Supp. 1109 (E.D. Mich. 1986).

APARTMENT SECURITY II: STANDARDS OF CARE AND CAUSATION

5

INTRODUCTION

If a plaintiff manages to establish that a duty exists, she or he must then show that the defendant breached this duty by not upholding an applicable standard of care. In an apartment setting, security standards may entail some combination of access control, sufficient lighting, effective locks, foliage control, strict tenant screening policies, key control, courtesy patrols, and other property-specific measures. A forensic criminologist can explain to a jury exactly which security measures should have been in place given the level of foreseeability that a crime would occur. A forensic criminologist can also evaluate whether the property meets the security standard of care given this level of foreseeability and whether there is a causal relationship between any shortcomings in the standard of care and the injuries suffered by the plaintiff. As an expert witness, a forensic criminologist must be able to examine a location's security measures, apply the case facts, and determine if those security measures were reasonable under the circumstances and conditions on the property at the time of the criminal assault. As we noted in Chapter 3, forensic criminologists can consult with appropriate standard-setting organizations and report to the court the precise contributions such organizations have made to clarify the duty owed to people that enter the premises (Calder and Sipes, 1992, pp. 75–77).

For apartments, several property management companies publish guides to landlords and identify standards of care. These guides include Texas Apartment Association (1995), Campbell (2000), French (1997), Kelley (2009), National Fire Protection Association (NFPA) (2018), Institute of Real Estate Management (IREM) (2014), and Sampson (2001). To evaluate whether a defendant met the standards of care, a forensic criminologist can access documents such as corporate manuals (e.g., training materials for employees, policy and procedures books, and security manuals); security or insurance audits; descriptions and records of security equipment; personnel files on in-house security staff; contracts and post orders outlining the specific duties that are to be performed by security services provided by outside agencies; and security manpower schedules (Harris, 2002; Talley, 2000). Given that the courts call for empirical precision in assessing the liability of landholders on whose premises criminal actions occur, establishing breach of duty by way of empirical, defensible, and legally relevant methods is paramount.

Practicing Forensic Criminology. https://doi.org/10.1016/B978-0-12-815595-0.00005-5

OPTIONS NOT STANDARDS: CCTV AND SECURITY GUARDS

At times, security experts may imply in their expert witness reports that video surveillance (e.g., closed-circuit television, CCTV) and security guards are widely acknowledged as standards of care in the multifamily housing industry. In some apartment cases, expert witnesses for plaintiffs may express opinions that the property where the criminal event happened is in a high crime area, argue that video surveillance technologies such as CCTV should have covered the entire property, and state that more security guards should have been deployed to patrol the property. The reports may conclude that the person injured on the premises would not have been assaulted or hurt had more and different security measures been in place.

In the following excerpts, we illustrate how a forensic criminologist can use extant criminological research and forensic evidence to address issues involving security options and security standards in the multifamily housing industry. The following two quotes are drawn from two different expert witness reports that challenge accounts offered by security experts that CCTV has a crime deterrent effect and thereby constitutes a standard of care.

> CCTV deployment in apartment complexes does not represent the current standard of care for apartment security because it cannot be demonstrated that CCTV deters violent crime. While there have been some successes with CCTV reported in England, research in the U.S. has not shown CCTV to be a deterrent [citation to Welsh and Farrington, 2003]. Even more specifically, CCTV has also failed to live up to expectations for security in residential areas [citation to Gill et al., 2007]. While CCTV can certainly be useful in documenting and investigating crime post event, it generally fails to deter crimes of violence. If one were to stop and think for a moment, virtually every robbery of a bank in the U.S. takes place on CCTV. Also, recall how many times one sees on regular television a violent crime which has taken place in front of video cameras.
>
> Plaintiff's experts imply in their reports that CCTV and security guards are widely acknowledged as standards of care within the "affordable" housing industry. This is not true. They are certainly options, but just two among many options. One reason why CCTV does not and cannot constitute a standard of care for the prevention of violent crime is that there is insufficient evidence to prove CCTV even works [citations to Musheno et al., 1978; Welsh and Farrington, 2003; Ratcliffe et al., 2009; Gill et al., 2007]. CCTV can be useful in documenting what has already happened for investigative purposes, but its value as a prevention tool is too precarious for it to constitute a standard of care. As further evidence, I reviewed three major sources of recommended property management practices. None identified CCTV as a standard [citations to Texas Apartment Association, 1995; Campbell, 2000; French, 1997].

The crime deterrent and security enhancing function of security guards can be as ambiguous and complicated as the effectiveness of CCTV. Ever since seminal research on police patrol, known as the Kansas City Study, was conducted in the early 1970s, the value of random preventive patrol has been questioned. In the Kansas City Study, neither doubling of patrols nor ceasing preventive patrol altogether impacted crime or residents' perception of crime (Kelling et al., 1974). According to a well-known expert on policing: "[t]he police do not prevent crime. This is one of the best-kept secrets of modern life. Experts know it, the police know it, but the public does not know it" (Bayley,

1994, p. 3; see also Weisel 1990, p. 5). In fact, on-view crimes are rare, and few crimes actually involve an incident where police officers observe a perpetrator in the midst of an attack (Felson, 1994, p. 11). Most police action results from notification by residents or by dispatchers. Random uniformed patrol is not demonstrably effective because so many crimes occur indoors, on impulse, or because perpetrators simply wait for a patrol to pass. The point is not that patrols can never be effective, only that their prevention benefit remains too uncertain to constitute a blanket mandate as a standard of care.

The following excerpt provides a rebuttal to a security expert's opinion that an individual at a large apartment complex would not have been shot had apartment management deployed armed security guards.

> With regard to the [apartment] property … there are additional concerns as to the possible efficacy of a uniformed security guard patrol. Police and security officers can actually cause problems by a perceived insensitivity toward juveniles [citation to Barocas, 1974, pp. 113–121], a group prone to challenge authority not only because of their age but also to the extent they share "street" values of independence, toughness, the need to maintain "face," and reluctance to submit to authority [citations to Wilson, 1987, pp. 36–39; Miller, 1958]. It can be quite risky to place security officers in a situation where they may have to confront youth on a property which is highly permeable due to public streets and public sidewalks. In other words, would this "preventive" measure create more problems than it solves? This was a major concern for apartment management given that 39 percent of their tenants were under the age of 18 and almost 49 percent were 21 and under. Some management companies may have decided reasonably to take this risk. [Apartment Management] decided reasonably not to. Given the circumstances as explained above, deciding against placing armed guards amongst such an adolescent population fell within the parameters of permissible and reasonable managerial discretion. Indeed, placing armed guards at [the apartment complex] could have worsened the security situation there due to ensuing resentment by many youths [citation to Sherman, 1993].

The previous points reveal how a forensic criminologist can draw on extant criminological scholarship and case-specific forensic evidence to provide relevant and helpful information to a fact finder. As the previous points show, the criminological research on the crime control effectiveness of public area surveillance measures is by no means settled and unambiguous. Rather, criminological findings suggest caution in interpreting the relationship among crime and security measures, especially in the context of rental housing developments. As we pointed out in Chapter 3, decades of criminological research show that the effects of different security measures are not only likely to vary by time and place but also by different social-spatial conditions. In their exhaustive and comprehensive review of the criminological literature, Welsh and colleagues (2015, p. 115) suggest that CCTV could even cause crime to increase. As they put it,

> In the case of CCTV, for example, its visible presence could give potential victims a false sense of security and make them more vulnerable if they relax their vigilance or stop taking precautions, such as walking in groups at night and not wearing expensive jewelry. CCTV may also encourage increased reporting of crimes to the police and increased recording of crimes by the police. If an offender is detected through CCTV, the offense may be recorded and detected at the same time, leading to an increase in police clearance rates as well as in crime rates.

In sum, forensic criminological theory and testimony can establish the criminal history of a property and evaluate whether the steps that the defendant took to protect the tenants or invitees were reasonable under the circumstances. While criminal behavior in a general sense may be foreseeable at an apartment complex, targeted violence is not readily foreseeable. CCTV and armed security patrols do not constitute a national standard of care, although some properties follow such practices. CCTV has not been proved effective in the U.S. context in preventing crime, and both CCTV and armed patrols may generate unforeseen security problems and negative consequences. Dain and Brennan (2003, p. 75) mention a major risk of CCTV: "if you install closed-circuit televisions and as a practice monitor them, but fail to monitor them at the time a violent act is committed on the premises, a jury may be more likely to find a breach of the duty of care than if the televisions had not been installed in the first place." For security guards, potential liability arises for assault and battery, which may occur during the course of attempting to stop or arrest a suspected trespasser on the premises. Liability, in exceptional circumstances, may also arise from the failure of a security guard to protect invitees and licensees on the premises.

CASE EXAMPLE: (IN)ACTIONS OF SECURITY GUARD

In the following excerpts, we analyze an expert witness report to illustrate how a forensic criminologist can use forensic evidence and criminological data to assess whether a defendant has violated a standard of care. Plaintiff Elma Lakewood (a pseudonym) was in her apartment with her son and others when a group of eight intruders pushed their way through her apartment door. Ms. Lakewood, fearing for the safety of her 4-year-old child, held him in her arms as she jumped from an open window to the street some twenty feet below. She brought suit against the apartment complex and the security company for injuries suffered during her escape from this home invasion. At issue were the actions or inactions of a security guard whose post orders had included registering and signing in all visitors to the property as well as notifying residents of the arrival of visitors. The security guard was not at his door post when the group of intruders arrived and entered the building. In an alternate version of the group's entry into the building, one of the offenders testified that the security guard was there at his post but simply waived them through. According to the forensic criminological report:

> I understand that duty issues are to be decided by the court as a matter of law. I also understand that foreseeability is a major consideration to be examined in making this decision. In this case, however, it seems a duty or obligation has been imposed on the ownership of [the apartment complex] by the elected officials of [the city], who passed an ordinance requiring the presence of an armed security guard for eight hours and an unarmed guard for the remaining sixteen hours in any building which contains over one hundred housing units. It is unlikely city leaders would have passed such a measure if they didn't believe that crime at these locations was sufficiently foreseeable to require such preventive measures. Of course, once such an obligation to guard a property exists, it should be carried out reasonably well and generally commensurate with an appropriate standard of care … I comment further on the matter of foreseeability since a higher level of crime foreseeability drives up the appropriate standard of care.

For this case, the following materials were reviewed: the local security guard ordinance, census tract data, the city police Calls for Service, and FBI Uniform Crime Reports for the city. The median family income for the census tract where the apartment is located is only 60% of the median family income for the broader metropolitan statistical area. The report also refers to newspaper coverage about drugs, gangs, and murders in the immediate area of the apartment complex. As the report details:

> This area [of the city] certainly appears to have been unsafe in 2009, and I am not sure how much had changed by 2015. The point of this commentary is that [local] legislators apparently had good reason to require a strong security presence in large multihousing buildings. Given the clear risk of crime, any security to be provided should have been provided in a most effective manner. This was not the case at [the apartment complex] on January 19, 2015.
>
> Among the material provided for my review is a [police department] 198-page CAD [Computer Aided Dispatch] printout of Calls for Service to the [apartment complex] which occurred from January 1, 2009, through June 6, 2015. There are approximately twelve entries per page, totaling just over 2,364 entries. These calls range from sick/injured person to stabbing in progress to shots fired to drug activity. Although specific inferences cannot be drawn from these incomplete accounts, they are suggestive of significant police responses to this address.
>
> Additional data sources which establish the need for effective access control at [the apartment complex] are the 149 incident reports produced by [the security firm] posted at the main door to the apartments. After reviewing the descriptions of incidents encountered by these security officers, it became clear that many attempted "visitors" to the property were unsavory characters who behaved aggressively and threatened security officers when they were denied entry. Their behavior clearly reinforced the need for effective access control at [the apartment complex].

The forensic criminological assessment then proceeds to discuss breach of duty and elaborates on violations of standards of care.

> A primary function of security personnel is access control, which is the regulation of movement into, out of, and/or within a designated building or area [citation to ASIS International 2012b, p. 387]. This can be done through a combination of locking devices, CCTV, direct visual observation, and personal contact with visitors and others. Post orders are used to indicate just how access control is to be accomplished, and care must be taken to ensure that no contradictory orders are in use [citation to ASIS International 2011a, p. 35]
>
> Based on my reading of the [security company] post orders for [apartment complex], security officers were to sign in all visitors and to notify tenants when they had a visitor. This could only be done if an officer was posted at the building's only point of entry for visitors, the main lobby doors. A visitor would enter into a foyer, identify himself or herself to a guard in an office area separated by a plexiglass barrier, and be buzzed in through an otherwise locked door if a tenant approves the visit. This function is so important that one of the post orders reads, "DO NOT LEAVE YOUR POST, UNLESS FOR A BRIEF PERIOD TO USE THE BATHROOM." Possibly in order to avoid distracting a security officer's attention from these screening duties (among other reasons), another post order reads, "DO NOT ACCEPT PACKAGES FOR TENANTS AT ANY TIME."

There are at least three practices which are highly frowned upon by security professionals. One is the use of "dummy cameras." The second is reducing the number of security officers at a location because nothing bad is happening (when the reason for no adverse activity is the presence of the guards). A third pet peeve is to use a security guard for non-security functions such as delivering towels at a motel or getting coffee for corporate executives. Such unrelated duties remove a security officer from his post and open the way for intruders. According to [the] building manager at [the apartment complex], a security officer would routinely be directed to receive loading dock furniture deliveries if maintenance personnel were "unavailable." This is a classic security negligence blunder chargeable to building ownership and management. Deliveries of this nature should only be scheduled when building maintenance personnel or porters are available to receive them.

[Security Company] is also culpable in allowing this post to be controlled by self-contradictory post orders. The importance of the screening function is clear, just as is the mandate that the post not be left vacant (other than for bathroom breaks). Such conflicts place a security officer in a difficult position and would certainly confuse any new officer rotated through the post. In order to avoid allegations of negligent supervision and negligent failure to direct, [security company] should have met with [apartment] management to clarify these post orders and to explain to them the breach of the security standard of care created by the use of [the security guard] as an off-post concierge or building porter. Post procedures are a collaborative effort and both the security company and the client share this responsibility [citation to Sorrells, 2016, pp. 50, 141–142].

The previous excerpts highlight the importance of conducting a thorough and detailed forensic investigation to assess whether or not there was a breach of duty by the defendant property owner. Breach of duty may be a failure to prevent reasonably foreseeable criminal events as well as a violation of standards of care. In the previous case, the failure to properly deploy the security guard and the decision to use him as a delivery person constituted a violation of existing security standards. The standard of care can also be defined by the customs and practices commonly followed within an industry. The standard may be further defined by state and local ordinance, industry publications and trade journals, and practices unique to a particular geographic area. Talley (2000, p. 3) contends that the "strongest standards are those that defendants impose on themselves in their policy and procedure manuals."

A forensic criminologist may also testify as to whether the breach of duty was the cause-in-fact of a crime in an apartment. A forensic criminologist might opine, for example, that an offender selected a particular apartment and victim because she or he believed they could gain easy entrance (poor locks), could not be seen doing so (poor lighting, overgrown foliage), and could likely make an unimpeded escape (no fencing on property). A forensic criminologist can draw on the theoretical variants of environmental criminology we mentioned earlier to explain the actions of criminals in these various circumstances. In addition, a forensic criminologist can also interpret the literature in such a way as to challenge a causal relationship between property conditions and a criminal's actions. That is, there must be a causal link between the breach and the incident. A forensic criminologist can provide the background knowledge and investigative research to help the jury ultimately decide whether a defendant's actions or lack of actions were a proximate cause of a plaintiff's injury.

A key factor in evaluating causality is whether security breaches, failures, or deficiencies more likely than not contributed to the criminal event. A property owner owes a duty to tenants to provide reasonable measures to protect them from foreseeable criminal attacks by third persons. The duty is not to guarantee safety, nor is it to ensure against all criminal attacks. To determine the reasonableness of an apartment complex's security measures, a forensic criminologist can examine industry standards and evaluate what security measures have been implemented by similar facilities. Characteristics unique to the particular apartment complex, such as location, layout, design, and type and level of activity are keys to the forensic criminological analysis. Causation may be difficult to establish if there were few or no cost-effective security measures that could have been implemented by the property owner that could have deterred the crime. The causal link is easier to make if the plaintiff can identify cost-effective measures (e.g., adequate key control, effective locks, functioning gates, attentive security guard) that were not in place at the time of the incident and that could have deterred the crime. Finally, a factor that makes a strong causal link is if the plaintiff can identify security inadequacies that contributed directly to the crime. If an offender enters a tenant's apartment through a defective door lock, for example, then assaults the tenant in the apartment, a strong causal connection is established between the breach of duty and the injury.

Continuing with the analysis of this case involving the plaintiff Elma Lakewood, who jumped out of a window to protect herself and her son from intruders, let us presume that the security officer was not at his post for at least twenty minutes because he was performing an errand for building management. The plaintiff would need to establish that this absence led to her being assaulted and suffering her injuries. Under a cause-in-fact analysis, *but for* the security officer's absence from his post, the offenders would not have been allowed entry into the apartment complex. More likely than not, the apartment tenant would not have given permission to the security guard to allow entry of the group of offenders. According to the forensic criminological report:

> In terms of proximate cause, "when doors are not physically controlled by a guard, there is a tendency for personnel to violate entry procedures. Violation of access control systems … may occur by 'tailgating' or 'piggybacking.'" A common loophole in an otherwise secure access control system is the ability of an unauthorized person to follow through a checkpoint behind an authorized person [citation to Baker and Benny, 2013, pp. 75, 105; Craighead, 2003, p. 143]. Even though front doors may be electronically locked to outsiders, piggybacking or tailgating will still occur unless a guard is there to stop it.
>
> Tailgating is a well-known and foreseeable problem for any electronic entry system not staffed by a security officer or other countermeasure. In fact, that is likely what occurred in this case, and this violation allowed the intruders to get through the main door and up to [the tenant's] apartment. Two women visitors were in the apartment prior to the intrusion. These two ladies left the apartment to get food and were to return. [Plaintiff] was not involved in opening her apartment door to the intruders. It was reasonable for [the tenant's brother] to assume that it was these same two visitors at the door when he opened it, given the policy that only "cleared" visitors are permitted entry to the building.
>
> [Security officer's] incident report of 11/19/2015 referring to the assailants reads, in part: "the people and or persons followed a tenant in through… the front door when security was away from the booth." There is no doubt that a security officer's absence from the booth post would increase the risk of interlopers gaining illicit entrance into the building. It was just this scenario that building residents had relied upon [the Security Company] to prevent.

The previous case reveals the linkages among crime foreseeability, breach of duty, and causation. The conclusion of the forensic criminological assessment is that the security guard charged with access control at the front door had left his post to receive a furniture delivery. During his absence, the assailants likely tailgated a resident and gained entrance illicitly since there was no guard present to stop them. The importance of staffing this post was based on a local ordinance requiring an armed guard at this building and due to the criminogenic nature of the neighborhood itself. The crafting of post orders is a function shared by the guard company, client, and the guard. The security guard should not have been tasked with a furniture delivery, thus removing him from this sensitive post. The security company operated this post under contradictory post orders, a substandard practice which should have been resolved through consultation with the client.

To establish proximate causation, a forensic criminologist can investigate whether the defendant's violation of the standard of care played a role facilitating the criminal event that caused the client's injury. Legal practitioners often define proximate causation as "that, which in a natural and continuous sequence, unbroken by any efficient intervening cause, produces injury, and without which the result would not have occurred" (Nolan and Connolly, 1983, p. 641). As noted in Chapter 3, this definition encompasses the notion of foreseeability. "In other words, not only must a crime be foreseeable for duty to attach, it must also be foreseeable that a given breach would lead to injury" (Kennedy, 2006, p. 133). To survive a motion for summary judgment, there must be a causal link between the breach and the criminal event. A jury ultimately decides whether a defendant's actions or lack of actions was a proximate cause of a plaintiff's injury. But a forensic criminologist's investigation will reveal the factual background that will allow the fact finder to determine causation and liability.

Researchers and scholars have long assumed that the presence of uniformed police or security personnel can provide a deterrent effect. Yet, as the previous example shows (and as we detail in other chapters), a crucial part of evidence development in a negligent security case is examining the premises, putting the security measures into context, and investigating whether the security company followed its own rules and procedures as a capable guardian. Standards of care do not mean much if the defendants did not follow them in the conduct of their duties. As independent contractors, security companies provide security guards and often utilize security cameras, video monitoring, and other surveillance techniques to reduce the risk of criminal activities and maintain the premises in a reasonably safe condition. Broadly, breakdowns and failures in following safety and security procedures can create opportunities for criminal acts and subsequent litigation. Thus, an analysis of how and why a crime event happens will need to take into account where and when it happens.

CASE EXAMPLE: OFFENDERS, TARGETS, AND GUARDIANS

This case involves the shooting of Jose Ferrara (a pseudonym) by a group of two or three young men who approached him in the parking lot of an apartment complex at 8:00 p.m. one evening. Mr. Ferrara seems to have been doing mechanical work on automobiles under the direction of Maria Sanchez (a pseudonym), a resident of the apartment complex who was in the United States illegally, as was Mr. Ferrara. Mr. Ferrara did not know why he was approached or why he was shot. The assailants appeared suddenly, and the shooting happened quickly thereafter. The case involves liability issues pertaining to the proximate cause of the shooting. The forensic investigation focuses on whether there was a causal relationship between the management company's management of the apartment complex, specifically with regard to the security provided, and the injuries suffered by Mr. Ferrara. According to the forensic criminological report:

First, from a physical security perspective, this huge property [139 buildings spread over 70 acres] is virtually indefensible against outsider incursion because it has several public streets running through it over which no management company or security agency could exercise control. [See the security complications involving open access streets as well as the difficulties and implications involved with closing off these streets as discussed in Ronald Clarke, *Closing Streets and Alleys to Reduce Crime: Should You Go Down That Road* (Washington, D.C.: U.S. Department of Justice, 2005)]. The impracticality of effective access control is further evidenced by the lengthy perimeter of the property. It is well known to criminologists that the permeability of a property is directly related to the likelihood of crime being committed therein, other things being equal [citations to White, 1990; Schneider and Kitchen, 2007, p. 190].

In addition to the physical qualities of the property which contributed to this crime, certain social structural factors are ultimately responsible for creating the conditions which led to the shooting of Mr. Ferrara. [The city] and its environs [are] particularly attractive to illegal immigrants seeking work in the U.S. Due to a phenomenon known as "chain migration," immigrants will go to those locations where they have friends and relatives and where it will be possible to improve their economic situations without excessive concerns about being arrested [citation to Parillo, 1985]. Based on my review of case materials and information from property management, the [apartment complex] was a known magnet for illegal immigrants.

The presence of illegal immigrants is related to crime in a number of ways. Immigrant populations have been described as natural victims because of their somewhat vulnerable social position [citation to Doerner and Lab, 2002]. They also deal in cash since they cannot use banks; and they are reluctant to rely on police to protect them, given their illegal immigrant status [citations to Davis, 2001; Davis and Erez, 1998; Davis and Henderson, 2003]. Immigrant populations are thus susceptible to being victimized by those within their own population who are not controlled by social bonds and by local homegrown thugs who routinely prey upon the socially helpless wherever they can be found [citation to Martinez and Valenzuela, 2006, pp. 1–19]. This already criminogenic situation was exacerbated by the occasional raids by immigration authorities. These federal government actions resulted in a high turnover of Latino residents at [the apartment complex] as they reacted to such raids by quickly moving away, only to have others move in due to the notion of chain migration mentioned earlier. Such a high turnover means there is little neighborhood "collective efficacy," where neighbors look out for one another and exercise some form of territorial control and concern for the property [citation to Morenoff et al., 2001]. This form of natural surveillance is the primary means of security in any neighborhood, yet the social dynamics of a transient population prevent this natural form of security from developing. The large number of vacant units (80 percent) made it even more unlikely that neighbor could effectively look after neighbor. As I indicated earlier, this was not a conventional apartment complex; therefore, the unique problems involved with improving the entire property must be taken into account when assessing the reasonableness of management decisions.

The forensic criminological investigation then turns to matters of causation and opines that neither the presence nor absence of two proposed security measures—enhanced security patrols or video surveillance—were causally related to Mr. Ferrara's injuries. We have already commented before that video surveillance is not a security standard of care and there is no evidence that CCTV prevents violent crime. The forensic report provides a rebuttal to an expert witness report submitted by opposing counsel.

[The expert witness] has also recommended increased security patrol for the [the apartment complex]. This issue is also more complicated than one might think. First, there was a very active patrol service in effect on the evening of March 28, 2007. My review of many pages of [the security company] Daily Activity Reports tells me these fellows were doing an active, professional job. Yet, the shooting still occurred, even though the intensity of patrol on the property was six times greater at [the apartment complex] than for the city. Consider two officers patrolling seventy acres on one shift at [the apartment complex] versus 600 [city] officers (one third of entire city force for one shift) patrolling 134,592 acres of [city] proper. Even had the [security company] patrol force been doubled in number, proper deployment would not have placed the second vehicle near the original scout car on duty. Since the patrol vehicle in service that night was quite close to the shooting, the second vehicle would not have been near the shooting and would not have deterred it anyway. Also, please note that probably only one percent of crimes involve an on-view incident where police officers observe the perpetrators just as they launch their attack [citation to Felson, 1994].

The fact of the matter is that overall crime rates are generally not directly affected by the number of police on patrol [citation to Kelling et al., 1974; Bayley, 1994]. Too many crimes occur indoors, or on impulse, or after perpetrators have waited for a patrol car to pass. While police in certain circumstances can be credited with reducing crime, the effect may be fleeting; or police may simply have displaced criminals to the next block [citation to Di Tella and Schargrodsky, 2004]. Criminologists continue to debate reasons for the recent national decline in violent crime. Some credit more police, others do not. One problem in measuring the impact is one of simultaneity, known as reciprocal causation. If a community has more crime, it often puts on more police, so more police often means more crime [citation to Blumstein and Wallman, 2006]. My point is not to deny that police officers can have a deterrent effect on crime. It is simply that we do not know enough about the exact causal relationship to conclude that, in this case, a few extra security officers on patrol at [the apartment complex] would have deterred the shooters unless these officers happened to be standing right next to Mr. Ferrara.

This leads me to my last point on causation. Would extra patrol officers, CCTV, or even a little more light have convinced these two (or more) thugs not to attack? I believe not. I don't know at this point that robbery was the sole or primary motive, but I do know that two or more armed young men [may] have an inflated sense of power and often act as much to impress each other as they do to secure a substantial financial reward from robbery [citation to Erickson, 1996, 2003].

Clearly, [this case] is more complex than many cases involving premises liability for negligent security. [The apartment complex] was a somewhat indefensible property because of the public streets running through the complex, its high vacancy rate, and the lengthy perimeter created by a 70-acre parcel of land. This permeability problem was greatly exacerbated by a high tenant turnover occasioned by the large number of undocumented immigrants attracted to and moving about the [urban] area. Undocumented immigrants are particularly susceptible to crime victimization for reasons beyond the control of any management company. Anonymity and high turnover rendered the primary security benefit of any community, neighbor looking after neighbor, simply inoperative at [the apartment complex]. Such conditions can be improved upon only over an extended time period and only with the full cooperation of local authorities. The sudden and unprovoked shooting of Mr. Ferrara by one of the robbers suggests the perpetrators were unlikely to be deterred other than perhaps by the immediate presence of armed security personnel. Since no standard of care requires this level of personal protection, there was no causal relationship between the reasonable deployment of security personnel and the injuries suffered by Mr. Ferrara.

The previous case suggests several implications for investigating the actions and motivations of an offender, the status of the target victim, and the absence or presence of capable guardians in explaining a criminal event. First, of central importance in a forensic criminological investigation is an evaluation as to whether or not, with reasonable security measures, a crime could be deterred or prevented. To address this issue, a forensic criminologist can examine whether a criminal act is one of "opportunity" or "victim-targeted," a central question that can aid a jury in evaluating the issue of causation. Criminologists have generally found the criminal who acts instrumentally (theft, burglary) to be more deterrable than one whose crimes tend to be expressive (assault, sexual victimization) (Turvey, 2014, p. 443).

Jacobs (2004) has offered several factors to consider in evaluating whether an offender is more or less risk sensitive and therefore deterrable by various security measures. Impulsive offenders tend to be less deterrable as are those who conceal their appearance and identity to render them anonymous. The presence of bystanders can deter some criminals, while crime sprees generally reflect risk insensitivity. Other considerations include presence of a prior record, intoxication, whether an offender is "dared" to do a crime, and whether there are perceived wrongs or injustices to be corrected. These factors, according to Jacobs (2004, p. 19), "can distort the perpetrators' calculation of risks and rewards and potentially dull sensitivity to sanction threats." In addition, if the assailant knew the victim, or if the assailant targeted a particular victim, the incident becomes less foreseeable and the relationship among inadequate security measures and the injury becomes more difficult to establish. If the crime is of a random nature, however, and is similar to prior incidents on the premises, the relationship becomes less challenging to establish. Thus, the determination of undeterrability becomes relevant when the offense is legally foreseeable. According to Jacobs (2004, p. 19), foreseeability and deterrability are conceptually separate and analytically distinct. Each must be assessed independently to evaluate the preventability of crime and the liability of the businesses at which a crime occurs.

Second, forensic criminologists can inquire into the status of the target victim and investigate relationships between the victim and offender, and the victim and the place of the crime. Much criminological research has examined the relationship between lifestyle-routine activities and victimization. According to the lifestyle exposure perspective, "individuals' lifestyles influence victimization due to the extent to which these lifestyles expose them to high-risk places and people during times when crime is most likely to occur, bringing them into contact with potential offenders" (McNeeley, 2015, p. 32). Criminological research suggests that demographic characteristics such as age, sex, race, marital status, income, education, and occupation affect lifestyles because these characteristics can affect role expectations—or behaviors that individuals are expected to engage in. Those individuals with demographic characteristics similar to potential offenders (e.g., males, minorities, and young people) are likely to be at greater risk of victimization due to exposure to criminogenic environments.

Finkelhor and Asdigian (1996) developed the concept of *target congruence*, or the extent to which targets' characteristics match up with offenders' needs, motives, or activities. Target congruence consists of three components: target antagonism (characteristics of the victim arouse the offender's anger or jealousy), target gratifiability (characteristics of the victim lead to victimization because they are qualities that the offender wants to obtain or use), and target vulnerability (characteristics of the victim that demonstrate an inability to resist or deter victimization). The importance of target suitability in determining victimization has received support in the literature (e.g., Fisher et al., 1998; Miethe and McDowall, 1993; Miethe and Meier, 1990; Peguero and Popp, 2012; Peguero et al., 2015; Sampson and Wooldredge, 1987; Wilcox et al., 2009; Rountree et al., 1994).

The final part of the analysis of causality is the examination of the role of the immediate environment in creating or intensifying criminal opportunities and activating criminal motivations in offenders. Drawing on research from social, behavioral, and cognitive psychology, Wortley (2001, 2008) proposes four ways that immediate environments can actively precipitate crime.

> First, immediate environments can present cues that prompt the individual to perform criminal acts. For example, exposure to weapons and other symbols of violence can increase access to aggression-related thoughts and feelings and thus prime the individual for violence. Second, immediate environments can exert social pressures to offend. Social influences include the tendency for individuals to conform to group norms, to obey authority figures, and to engage in herd behavior. Third, immediate environments can interfere with moral judgments and permit the performance of normally proscribed acts. Individuals may blame alcohol, rule ambiguity, depersonalizing social systems, or other environmental circumstances for their actions. Finally, immediate environments can create aversive emotional arousal that provokes a criminal response. Being thwarted, constrained, insulted, threatened, annoyed, overwhelmed, or discomforted may be accompanied by emotional responses such as irritability and frustration, and behavioral responses that include aggression (Sidebottom and Wortley, 2016, p. 173).

Recent research in environmental criminology has focused on situational precipitators to address the crime–environment nexus (Wortley, 2001). Situational crime prevention (SCP) addresses opportunity-reduction measures that "(1) are directed at highly specific forms of crime, (2) involve the management, design and manipulation of the immediate environment in as systematic and permanent a way as possible, (3) make crime more difficult and risky, or less rewarding and excusable as judged by a wide range of offenders" (Clarke, 1997, p. 4). Proponents of SCP propose three basic types of offender. The first is the antisocial predator, a criminally motivated individual who actively seeks out or creates crime opportunities. The second, the mundane offender, is an individual characterized by low self-control who opportunistically responds to easy criminal temptations. The third category is the provoked offender, an individual who reacts to situational stresses and frustrations to commit a crime she or he would not have otherwise committed. In 2003, Cornish and Clarke added a set of new situational crime prevention strategies under the heading of "reducing provocations" to address the crimes of the provoked offender (see Table 3.3). "Since perception of opportunity to commit specific types of crime is a function of environmental factors (e.g., risks and rewards) in the immediate setting of the criminal event," according to Welsh and colleagues (2018, p.152), "the theoretical development of SCP has largely been a development of conceptualizing this situational opportunity and how it can be effectively reduced" (Smith and Clarke, 2012).

In short, the courts, social scientists, and legal scholars debate whether or not a specific type of criminal act can be deterred by reasonable security measures. There are no hard and fast rules regarding causality and issues of foreseeability and deterrability must be addressed on a case-by-case analysis. In many instances, the property owner and/or manager may have failed to put in place policies and procedures that ensure that the premises are kept reasonably safe. Important questions to address include: Were the plaintiff's security policies, procedures, and actions reasonable under the circumstances? Did the perpetrator target the victim or the property? Did the perpetrator take precautions against being identified? Are there indications that the perpetrator could have been easily deterred from attacking the plaintiff? (Talley, 2000). Whether or not the plaintiff contributed to the injury may be considered by the jury during trial and balanced against actions taken by the defendant to deter criminal activity on the property.

SECURITY CHALLENGES AND STANDARDS OF CARE IN LOW-INCOME HOUSING

Over the decades, scholars and researchers have focused on the complex and complicated relationship between crime, security, and low-income housing developments. Research has shown a moderate-to-strong positive relationship between the location of subsidized housing in cities and crime hot spots (Galster et al., 2002; McNulty and Holloway, 2000; Roncek et al., 1981; Suresh and Vito, 2009). Popkin and colleagues (2000) and Venkatesh (2000) suggested that opportunities for involvement in gang violence and drug sales, among other kinds of offending, are more readily available to youth who reside in low-income housing developments than to those who live elsewhere. Low-income housing residents also experience increased levels of criminal victimization relative to people that do not live in low-income housing developments (DeFrances and Smith, 1998; DeKeseredy et al., 2003; Griffiths and Tita, 2009; Holzman et al., 2001; Kling et al., 2005). In a comprehensive review of scholarship on low-income housing and crime, Lens (2013) finds that "subsidized households have too frequently lived in violent housing developments and neighborhoods …[T]he spillover effects on crime in surrounding neighborhoods are typically very small … [and] [a]lthough the precise mechanisms through which subsidized housing may affect crime are less clear, it is most likely that concentrated disadvantage plays the biggest role when effects are observed, rather than the physical attributes of subsidized housing."

Crime in low-income housing developments can be a problem for landlords, property management companies, and residents (Mazerolle et al., 2000; Roncek et al., 1981; Popkin et al., 2000). At issue for the forensic criminologist is the nature of this crime and whether it is preventable by conventional crime prevention measures. Much of the violence in subsidized housing is committed by the residents themselves, so controlling the perimeter of a property might have little to no effect on violent crime incidents or rates (Brantingham and Brantingham, 1993). Also, sexual assault and violence against women in low-income housing are generally committed by intimate partners, a problem that rental housing management cannot readily address using conventional physical security measures (Menard, 2001; Raphael, 2001).

In addition, to assess prevention possibilities, one must consider the specific crime in question and address whether a criminal act was a random act or whether it was targeted. Targeted violence is not necessarily a foreseeable outcome of the condition of a property but, rather, could be a product of pre-existing animosities. There is also the question of the deterrability of targeted violence. Environmental crime deterrents such as physical security measures are not likely to be effective in the case of a highly motivated planned murder or in the case of an impulsive, emotionally motivated murder. Planned murders are often predatory, methodical, and instrumental in nature. Expressive homicides are often impulsive. The former homicide often involves conscious planning and while the latter homicide tends to be spontaneous. In both cases, the actions of the highly motivated offender may be effective in neutralizing the possible deterrent effect of existing security measures (Levi et al., 2010; Salfati and Canter, 1999; Chambliss, 1967).

In the following three examples, we draw on expert witness reports to show how a forensic criminologist may address the issue of standards of care in low-income housing developments.

CASE EXAMPLE: MANAGEMENT DEFICIENCIES AND SECURITY ROLE CONFLICT

This case involves the shooting of a female ice cream truck driver in a low-income housing development. The driver was shot and rendered quadriplegic by the offender during his attempt to rob her. The offender's mother was a lessee but the shooter was not a resident of the apartment complex. The following materials were reviewed: the police report of this crime, calls for police service to the apartment complex, crime scene photos, the civil complaint, amended complaint and answers, the offender's file, tenant notes to management, police department incident reports, production of documents materials, answers to interrogatories, and depositions of plaintiffs and defendants. Also reviewed were demographic trends as well as current professional literature on crime problems attendant to subsidized housing properties. Finally, the forensic criminologist visits the apartment complex and conducts an assessment of the apartment security measures, policies, and procedures. We quote at length to demonstrate the importance of providing a thorough and detailed forensic criminological investigation and report to assist a fact finder in determining the facts of a case.

As will be demonstrated below, the occurrence of a violent crime at [the apartment complex] was readily foreseeable to property management. Management of [the apartment complex] fell beneath the standard of care for a subsidized housing complex in several respects. Finally, had [the apartment complex] management met the standard of care, it is more likely than not that [victim] would not have been shot and rendered quadriplegic.

Police officials, professional property managers, and housing professionals have long known that subsidized rental properties can become havens for crime if not properly managed [citations to French, 1997; Clarke and Bichler-Robertson, 1998]. Social problems tend to come in bundles in that economic problems are often accompanied by sporadic income histories, residential mobility, health issues, and family behavioral problems. Sadly, crime problems have long plagued low-income housing and other forms of subsidized housing such as Title 42 Low Income Housing Tax Credit and Section 8 programs [citations to Bryson and Youmans, 1990; Popkin et al., 2000; Suresh and Vito, 2009; Roncek et al., 1981].

An examination of the history of crime at [the apartment complex] reveals a property with a significant history of violence. For example, from 2001 through 2004, three people were shot, six people were robbed, over six home invasions occurred, and several instances of shots being fired were reported. Police responded to numerous instances of domestic violence, at least forty-four burglaries, and three drug detentions. These criminal incidents reflect only a sampling of the total calls for police service and do not include any incidents known to property management or its agents.

As a criminologist, I am also interested in what police officers familiar with a property have to say about it. Metro Officer Harry James [a pseudonym], one of the first police officers on the scene, believes [the apartment complex] was crime infested and had a real problem with drug trafficking and with gangs [citation to Harry James deposition]. Detective Mike Johansen [a pseudonym] described [the apartment complex] as having a crime problem, a drug problem, and a gang problem [citation to Mike Johansen deposition]. Wherever drugs are sold and used, there is a greatly increased likelihood of criminal violence. Violence among dealers and customers accounts for "systemic" violence. Violence by users who are high on drugs is described as "psychopharmacological" violence. "Economic" violence is caused by users robbing to get money to buy drugs [citation to Goldstein, 1985; Chaiken and Chaiken, 1990].

Given the high level of crime foreseeability at [the apartment complex], it is my opinion that apartment management should have attended very closely to known property crime prevention policies and procedures [citations to Sampson, 2001; Campbell, 2000; Wiesel, 1990; Webster and Connors, 1992]. More specifically, potential tenants must be thoroughly screened before being allowed to take up residence. Once tenants have moved into a property, notice must be taken of possible antisocial behavior exhibited by any members of the household or any guests of the household. Management must follow up with evictions should any residents violate property rules or lease provisions. Of course, appropriate physical security practices (lighting, access control, mechanical and organized surveillance, etc.) should also be followed [citations to Reid, 2005; Fennelly and Lombardi, 1997].

My review of [the offender's mother tenant file] indicates that her prior landlord was never contacted and that various inconsistencies between her credit report and her tenant application were never resolved. I also understand that [the offender] assaulted his sister and others on three occasions and police were called to the property on these various occasions. Given management's knowledge of [the offender's] history of incarceration, these instances of violent behavior should have resulted in [the offender] being barred from the property or his mother being evicted under the "One Strike" policy. Note also that [the offender] was arrested for robbery while living at [the apartment complex] and yet was allowed to return to live at his mother's apartment without being listed on the lease even though he was over twenty years old at the time. This happened within days of [the victim's] victimization. Several months after the shooting, [the offender] was still "hanging around" the property and, in fact, was arrested there for the shooting of [the victim]!

Management of a subsidized housing development must be attuned to the possible presence of troublemaking younger family members and other visitors who tend to be responsible for much of the disorder in the housing community. It is generally not the leaseholder but some of her children or her male friends who cause the problems [citation to Popkin et al., 1999].

Active, involved, and somewhat "nosy" property managers, with the assistance of observant security officers, can generally determine who lives and who does not live on a property, and who behaves appropriately while visiting.

In my opinion, CSS [Community Support Services] could not serve as recreation leaders while at the same time be known as the "eyes and ears" of management. Criminologists would refer to this as a role conflict. Furthermore, I understand that Mr. McLeod's [a pseudonym] criminal history should have precluded his employment in such a capacity anyway. As it turns out, on-site property manager Mrs. Robertson [a pseudonym] also may have been unable to do her job effectively as she did not want to draw too much attention to herself by evicting troublesome residents. To do so may have called attention to her own embezzlement activities. Given the criminal history of this property, an effective, closely supervised, and well-trained security patrol should have been in place as opposed to reliance upon a "recreation leader." While Mr. McLeod testified that he passed on security information to Mrs. Robertson, I do not see where such information led to any evictions or to a reduction in the level of crime at the property. In fact, it seems crime at [the apartment complex] had been on the rise within the year or two before the shooting.

The previous excerpts reveal several security deficiencies at the low-income housing development. First, the previous reference to "role conflict" draws attention to the conflict inherent in having McLeod act as friend and coach to the young people while at the same time serving as the apartment management's main security official. Second, while it appears that a tenant background screening company provided information to management of the apartment complex, management did not analyze or act on adverse tenant information in the case of the tenant mother of the offender. In this apartment complex, tenants were required to sign a crime-free lease addendum but the shooter was not on the lease and yet was allowed to live on the property even though the police had been called at least three times concerning violence in which he was involved. The apartment complex was a busy place for local police and local police department crime records illuminate the serious crime problems at the low-income housing development. From 2003 to 2005, there were 12 shooting reports at the property. And there were 2553 Calls for Service for the years 2000–2004. Depositions of police officers and detectives describe the apartment complex as crime infested with drugs and gangs.

In conclusion, the evidence presented in this case suggests that the commission of a violent crime against the ice cream truck driver at the apartment complex was reasonably foreseeable. Property management did not take sufficient precautions to screen out violent residents, nor did it sufficiently monitor the property to evict or prevent from loitering those individuals likely to cause harm to others. Had the mother of the offender not been allowed to move into the apartment complex, or had her son been effectively barred from the property, it is likely that the victim would not have been harmed. In short, the evidence suggests that the above management failures of the property managers and owners were a substantial factor in the injuries sustained by the victim.

CASE EXAMPLE: SECURITY FORCE REDUCTION AND PARKING LOT CONTROL

This case involves the shooting death of a 19-year-old man in his car in a parking lot of a low-income housing development. This housing development is a Section 8, multifamily, low-income housing building with over 200 rental units and owned by Associate Court Tempest (ACT) (a pseudonym). At issue is whether the property owners/managers and the security company—Metropolitan Security Services (MSS) (a pseudonym)—were negligent in providing security services at the location. The plaintiffs in the case brought a survival action and asserted claims for negligence, nuisance, intentional infliction of emotional distress, and wrongful death. Plaintiffs sought compensatory and punitive damages. By the early 1990s, the apartment complex had become a building plagued by "problems of loitering and drug sales and all of the ramifications associated with that kind of activity" according to the property manager in a questionnaire filed with the regional Department of Housing and Urban Development (HUD) Field Office.

There were three major points of contention in the case. The first was whether the parking lot where the defendant was shot was part of the premises of the apartment complex and therefore an area of the security patrol assignment of MSS. Several months before the shooting, the building owner and manager had hired a security firm to provide a patrolling officer to safeguard users of the parking lot. As such, the parking lot was part of the common area for which the defendants had assumed responsibility to safeguard from foreseeable criminal acts by others. According to the premises liability law of the jurisdiction:

The landlord of a multi-unit apartment building owes to tenants and others foreseeably on the premises a duty of ordinary and reasonable care to provide protection against foreseeable criminal acts of third parties. A landlord's obligation to tenants is to exercise prudent care, not only in his own pursuits, but also to identify and safeguard against whatever hazardous acts of others are likely to occur upon the premises. A landlord has a duty to make himself aware of the condition of the premises, including the activities of the tenants, which would affect the safety and well-being of other tenants. A landlord who rents different parts of his property to various tenants has a duty to maintain the common areas of the property, such as the parking lot, in a reasonably safe condition for use by tenants and other persons lawfully on the premises. Persons lawfully on the premises include not only the tenants, but also any person who is on the premises at the request or invitation of a tenant.

In determining a landlord's duty to protect tenants against criminal activity, a landlord must "use reasonable care to keep safe those common areas of the building retained under his control."

A landlord cannot escape the consequences of his own negligence merely because another person, with whom he has no connection or over whom he has no control, may have contributed to the injury by his wrongful act. It is no defense to a landlord to assert that he had not foreseen the precise injury, nor should he have notice of the particular method in which a harm would occur, if the possibility of harm was clear to the ordinarily prudent eye.

The second issue of contention was the consequences of a reduction in the security budget of the apartment complex, a major budgetary consideration in determining negligence. Evidence presented in this case showed that between 1999 and 2003, the property owner of Associate Court Tempest (ACT) reduced its spending on security services from $209,000 to $160,000. In the following excerpt, the forensic criminological investigation illustrates that the reduction in the security budget for the apartment complex occurred in a context of high crime foreseeability.

In December 2002, the owner and manager of the building, over the objection of [MSS], reduced the security force by halting patrols in and around the building after 2:00 a.m. Thus, there was no armed special police officer on patrol in the parking lot at the time of this incident. Records from the [Crime Analysis Unit of the local police department] reflect that within 1000 feet of this incident, approximately 1,600 crimes had occurred in the period from January 1, 1997 to December 31, 2003. Among other offenses, 12 homicides had been recorded during that period.

Blake and Bradley (1999, p. 46) suggest that budget reductions in security may indicate that management is deliberately or inadvertently sacrificing security measures in favor of redirecting resources to other areas, or they are interested primarily in maintaining or increasing revenues. A disproportionate decrease in security expenditures may suggest that management does not feel that the loss-preventive security capabilities are important to the organization or facility. In times of fiscal retrenchment and austerity, the security budget can be an easy financial target since the security department typically is not a direct revenue generator for an organization or facility.

The third issue in this case is whether the security measures employed at the apartment complex were reasonable in application and sufficiently adequate to provide a requisite degree of protection based on the foreseeability of a criminal event occurring. In a negligent security case, the failure of the organization to implement reasonable security measures as well as properly use existing security measures can expose the organization to claims of negligence. The security challenge for any organization is to properly identify the appropriate security measures and consistently apply and manage them. As the forensic criminological investigation concludes:

> Based on the prior history of crime and testimony concerning drug traffic on the premises of [the apartment complex], it is my opinion that a crime of violence was foreseeable on the evening of March 16, 2003. Given the foreseeability of such a crime, appropriate security measures should have been in place. Specifically, tenants should be properly screened by checking with prior landlords and verifying employment. Persons not on the lease should not be allowed to reside in the apartments. Furthermore, tenants violating community rules should be evicted. I have not been provided with any evidence that suggests these preventive measures were in place.
>
> Additionally, reasonable efforts should be expended to control trespasser access both to the parking lot and to the apartment building proper. I understand that the external CCTV camera was not working, that no patrol was in place to discourage loitering at the time of the shooting and that the shooter freely accessed the apartment building in order to purchase drugs on the second floor of [the apartment complex]. The one guard on duty was on the other side of the building and was unable to effectively surveil this activity. This guard was not expected to patrol the property but to maintain his post at the front door in order to register visitors. It is unclear at this time whether he effectively performed even these duties in that there are no entries on the visitor log for that evening.
>
> In my opinion, portions of [the apartment complex] constituted an open drug market which constitutes a nuisance and threat to people in the general area. Drug trafficking is predictably associated with violence to innocent people and played a causal role in [the victim's] death.

In sum, any effective premises security program depends on close coordination and communication between building owner, management, security personnel, and residents. The previous case suggests poor or nonexistent communication among these different groups, a situation that appears to have contributed to poor record keeping and weak implementation of existing security measures. In 2000, the defendants applied for a HUD Multifamily Housing Drug Elimination Grant. According to the plaintiffs, the application was denied because one of the applicants lacked the police record evidence and crime statistics necessary to satisfy the agency's "objective crime data" requirements. Decisions to reduce the security budget may have contributed to lax crime data collection and analysis.

Security budgets are a major security concern since budget shortages can result in security personnel cutbacks, heightened risk of security breaches, and deficient security data collection and analysis. Reductions in the security budget of an organization can cause administrative inefficiencies and dysfunction. As part of any forensic criminological investigation, it is important to establish whether there is evidence that the landlord or property management company reduced the security budget over time. If so, a forensic criminologist would investigate whether any security budget reductions contributed to security deficiencies or failures to maintain residential premises in compliance with building, housing, and health codes. The next step in the investigation would be to evaluate whether any security deficiencies proximately caused the criminal act to occur.

CASE EXAMPLE: TENANT SCREENING AND THE PRINCIPLES OF CRIME PROTECTION THROUGH ENVIRONMENTAL DESIGN (CPTED)

This case concerns the shooting of a young man who was socializing with friends outside an apartment building when he was called away from them by an individual who, it is presumed, subsequently shot him in the back of the head. After analyzing the foreseeability of crime at the property, the forensic criminologist evaluates whether the property met or violated the security standard of care for the level of foreseeability. The forensic criminological investigation addresses several security standards of care applicable to the apartment complex that were in place.

Tenant screening is probably one of the most important aspects of apartment security management. Based on my discussions with [the management company], I learned that potential tenants are screened for criminal histories. Where possible, their prior living quarters are inspected and their financial reliability with regard to honoring rent payment schedules is also checked. They are expected to sign a comprehensive lease which contains recommended security-related behavioral requirements. This lease contains the essence of a "crime free addendum" which is recommended by a leading crime prevention group dealing with apartment security known as the "International Crime Free Association." There is active lease enforcement and management will definitely evict for reasons other than nonpayment of rent.

Management maintains active and ongoing communication with metro police and provides apartments for its use. Police meet with management on a monthly basis. Management also realizes how important it is to be aware of behavior on its premises and thus maintains a rapport with several long-term residents in order to keep itself apprised of any developing problems. Likewise, at least six management company employees live on the property and serve as additional "eyes and ears" of management in order to further provide for the security of residents.

[The management company] also realizes the importance of image to the security of a residential property and operates an active maintenance schedule on the property. Fencing is extensive throughout the property and serves to guide the flow of inevitable foot traffic and to enhance a sense of territoriality, thus giving many residents a personal stake in maintenance and protection of the property [citation to Cozens et al., 2005].

Of paramount importance to security planning at [the apartment complex] is the concept of "supportive housing." Supportive housing was chosen as an alternative to guard patrols as a means of addressing certain adolescent and other resident problems on the property. Supportive housing provides special services for the elderly, substance abuse education for youngsters, academic and education assistance, youth programming, ministerial outreach, high-risk youth counseling, HIV education, and a variety of other services for special needs populations. Supportive housing programs will vary in focus from property to property, but the aim is to deal with many of the social problems suffered by low-income housing residents [citation to Galster et al., 2002].

These and other programs too numerous to list here are either funded by or otherwise supported by [the apartment complex]. These programs seek to provide elders with support and young persons with constructive activities and role models who are more appropriate than street criminals. [Management company] even supported the election of its employee …, Community Relations Coordinator, to the office of Advisory Neighborhood Commission so that he could bring additional social services resources to this residential community. Few private properties engage so actively in the provision of so many "wrap around" services to their community residents.

There remains, of course, the question of target hardening. [The apartment complex] residents enjoy the security benefits of locked vestibules in each building, metal-covered apartment doors, deadbolt locks on unit entry doors, peepholes, and secondary locking systems and/or gating on patio doors at ground level. Such target hardening devices are to be expected at any well-run property, and they are in place at [the apartment complex].

The previous findings provide insight into how residential rental property ownership and management characteristics can affect crime. Tenant screening, lease enforcement, image awareness, territoriality, security awareness, and specific target hardening measures are important to security efforts as recommended by proponents of Crime Prevention Through Environmental Design (CPTED) (see Fig. 4.1) (for an overview, see Cozens and Love, 2015). Target hardening can increase the effort and risk of offending as well as reduce the rewards associated with the commission of a crime. As a long-established and traditional crime prevention technique, target hardening focuses on denying or limiting access to a crime target through the use of physical barriers such as fences, gates, security doors, and locks.

The notion of supportive housing described above interconnects with the second-generation CPTED concepts of social cohesion, community connectivity, and community culture. Supportive housing programs that provide support services to special needs populations in conjunction with housing assistance can help to create and reinforce an environment of positive relationships between people of different backgrounds. In theory, a more empowered, well-connected, and integrated community will have a stronger sense of place. This connectivity can help to encourage and maintain community self-policing to potentially discourage crime and deviant behavior.

Just because an apartment complex uses CPTED "target hardening" techniques does not mean that crime will be eliminated. An overreliance on target hardening can produce a "fortress mentality," where citizens and communities withdraw behind walls, fences, and overfortified homes. Resident anonymity and isolation can work against CPTED concepts directed at supporting social interaction and community engagement. Cozens (2014) maintains that treating CPTED as a simplistic design outcome has resulted in the development of a range of assumptions about CPTED that may not always be correct. These include the belief that "eyes on the street" (Jacobs, 1961) always reduce crime; the assumption that permeable streets always reduce crime; the assumption that high densities of people always reduce crime; the assumption that mixed-use developments always reduce crime; the assumption that CCTV always reduces crime; and the assumption that improved street lighting always deters crime (Cozens and Love, 2015, p. 12).

The previous points corroborate research by Santiago and colleagues (2001), Dillman and colleagues (2017), and Albright and colleagues (2013) who find that low-income housing projects can be safe and secure with effective place management. Strict tenant selection and monitoring processes and procedures, on-site staff, and engagement with local police are the requisites for promoting safety and security. Albright and colleagues (2013) suggest that active information sharing and place monitoring by residents are informal mechanisms of social control that can promote safety on-site and in the community. Property management's conscientious maintenance of the buildings and grounds, tenant screening and monitoring efforts, responsiveness to community concerns, and ongoing communication with nearby residents and property owners can be effective crime-deterrent activities. The takeaway here is that with proper and effective property management, low-income housing developments can be safe and secure places to live (Dillman et al., 2017).

CONCLUSIONS

Over the decades, the field of apartment security litigation has been undergoing a profound transformation as a result of socioeconomic and demographic changes, evolutions in tenant screening, alterations in landlord–tenant laws, decline of the mom-and-pop landlord, professionalization of apartment management, and proliferation of private security companies and security guards (Thacher, 2008). Crime victims, perhaps once hesitant to go public with information about their victimization, are now eager to seek redress and justice through litigation. In addition, attorneys fervently pursue negligent security cases because of the potential for large recoveries. As applications of security law have become more complex, the types of apartment security cases have become more diverse and sophisticated. Owners of apartments are not alone in being targeted as defendants in negligent security actions. Claims against property managers, security companies, alarm system companies, and maintenance personnel have proliferated over the decades.

One emerging area of security litigation is the "ban-the-box" movement which seeks to remove the "box" that refers to the question on job applications that asks applicants whether or not they have ever been convicted of a crime. Ban-the-box laws require employers and landlords to remove this question—as well as any other queries about criminal history—from job applications. Ostensibly, ban-the-box laws seek to prevent employment discrimination and housing discrimination against individuals with criminal records. Since 2012, the Equal Employment Opportunity Commission (EEOC) has strongly urged employers to make decisions based on the qualifications of individual applicants rather than immediately disregarding applicants with a criminal history. In recent years, the Department of Housing and Urban Development (HUD) has declared that landlords may be in violation of the Fair Housing Act if they institute blanket bans on tenants with prior arrests or criminal convictions. This shifting legal landscape is creating new security challenges for employers and landlords. On the one hand, failure to comply with EEOC and HUD guidelines can lead to a lawsuit filed by the federal government. On the other hand, failure to properly screen out potentially dangerous applicants can lead to a negligent security lawsuit or a workplace violence incident if that person commits a violent crime.

The forensic criminological theories and methods we have described in apartment security litigation can be applied by researchers and forensic experts to other kinds of properties. Questions of crime foreseeability, standards of care, and causation are central elements of a tort that can apply to different circumstances and facilities including entertainment venues, tourist attractions, grocery stores, schools, among other commercial areas. Prior crime history, access control, guarding, surveillance cameras, and screening of employees can be critical issues in negligent security cases involving hotels/motels, parking lots, garages, malls, convenience stores, fast food restaurants, and apartments. Armed with knowledge of criminological theories, a forensic criminologist can use variants of environmental criminology to examine crime, criminality, and victimization as they relate to particular places and to the ways in which individuals and organizations shape their activities spatially. Armed with knowledge of criminological methods and analytical techniques, a forensic criminologist can draw on reliable crime data, prior incidents or complaints, industry standards, and company security policies and procedures to evaluate breach of duty and violation of standards of care.

Policy makers, law enforcement officials, decision makers, and the courts are increasingly looking to criminological research methods and theories to understand the etiology of crime events, patterns of crime, and the opportunity factors related to crime. As we have detailed in the previous two chapters, forensic criminology has a variety of analytical, methodological, and theoretical resources that a trained researcher can use to investigate a negligent security case pertaining to apartments as well as other establishments including hotels, restaurants, shopping malls, bars and taverns, concert venues, casinos, convenience stores, and education institutions. In most cases involving apartment security, an expert witness is needed to explain to the fact finder the issue of negligence and delineate the connections among duty, breach of duty, and causation.

Like forensic criminologists, security experts may also focus on issues involving crime foreseeability, violations of standards of care, and causation. Yet a forensic criminologist offers a unique perspective in which she or he "imagines a world where a single act or event is embedded in a complex array of spatial, temporal, historical and interpersonal contingencies and conditions," according to Voigt and Thornton (1996, p. 189). When it comes to understanding the intersection of context and criminal event, the picture that emerges is dualistic: on the one hand, offenders can show reason, rationality, and an ability to calculate; on the other hand, that calculation is bounded by factors such as environmental cues, perceptions of the capability of guardians to deter deviant acts, time pressure, and emotions. By examining the subjective basis of risk/reward perceptions, opportunity construction, and related constructs that frame criminal choice and offender decision-making, a forensic criminologist can assist the fact finder on seemingly unrelated patterns and occurrences connected to the determination of the facts of a case.

CRIME AND BUSINESS I: NEGLIGENT SECURITY LITIGATION CONCERNING PARKING FACILITIES AND HOTELS/MOTELS

6

INTRODUCTION

This chapter and the next chapter analyze expert witness reports related to negligent security cases involving criminal incidents that occur on commercial land uses. We focus specifically on parking facilities and casinos/hotels in this chapter, and shopping centers and bars/taverns in the next chapter. We have two goals. First, we demonstrate the utility of environmental criminology in directing a forensic criminologist's attention to the role of place and situational opportunities in the etiology of criminal events. In this theoretical perspective, criminologists recognize that the production of crime is influenced by the intersection of criminal motivation and situational context, for example, where the crime occurs. Criminal motivation or propensity to commit crime is neither static nor exists in *a priori* fashion. Rather, to quote Weisburd and colleagues (2016, p. 70), "the (criminogenic) setting within which individuals make their decisions is just as important for criminal involvement as their propensity for crime." Thus, if commercial facilities and places offer more opportunities for criminal activities, *ceteris paribus*, individuals are then more likely to commit crime in these areas. Connecting the crime-committing propensities of offenders to sociophysical settings expands the scope and explanatory power of criminological theories.

Our second goal is to demonstrate how a forensic criminologist develops expert opinions regarding foreseeability in the context of a special relationship (as an element of duty), standards of care (as they may pertain to breach of duty), and causation (cause-in-fact and proximate cause). Foreseeability is the key element establishing a business owner's duty to maintain the security of the premises. A court cannot impute a crime's foreseeability to a defendant business owner without determining whether the evidence establishes foreseeability under the jurisdiction's controlling test (e.g., imminent harm, prior similar acts, totality of circumstances, and balancing test). Lack of evidence sufficient to establish foreseeability, violation of a standard of care, or causation can be fatal to a negligence claim. When the plaintiff claims that the defendant failed to protect the plaintiff from harm, a forensic criminologist can articulate and reference a standard of care or other measure of reasonableness by which the fact finder can measure the defendant's actions.[1] Moreover, a forensic criminologist cannot merely rely upon a general duty of care to establish an objective standard requiring specific conduct. Nor may

---

[1] See *Beckwith v. Interstate Management Company.* 82 F.Supp.3d 255 (2015). District of Columbia. Civil Action No.: 14-00214 (RC); *Varner v. District of Columbia,* 891 A.2d 260, 269 (D.C.2006).

the plaintiff rely on a forensic criminologist's own *ipse dixit*, conclusory opinion, without any evidence showing that the proffered standard has been promulgated or is generally known.[2] Whether the injuries sustained at a commercial premises were causally related to the condition of the property must also be determined, ultimately by a jury, of course, but often informed by research and investigation done by a forensic criminologist. Even if a civil suit is settled and never goes to trial, a forensic criminologist can often help to shape much of the settlement terms and discourse between plaintiff and defense attorneys.

We first discuss the extant theoretical criminological research on risky facilities, a concept that criminologists can use to describe the uneven distribution of criminal events across commercial facilities of the same type. We then examine the linkages among commercial activities and crime. Next, we introduce the 80/20 rule which postulates that, in theory, only a small proportion (e.g., approximately 20%) of any commercial facility type will be responsible for a majority (approximately 80%) of crime experienced or produced by this group of commercial facilities. We then examine expert witness reports pertaining to parking facilities and hotels and motels. It would be impossible to cover all the major areas of sociolegal and criminological concerns in the field of negligent security involving commercial properties in this chapter and the following chapter. Thus, we want to stress to the reader that our coverage of the field only addresses a few areas of inquiry. Our analysis of commercial land use leaves out many areas of litigation such as gas stations, cruise ships, music festivals, special events, police actions, security guard actions, and of course, the many areas of criminal forensic criminology. Still lessons learned and general principles discerned in one security context can often be transferred to other settings.

MASS PRIVATE PROPERTY, RISKY FACILITIES, AND THE 80/20 RULE

Over the last century, the United States has witnessed a proliferation of commercial land uses (properties) and businesses specializing in producing and delivering a variety of products and services for people. During the 19th century, private property was mostly owned and controlled by individuals, small merchants, and state and local governments. Over the decades, population growth, urbanization, expansion of governments, new forms of real estate financing, and the development of large corporations have spurred the growth and differentiation of private properties on a mass scale (Shearing and Stenning, 1983). A major implication is that the modern development of mass private property and attendant spread and propagation of commercial activities means that more and more public life now takes place on property that is privately owned and operated.

Over the decades, the growth of mass private property and the diversification of commercial activities and land uses have created new opportunities for third-party lawsuits against business owners (Kennedy, 2013, p. 237; Savard and Kennedy, 2014, p. 266). From a routine activities perspective, the proliferation of hotels and motels, convenience stores, bars and taverns, shopping centers, and many other commercial properties have fostered the development of spaces that offer high potential for convergence between motivated offenders and suitable targets. In their pioneering work on the

---

[2]*Clement v. Peoples Drug Store, Inc.*, 634 A.2d 425 (D.C. Cir. 1993); *Varner v. District of Columbia*, 891 A. 2d 260 - DC: Court of Appeals 2006—when "the defendant is alleged to have failed to protect the plaintiff from harm, the expert must 'clearly articulate and reference a standard of care by which the defendant's actions can be measured'" (*Casey v. Ward*, 211 F. Supp. 3d 107 - Dist. Court, Dist. of Columbia 2016).

crime-generating nature of commercial land uses, Roncek and colleagues analyzed the proximal effects of bars/liquor establishments in generating criminal opportunity in the Cleveland and San Diego areas. They found that adjacency to these establishments was connected to higher levels of crime, including murder, assault, and robbery. For Roncek and colleagues, opportunity is the key explanatory mechanism that connects commercial activity with criminal events. Patrons that frequent bars and taverns create high traffic in the immediate environment, including a high density of adolescent or young adults (sometimes under the influence of alcohol). The high traffic and density offer a lucrative opportunity for motivated offenders to victimize targets for criminal gain (Roncek et al., 1981; Roncek and Fagianni, 1985; Roncek and LoBosco, 1983; Roncek and Maier, 1991).

Several elements of routine activities theory can help explain the linkages among commercial areas and crime. First, patrons of businesses such as casinos, bars and taverns, convenience stores, and so on, are likely to have cash with them and thus be easy targets for victimization. According to Roncek and Maier (1991, p. 726): "[b]eing inside the tavern may make individuals inaccessible to predators outside, but items of value (including the bodies of individuals) can become available, visible, and accessible as individuals are going to or from such businesses and their inertia in terms of resisting crime or escaping may have been lowered."

Second, many commercial facilities including shopping malls, bars and taverns, and convenience stores typically have many desirable and highly valued goods that people can directly sell or consume. As businesses that are open to and dependent on the public, casinos and taverns themselves are accessible (although dress codes and entrance fees can restrict the clientele), and they typically have signs on them to attract customers. The spatial concentration of consumers can also attract potential offenders in their searches for vulnerable victims or targets. Quoting Roncek and Maier (1991, p. 726), "patrons and the businesses have all the components of target suitability (Cohen and Felson, 1979, p. 591), namely, value, visibility, low inertia, and accessibility."

Third, commercial businesses face the challenge of providing capable guardianship to deter criminal threats. Capable guardianship operates to communicate to consumers that the business establishment is a safe and secure place to do business and consume goods and services. Capable guardianship also provides surveillant deterrence functions that operate as disincentives for offenders to engage in deviant acts that could threaten business profitability. Opportunities for crime can proliferate when motivated offenders come into contact with suitable targets in the absence of capable guardians.

Much criminological work over the decades supports the notion that a variety of commercial land uses are related to crime at micro-spatial units of analysis (Kurtz et al., 1998; White and Muldoon, 2015). Sherman and colleagues' (1989) seminal study of calls for service in Minneapolis noted that commercial spaces can be susceptible to becoming hot spots. Their analysis of all calls over a 1-year period showed that most places in the city experienced no crime while a few locations were responsible for a disproportionately high number of calls about crime. In fact, 50% of all calls for service in Minneapolis were associated with just 3% of the city's places. Commercial places such as department stores, bars, and convenience stores were among the places with the highest numbers of calls. Deryol and colleagues' (2016) research using data from Cincinnati suggests that crime-generating nodes and/or paths (carry-out liquor stores, on-premises drinking establishments, and bus routes) are negatively related to place-level crime counts, especially in neighborhoods with high levels of commercial density. Bernasco and Block's (2011) study of the spatial pattern of street robberies in Chicago finds that small bars, fast food restaurants, liquor stores, and laundromats have a positive relationship with the number of robberies. Drawing on a dataset from Chicago over the period from 2008 to 2013,

Twinam (2017, p. 104) finds that "commercial uses lead to more street crime in their immediate vicinity, particularly in more walkable neighborhoods." However, this effect is offset by population density and dense mixed-use areas tend to be safer than residential areas. Additionally, some liquor stores and late-hour bars drive much of the commercial effect.

Criminologists have long known that the relationship among criminal events and commercial land uses is multifaceted and nuanced. Blair and colleagues (2017, p. 61) argue that "facility type may not matter and that specific characteristics and contexts associated with crime opportunity at places should be measured as opposed to assuming that broad categories of land uses typically generate crime." As Clarke and Eck (2007) and Eck and colleagues (2007) point out, in any large city just a handful of commercial businesses including bars, schools, convenience stores, and parking facilities give the police far more trouble than all the rest put together.

This phenomenon—called "risky facilities"—has several important implications for investigating negligent security claims. One implication is that criminal events are highly concentrated among particular people, places, and activities. A second implication is that most facilities of any type are not at high risk for criminal events. A third implication is that "only a small proportion of any specific type of facility will account for the majority of crime and disorder problems experienced or produced by the group of facilities as a whole" (Clarke and Eck, 2007, p. 4). This pattern is so common that Wilcox and Eck (2011) term it the "iron law of troublesome places," and Weisburd and colleagues (2016) refer to it as the "law of crime concentration at places." Clarke and Eck (2007, pp. 4–5) and Eck and colleagues (2007, p. 228) elaborate on what is known as the 80/20 rule in describing the theory of risky facilities:

> As a rule of thumb, about 20 percent of the total group will account for 80 percent of the problems. This is known as the 80/20 rule: in theory, 20 percent of any particular group of things is responsible for 80 percent of outcomes involving those things. The 80/20 rule is not peculiar to crime and disorder; rather, it is almost a universal law. For example, a small portion of the earth's surface holds the majority of life on the planet; a small proportion of earthquakes cause most earthquake damage; a small number of people hold most of the earth's wealth; a small proportion of police officers produce the most arrests; and so forth. In practice, of course, the proportion is seldom exactly 80/20; however, it is always true that some small percentage of a group produces a large percentage of any particular result involving that group.

A forensic criminologist can begin with the 80/20 rule as a general and useful initial assumption when investigating crime foreseeability in a negligent security case. That is, criminal events are created by a few individuals at a few places. Clark and Eck (2007, p. 5) maintain that "[a]lthough this first approximation is not always correct, it is probably correct more often than assuming that the problem is spread evenly across individuals, places, or events. Careful analysis can then test whether this starting assumption is correct." That is, crime is neither random nor evenly distributed across different land uses. Rather, the concept of risky facilities suggests that criminal events are highly concentrated in space and time and crime risk is concentrated among certain commercial facilities. A forensic criminologist can draw on the theoretical resources of risky facilities to compare the socio-spatial characteristics of high crime facilities to those of low crime facilities that are suggestive of high or low crime foreseeability (Eck et al. 2007; Eck and Eck, 2012). In addition, she or he can use comparisons of risky and nonrisky facilities to point to the role played by place management (e.g., landlords, landowners, security officials, and so on) in preventing criminal events or creating and exacerbating criminogenic conditions (e.g., Clarke and Bichler-Robertson, 1998; Hannah et al., 2007; Madensen and Eck, 2008; Mazerolle et al., 1998).

PARKING FACILITIES

Parking facilities are locations of real estate that play a vital role in supporting the economy of U.S. cities and metropolitan areas. Parking facilities come in all shapes and sizes, from vast tracts of black-top, to multilevel garages (both above and below ground), to simple dirt facilities. Many people take it for granted that parking facilities are supposed to be safe and secure places for motorists to leave their cars while they go about their busy lives. Yet some parking facilities can become criminogenic places. The U.S. Department of Justice, Bureau of Justice Statistics analyzed violent crimes occurring between 2004 and 2008 and concluded that during the 4-year period, there were more than 400,000 violent assaults committed nationwide in parking facilities. According to the latest National Crime Victimization Survey (NCVS) conducted by the U.S. Bureau of Justice Statistics, more than 1 in 10 property crimes—including motor vehicle theft and property theft—occur in parking facilities or garages. Survey findings from the NCVS suggest that 7.3% of all violent crimes are reported to occur in these facilities. Of those crimes, 16% were violent victimizations, such as assault, rape, and robbery (Bureau of Justice Statistics, 2016). Referring to data from the Bureau of Justice Statistics, an Urban Institute study reported that almost one-quarter (23.7%) of car thefts and nearly 12% of all thefts happen in parking facilities and nonresidential garages (La Vigne and Samantha, 2011).

Criminologists have used the concept of "critical intensity" to examine and explain the criminogenic nature of parking facilities. Critical intensity refers to the number of people in a geographical area that would be enough to attract a motivated offender searching for targets but not enough to deter the offender. Too few targets would mean less opportunity to commit a crime, whereas too many targets could raise the likelihood of getting caught in a criminal act. In his classical work on the relationship between the socio-spatial environment and crime, Angel (1968) asserted that crime was inversely related to the level of activity on the street, and that the commercial strip environment was particularly vulnerable to crime because it thinned out activity, making it easier for individuals to commit street crime. As we mentioned previously, the concept of "Critical Intensity Zones" refers to areas where pedestrian circulation is intermediate such that there are ample potential crime victims but not a sufficient amount to provide a surveillance or deterrent function. As intensity of use increases and streets become more populated, they become safe again (Angel, 1968). These zones tend to have specific physical environmental characteristics and land uses that provide opportunities for offenders to target and victimize others. Examples include open parking facilities in isolated areas, commercial areas backing residential areas, and structures that provide poor pedestrian circulation.

Some features of parking facilities can provide criminogenic conditions and opportunities for crime. The physical configuration can provide many hiding places (pillars, ramps, building corners, and the vehicles themselves) that can limit a patron's field of vision or perspective, and limit the number of directions a patron can use to escape predation. The walls and internal structure can also limit the ability of passersby to monitor or surveil the parking areas within, thus removing the deterrence capacity potentially offered by the visual presence of other people. Patrons are often alone when going to or coming from their cars. Drawing on the principles of CPTED, Smith (1996, p. 1) maintains that ensuring safety can be difficult in parking facilities since cars can provide hiding places and impede the distribution of lighting. Most parking facilities are open to the public, a situation that can bring motivated offenders into contact with vulnerable targets. Moreover, an offender's car is not likely to be noted as strange or memorable in a public parking facility. That said, some parking areas will be more criminogenic than others, depending on size, location, history, mix of tenants, characteristics of facility users, proximity to a school, accessibility to public transportation, and the real or perceived efficacy of security measures (Brantingham et al., 1990; Calder and Sipes, 1992, pp. 68–69).

CASE EXAMPLE: ABDUCTION AND MURDER IN A CASINO HOTEL PARKING LOT

This case involves the abduction of Carl Martino (a pseudonym) from the main parking structure at the Trip Casino Hotel (a pseudonym) one night at approximately 10:30 p.m. Mr. Martino had just dropped his wife off at the hotel/casino entrance and drove to the third floor of the parking structure to park. He was approached by Andre Cello and Jane Kibry (both pseudonyms) who forced him into the trunk of his car, drove him off the property, and then stabbed and killed him. The family of the deceased brought a wrongful death suit against the casino hotel.

The forensic criminologist was asked by counsel for the plaintiff to review the facts of this case and render opinions regarding any security issues which may have played a role in this tragedy. The following materials were reviewed: the local police department investigative file and calls for service, prosecutor's file, court transcripts, newspaper coverage, civil complaint, security reports of criminal incidents on the Trip Casino Hotel property, Trip Company internal documents (e.g., roster and security manual), discovery information, demographic data on the casino's environs, video recordings of the parking structure, and numerous depositions. The garage and hotel/casino premises and the immediate neighborhood were inspected during daylight and evening hours. Below are excerpts from the forensic criminological report.

> Among the most important issues in any negligent security case is the question of foreseeability [citation to Kennedy, 2006]. Utilizing a "totality of the circumstances" perspective, there are several reasons why a criminal attack in the casino garage was reasonably foreseeable. A "risky facility" is a location where one might come to expect repeat criminal activity and which may be designated a crime "hot spot." A parking facility such as a parking structure is one such example [citation to Eck et al., 2007]. Note, however, that parking structures are not automatically dangerous unless they possess additional characteristics. However, the Trip Casino Hotel parking structure possesses such risk factors. The structure is located in a higher-risk neighborhood that is a high-crime area. This was confirmed by my visual inspection of the immediate neighborhood in the area surrounding the Trip Casino Hotel as well as available socioeconomic census data I reviewed.
>
> Census data for 2010 show the census tract residents for tract code 0024.00 to have a median family income of $19,375 compared to the overall [city] area median of $65,400 for 2013. The tract's "poverty" rate was about 50 percent of the tract population. A number of subsequent, highly publicized crimes at the Trip Casino Hotel and within a one-mile radius do nothing to dispel one's image of the neighborhood.
>
> The parking garage also had a crime history, including a recent violent attack. Demonstrating that this event was not a unique occurrence, following the Martino carjacking and murder, the exact crime occurred again in the parking garage in September 2011, when [another person] was murdered.

In fact, prior to the Martino carjacking and murder, the Trip Casino Hotel recognized that its garage cashiers required an escort while walking inside the garage.

The parking structure is obviously designed for patrons of the hotel/casino. The "place and character of the business" are identified as criminogenic by various courts which have taken judicial notice that "a gambling casino where cash and liquor are constantly flowing may provide a fertile environment for criminal conduct such as robbery and assault … in areas … which are removed from the protection offered by crowds" [citation to *Doud v. Las Vegas Hilton Corp.*, 864 P.2d 796 (Nev. 1993)]. Indeed, the perpetrators of this crime went to the property looking for someone to rob. Further highlighting the risks that were present at the Trip Casino Hotel, please note that the [other expert witness] report provided to you in this matter identifies two murders, three aggravated assaults, and 66 assaults as having been committed on the property between January 1, 2006 [until the day of the murder in 2010].

The basic design of many parking structures allows for various hiding places and, owing to parked cars, ramps, pillars, and walls, limits a victim's ability to visualize a wide area. Such structures can have many nooks and crannies which hinder surveillance and can even make exit/escape routes hard to locate [citations to Fisher and Nasar, 1992; Smith, 1996, referring to the concepts of blocked prospect, blocked escape, and opportunities for concealment]. The construction of this particular garage posed additional security concerns that should have been recognized by the Trip Casino Hotel. The garage is not only of significant size, but each level of the garage has a number of perpendicular aisles. The design of the garage should have caused the Trip Casino Hotel to concentrate even more of a security presence in this potentially dangerous area. Illustrating the maze-like nature of the garage, Mr. Martino's vehicle was parked behind a wall which partially obscured the digital recording of the actual abduction. Lighting and signage can also serve as a deterrent to criminal activity, especially in more remote areas of a hotel casino. Following the carjacking and murder, the signage and lighting were upgraded; this is a further indication that the security risks posed by the garage were not recognized by the Trip Casino Hotel.

As we noted earlier, the concept of "critical intensity" refers to that number of pedestrians in the garage which would be enough to attract a predator looking for a "straggler" but not enough to deter the miscreant. In the case of the casino hotel, there were enough potential victims to provide a target but not so many potential victims as to deter a criminal by virtue of their numbers (Kennedy, 1990, p. 245 discussing the concept of critical intensity). From what could be determined from a digital recording, Mr. Martino was alone in the area of his parking space at the time of his abduction, although there may have been some activity throughout other areas of the multilevel parking structure and perhaps even in other aisles of the same level. This is often the pedestrian and vehicle traffic pattern in large parking facilities and explains why they may present such a hazard for patrons of a hotel/casino. As an additional example, parking facilities surrounding shopping center buildings are often the location for crimes against both vehicles and persons leaving or returning to their automobiles. Security concerns are even more heightened in casinos as there is an expectation that patrons may be carrying significant sums of money, especially as they enter the premises.

As the forensic criminological report concludes:

Finally, the foreseeability of crime in this parking structure can also be established by the history of adverse events on the property. I have reviewed the very limited security reports provided by the Trip Casino Hotel for the garage, as well as calls for service from the [City] Police Department. I have also reviewed the crime analysis report of [an expert witness], as well as the data on which his report was based. The Trip Casino Hotel should and would have been able to provide reports of murder, robbery, and assaultive crimes on the Trip Casino Hotel property, including Lot A, Lot B, the Bus Lobby, Valet Parking, and the perimeter of the property. All security reports for these same areas, as well as the Self-Park Garage, for the years immediately prior to Mr. Martino's abduction would have been relevant.

However, even though I only had security reports for the garage 2006–2009 and not for other areas of the property, there were still enough prior crimes to put Trip Casino Hotel management on notice that a crime was foreseeable. From this limited data, we know that there were at least eight reported robberies in the parking structure between June 25, 2006 and January 4, 2009. Given these robbery incidents together with the other factors previously mentioned, I reiterate that a violent crime was reasonably foreseeable at the time of Mr. Martino's abduction and subsequent murder.

Criminologists have long examined the impact of land use on crime, particularly the effects of non-residential land use in the form of commercial facilities. Places like bars, motels, schools, convenience stores, and check-cashing centers have been examined in relation to crime and research suggests that these facilities can have criminogenic features. In this conception, places of a particular type are assumed to inherently offer crime opportunity. Yet Blair and colleagues (2017, p. 62) have argued that "[a]lthough it makes intuitive sense that certain types of facilities may attract undesirable clientele or produce greater opportunities for crime, there are problems with focusing on certain facility types as generating crime—whereby the facility type itself is essentially used as a proxy measure for crime opportunity." Blair and colleagues suggest that criminologists should measure the specific characteristics and contexts associated with crime opportunity at places and not assume that broad categories of land uses or facility type automatically generate crime (Blair et al., 2017).

Drawing on environmental criminology, the previous excerpts from the forensic criminological investigation suggest that parking facilities are not inherently criminogenic. Rather, it is the coalescence of several factors that explain why a parking facility can become a hot spot of crime. In the case above, these factors include location in a high crime area, past history of criminal events, presence of cash-rich suitable targets, and physical design features that allow for various hiding places. The findings of the forensic criminological investigation resonate with the work of Brantingham and Brantingham (1999) who theorized that hot spots are most likely to form where three "layers of crime potential" intersect: busy nodes, high-traffic paths, and opportunistic backcloth or contextual features of an area in which a place is situated. In similar fashion, Felson (2006) explained that "thick crime habitat" exists where multiple nodes, paths, and unowned vacant spaces cluster without any available buffers from "crime-neutral" spaces. The theoretical notion that crime concentrates at the confluence of "layers of crime potential" is consistent with the findings of the forensic criminological report discussed before and with empirical work showing the effects of certain land uses vary depending on street or neighborhood context (e.g., Deryol et al., 2016; Hart and Miethe, 2014).

VIOLATION OF STANDARD OF CARE

After investigating foreseeability, a forensic criminologist can determine whether the property owner breached any standards of care. Below, we provide excerpts from the forensic investigation that considers whether the Trip Casino Hotel had actual or constructive knowledge that a person was at risk of becoming a crime victim. In any negligent security case, a property owner may be liable if he or she breached the standard of care and if his or her actions—or lack of actions—were a cause-in-fact and a proximate cause of the criminal event.

According to the forensic investigation:

Experienced, well-trained, uniformed foot, motor vehicle, and bicycle patrols of a casino parking structure on a regular basis constitute a reasonable standard of care. The hospitality/gaming industry literature endorses the importance of routine patrol and posits that "…the size, shape, design, and environmental conditions will dictate the level of security required in the parking area and the number of security officers that should be assigned to patrol it" [citations to Boss and Zajic, 2011, pp 154–155; Clifton, 2012]. I understand that the Trip Casino Hotel would routinely schedule three outside patrol officers on weekend evenings as these were particularly busy times. On the night Mr. Martino was abducted and murdered, however, there was only one mobile patrol officer on duty, and he had to cover, in addition to the parking structure, the entire perimeter of the property, two surface parking facilities, valet parking areas, porte cochere entrance, and the Bus Lobby as well as provide parking booth cashier escorts. A second officer who should have been on patrol was off due to a prescheduled vacation, yet no replacement officer had been scheduled. I do not know why a third officer was not even scheduled on the weekend evening in question.

On the evening of my site inspection, I counted four points of unattended pedestrian entry into the parking structure from surrounding streets. Given the questionable nature of the Trip Casino Hotel neighborhood, this lack of access control would make comprehensive security patrols even more important.

The lack of proper security staffing in the parking garage was consistent with the lack of an adequate security plan for the parking structure. It does not appear that in formulating a security plan for the structure, the Trip Casino Hotel considered any of the prior crime history or that the parking structure presented the greatest single risk to patrons. There should have been evaluations of high-risk areas as well as security audits on a regular basis; none were performed. Instead of recognizing the risk present in the parking structure in the years leading up to the Martino carjacking and murder, the Trip Casino Hotel slashed the security budget. The lack of or failure to execute a security plan was also evident in the assignment of a single security person in the fire command center to scroll through and monitor the 1,000 plus security cameras located on the hotel side of the operation. Of course, this stands in stark contrast to the manner in which surveillance is conducted on the casino floor.

The lack of an adequate security plan for the garage and the intentional and deliberate decision of the Trip Casino Hotel to have just one security person assigned to the parking structure, property perimeter, surface parking facilities, valet parking areas, porte cochere entrance, and bus lobby was below the standard of care, especially as it was foreseeable that casino patrons could suffer harm as a result of the inadequate security in the parking structure. You have asked me whether the actions or inactions of Trip Casino Hotel security management could be described as reckless in their failure to provide adequate patrol coverage in the garage. Given that the foreseeability of a violent event in this facility was so high and the failure to plan for a known future security officer absence was so egregious in its implications, I would have to describe management behavior as reckless. There is no justifiable explanation that could be offered by the Trip Casino Hotel as to why the riskiest areas of the property were likely to be the least patrolled by security or supervised by regular employees in the course of their duties.

The forensic report concludes that the Martino carjacking and murder that occurred at the Trip Casino Hotel parking structure was reasonably foreseeable and should have been recognized by the Trip Casino Hotel if an adequate security plan for the garage had been in place. The Trip Casino Hotel violated its own standard of care by failing to sufficiently staff its garage patrol force on the night in question. This staffing shortfall created a high risk of danger to patrons such as Mr. Martino.

These findings resonate with three oft-cited cases. First, in *Hanewinckel v. St. Paul's Property and Liability Ins. Co.*, 611 So.2d 174 (La. Ct. App 1992) the court determined that there were too few guards on duty to patrol the property where an attack occurred. The court stated that "reasonable security requires continuous, random patrolling" of all areas. The court found the security guards negligent and the property owners breached their duty to protect the plaintiff and others on the property from harm.

Second, in *Doe v. System Parking, Inc.*, 79 Ohio App.3d 278 (1992), the court noted that the place and character of appellee's business are such that appellee should have anticipated criminal conduct on the part of third persons. According to the court, the character of appellee's business, including the concentration of parked cars and customers who often return to their cars alone, provides targets for criminal activity. The court reversed judgment and remanded the case for a new trial.

Third, in *Romaguera v. Piccadilly Cafeterias, Inc.* (648 So. 2d 1000—La: Court of Appeals, 5th Circuit 1994) a cafeteria patron who was shot by an armed robber in the restaurant's parking lot brought suit charging that the restaurant should have been aware of the potential for crime and the likelihood of this type of crime. The Court of Appeals of Louisiana, Fifth Circuit, affirmed the district court's ruling that the restaurant had a duty to provide security in its parking lot and the restaurant breached that duty. According to the court of appeals, "[i]n the modern urban environment a business which undertakes to provide parking for its customers should determine whether security is required for the parking area and, if so, should ensure that adequate security is provided. Increased expense is a small sacrifice to make for protection of human life."

The Trip Casino Hotel case also suggests that businesses should seriously consider the possible negative consequences of cutting the security budget and reducing existing levels of security, a point we raised in the last chapter. During the years before Mr. Martino's abduction, the Trip Casino Hotel reduced the security payroll and related expenditures from $9,574,419 in 2006 to $6,646,017 in 2010. Inadequate security staffing may have been the result of cutbacks to the security budget. Ultimately, the responsibility for protecting the assets of a business rests with leadership. Departments such as security, legal, operations, human resources, information technology, and other functions assist in developing, implementing, and supporting the asset protection functions of a business. In any business firm, senior management views business operations from a financial perspective and may look to cut the budget of the security department to save money or redirect resources elsewhere to increase profit. Typically, security departments are not direct revenue generators and senior management may view security programs and activities as a business cost rather than an area of investment (ASIS International 2012a, p. 109). Gutmacher (2016) notes that a business might find it tempting to reduce existing levels of security at the property. But reducing the level of security can expose the business to costly litigation especially if there is a criminal incident on the property and the victim sues. "[A]dmitting that it reduced security for cost considerations is unlikely to go over well in the courtroom" (p. 3).

CASE EXAMPLE: PARKING LOT ABDUCTION

In this case, Mr. Bill Lawrence (a pseudonym) was abducted from the parking lot of an office building after leaving his job at about 6:30 p.m. Two offenders on a crime spree happened upon Mr. Lawrence as he was walking to his parked car and carjacked him. He was later forced out of the vehicle at the side of an expressway and shot. Fortunately, he survived his wounds. The forensic criminologist is asked by counsel for the defense to review the file and to comment on any liability issues and issues of security negligence from the perspective of a forensic criminologist. The following materials were reviewed: FBI Uniform Crime Reports, census data, police crime printouts, carjacking data, depositions given by five individuals (including the plaintiff, Bill Lawrence), expert reports of two plaintiff expert witnesses, maps of the property, court documents pertaining to the prosecution of the perpetrators, and case reports generated by the local police department. The property was also inspected during daylight and nighttime hours. Following are excerpts from the forensic criminological investigation.

First, I shall discuss foreseeability. Either under a prior similar acts test or under a broader totality-of-the-circumstances test, the crime against Mr. Lawrence was not foreseeable. The best predictor of future acts is prior acts [citations to Gabor, 1981; Kennedy, 2006], whether referring to an individual's behavior or to the likelihood of crime occurring on a property. The office complex … had absolutely no history of prior crimes against the person. There had never been any violence reported to the authorities at this property.

This office complex is located in a very stable and financially secure area of [the city]. For example, the median household income in the area around the office complex is approximately $85,281, compared to the [state] median of $66,961 and a [central city] median of $35,493. The median value of a house in the state … [is] $170,800 and $137,400 in [the county] in the year 2000, compared to $205,532 in a one-mile radius of the office building parking lot. This was not the kind of questionable neighborhood where one could foresee threats from the social environment. Furthermore, the office complex cannot be described as a crime magnet based on land use [citation to Kennedy, 1990], nor can it be described as a crime attractor (e.g., known open-air drug market, widespread prostitution) or crime generator (e.g., hundreds of thousands of visitors to the property, some inevitably committing crimes) [citation to Brantingham and Brantingham, 1995].

My opinion concerning the absence of foreseeability in this matter is further buttressed by a consideration of the community itself. [The city] enjoys a low crime rate when compared to other communities across the country. For example, in 2005 the robbery rate for the U.S. was 140 per 100,000 versus the [city's] rate of 44 per 100,000. The rate of aggravated assault was 291 per 100,000 for the U.S. versus 42 per 100,000 for [the city]. The bottom line is that the office building … was not a "risky facility," and a violent crime simply was not foreseeable there [citation to Eck et al., 2007].

Given there was no foreseeability of criminal attack at this property, security measures would ordinarily not be required. Nevertheless, Rolling Hills Realty Trust [a pseudonym] managed this facility with an attention to security even beyond what was called for. For example, given the absence of crime foreseeability, nighttime lighting sufficient for safety purposes, to avoid trips and falls, would be all that was required. Rolling Hills, however, illuminated the lot in full compliance with lighting levels recommended by the Illuminating Engineering Society of North America. The local lighting ordinance requirement was also fully met. These conclusions are based on the measurements and opinions found in the expert report of Garrison Gethem [a pseudonym]. Please note that plaintiff's lighting expert wrote an eight-page report without mentioning any measurements or reporting on how many footcandles of lighting actually fell on the pavement at the [office complex]. [The plaintiff's expert] did not mention the quantity of lighting, nor did he mention the quality of lighting. Based on my visit … both were reasonable.

Additionally, the office building was equipped with a sophisticated card access-control system, clear sight lines provided for natural surveillance of the parking lot from the building's interior, and the property was well maintained so as to project the image of a property which would be defended. Properly maintaining a property is the cornerstone of "Broken Windows Theory," first introduced to the public by George Kelling and James Q. Wilson in their seminal article in *Atlantic* magazine, March 1982. Sight lines and image remain central considerations within the body of theory known as Crime Prevention Through Environmental Design [citation to Crowe, 1991].

William Dobbins [a pseudonym], a Rolling Hills maintenance employee, would regularly check parking lot lights for any maintenance issues. He recalls no security issues at the property except for a call or two about vehicle vandalism which occurred in the late 1990s. Mr. Dobbins also testified at deposition that emergency phones programmed to dial 911 are located at the front entrances to the buildings. Property manager Michelle O'Keefe [a pseudonym] reported no security complaints from tenants and followed a policy of tenant notification of any significant problems. Ms. O'Keefe did not post security officers at this property because she saw no need to do so, and I completely agree with her in this regard.

Turning to causation, note that the perpetrators of this crime were driving from [another state] and were unfamiliar with this area. They got off the … Turnpike in order to find someone to rob. Neither criminal knew where they were, and they certainly did not begin their journey with the intention of going to the [office building]. They wound up there by chance and, unluckily for Mr. Lawrence, fell upon him by pure happenstance. It appears they had been on a crime "run" for at least a couple of months. Criminals on a crime spree or "run" do not generally specifically plan their offenses, are rank opportunists, and pay little attention to the longer-term consequences of their actions. It is as if they know at some level they will be caught anyway so they throw caution to the wind and live for the moment. Such sociopaths are unlikely to be deterred by an extra footcandle of light and, being armed, are unlikely to be worried about an unarmed civilian security officer [citations to Hochstetler, 2001; Erickson, 1996]. In other words, this crime was unrelated to the condition of the property at the [office building] and could have occurred virtually anywhere these criminals happened upon a solitary individual.

I turn now to a brief commentary on the report prepared by plaintiff's security expert. After much discussion of general security principles, plaintiff's expert report essentially concludes this crime was foreseeable because it happened in a parking lot and that parking lots can be dangerous places. Certainly, *some* parking lots can be dangerous, but not *all* parking lots are foreseeably dangerous. Plaintiff's expert then suggests "other strategies" could have prevented a carjacking without mentioning *what* specific strategies were required. Plaintiff's expert then lists CCTV and emergency telephones, neither of which constitutes a required standard of care, as measures which would have prevented this occurrence. CCTV has not proved effective in preventing crimes of violence such as this [citation to Welsh and Farrington, 2003], and I doubt [the] perpetrators … would have stood by and allowed Mr. Lawrence to contact police on an emergency land line. Plaintiff expert's citation to an article appearing in *Access Control & Security Systems* must be placed in perspective. This magazine is circulated free of charge and is paid for by advertisers selling security equipment such as CCTV.

As the above excerpts show, the crime committed against Mr. Lawrence was not foreseeable and security measures at the office building appeared to be appropriate under the circumstances. The reference to "broken windows theory" focuses on the importance of maintaining and managing spaces to diminish opportunities for committing crime. In formulating "broken windows theory," Wilson and Kelling (1982) suggest that an abandoned building can remain in its present state indefinitely, but once the first window is broken, the building is quickly vandalized. To paraphrase the ASIS International's *Guideline on Facilities Physical Security Measures*, maintaining a building and its physical elements (such as lighting, landscaping, paint, signage, fencing, and walkways) is critical for supporting and controlling desired and acceptable behaviors in the area (ASIS International, 2009a, p. 6).

Using a variety of data sources, the forensic criminological report suggests that the crime committed against Mr. Lawrence was opportunistic in nature and not related to the condition of the property or any claimed security deficiencies. This conclusion is based on using two tests of foreseeability: prior similar acts test and the totality of circumstances test. Under either of these two tests, plaintiff has the burden of establishing the premises owner knew or should have known the criminal act was foreseeable. Under both tests, foreseeability is required before the premises owner owes any legal duty to the injured guest. Under both tests, the court determines, as a matter of law, whether a duty is owed or summary judgment is appropriate. The "totality of circumstances" test is less restrictive than the "prior similar incident" test because plaintiff has additional factors to use in establishing foreseeability under the former test.

The last paragraph of the previous forensic criminological report provides a rebuttal to several plaintiff's expert witness claims concerning foreseeability and standards of care. Courts have ruled that where the plaintiff alleges that the defendant negligently failed to prevent a third party's injurious criminal act, she or he must prove that the criminal act was so foreseeable that it became the defendant's duty to guard against it by adhering to a recognized standard of care.[3] In addition, the plaintiff must prove with a preponderance of evidence that the defendant breached a recognized standard of care, and that the failure to exercise due care proximately caused the injury. Referring to "best practices" may not constitute a standard of care in some jurisdictions because "best practices" can be tantamount to "aspirational" industry standards.[4] Furthermore, courts have generally concluded that a landholder is not required to employ the "best" security practices but must employ those that are reasonable.

The previous excerpts suggest that the plaintiff's expert in the case offered only his own conclusory *ipse dixit* (unproven statement) or personal standards opinion that the parking lot's security measures were inadequate in various ways—that the defendant should have had "other strategies" such as "CCTV" and "emergency telephones." None of these security measures are recognized standards of care. Courts have ruled that because inadequate standard of care evidence can be fatal to a negligent security claim, then summary judgment will be granted to a defendant even if an assault was deemed

---

[3]*Beckwith v. Interstate Management Company*. 82 F.Supp.3d 255 (2015). District of Columbia. Civil Action No.: 14-00214 (RC); *Clement v. Peoples Drug Store, Inc.*, 634 A.2d 425, 427 (D.C. 1993); *Smith v. Hope Village, Inc.*, 481 F. Supp. 2d 172 - Dist. Court, Dist. of Columbia (2007).

[4]*Briggs v. Washington Metropolitan Area Transit*, 481 F.3d 839 (D.C. Cir. 2007); *Varner v. District of Columbia*, 891 A. 2d 260 - DC: Court of Appeals (2006).

foreseeable.[5] In *Perez v. DNT Global Star, LLC*, the court noted that neither the plaintiff's expert witness nor the defendant's expert witness "could say that additional security measures would have deterred the criminal in this case," a finding that means that "there is no evidence that the lack of security measures was a cause in fact of the murder."[6] In *Lee v. Borman's Inc.*, the court noted that "reasonable care" is a question of law for the court to determine, and reasonable care does not necessarily include the providing of armed guards. The court also held that the business owner is not required to provide its invitees with notice that the armed guards were no longer being used. The court affirmed the trial court's dismissal of the case.[7]

Criminologists have long known that some parking lots can be places that afford offenders refuge and give victims limited prospect and escape. According to prospect-refuge theory, "potential offenders desire a refuge, a hiding place, from which they can await, attack, and, if need be, take the victim out of sight" (Fisher and Nasar, 1992, p. 38). Some parking lots can offer a potential offender a place of concealment while awaiting a potential victim. This view of the desirability of concealment resonates with views such as those of Jacobs (1961), Newman (1973), and Jeffery (1971), who discuss the relationship between criminal behavior and environmental design. Research on crime on college campuses and bank robberies suggests that offenders often look for site-specific cues in the built environment when selecting their targets (Taylor and Nee, 1988). Some parking lots can have characteristics that make them attractive targets for criminals and that generate fear of crime. The diversity of suitable targets moving through a parking lot, as well as their transient tenure and belongings, gives potential offenders opportunities for theft and assault. Some parking lots tend to have easy access, free movement at all hours, and lack of capable guardians that allow offenders to remain unnoticed. Parking lots can have an abundance of "lurk zones" (Goffman, 1979) or "blind spots" (Warr, 1990) that demarcate zones beyond or behind an individual's line of sight. Archea (1985) argued that offenders tend to embrace an access and exposure model to the extent that they select targets and follow a path of offending that lets them see as much as possible while remaining unseen. In this sense, some parking lots can create crime opportunities that allow offenders to operate from locations with "enough visual access to gain and maintain control" and "low visual exposure from areas not in direct control" (Archea, 1985, p. 249).

The previous theoretical points can be helpful to a forensic criminologist in the assessment of crime foreseeability in a parking lot. As described in *Protection of Assets (POA) Physical Security*, published by ASIS International (2012b, p. 67), generally in the United States, the "standard of care dictates that the [vulnerability] assessment includes a criminal history of the site; a review of landscaping, lighting, stairwells, elevators, surveillance capabilities, access control equipment, signage, and restrooms." A forensic criminologist can also investigate the policies and procedures of the parking facility including operation and staffing. Additional concerns include the users of the parking facility (shoppers, commuters, students, or employees); the number of cars that travel into the facility per day/month

---

[5]*Briggs v. Washington Metropolitan Area Transit*, 481 F.3d 839 (D.C. Cir. 2007); *Clement v. Peoples Drug Store, Inc.*, 634 A. 2d 425 - DC: Court of Appeals 1993; *Workman v. United Methodist Committee on Relief*, 320 F.3d 259 (D.C. Cir. 2003).
[6]*Perez v. DNT Global Star, LLC, 339* S.W.3d 692 (Tex. App. 2011); see *E. Tex. Theatres, Inc. v. Rutledge*, 453 S.W.2d 466, 469 (Tex.1970) (holding no cause-in-fact because no evidence to show that, had theater employed sufficient security measures, bottle would not have been thrown); see also *Price v. Ford*, 104 S.W.3d 331, 333 (Tex.App.-Dallas 2003, no pet.) (holding no cause-in-fact absent evidence that additional security measures would have prevented injury).
[7]*Lee v. Borman's, Inc.*, 470 N.W.2d 653, 188 Mich. App. 665 (Ct. App. 1990).

and the rate of turnover of spaces; the degree to which lines of sight are clear or blocked by walls, columns, or ramps; the hours of operation of the parking facility and the effect of those hours on the user environment; the degree to which light is natural and/or artificial; the location of lighting fixtures (ceiling height, color of ceiling, and placement of lights); use of video surveillance and the details of the video surveillance system; and the degree to which the parking facility has ground-level protection such as gates, screens, or other barriers. All these issues can be important in evaluating the security of a parking facility.

HOTELS/MOTELS

Many travelers view hotels and motels as a home away from home, a place where a guest can relax while on a business trip or vacation. While hotels are meant to provide luxury and comfort, they can also become criminogenic places if hotel managers and business owners do not properly care for and maintain the facility. Poor physical design, weak informal social control, inadequate guardianship, and the presence of many motivated offenders and many targets can foment crime opportunities (for an overview, see Weisburd et al., 2016, pp. 46–50). Hotels have an affirmative duty to exercise reasonable care for the safety and security of their guests and protect their guests and employees from reasonably foreseeable criminal acts of third parties. Evidence relevant to establishing foreseeability includes the general likelihood of harm to the guest, past criminal activity on the premises and in the immediate vicinity, and security measures taken by the owner of the premises. Quoting *Meyers v. Ramada Hotel Operating Company* (1987), "When a plaintiff-victim seeks to be compensated by the innkeeper as a result of an intentional attack or assault by a third person, the burden is ordinarily upon plaintiff to establish that the innkeeper knew, or should have known, about the assailant's dangerous propensity and/or the innkeeper knew, or should have known, that the attack upon plaintiff was imminent."[8]

A forensic criminologist can investigate whether a pattern of prior disturbances or crimes existed at or near the premises, which should have put the hotel owner or manager on notice of a risk of criminal assault. One significant outcome of the Connie Francis Garzilli case was that the decision "signaled that courts would now increase the duty of care owed by the hotel industry by expanding the scope of constructive notice regarding any prior criminal incidents that had occurred on the hotel/motel property, even if such crimes were different than those inflicted upon the plaintiff" (Addicott, 2017, pp. 862–863). The court in the *Garzilli* case observed that four previous burglaries on the premises put Howard Johnson's Motor Lodge on constructive notice to take a higher level of what it had previously considered to be "reasonable care" for its guests. According to the court, it was not enough that Howard Johnson's had ordered new locks. Rather, what was the important and determining factor in the case was that the motor lodge had not installed the locks at the time of the rape.

Hotels and lodging constitute a multibillion-dollar global industry, with over five million hotel rooms across 53,554 properties in the United States alone (as of 2015), according to hotel census firm STR (Sickel, 2015). Standards of care and best practices are generally defined in operating or "standards" manuals published by each hotel chain or individual proprietor. Many states have enacted laws

---

[8]*Meyers v. Ramada Hotel Operating Company, Inc.* 833 F.2d. (11th Cir. 1987).

that regulate or impose minimal operating requirements. Organizations such as the American Hotel and Lodging Association (AH&LA) have defined "best practices" to which hotel managers and management companies should adhere to further promote the safety and welfare of guests. The Gale Encyclopedia of Everyday Law (2013) suggests several minimum safety and security measures that indicate compliance with "standard practices" and have been used by courts to establish legal precedent. These include access control, deadbolt locks with one-inch throws, viewing devices (peepholes) on room doors, chain locks, communication devices (telephones to enable emergency calls for assistance), and track bars for sliding glass doors. The standard test in establishing hotel liability is whether the hotel had taken reasonable steps to prevent certain crimes in light of the relevant facts and circumstances surrounding the particular crime event.

CASE EXAMPLE: ASSESSING FORESEEABILITY AND STANDARDS OF CARE IN A LOCALLY OWNED HOTEL

In this case, Gerry Oscar (a pseudonym) was shot one morning through the glass window of his rented motel room by Carl Royal (a pseudonym). Mr. Oscar was in Room 217 with a companion when he heard a knock on the door. As Oscar opened the curtains, Mr. Royal shot him through the window. Royal then entered the room, pointed his gun at the occupants, suddenly turned the gun on himself, and shot himself in the head. No motives for these criminal acts were ever established. Mr. Oscar suffered a chest wound in this incident and brought suit against the St. Charles Motel (a pseudonym) for negligent security.

The forensic criminologist was asked to review the case materials and investigate the foreseeability of crime at the property, evaluate whether security systems were commensurate with the level of foreseeability, and to determine whether any shortcomings in security operations were causal factors proximately related to injuries suffered by the crime victim. The following materials were reviewed: depositions given by five people, the police investigation along with witness statements as well as medical findings, reports of incidents of prior crime at the motel, and photographs taken from the CCTV system in use at the property at the time of the incident. The property was also inspected.

Following are excerpts from the forensic investigation:

> Due to their low cost and anonymous and transient nature, budget motels have a potential for crime and disorder and must be managed carefully if injury to guests and employees is to be avoided [citations to Schmerler, 2005; Kohr, 1991]. If a property has a history of illicit drug use, violence on that property is foreseeable due to disputes among sellers and buyers, the psychopharmacological effects of the drugs and the need for cash to make drug buys [citation to Goldstein, 1985]. My review of police reports produced by the [City] Police Department revealed three different drug arrests associated with this motel, including possession with intent to distribute.
>
> Where prostitution exists on a property, it is also foreseeable there will be violence. Violence may be directed against the prostitute herself, or the client may be robbed either by the prostitute acting alone or with the assistance of pimps or other male conspirators. Clients are frequently the victims of "trick rolls" and have been drugged, beaten, and even murdered. Lt. Getty [a pseudonym], a knowledgeable police executive, has testified that the St. Charles Motel sits within a known zone of prostitute activity [citations to Scott, 2001; Miller, 1998; Wright and Decker, 1997].

To the extent prostitution occurred at the St. Charles Motel itself, a crime of violence was also reasonably foreseeable. In addition, I should note that a strong predictor of future violence at a property is prior violence at a property. The St. Charles Motel has had at least six violence-related crimes on its premises dating back [four years from the time of the incident]. For the above reasons, then, it is my opinion that a crime of violence was reasonably foreseeable at the St. Charles Motel.

Not only was a violent crime foreseeable in a general sense, but there was imminent notice that a potentially dangerous man was present on the property well before Mr. Oscar was shot by Carl Royal. Royal had knocked on the door of Room 202 between 7:00 and 7:30 a.m. and wanted to come inside to look for a wallet he supposedly had left there. Wisely, the room's occupant, Steve Warren [a pseudonym], did not let him in. Mr. Magana [a pseudonym] also reported that someone had knocked at his door during the early morning hours, but he did not answer it. The St. Charles Motel housekeeper, Valeria Tico (a pseudonym) was grabbed by Mr. Royal as she was going about her cleaning duties sometime around 7:45 a.m. She believed she was about to be killed and screamed to be set free. He told her he had a gun and then ran upstairs just as she struggled free.

Photos reproduced from the CCTV system show Mr. Royal hanging about the motel walkways during the early morning hours and even depict him peering into a motel room not his own. Even given these inappropriate and threatening behaviors, the police were not notified of Mr. Royal's presence until after he shot Mr. Oscar. It appears that the first telephone call did not come into the [City] Police Department until 8:14 a.m.

Given the general foreseeability of crime at the St. Charles Motel, all employees would have benefited from "security awareness" training designed to instill in them the notion that all employees are responsible for premises security. Housekeeper Valeria Tico should have reported any initial suspicions she may have had about Mr. Royal when he first asked her for a cigarette. Once he grabbed her, she should have immediately contacted the front office after she pulled away, and police should have been notified without delay. To do anything less would be a violation of the standard of care for employees of the hospitality industry. It is unclear as to her activities from the time Mr. Royal first accosted her around 7:45 a.m. until the police were called around 8:14 a.m.

Desk clerk Parekh Barrain [a pseudonym] had never had any training in security emergencies (yet he would be responsible for responding to fire, medical, and crime-related incidents). Although Mr. Barrain claims to have watched the CCTV monitors, he apparently did not observe Mr. Royal loitering about the motel walkways in a suspicious manner at different times between 3:00 and 8:00 a.m. Recall also that Mr. Royal had reportedly been knocking on doors and peered into two motel rooms which were not his. He had also been personally to the front desk, so his presence on the property was definitely known to the night clerk. All in all, neither housekeeper Tico nor desk clerk Barrain responded in a timely or efficient manner to Royal's ominous presence on the property before Royal shot Mr. Oscar. It is my opinion that one or more of these failures to act was a contributing factor to the injuries suffered by Gerry Oscar.

The previous investigation offers several lessons for forensic criminologists. First, the examination of the case materials reveals the multiple ways in which a forensic criminologist can draw on forensic evidence to evaluate foreseeability. In the above case, crime data and other information are analyzed to assess foreseeability based on the prior similar acts test and an imminent harm test that a potentially dangerous man was present on the property. As explained in the previous excerpts, a crime of violence was reasonably foreseeable at the St. Charles Motel. It would also appear that motel employees were not properly trained in security awareness and did not respond appropriately to the threat posed by Mr. Royal based on his prior behavior at the property. Had Mr. Royal been approached by motel staff before the shooting or had police been called in a timely fashion, it is more likely than not that Mr. Oscar would not have been shot as he looked through the window of his room.

Second, the case suggests that while a landowner's duty may arise based on previous criminal events, it may also arise based on the landowner's knowledge of events that are currently unfolding on the property. In *Corinaldi v. Columbia Courtyard, Inc.*, a hotel was sued by the family of a man who died when a fellow guest fired a pistol at a party in the hotel. The trial court granted summary judgment for the hotel, ruling that as a matter of law the harm to the decedent was unforeseeable. The Court of Special Appeals overturned the ruling. While the court acknowledged that the hotel had no previous interaction with the shooter, the record showed that the hotel staff was advised at 10:45 p.m. that one of the guests had a gun. Nevertheless, the hotel staff did not call the police until 10:55 p.m. The shooting occurred between 10:53 and 10:55. The court ruled that even though hotel staff waited only ten minutes to call the police, "a reasonable jury could find that imminent harm was foreseeable when appellees were advised that an attendee of the party had a gun." Moreover, "[i]n light of the fact that an officer responded within three minutes of the 911 call, a reasonable jury could also find that the harm was preventable if appellees' agents had made the call to police immediately upon discovering that someone had a gun."[9]

Third, the reference to "security awareness training" connects with long-standing guidelines from ASIS International (2012a, pp. 291–301) that employee training and awareness of security issues can be cost-effective asset protection tools. The notion that all employees have a security function is well established among security professionals and in the hospitality industry (Newland, 1997, p. 174; Fay, 2002, pp. 373–376). Moreover, security awareness training is a standard of care in the hospitality industry. Emison (2013) suggests that one of the most significant obstacles to a successful defense of a premises security case is when an employee testifies that there was no training from the owner on customer safety. Even more damaging is when an employee cannot explain the physical security measures that were in place, given the level of risk.

CASE EXAMPLE: SHOOTING OF A HOTEL EMPLOYEE BY A GUEST

This case involves the shooting of a hotel employee by a guest. Gabby Land (a pseudonym) worked as a desk clerk during the day shift at the Country Inn (a pseudonym). For some unknown reason, she knocked on the door of motel guest Larry Estilla (a pseudonym) one night around 3:00 a.m. Mr. Estilla, assuming Ms. Land was an assailant he believed to be hunting him, fired several times through the door, killing Ms. Land. Plaintiff expert opines that the Country Inn was a "hotbed" of prostitution and drug sales and that Estilla and others paid hotel owner Manson Gomi (a pseudonym) and the deceased, Gabby Land, not to interfere with these illicit activities. It appears Ms. Land may have had some involvement with these kinds of behaviors in the past. Her estate brought suit over her death.

The forensic criminologist was asked by attorneys for the defense to investigate issues regarding the foreseeability of crime, standards of care (as they may pertain to breach of duty), and causation

---

[9]*Corinaldi v. Columbia Courtyard, Inc.* 162 Md. App. at 207, 873 A.2d at 483; 492; 495.

(cause-in-fact and proximate cause). The following materials were reviewed: census data for the Country Inn neighborhood, appropriate state case law, newspaper articles about the criminal event, the Affidavit for Warrant of Arrest, numerous motel guest portfolios, the plaintiff's petition, answers to various interrogatories, and responses to requests for production of documents. Also reviewed were four depositions of plaintiffs and defendant witnesses, video recording of a statement given by Mr. Estilla, affidavits/reports by plaintiff expert witnesses Bill Bertrand and Daniel Ellington (both pseudonyms), Plaintiff's 5th Supplemental Response, and Defendant's Motion for Summary Judgment. Also examined was the police investigation report which included witness interviews, plaintiff's expert declaration (unsigned), the criminal history of Gabby Land, and a video disk of the shooting recorded by the property's CCTV system. In addition, the property was inspected one evening and one morning where the forensic criminologist also talked with Mr. Gomi. Below, we include excerpts from the forensic criminological report.

Foreseeability

Plaintiff experts Bill Bertrand and Daniel Ellington seem to rely on a review of police Calls for Service (CFS) and Bertrand's own knowledge of the [local area of the city] in order to conclude that the shooting was foreseeable. Relying on CFS instead of actual police incident reports can be quite problematic in that 911 errors and misuse constitute a potential source of error when assuming CFS represent a true crime or disorder problem [citation to Sampson, 2004]. Technical errors, 911 misdials, hang-up calls, pranks, lonely heart calls, and exaggerated emergency calls are just a few of the problems associated with interpreting CFS. For example, the vast majority of CFS have nothing to do with crime [citation to Adams, 1988, p. 14] and often relate to events which did not even occur on the property to which the CFS were logged. For these reasons and others, analysis of crime based on CFS can be misleading [citations to Boba, 2009, p. 85; Boba, 2004] and it is premature to wholeheartedly embrace CFS as a valid measure [citation to Klinger and Bridges, 1997]. While CFS are of interest to police management, "…calls can be verified and reliably enhanced only when CFS are used in conjunction with the local law enforcement agency's offense or incident reports…" [citation to Vellani and Naoun, 2001, p. 29].

I was provided with 26 police narrative reports of crime on the premises of the Country Inn for the dates July 9, 2014 through July 21, 2015. There were thefts, possibly by prostitutes from their "customers," five instances of domestic violence, and a nasty struggle involving police officers and a man who was beating up his girlfriend. However, there were no robberies, stabbings, or stranger-on-stranger violence included in these 26 reports. Nobody was shot, and I saw no record of any firearms discharged. No hotel guest was known to have fired a handgun at or through a unit door due to a perceived threat. Based on my understanding of negligent security issues in [the state], I would conclude the shooting of Ms. Land, particularly given the bizarre circumstances in which it happened, would not have been foreseeable.

Plaintiff expert Bill Bertrand describes the general area in which the Country Inn is located as having a high level of drug dealing and prostitution relative to other parts of the city. No empirical data are provided to support this notion. On the other hand, Detective Manny Esteban [a pseudonym], who is also familiar with the area, believes the neighborhood has been somewhat revitalized and uplifted and that it looks better as it gets trendier. Nevertheless, the census tract in which Country Inn is located still seems economically depressed compared with the rest of the city.

Although some businesses and other properties may be improving, roughly 25 percent of the resident population remains beneath the poverty line. FFIEC Geocode Census Report for tract 0048.00 shows the median family income for 2015 estimated at $37,210, which is just about half of city-wide median family income. Given its location and the reputation of the area, it would not be surprising to find undesirables visiting this property from time to time.

Standards of Care

Any discussion of security practices at Country Inn must bear in mind that it is a small, privately owned property which will never have the resources of a large national chain such as a Motel 6 or Day's Inn. Nevertheless, the Country Inn meets or exceeds the single most important hospitality standard: access control. As any knowledgeable security specialist will attest, access control is of primary importance in any hospitality setting [citations to Beaudry, 1996, p. 71; Burstein, 2001, p. 28]. Manson Gomi, the property owner, had installed fencing to ensure that all visitors and guests must enter the property from the front of the motel, where they can be plainly observed directly through the windows of the motel office and via the 16-camera CCTV system installed throughout the property. The property is surrounded by metal fencing and/or cyclone fencing on all sides. Plaintiff's expert, Mr. Ellington, believes the most important preventive measure Mr. Gomi could have taken would have been to hire a security guard. Aside from a burdensome cost of $41,600 per annum, such a guard would not have prevented tenant and employee Gabby Land from knocking on guest Larry Estilla's door and being shot from within the room.

Access control and security for each guest room are also established by furnishing each room with an outside-line telephone (to call 911), a metal-skin room door, a deadbolt with one-inch throw, and a peephole on each of the doors. These access controls are enhanced by the presence of very effective night lighting throughout the premises.

Mr. Gomi has installed 400 watt floodlights at numerous locations on the motel building walls and there are automatic lights placed next to the door of each guest unit. The property also benefits from ambient lighting from municipal light poles, a nearby signaled intersection, and the very bright pole lights of an automobile dealership just across a sidestreet.

There were a number of additional security measures in place on the night of Ms. Land's death. Three employees were on the property at the time, and two of them lived on the premises (thus incentivized to maintain order). No trespassing signs were clearly posted as were the rules of the property. Such postings make it easier to deal with defiant trespassers when calling the police.

Mr. Gomi indicated during my interview with him and during his deposition that his staff was instructed not to rent to known troublemakers and to require photo I.D. when renting a room. Locks are changed whenever a key is lost. Outside contractors keep the shrubbery trimmed on a regular basis, trespass notice copies are kept on file, and Mr. Gomi walks the property two or three times each night. Mr. Gomi indicated he cooperates fully with any police officer who enters his property for investigative purposes and has always done so. Mr. Gomi also indicated he has greatly improved the property since he acquired it in 1997 rather than allow its deterioration (e.g., new cameras and all new windows in 2009). Mr. Gomi also asserts that his property has more security measures in place than other similarly situated motels in his immediate market area.

Causation

It is my intention to leave any "cause-in-fact" discussion to others and to comment on the issue of proximate cause. I understand that in [the jurisdiction] in order to be a proximate cause, an act or omission complained of must be such that "…a person using ordinary care would have foreseen that the event, or some similar event, might reasonably result therefrom" [citation to Kirkland, 2011, p. 994]. After over fifty years as a student, practitioner, professor, and consultant concerning matters of criminal and civil justice, I do not recall encountering a case like this one. While violence is not unheard of in association with drug markets, I have never known of a possible co-conspirator shot through a door due to mistaken identity. Possible, yes, but foreseeable, I think not. Here I must agree with the police officer who investigated this homicide, Detective Manny Esteban, who testified to the effect that a shooting under the circumstances of this case was not foreseeable [citation to Esteban deposition, pp. 53–56]. The fatal shooting of Gabby Land, which occurred through a door as a result of mistaken identity, was certainly not the result of a "natural and continuous sequence" of whatever was occurring at the motel.

The forensic investigation concludes that, given the circumstances surrounding Ms. Land's murder, there was no foreseeability under a proximate cause analysis. Country Inn is an older property located in an economically depressed area of the city. As such, one might expect a certain amount of crime. In the previous case, although there had been reports of drug dealing and prostitution, the forensic analysis of police incident reports for the property reveals no significant pattern of violent crime on the premises.

The forensic investigation suggests that the relative absence of violent crime at the premises could be a function of the implementation of several place management strategies including strong access control measures and high lighting levels which had been put in place by Mr. Gomi. The ASIS International's (2009a, p. 17) *Guideline on Facilities Physical Security Measures* maintains that a "comprehensive access control system is designed to permit only authorized persons and vehicles to enter and exit; detect and prevent the entry of contraband material; detect and prevent the authorized removal of valuable assets; and provide information to security officers to facilitate assessment and response." Included in an access control system are the technologies, procedures, databases, and personnel used to monitor the movement of people, vehicles, and materials into and out of a facility (p. 18).

Courts have struggled to clarify what security measures are adequate to prevent guest-on-guest or guest-on-employee crime. "Obviously a perimeter defense has no value against a criminal guest. And a hotel could hardly be required to have security guards watching every inch of the lobby every second of the day and night."[10] A security camera trained on the hotel room or floor where the shooting of Gabby Land occurred probably would not have been effective in preventing the crime. Had there been a security camera trained on the room, the shooting would have been completed long before a guard, alerted by what the camera showed, would have arrived on the scene. Hotel ownership or management could become liable for guest-on-guest crime or, in the previous case, guest-on-employee crime, when these types of criminal events become reasonably foreseeable. There is no evidence that the Country Inn management had reason to think that one of its guests would shoot an employee.

---

[10]*Shadday v. Omni Hotels Management Corp.*, 477 F.3d 511 (7th Cir. 2007) at 516.

CONCLUSIONS

In cases of crime and security at commercial land uses and facilities, courts may expect forensic criminologists to opine on questions of crime foreseeability and security standards of care considering this foreseeability. A forensic criminologist may also address the causal relationship between any alleged breach of standards and the damages suffered by a plaintiff. We have discussed in previous chapters that it is important for forensic criminologists to understand local case law to identify the appropriate foreseeability test used by a court in a particular jurisdiction. As criminologists know, the best predictor of future crime is past crime, whether we are speaking of individuals or of locations (Chainey et al., 2008; Walters and DeLisi, 2013; Kennedy, 2006). The context of the specific environment in the face of crime risk and the use of various risk management strategies are, of course, contingent upon and unique to the commercial facility in question.

A forensic criminologist should not just rely purely on incidents that have been reported in the recent past to investigate the foreseeability of criminal acts. Emison (2013) suggests, "there can be many changes to or developments at or near the property to alter the analysis, such as a change in the use of a facility, new or inexperienced management, new construction, and rapid changes in the neighborhood's character." Just because a hotel is considered safe one year does not mean that hotel owners have no obligation to adapt to changes in the neighborhood. Sociodemographic conditions and spatial features of neighborhood can change dramatically in a short time. Hotel management should be aware of any major neighborhood changes. According to the court in the *Timberwalk* case:

> The publicity surrounding the previous crimes helps determine whether a landowner knew or should have known of a foreseeable danger. A landlord often has actual knowledge of previous crimes occurring on the premises through tenants' reports. Actual notice of past incidents strengthens the claim that future crime was foreseeable. However, unreported criminal activity on the premises is no evidence of foreseeability. Previous similar incidents cannot make future crime foreseeable if nobody knows or should have known that those incidents occurred. Property owners bear no duty to regularly inspect criminal records to determine the risk of crime in the area. On the other hand, when the occurrence of criminal activity is widely publicized, a landlord can be expected to have knowledge of such crimes.[11]

Even without prior similar crimes, premises owners do not get a free pass because foreseeability may be established in other ways. In the oft-cited case, *Trammel Crow Central Texas v. Gutierrez*, the court noted that a focus solely on foreseeability overlooks other factors that are pertinent to the existence and scope of a duty. These factors include the risk, likelihood of injury, and the consequences of placing the burden on the defendant.[12] Leesfield and Peltz (2013) suggest, for example, a hotel's recognition that it

---

[11]*Timberwalk Apartments, Partners, Inc. v. Cain*, 972 S.W.2d 749 (Tex. 1998).

[12]*Trammell Crow Cent. Texas v. Gutierrez*, 267 SW 3d 9 - Tex: Supreme Court 2008); *Timberwalk*, 972 S.W.2d at 756 ("Foreseeability is the beginning, not the end, of the analysis in determining the extent of the duty to protect against criminal acts of third parties'") (quoting *Lefmark Mgmt. Co. v. Old*, 946 S.W.2d 52, 59 (Tex.1997) (Owen, J., concurring); *General Elec. Co. v. Moritz*, 257 S.W.3d 211 (Tex.2008).

needs to hire security guards or take other safety precautions may help establish foreseeability.[13] Security measures taken by the business owner prior to the criminal act may establish that the business owner foresaw criminal activity and had tried to guard against it.[14] That said, in *Lau's Corp., Inc. v. Haskins*, the court ruled that "undertaking measures to protect patrons does not heighten the standard of care; and taking some measures does not ordinarily constitute evidence that further measures might be required."[15] Likewise, where activities could be associated with criminal conduct, the premises can be put on notice of the need for security measures. As one of the previous cases that we discussed shows, employees' observations of conduct or events immediately before the crime, such as a suspicious person in the wrong place, may also give rise to notice.

One court maintains that the possibility of a criminal event occurring is "present in almost every aspect of daily life," and in that sense, "the possibility of a violent attack is always able to be foreseen."[16] Yet, decades of criminological research have shown that crime is not randomly distributed but tends to be concentrated at particular facilities, that is, the 80–20 rule. Moreover, a forensic criminologist should evaluate foreseeability on a continuum from high foreseeability to low foreseeability. Assessing the degree of foreseeability (as well violation of standard of care and causality) can be challenging. For a forensic criminologist, conjecture and speculative expert testimony are not admissible but absolute certainty is not required. A lesson in forming expert opinions is that forensic criminologists should aim to provide expert testimony that is stated to a reasonable degree of certainty. In the end, a forensic criminologist's opinion is only as strong as the facts and data upon which it is based (i.e., the expert's investigation).

---

[13]*Holley v. Mt. Zion Terrace Apts., Inc.*, 382 So. 2d 98, 99-100 (Fla. 3d Dist. App. 1980); *Daniel v. Days Inn of Am., Inc.*, 356 S.E.2d 129 (S.C. App. 1987).

[14]See *Cross v. Wells Fargo Alarm Services*, 412 N.E.2d 472, 82 Ill. 2d 313, 45 Ill. Dec. 121 (1980) (defendant had hired security for certain hours of the day and not for other hours, arguably making the premises more dangerous during the hours the plaintiff was present).

[15]*Lau's Corp., Inc. v. Haskins*, 261 Ga. 491, 492, 405 S.E.2d 474 (1991).

[16]*Whittaker v. Saraceno, 418 Mass.* 196, 635 N.E.2d 1185, 1188-89 (1994).

CRIME AND BUSINESS II: NEGLIGENT SECURITY LITIGATION CONCERNING SHOPPING MALLS AND BARS/TAVERNS

INTRODUCTION

This chapter continues the analysis we introduced in the last chapter concerning negligent security matters involving commercial facilities and land uses. In this chapter, we focus specifically on the unique security concerns of shopping centers/malls and bars/taverns. Throughout our book, we have stressed the importance of gathering evidence of prior similar incidents on the premises to evaluate whether the owner was aware or should have been aware of the need for increased security. A 2012 case from the Georgia Court of Appeals serves as a reminder that a plaintiff must prove with a preponderance of evidence that security was negligent. In *Yearwood v. Club Miami Inc.*, the Georgia Court of Appeals affirmed a trial judge's grant of directed verdict for the defendant night club in a personal injury lawsuit arising after the plaintiff Yearwood was shot in the defendant's club. Yearwood, a patron at the defendant's Club Miami nightclub, was on the dance floor when a fight broke out and a gun went off. Yearwood was shot and filed suit against Club Miami for negligence. A jury awarded Yearwood $500,000 but the judge granted Club Miami's request for a directed verdict. Yearwood then appealed. At the club, Club Miami personnel used a two-step security procedure involving four to eight security guards and uniformed police. Customers were patted down and scanned with a metal-detecting wand before admission. Yearwood argued that Club Miami's procedures should have prevented weapons from being brought into the club and therefore the club was negligent.

During the trials, the plaintiff Yearwood could not prove that the injury inflicted was due to the insufficient security measures taken by Club Miami. According to the appeals court, "[c]ontrary to [Yearwood's] argument, in a negligence action, it is not enough for [Yearwood] to merely present evidence of his injury as evidence that [Club Miami] performed its security screenings in a negligent manner … To succeed on this claim, [Yearwood] had the burden to present evidence at trial of how specifically [Club Miami's] measures made the security situation worse, or how those measures were inadequate or insufficient such that negligence could be established." According to the appeals court, "Yearwood presented absolutely no evidence that the security measures in place were performed in a negligent manner or worsened the situation." In addition, "[n]o witness testified that the security personnel should have done anything differently. Yearwood himself testified that he thought the security was sufficient. Nor did Yearwood present any evidence of any prior criminal activity on the premises that may have put Club Miami on notice that its security measures were inadequate."

The plaintiff Yearwood's case was essentially built on the assumption that Club Miami was liable because an offender was able to get a gun through the club's security measures. But a breach in security is not enough to prove negligence. The appeals court therefore affirmed the directed verdict for Club Miami.[1]

The lesson in this case is that a forensic criminologist must investigate prior similar criminal acts on and around the premises, conduct detailed discovery and investigation about the security measures that the defendant did or did not use, and present expert testimony showing exactly why the defendant's conduct was adequate or inadequate for the standard of care under the circumstances. According to Bates and Frank (2010, p. 207), "[t]he failure to provide an adequate explanation as to the relationship between the injury that occurred and the security of the premise (or lack thereof) is a fatal mistake on the part of the expert because it forces the jury 'to engage in idle speculation, which is prohibited.'"[2] In addition, it is not enough for a plaintiff's expert witness simply to declare that a defendant violated some sort of standard of care. Rather, the expert must clearly articulate and reference a standard of care by which the trier of fact can measure a defendant's actions. Some courts require the expert to clearly relate the standard of care to the practices generally followed by other comparable facilities or to some standard nationally recognized by such units.[3]

SHOPPING CENTERS/MALLS

Shopping centers are places that place managers have explicitly designed to bring people together to buy and sell goods and services. Sociologist Ritzer (2005) refers to shopping malls as "cathedrals of consumption" since commercial displays are meant to inspire awe, wonder, and enchantment in the consumer. Malls do not just sell merchandise but are places where sophisticated corporate advertising and marketing converge to "sell" individual taste, style, and fashion. The International Council of Shopping Centers (ISCS) (2018) categorizes U.S. shopping centers as either general purpose or specialized purpose. General-purpose centers are open-air (convenience, or neighborhood and community centers) or enclosed malls (regional and super-regional). Generally, smaller open-air centers offer convenience-type goods, while larger ones integrate apparel with general merchandise and fashion-oriented offerings. Specialized-purpose centers—for example, lifestyle, factory outlet, theme/festival—have specific types of tenants with a well-defined concept.

---

[1]*Yearwood v. Club Miami, Inc.*, 728 S.E.2d 790, 316 Ga. App. 155 (Ct. App. 2012).
[2]*Hughes v. District of Columbia*, 425 A.2d 1299, 1303 (D.C. 1981) (stating expert testimony is required to aid the jury in making a determination and avoid forcing the jury to speculate).
[3]See *Briggs v. Wash. Metro. Area Transit Auth.*, 375 U.S. App. D.C. 343, 350, 481 F.3d 839, 846 (2007). In *District of Columbia v. Carmichael* (577 A. 2d 312, 314-15—DC: Court of Appeals 1990), the District of Columbia Court of Appeals concluded that appellees' expert witness on prison security failed to establish an adequate standard of care to determine whether the District was negligent in controlling contraband weapons within its prison. Specifically, his conclusion that there were "too many shanks" (prison-made weapons) was based primarily on his own experiences, and his references to national and District of Columbia standards were too general, and he did not mention a specific standard or regulation the District had breached. In contrast, in *District of Columbia v. Price* (759 A.2d 181, 183–84 (D.C.2000)), the District of Columbia Court of Appeals concluded that appellee's expert on police practices sufficiently established the standard of care assigned to police when a prisoner in custody is ill or intoxicated.

Shopping centers and malls are enormously popular places that attract millions of residents a year. Twerski and Shane (2018) note that the average size of the thirty largest malls in the United States is 2.07 million square feet of gross leasable area (GLA). The average yearly attendance per mall is almost 19.3 million visitors. Based on being open for business an average of 6.5 days per week each year, average daily attendance is 56,844. Over the decades, place managers, architects, urban planners, and real estate officials have spent much time and effort researching the relationship that shopping centers have to the socioecological environment. A major challenge has been to design esthetically pleasing shopping centers that attract consumers while also minimizing opportunities for criminals to victimize shoppers and others at the site (Kennedy, 1990, 1993; Savard and Kennedy, 2014). To reduce the likelihood of on-site criminal events, place mangers have at their disposal a repertoire of crime prevention techniques including Crime Prevention Through Environmental Design (CPTED) (for an overview, see Cozens and Love, 2015), environmental criminology (Brantingham and Brantingham, 1981), and situational crime prevention (SCP) (Cornish, 1994; Clarke, 1997).

Shopping malls can present security challenges for mall managers and individual merchants since the large volume and high concentration of goods, consumers, and merchants can create opportunities for motivated offenders to victimize targets. That said, like parking facilities and hotels/motels, shopping malls are not inherently criminogenic. Criminologists recognize that some locations will inevitably have a certain number of criminal incidents simply because so many people come to the property (crime generator) as opposed to those locations which attract criminals because illicit activity is tolerated there, such as a parking lot where drugs are known to be sold (crime attractor) (Clarke, 1997, p. 108).

In studying the criminogenic features of a place, including a shopping mall, a criminologist should understand the difference between the possibility and probability of criminal events. Just because a criminal event is possible does not mean that it is probable. On the one hand, wherever many people conglomerate, there will be an increased possibility of criminal events occurring. On the other hand, an individual's risk of becoming a crime victim is greatly reduced because whatever crimes do occur are distributed among so many people. For example, let us say there were approximately 25 assaults over a 5-year period at a shopping mall with about 50,000,000 customer visits during that same 5-year period. An individual's risk of being assaulted at this shopping mall during a visit would thus be one in 2,000,000. Thus, the odds of victimization are low at shopping malls. In this hypothetical case, an individual is statistically three times more likely to be struck by lightning during the coming year than to be attacked while visiting the mall (Baer, 2003, p. 87).

CASE EXAMPLE: ATTACK AND MURDER BY HOMELESS MAN IN STRIP MALL

This case concerns an attack against two senior citizens—Bill Baldwin and Will Willings (both pseudonyms)—outside a donut shop in a strip mall. As the two senior citizens left the donut shop, they walked past Mr. Eugene Warner (pseudonym), a homeless man who frequented mall premises but was never known to cause a disturbance. One morning, however, he suddenly turned violent and attacked the two folks with knives, killing one of them and seriously wounding the other. No motive for this attack was ever established. Mr. Warner was found Not Guilty by Reason of Insanity and was institutionalized. A lawsuit was brought against strip mall ownership and one of the merchant tenants. The forensic criminologist was asked by counsel for the defense to review the case for possible security-related negligence. The following materials were reviewed: newspaper articles covering the stabbings, census data concerning the neighborhood in which the mall is located, relevant crime data for the city, and autopsy results and investigative reports from the local police department and county prosecutor's office. Also reviewed were miscellaneous insurance documents, lease agreements, security background reports, a building underwriting report, four depositions, multiple crime scene photos, psychiatric evaluations, the commitment order, and other court documents concerning Mr. Warner. Finally, the property was analyzed using a DVD of the property, multiple photographs, and a virtual tour through Google Maps. Following are excerpts from the forensic report:

Duty (Foreseeability)

The murder of Mr. Baldwin and the wounding of Mr. Willings were completely unforeseeable. Whether analyzed from an imminent danger perspective, from a prior similar acts perspective, or from a totality of the circumstances perspective, no one could have foreseen this attack. A sudden, unprovoked attack such as that perpetrated by Mr. Warner is known as "sudden murder," "homicide without apparent motive," "catathymic" murder, or "psychotic homicide." Such an attack is entirely psychogenic in nature and not predictable in any practical sense [citations to Holcomb and Daniel, 1988; Blackman et al., 1963; Schlesinger, 1996]. Indeed, Mr. Warner's attack had the prominent characteristics of a "schizophrenic and psychotic violent crime" as described in the literature [citation to Schug and Fradella, 2015, pp. 190–1].

Mr. Willings himself testified there was nothing unusual about his walk back to his car from the coffee shop, just before he was stabbed [citation to Willings deposition, p. 46]. Off-duty police officer David Strang [a pseudonym] was unaware of any problem as he left [the donut shop] until the fatal attack began [citation to Strang deposition, p. 25]. Based on Mr. Willings' description of events, what Strang describes as an argument or "discussion" was actually the victim's initial protestations over the first stabbing. Most fatal arguments tend to escalate through a series of face-saving verbal stages until an actual assault begins [citation to Luckenbill, 1977]. This encounter began with the attack rather than ended with it. It was not foreseeable.

Another approach to foreseeability involves an evaluation of prior similar acts at a given location. There were none. In fact, it is my understanding there is no history of violent crime at this strip mall preceding the sudden attack on Messrs. Baldwin and Willings. According to a common criminological adage, the best predictor of future events is past events. Since there is no prior pattern of violence at [the mall] prior to the attack on Mr. Baldwin and Mr. Willings, none could have been predicted (i.e., foreseen). Whether talking about offenders or locations, past history of crime is important in the prediction of future crime [citations to Martinez et al., 2017; Johnson and Bowers, 2004a].

It is my understanding that [the jurisdiction] utilizes a "totality of the circumstances" approach to the question of foreseeability. This would call for an additional analysis of land use and city/neighborhood socioeconomic status to determine the presence of criminogenic characteristics at the…strip mall. Let me start with a description of the city … itself. The median household income for [local] residents was approximately $66,382 per year. This was significantly higher than the U.S. average at $52,250. The … strip mall itself is located in census tract 1243.23, which had a median household income of $58,214. Surrounding tracts had incomes ranging from $81,333 to $111,220, so the neighborhoods around the mall were thriving middle-class communities. These data are taken from the American Community Survey for 2009–2013.

The economic stability of [the city] is likely one of the reasons the city benefits from a low crime rate. Mr. Baldwin was the only homicide in the city during 2014, and there had been no others in 2013 or 2012. [The city's] violent crime rate of 206 per 100,000 compares favorably to the national average of 368 per 100,000. My sources are the FBI's Uniform Crime Reports for 2011, 2012, 2013, and 2014.

With regard to violent crime at the…shopping center itself, I am unaware of any violent crimes at that location prior to the unprovoked and sudden murderous attack on Mr. Baldwin and Mr. Willings. Given that this attack was unforeseeable, there was no obligation to provide for security measures.

Breach (Violation of a Standard of Care)

Assuming for the sake of argument that security measures should have been in place at [the mall], what would this entail? Given that foreseeability drives the standard of care, little or no foreseeability would negate the need for security guards to be stationed at this neighborhood mall. In fact, strip malls like [the one here] do not generally utilize the services of guard personnel as such is not the standard of care [citation to Twerski and Shane, 2018]. Instead, security assumes a more subtle form referred to as "defensible space theory." Here, maintaining a property in a neat and clean condition deters potential criminals because they can sense that property management is attentive and likely intolerant of crime, petty or otherwise [citation to Murray, 1983]. [One person] would routinely clean the parking lot and monitor the property on a daily basis. Phillip Pascal [a pseudonym] [the owner of the strip mall] is at the property two and a half days a week and walks the property.

The forensic criminological report points out that merchant tenants at the mall serve as the "eyes and ears" of management. Given the glass storefronts found in strip malls such as this one, employees at the various shops can monitor the sidewalks and parking lot areas in front of their establishments. Through a process known as "natural surveillance," merchants and their employees would either call the police or report potential problems directly to mall management. The report also notes that the city police department is located just down the street. The close proximity of the police station to the mall could allow police frequent opportunities to observe the mall as they go to and from work or drive out to their patrol areas. The report points out that there were no "problem" tenants at this mall which would attract troublemakers to the property. In addition, there were no "fighting" bars, video arcades, drug counseling centers, or other potential magnets for disorder. In fact, this mall was judged safe, thus adequately secured, by police officer David Strang, who arrested Mr. Warner at the scene. According to Officer Strang, who grew up in the neighborhood, his wife, children, and mother all frequent the mall, and he has no problem with them visiting the area.

In opining on the issue of causation, the forensic criminological report comments that just as this heinous attack was unforeseeable, and there was no breach of a standard of care, the facts of this case do not establish either of the two types of causation (cause-in-fact and proximate causation). According to the report:

The plaintiff's expert may argue that a security guard's presence would have prevented this attack. This is not true. Mr. Warner attacked Messrs. Baldwin and Willings without concern for the presence of witnesses in that police officer Strang and mall patron Louis Ventura [a pseudonym] were in the immediate area of the attack. Their presence did not deter Mr. Warner as he carried out his attack in broad daylight with no apparent concern for the consequences to himself. Even had a security guard been assigned to the property, he may not have been posted so early in the morning given scant customer traffic, and he very well could have been at a location more distant from the attack site. The presence or absence of a security person simply would not have mattered. One cannot establish that but for the absence of a security guard, this crime would not have occurred.

Plaintiff may also argue that Warner should not have been allowed to loiter about the premises. In fact, Warner was known to purchase goods and services so he was not readily designated as a mere loiterer. The fact that he was homeless and sometimes talked to himself did not establish that he was a danger to others. Allowing an otherwise inoffensive homeless person to patronize various businesses and spend a considerable amount of time on the premises does not render an attack foreseeable.

Violence is not a natural, foreseeable consequence of mental illness. Where violence is associated with mental illness, other factors are also usually involved such as substance abuse, a history of violence, and being young, male, and the product of a subculture of violence [citation to Stuart, 2003; Monahan, 2006]. I do not deny that, under certain conditions, mentally ill persons may engage in more violence than similarly situated nonmentally ill controls. These "conditions," however, did not apply in Mr. Warner's case. In particular with regard to Mr. Warner, he had been patronizing this mall for many years without incident, was an older man, did not appear disheveled, and was believed by nobody appearing in my file review to constitute a danger to others [citations to depositions of four eye witnesses].

The forensic criminological report concludes that the assaults were not foreseeable under any test of foreseeability. The report opines that there is little evidence that any additional security measures would have prevented the murder of Mr. Baldwin. As discussed by Bates and Frank (2010, pp. 206–7), establishing a causal relationship between a violation of standard of care and injury is no easy task. To do so, the expert witness must "provide a detailed explanation of how the injury would have been prevented had the defendant employed recommended security precautions." Alternatively, if the security expert finds no causal relationship, as is the case before, then "he or she must provide an adequate explanation as to why the injury would have occurred regardless of whether suggested security precautions were in place prior to the injury."

Essentially, the forensic criminologist argues that any breach the plaintiff may have committed is not actionable because it was not the proximate cause of Mr. Baldwin's murder. Rather, the murderer's conduct was the intervening cause. The presence of police officer Strang and mall patron Louis Ventura in the vicinity did not discourage the murderer from acting on his impulses. Based on an analysis of multiple data sources, there was no atmosphere of violence in the area. In sum, the forensic criminological report opines that the shopping center management did not violate any standard of care because the murder and assault were unforeseeable. Any failure on the shopping mall's part to provide adequate security did not proximately cause injury and death.

CASE EXAMPLE: ASSAULT IN SHOPPING MALL RESTROOM

This case concerns an assault of a young female in a family restroom area of the River Springs Mall (a pseudonym) one evening. Canterbury Coffee Shop (a pseudonym) employee Jamie Paula (a pseudonym) was accosted by Javier Otero (a pseudonym). While attempting to use the restroom during a break, Mrs. Paula was pushed into the bathroom by Otero, who closed the door behind them and threatened her with a knife while undoing his belt buckle. Mrs. Paula suffered defensive wounds and a cut to the neck during the assault. Fortunately, Otero was dissuaded by her screams from continuing the attack and escaped through a corridor door leading out of the mall. The forensic criminologist was asked by the counsel for the defense to review the file and to comment on possible liability for negligent security practices on the part of CCC Security Company (a pseudonym) and River Springs Mall. The following materials were reviewed: the Complaint, Answer, police incident report and investigation, answers to interrogatories, criminal trial transcripts, CCC reports, a DVD of the restroom area, a series of security and police incident reports, General Growth crime reporting forms and portions of a CCC manual, depositions from seven people, and the report offered by plaintiff's security experts Michael Paul Janesko and Gregory Albert Kahn (both pseudonyms). The family restroom area of the mall was inspected one evening and one morning. Below are excerpts from the forensic criminological report.

[I]t is my opinion that the sexual attack on Mrs. Paula was not foreseeable, that CCC and mall security practices as they related to the family restroom area were reasonable under the circumstances, and that there was no causal relationship between mall security and Javier Otero's decision to attack Mrs. Paula. More specifically, his cognitive and emotional state, from a criminologist's perspective, did not render him responsive to conventional security deterrent measures in place at the mall generally or in the family restroom area particularly.

With regard to foreseeability, this case involves the sexually based attack on a woman in the family restroom area of River Springs Mall in June of 2007. There had been a prior incident in February of 2004 where a young man forced a young woman into a restroom and tried to pull down her shirt. She kicked him in the knee and ran out of the restroom. Thus, one assault on a female in a restroom occurred in 2007 out of 6,947,000 customer visits to the mall and 1,400,000 customer visits to the AMC Theatres that year for a total of 8,347,000 visits.

Mall marketing folks estimate River Springs Mall receives 6,947,263 visits per year while AMC River Springs 24 Theatres estimate the cinema receives 1.4 million visits per year (estimates provided by Colby Springer of Mall Business Development and Marketing and Zack Dominick (a pseudonym), AMC General Manager). If one's chances of being struck by lightning are one in 600,000 during any given year, it is fair to say that a mall visitor is almost fourteen times more likely to be struck by lightning than to become the target of a restroom sexual attack during any given visit to the mall.

I am aware that statistics can be analyzed in many ways. Plaintiff's experts in their report identify an incident which occurred in 2003 near the food court restroom wherein someone was punched and, also in 2003, a robbery which occurred in the family restrooms. Adding these two incidents to the shirt-pulling incident totals to three restroom incidents for the years 2003–2006 and the first five months of 2007 (up to the day of Mrs. Paula's attack). During this four-year time period, at least 32,000,000 people visited the mall/theater; there were 40,800,000 if we add in the first five months of 2007. Thus, the chances of a restroom attack were three out of 40,800,000 or one out of 13,600,000. If only half of the visitors even used the restrooms, the chances would still be only one out of 6,800,000.

I conclude that while a restroom sexual assault is certainly possible, and it has happened at this and other malls, it is not reasonably foreseeable, i.e., reasonably likely to occur or having an "appreciable chance" of occurring. Given these incredibly low odds, suggestions that River Springs Mall was negligent because it did not have a guard posted outside the bathroom or an emergency alarm button inside the bathroom are simply not credible or reasonable.

Plaintiff experts seem to argue that there was imminent notice of danger in the area of the family restroom because Public Safety Officer Gary Wisniewski [a pseudonym] became aware of a male acting "strangely." He did observe this male but took no further action such as approaching him to offer assistance. Wisniewski does not remember the nature of this man's behavior and did not identify this man as the same person who later attacked Mrs. Paula. Basically, then, we do not know who this man was nor do we know the nature of his behavior. Appearing "strange" is not the same as appearing or acting dangerous. Wisniewski may not have approached the subject because there appeared to be nothing to fear from him. Ever since *O'Connor v. Donaldson*, 422 U.S. 563 (1975), which led to the virtual emptying of state mental hospitals, many "strange" people may be found in public places. Unless dangerous to self or others, or unable to care for themselves, people with various mental afflictions have a right to access public accommodations and places open to the public just as everyone else does. Recall [a police officer] stating in his deposition that "they encounter a lot of strange persons in the mall; and unless they feel they're a dangerous threat immediately, they don't contact us" [citation to deposition, pp. 63–69].

Unless there was some reason to suspect this individual posed a threat to the mall or its customers, Wisniewski violated no standard of care by not interfering with him or asking the CCTV operator to track him. Indeed, CCTV operators must be responsive to the concerns of many members of the public that they may be "tracked" in a retail setting merely because of their ethnicity. Such discrimination would not constitute appropriate security practice [citations to Gabbidon, 2003; Gould, 2006]. Furthermore, any recollection or identification of suspicious traits a witness remembers primarily after the witness has learned of an incident involving a subject may fall prey to the hindsight bias known as "omen formation" or "retrospective presifting" [citations to Terr, 1983; Schwarz et al., 1993].

At this point in my report, I need to highlight an inconsistency in plaintiff experts' reports. On page 4 of their report, they discuss Public Safety Officer Gary Wisniewski's testimony wherein Wisniewski testified he "called the incident in" (referring to the male in the management hallway). The actual wording is found on page 100 of Wisniewski's deposition. Yet, on page 6 of Janesko and Kahn's expert report, they state that "Wisniewski did not report the suspicious activity that he encountered in the forty minutes prior to the incident to management…" There is an implication that Gary Wisniewski violated a security procedure by not informing dispatch about this "strange" mall visitor. Actually, then, Wisniewski *did* report him to the dispatch/CCTV operator who apparently viewed the scenario and cleared it as not requiring further security action.

Plaintiff experts further opine that CCC and River Springs Mall should have had an officer proactively monitoring the 49–50 cameras and that had an officer been doing nothing but watching these screens, he or she "would have observed the suspicious activity at the time of Jamie Paula's attack …" This is speculation. Given the well-known human limitations such as video blindness, change blindness, and vigilance decrement, most CCTV operations involve reactive monitoring rather than the sort of proactive monitoring suggested by Messrs. Janesko and Kahn [citations to Strauchs, 2008; Wallace and Diffley, 1998; Scott-Brown and Cronin, 2008; Crowe, 1991, pp. 29–34].

Plaintiff experts also opine that the corridor door to the loading dock should have been locked. This opinion ignores fire emergency escape routes, the need to move people and goods through these doors during the day, and the fact that people moving through these doors provide for a kind of natural surveillance of the family restroom area, which serves as a crime deterrent [citation to Crowe, 1991, pp. 29–34]

I next address the question of causation. In my opinion, Mr. Otero's assault on Mrs. Paula was an expressive crime characterized by impulsivity and anger [citations to McCabe and Wauchope, 2005; Siegel, 2004, pp. 63, 124]. Otero was a substance abuser with mental health problems who knowingly engaged in a high-risk crime without particular regard for the consequences to himself or his victim. Otero's desperate emotional state was further suggested by his suicidality and the perception by arresting officers that Otero needed to be evaluated by mental health professionals before jailing him. Such an individual is not likely deterred by conventional security measures which suggest to the rational offender he should not commit an act because it is likely to bring him unpleasant consequences. It seems that Otero was more interested in venting his anger through sexual assault than worrying about his future.

This report would not be complete without comment on the overall security profile in place at the River Springs Mall on the evening of [the assault]. In my opinion, mall security was more than reasonable and violated no standards promulgated by the International Council of Shopping Centers or other relevant professional associations. CCC and mall management assigned three uniformed…police officers and eight security officers to patrol duty on the night in question. CCC Public Safety Officer Pierre [a pseudonym] was on duty in Zone 4 just down the main corridor from the family restroom hallway and … officers were nearby patrolling the AMC Theatres area.

There was CCTV coverage throughout the property, which itself was well lit. CCC also carried out frequent and random patrols. Even though there was no pattern of problems in the family restroom area, a CCC officer patrolled this area specifically as part of a patrol pattern, and a dedicated CCTV camera covered the family restroom waiting area. Housekeeping personnel also visited the restrooms on a regular basis. The family restrooms were only about forty feet off a main corridor and certainly within earshot of passersby. Finally, CCC training and record keeping practices are among the best in the industry and cannot reasonably be criticized as causal factors in the events of that evening.

An important lesson from the previous case is that forensic criminologists should understand the role of individual behavior in the cause of an injury, the efficacy of conventional security measures in preventing criminal events, and an offender's susceptibility to deterrence. One fundamental assumption of all security plans and activities—whether for apartments, parking lots, bars and taverns, hotels and shopping malls, among other premises—is that security measures can deter otherwise motivated offenders from committing crimes. This basic assumption is the foundation of rational choice/deterrence theories which posit that offenders are volitional and calculating. That is, would-be offenders weigh the anticipated costs of offending against the expected rewards and decide to offend when the benefits appear to be greater than the liabilities (Becker, 1968; Piliavin et al., 1986). From this cost–benefit standpoint, criminality is not a disposition but the result of purposeful, freely made decisions. Crime happens when offenders judge it to be profitable and pleasurable to do so. Generally, the greater the risks and costs of crime, the less likely a crime will happen.

Criminologists and security experts know that even the best designed, most sophisticated security operations can be and have been breached by highly motivated offenders that are not risk averse and are not swayed by ostensible threats of sanction. In his theorization of the "undeterred offender," Jacobs (2004, p. 19) argues that these "offenders are either undeterrable or so difficult to deter by conventional measures." They are "functionally undeterrable." These types of offenders are not dissuaded by risks of criminal acts because they are "impulsive, shortsighted, and focused on anticipated rewards rather than delayed consequences" (Jacobs and Cherbonneau, 2018, p. 181). The factors a criminologist might consider in whether a criminal could be deterred would be (1) whether the crime was planned or impulsive; (2) whether the criminal made efforts to conceal herself/himself; (3) whether there were bystanders; (4) whether the crime was part of a crime spree; (5) whether the perpetrator had a criminal record; (6) the perpetrator's mental state; and (7) whether the perpetrator was intoxicated.[4]

In the previous case, the evidence presented appears to reflect and reinforce the empirical applicability of the concept of the undeterred offender. When discussing causation, the forensic criminological report suggests that the assault was an expressive crime rather than an instrumental crime. Expressive crimes are violent acts that are not directed at the acquisition of anything tangible or designed to accomplish anything specific other than achieve a violent outcome. Instrumental crime, on the other hand, involves criminal behavior that has a specific, tangible goal. Criminologists have generally found the criminal who acts instrumentally to be more deterrable than one whose crimes tend to be expressive in nature (Nettler, 1989). In the previous case, it appears that the offender (Otero) was acting in an expressive manner and relegated the risk of committing a crime to the hinterlands of decision-making. He appears to have given little or no thought to the possibility of arrest and does not appear to have been deterred by existing guardianship or conventional security measures at the mall. Because an undeterred offender may not think about consequences before she or he acts—or think about consequences only to dismiss them—then she or he represents a major impediment and hindrance to security in the public realm. Nevertheless, it is important to remember that "absolute security" is an impossible and unobtainable goal. Thus a business owner, property manager, law enforcement officer, and security professional all face challenges both in responding to reasonably foreseeable criminal events and in responding to incidents committed by "undeterrable" offenders.

BARS AND TAVERNS

Over the decades, drinking establishments such as bars, taverns, and nightclubs have generated a great deal of litigation sparked by alcohol-fueled violence. Criminologists and other social and behavioral scientists have built a substantial literature on the relationship between alcohol and violence (Felson and Staff, 2010; Graham et al., 1996; Graham and Homel, 2008; Greenfield, 1998; Hughes et al., 2008; Lang et al., 1995; Saitz and Naimi, 2010), the unequal distribution of violence across drinking establishments (Madensen and Eck, 2008), and how to mitigate the alcohol–violence relationship in the hospitality industry (Berkley, 1997; McManus and O'Toole, 2004; Scott and Dedel, 2006). For example, the amount of aggression expressed in bars is partly a function of the level of aversive stimuli present (the "toxic environment" theory of barroom aggression). Aggressive behavior is a typical response to many forms of pain, threat, or extreme discomfort. Bars and nightclubs can create an atmosphere that stimulates aggression as a function of such characteristics as loud, thumping music, heat, flashing lights, excessive noise, smoke, poor ventilation, slow service, crowded lines for restrooms, intoxication, lack of seating, poor bar design leading to foot traffic chokepoints, counterflows of foot traffic, dancing in congested areas, and overcrowding (Boyatzis, 1981; Graham et al., 1980; Homel and Clark, 1994). Add to this mix the presence of young adult males who are strangers to each other, a sexually

---

[4]See *Perez v. DNT Global Star, LLC*, 339 SW 3d 692—Texas Court of Appeals (2011).

charged atmosphere, and a generally permissive managerial philosophy then interpersonal violence can become foreseeable (Quigley and Leonard, 2004/2005). Conditions of crime foreseeability do not happen by accident or serendipity. Rather, following the insights of Madensen and Eck (2008), place managers can create environments that suppress or facilitate violence through business-related choices and decision-making.

CASE EXAMPLE: STABBING IN A COLLEGE BAR/NIGHTCLUB

This case concerns the stabbing of a patron in a college bar. One evening, Sean Ryan (a pseudonym) and a group of other college football players were drinking and socializing at the P.W. Pub (a pseudonym). As Friday night turned into Saturday morning, Mr. Ryan struck up a conversation with a young lady who happened to be the girlfriend of pub patron James Nicholas (a pseudonym). Ryan and Nicholas exchanged words, which led to the sudden explosion of a pushing and punching match. The much smaller Nicholas stabbed Ryan in the neck with a pocketknife. Nicholas was subsequently convicted of this assaultive crime. Ryan believed faulty security at the P.W. Pub ultimately led to his injury and he initiated a lawsuit against the establishment's owners. The forensic criminologist was asked by the law firm retained by the defendant bar owners to opine on liability issues raised by the plaintiff in this case. The following materials were reviewed: the Complaint, employee incident reports and statements, the local county police department reports, Probable Cause Statement, newspaper articles, employee manual, dress codes, and miscellaneous criminal court documents. Also reviewed were the criminal trial transcripts and the depositions of eleven people, transcripts of jail conversations between Nicholas and his girlfriend, video camera footage of the incident, and the forensic report of the plaintiff's expert witness. The premises was also inspected one evening. According to excerpts from the forensic criminological investigation:

> The stabbing of Mr. Ryan was simply not foreseeable, whether assessed from an imminent harm, prior similar acts, or "totality of the circumstances" perspective. With regard to imminent harm or imminent danger, an analysis of P.W. Pub video recordings reveals what appears to be the plaintiff Mr. Ryan and his assailant Mr. Nicholas standing and talking at the bar. Suddenly there is some pushing, and Mr. Nicholas is observed swinging his arm toward Ryan's neck within the first few seconds of the altercation. Bartender Martin Dimitri [a pseudonym] had just served Mr. Ryan some drinks and was turning around to put the payment into the cash register. As he was turning back around with change, the fight suddenly erupted without any notice [citations to depositions of bartender and two security employees]. The video recording will speak for itself.
>
> In terms of prior similar incidents, it is my understanding that nobody had used weapons offensively on the premises in the memory of any employees [citations to deposition of security employee and security director]. None of the police CAD [computer-aided dispatch] reports revealed any history of weapons use. To be sure, there have been instances of disorderly behavior and, perhaps, the occasional shoving match, as one would expect in any bar where young men are drinking alcohol and competing for the attention of young women. Given that this establishment serves well over 100,000 patrons a year, the number of security incidents is notably small.

Industry Standard Opinions

Elaborating on a "totality of circumstances" perspective, this is a somewhat upscale bar with extensive food service. There is clean and attractive decor as the interior had been remodeled after a fire a few years ago. The importance of decor in setting the behavioral tone of a bar is found in the work of K. Graham and R. Homel, *Raising the Bar: Preventing Aggression in and Around Bars, Pubs, and Clubs* (Willan Publishing, 2008). Decor relates not only to foreseeability but also to standard of care.

The management of this establishment values its civic role and donates money to [the local] University's athletic program and food to [a local] breakfast program. Donations are offered to multiple charities, and fundraisers are held for a local school [citation to deposition of part-owner]. This is no "dive," "punch palace," or "fighting bar" where knife violence is to be predicted or foreseen. This is a college bar located in a reputable entertainment district in the heart of [the] downtown.

It is my opinion that the P.W. Pub met and exceeded applicable standards of care for the hospitality industry with particular regard to bars and/or nightclubs. Serving staff were trained in responsible alcohol service, and security personnel were trained in crowd control techniques. Security staff were also given on-the-job training and training from county police. Security personnel were selected based on past related experience and staff recommendations. Interpersonal relations and communication skills were preferred to muscle mass, and physical controls were to be used as a last measure. Bar security personnel were distributed throughout the facility and were closely supervised by [the] security manager…and [the] evening manager.

Security staff wore clearly marked clothing identifying themselves as security and were deployed in more than sufficient numbers to maintain surveillance and respond to potential incidents. After studying the duty roster for the night in question, [the security director] indicated 14 security personnel were on duty at the time of the incident. Even if the P.W. Pub was at full capacity of 600 (which it likely was not since security uses "counters" to keep crowd density down so as to allow fluid movement of security personnel), this would result in a ratio of one security person per 43 patrons. The New York Nightlife Association and the New York Police Department recommend one security person per 75 club patrons. In other words, the P.W. Pub had almost double the number of security personnel a reputable hospitality industry association called for after much study of the subject. See [New York Nightlife Association] *Best Practices for Nightlife Establishments* (2nd ed. 2011), available on the Internet.

Attesting to this fact is that, by my estimate, a security staff member had Nicholas under control within close to twenty seconds of his unforeseeable act of violence. I note also, with some irony, that security staff member Michael Anthony [a pseudonym] reacted with alacrity and helped stem the flow of blood from Mr. Ryan's wounds (yet security staff are portrayed in this litigation as ineffective).

Other recommended practices in place at P.W. Pub include maintenance of a posted dress code, limiting access points into the venue, forming strong relationships with local police officers, and training all employees (not just security personnel) to keep eyes and ears open for trouble and to report immediately. Should any trouble develop, the DJ was expected to use the PA system to call for security after cutting the music. Also, an ID scanner was in use at the door, lines forming outside were closely scrutinized for potential troublemakers, and security team members met at the end of each night to assess the efficacy of their practices during the evening…IDs were checked carefully at the door. Approximately 48 CCTV cameras were deployed throughout the premises, and all security personnel were at their posts and in sufficient numbers when this incident occurred.

Causation Opinions

Even if one assumes that some action or inaction of P.W. Pub preceded the injury suffered by Mr. Ryan, the issue of proximate cause must be addressed. Had there been an intervening act on Mr. Ryan's part which broke the causal chain between P.W. Pub's actions or inactions and Ryan's subsequent injuries? Ultimately, this will be a factual issue to be resolved elsewhere rather than in the pages of this report. There is evidence, however, that Mr. Ryan took the first offensive or aggressive actions directed at the much smaller Mr. Nicholas leading to Nicholas's illegal overreaction and, thus, to his conviction and incarceration.

It is not unusual for an individual to initiate a series of events which lead to his own injury. In other words, one whose actions start a fight can often be a victim of his own aggression. The classic criminological study of this phenomenon is Marvin Wolfgang, "Victim Precipitated Criminal Homicide," *Journal of Criminal Law, Criminology, and Police* Science 48 (1957) 1–11. In his study of 588 criminal homicides, in 150, or 26 percent of these cases, the ultimate victim initiated the aggression.

For example, bartender Martin Dimitri recalls seeing Mr. Ryan grab Mr. Nicholas and start shoving him. Nicholas and his friend, Ed Nelson [a pseudonym], also claim that Ryan was the first to become physically, if not verbally, aggressive. Nicholas's girlfriend, Melanie Ashner [a pseudonym], stated to police that Ryan "grabbed Nicholas around the shoulders." These observations were recorded by police interviewers. Even Ryan states he tapped Nicholas on the shoulder twice because Nicholas was invading his space, and he, Ryan, then shoved him. Let me reiterate that I have no opinion as to the veracity of any of these statements as experts do not opine on witness credibility. Furthermore, even if Ryan's actions constituted the initial physical aggression, Nicholas's response was clearly excessive, even given the size imbalance, and should not have involved the use of potentially deadly force against Ryan.

One important lesson from this case is the importance of investigating a premises' security plan, training components of the security plan, and identifying applicable industry standards (Bates and Frank, 2010, pp. 204–5). Some commercial facilities may employ security guards, so the guards' quality and training often are important issues in a case. Guards can be armed or unarmed and uniformed or dressed in plain clothes, and their numbers and deployment plans vary greatly. Many states offer certification programs for guards, but their requirements run the gamut—some states certify guards after only a background check. Other states require extensive training. When a commercial facility such as bar or shopping mall employs security guards, the issue shifts from whether there was a need for them to how adequate their performance was.

ASIS International recommends that training for security personnel include such topics as use of force, evidence preservation, powers of arrest, criminal law, patrol techniques, and safeguarding proprietary information (see ASIS International, Protection of Assets (POA), *Security Officer Operations*). ASIS International recommends several published standards including *Security and Resilience in Organizations and their Supply Chains—Requirements with Guidance* (ORM.1); *Security Management Standard: Physical Asset Protection* (PAP); *Management System for Quality of Private Security Company Operations—Requirements with Guidance* (PSC.1). Doormen and concierges do not receive such training, nor do they expect to. Liability can be predicated on a commercial facility's lack of adequate procedures as well as its failure to comply with its own standards, even when they are sufficient on their face.

Like the case we discussed earlier on the murder of a shopper by a homeless man, the previous case addresses both cause-in-fact and proximate causation. Importantly, causation "need not be demonstrated by conclusive proof establishing that specific additional safeguards would have prevented the crime. It is sufficient for the plaintiff to prove that it is more probable than not that the crime was the result of the negligent failure to provide security" (Leesfield and Peltz, 2013, pp. 1–2). Some courts have articulated the rule by stating that the guest may recover if he or she can simply prove that the negligence "unreasonably enhanced" the risk of injury due to criminal activity.[5]

If we apply these insights to the previous case, it is difficult to interpret the security operations of the bar as enhancing the risk of injury to patrons in general. With regard to supervision, the bar personnel appeared to be very "hands on" and constantly circulating throughout the pub to ensure that things were running smoothly. All employees had a clear post assignment, there was a dress code for patrons, security personnel wore clearly marked clothing, IDs were checked at the door, and inebriates were not allowed to enter. The parking lot was well lit, comprehensive food service was provided throughout the night, alcoholic drinks were premeasured, there was often a cover charge to encourage responsible patronage, and security staffing was increased if a larger customer count was anticipated.

CASE EXAMPLE: STABBING AND MURDER OUTSIDE OF A SPORTS BAR

This case concerns the stabbing death of Kevin O'Neil (a pseudonym) by Dan Vincent (a pseudonym) in a parking lot outside of Big Belly's Sports Bar and Grill (a pseudonym) one night at about 8:10 p.m. Verbal conflict inside the bar between the two men had been escalating for several minutes, likely because of Dan Vincent's hostile and unsportsmanlike behavior triggered by his disappointment over the results of a televised football game. After a series of verbal exchanges, O'Neil left the bar, whereupon Vincent followed him outside and murdered him in the parking lot.

The forensic criminologist was asked by counsel for the plaintiffs to evaluate whether a violent crime directed at a bar patron was a foreseeable event at Big Belly's on the evening in question. The following materials were reviewed: depositions of eleven individuals, the complete city police department investigation with multiple witness statements, internal documents from Big Belly's, numerous city police department incident reports, criminal prosecution documents, autopsy report, camera and cell phone recordings, and pertinent criminological literature cited in the forensic report. The premises was inspected one morning and one evening. Below are excerpts from the forensic criminological investigation.

> **Foreseeability Under a "Totality of Circumstances" Test**
> As a general proposition, many bars can be described as "risky facilities" [citation to Clarke and Eck, 2007] based on violent confrontations or unacceptable drunken behavior which often takes place in and around them [citations to Scott and Dedel, 2006; Roncek and Maier, 1991]. The relationship between alcohol consumption and violence is sufficiently well established even though explanations may vary. The most concise explanation of causal relationships is K. Graham, "Aggression and Barroom Environments" *Journal of Studies in Alcohol* 41 (1980) 468–485. A unique twist in this case, however, is that Big Belly's is a "sports bar;" and the killer, Dan Vincent, can be reasonably described as a highly excitable and aggressive "sports fan."

---

[5]See e.g. *Nebel v. Avichal Enters., Inc.*, 704 F. Supp. 570, 577 (D.N.J. 1989) (quoting *Brahman v. Overlook Terrace Corp.*, 346 A.2d 76, 84 (N.J. 1975)).

While most sports fans behave appropriately for the setting, there is a subgroup described as "highly identified dysfunctional fans" who can become loud, obnoxious, angry, and physically aggressive toward others if they are displeased with their team's progress [citation to Wakefield and Wann, 2006]. They also tend to drink too much and can be fairly described as bullies [citations to Courtney and Wann, 2010; Nelson and Weschler, 2001, 2003]. This would certainly be an apt description of Dan Vincent's behavior on the night he murdered Mr. O'Neil. More will be said about Mr. Vincent's behavior in the next section of this report.

Given the nature of many bars in general and of sports bars in particular, it is instructive to look at the history of police activities at, nearby, or otherwise generated by the Big Belly's Sports Bar and Grill. There were a total of 352 calls-for-service during the years 2006–2008 [at the intersection where the bar is located]. While the records will not allow me to conclude these calls were all related to Big Belly's, as doubtless they were not, at least four involved fights and/or arguments. A review of police narrative incident reports revealed a major fight involving seven men around the pool table at Big Belly's on September 28, 2006.

More telling than formal police reports, however, are the employees' descriptions of customer behavior, including: starting fights with bouncers, customer slapping customer, threats of battery, insults to staff, manhandling staff, obnoxious behavior, loitering outside, overservice, fights with pool sticks, theft from table tops, stealing drinks from other customers, and fighting outside on the sidewalk. This sampling of events is taken from internal managers' logs, Big Belly's guest incident reports, handwritten reports, and "note to file" documents. Given the nature of this bar and the behaviors just described, it is not difficult to conclude that a violent act was generally foreseeable at this location.

Foreseeability Under an "Imminent Harm" Test

Even notwithstanding past behavior at this bar, given Dan Vincent's behavior on the night in question and, to a certain extent, O'Neil's initial reaction to Vincent, a violent altercation should have been foreseeable to Bully's staff under an "imminent harm" analysis. According to various depositions and witness statements, Dan Vincent was drunk or "high on something," acting obnoxiously, "acting crazy and incoherent," "drunk and out of control" [deposition of Cindy Waterfield (a pseudonym)]. Particularly telling are the statements made to police by witness Adam Michaels [a pseudonym], who was consternated to see [bar manager] Donald Robertson [a pseudonym] allow Dan Vincent to "bend him over the bar" and "scream in his face like that" [citation to Michael's witness statement to … police department, p. 11] … Bar management is expected to set the tone for an establishment. If Vincent could get away with bullying manager Robertson so easily, he would have reason to believe he could do what he wanted with impunity [citations to Madensen and Eck, 2008; Graham et al., 2005].

[U]ltimately, Vincent engaged in name calling (e.g., "bitch") directed at O'Neil. Name calling rapidly degenerates into violence. By this time, violence was foreseeable. It should be noted that this kind of altercation tends to escalate in somewhat predictable phases, which would often allow for effective managerial intervention at various points [citation to Luckenbill, 1977]. Unfortunately, no such effective intervention was forthcoming either from bar manager Robertson or bartender John Mosgrove [a pseudonym]. Finally, when O'Neil left the bar and Vincent got up and followed him outside shortly thereafter, it was again foreseeable that violence would ensue.

In sum, the forensic criminological report opines that a crime of violence was foreseeable based not only on a "totality of the circumstances" test but also on an "imminent harm" analysis. Failure to detect readily audible or visual signs of a developing altercation can lead to liability on the part of a liquor or gaming establishment (Kennedy, 2013). In other words, if bar or casino security personnel were, or should have been, in a position to detect signs of an escalation of threats and yet failed to intervene, then a strong case could be made that they were on notice of an imminent danger to patrons. Obviously, if an establishment is so overcrowded that monitoring is difficult and getting to the scene of a dispute even more so, then a liability argument also exists.

Even if security intervenes in a dispute in a timely fashion, the standard of care has evolved from the days when a bartender could simply declare, "Take it outside!" It is now more appropriate for security personnel to separate combatants, isolate them from each other, and evict them through different doors at different times. The idea, of course, is to take reasonable steps to discourage the fight from reigniting outside on the premises of the business. A landholder's obligation to an invitee does not automatically end when she or he walks out the door but generally when she or he leaves the property altogether. Where the assailant was in fact ejected, it will be important for the defendant to show that it fully ejected the assailant from its premises or areas over which it had control.[6]

The previous points concerning bars and taverns have implications for premises security at other commercial facilities. In some cases, a landholder may be expected to provide reasonable security where many guests are known to park even if such parking area is not owned by the principal landholder (Zinober, 2015). In fact, a landowner may be held liable for an injury occurring to a patron on adjacent property not owned by the landowner.[7] In the 1990s, Florida adopted a "foreseeable zone of risk" standard, under which the courts will inquire as to whether the landowner has created a foreseeable zone of risk beyond the boundaries of his property. If so, the landowner may be liable for injuries to invitees that occur off the premises (Lopez, 2000).

In a recent case, the Georgia Supreme Court reinstated a $35 million jury award given to a young man left permanently brain damaged after a beating he received while waiting for a bus after visiting Six Flags Over Georgia.[8] The court held that Six Flags could not escape liability simply because an attack that originated on Six Flags property was completed off property. In essence, this case recognizes that a "landlord's liability for an invitee's injuries from an attack that originates on the premises does not dissipate as soon as the invitee steps – or flees – off the property, so long as the invitee's injuries were proximately caused by the landlord's failure to exercise ordinary care in maintaining safety and security within its premises and approaches ... [A]lthough the landowner's duty is to maintain safety and security within its premises and approaches, liability may arise from a breach of that duty

---

[6]See *St. Phillips v. O'Donnell*, 137 Ill. App. 3d 639, 92 Ill. Dec. 354, 484 N.E.2d 1209 (2d Dist. 1985) (defendant who ejected unruly patron prior to assault acted reasonably under circumstances and, thus, was not liable for the plaintiff's injuries). See, for example, *Mata v. Mata*, 105 Cal. App. 4th 1121, 130 Cal. Rptr. 2d 141 (1st Dist. 2003), as modified, (Feb. 6, 2003) and review denied, (Apr. 23, 2003) (defendant did not exercise reasonable care in only excluding gunman from the interior of tavern; defendant owed the plaintiffs a duty to remove the gunman from the business premises, which included an exterior parking lot used by the tavern's patrons).
[7]See *Holiday Inns, Inc. v. Shelburne*, 576 So. 2d 322—Fla: Dist. Court of Appeals, 4th Dist. 1991 (finding Holiday Inns liable for death of bar invitee even though the incident did not take place on the hotel's property) (for an overview of this case, see Warner, 1991).
[8]*Martin v. Six Flags Over Georgia II*, LP, 801 SE 2d 24—Ga: Supreme Court 2017.

that proximately causes injuries even if the resulting injury ultimately is completed beyond that territorial sphere."[9] Other jurisdictions have followed this principle.[10]

CONCLUSION

Criminal events develop over time and at specific places (Felson and Steadman, 1983) as targets concentrate in a particular area and offenders realize new opportunities to victimize. As Felson (1987, p. 913) argued, potential offenders become aware of opportunities for crime in the general areas in which their routine activities take place. Over the decades, much criminological research has demonstrated that areas that generally suffer from high crime rates also tend to be areas that have high levels of repeat victimization, suggesting that chronic victimization can be one of the driving forces behind area-level crime risk (Johnson et al., 1997; for a comprehensive overview, see Weisburd et al., 2016, pp. 1–41). Chronic victimization in a particular area or place suggests the presence of socio-spatial conditions that generate and reproduce crime opportunities.

Criminologists have proposed two theories to explain patterns of repeat victimization. The first theory, flag theory, suggests that committing a crime allows the offender to learn information about the area that, in turn, enhances the vulnerability of the area. Burglars breaking into a house may become familiar with the weaknesses of neighboring houses and then use this information to burglarize more homes in the area. According to Bowers and Johnson (2004, p. 12), certain properties and their surrounding characteristics (e.g., disorder) "effectively advertise their vulnerability" which attracts opportunistic offenders. In this way, burglaries that occur at the same location are considered to be independent events, with the only thing in common being the property that criminals target. Second, boost theory suggests that repeat victimization is the consequence of a contagion-like process. If a home has been burgled on one occasion, the risk to the home is boosted, most likely because offenders will return to exploit good opportunities further (e.g., to steal replaced items or those left behind). Both

---

[9]*Martin v. Six Flags Over Georgia II*, LP, 801 SE 2d 24—Ga: Supreme Court 2017. *Id* at 31. See also *Double View Ventures, LLC v. Polite*, 326 Ga.App. 555, 560 (1), 757 S.E.2d 172 (2014) (where criminal attack took place along footpath between apartment complex and gas station, both apartment complex owner and gas station owner could be liable for their respective failures to provide adequate security, regardless of the precise location of the attack). See *Wilks*, 207 Ga.App. at 843, 429 S.E. 2d 322. See also, e.g., *Silva v. Spohn Health Sys. Corp.*, 951 S.W.2d 91 (Tex. Ct. App. 1997) (mere fact that appellant "had stepped across the imaginary line" separating appellee's property and public sidewalk did not as a matter of law remove appellant "from the ambit of appellee's duty").

[10]See, e.g., *Reynolds v. CB Sports Bar, Inc.*, 623 F.3d 1143, 1152 (7th Cir. 2010) (applying Illinois law, holding that sports bar owner could be held liable in connection with attempted criminal attack on bar patron more than a mile away from bar if bartender knew of plan to sexually exploit the plaintiff off-premises); *Osborne v. Stages Music Hall, Inc.*,312 Ill.App.3d 141, 244 Ill. Dec. 753, 726 N.E.2d 728, 733–34 (2000) (reversing directed verdict in favor of bar owner, holding that owner could be liable to bar patron for injuries sustained in assault on sidewalk outside bar's premises); *Silva v. Spohn Health Sys. Corp.*, 951 S.W.2d 91 (Tex. Ct. App. 1997) (reversing summary judgment, holding that hospital could be held liable for employee-invitee's injuries sustained when she was stabbed as she was entering an automobile on an adjacent street after leaving work); *Schneider v. Nectarine Ballroom, Inc.*, 204 Mich.App. 1, 514 N.W.2d 486, 488–489 (1994) (reversing summary disposition, holding that bar owner could be liable for injuries sustained by patron when altercation inside bar resumed outside bar after patron was ejected "into the waiting arms" of his assailants); *Udy v. Calvary Corp.*, 162 Ariz. 7, 780 P.2d 1055, 1060 (Ariz. Ct. App. 1989) (reversing summary judgment, holding that landlord could be liable for injuries sustained outside the premises if such injuries were reasonably foreseeable result of its negligence in operating the premises).

flag theory and boost theory recognize the importance of offender awareness or actual notice which refers to disorderly or criminal conduct which has already occurred at the property in question. Actual notice refers to historical fact or the basic "track record" for the general neighborhood or for the specific site. Actual notice is important to criminologists because the best forecaster of future crime events is past crime events. To determine what is likely to happen in the future, one looks at what has happened in the past, particularly the immediate past (Nettler, 1989).

An offender's decision to select a target is not a simple product of "opportunities" that offenders may discover or take advance of as they move through the built environment. Rather, the decision-making that goes into target selection involves a cacophony of practical and normative judgments that are contingent and context specific. Criminologists such as Jacobs (2010), Bennett and Wright (1984), and Topalli and Wright (2004) have developed the concepts *alert opportunism, motivated opportunism*, and *serendipity* to explain the dynamic interplay between risk, criminal desire and need, and criminogenic opportunity. *Alert opportunism* refers to offenders who face needs that are present but not necessarily pressing. Offenders are not desperate, "but they anticipate need in the near term and become increasingly open to opportunities that may present themselves during the course of their day-to-day activities" (Topalli and Wright, 2004, pp. 156–7). Criminologists have developed and applied the concept of *motivated opportunism* to describe criminal needs that are, or soon will be, acute. Attention and openness to possibilities can allow offenders to tolerate more risk. Based on goal seeking, opportunity taking, and rational planning, situations that previously seemed unsuitable for crime start to look better (Topalli and Wright, 2004, p. 157). According to Jacobs (2010), *serendipity* can be manufactured in probabilistic ways, and this manufacturing process need not flow from desperation or truncated rationality. Indeed, offenders "construct criminal opportunity by comparing recently formulated understandings [against] developing events and adjusting situations to make events and understanding correspond" (Hochstetler, 2001, 2002, pp. 747, 756). By definition, uncertain events rarely occur in predictable frequencies, but emergent cues can be recognized, processed, and manipulated for productive ends. Serendipity hinges on the interplay of agency and constraint. When action and receptivity interact in such a way, favorable outcomes result from unexpected and even negative events.

The previous insights inform our forensic criminological work and help to demonstrate the ways in which criminal actions connect with changing criminogenic opportunities. A major lesson of our analysis is that place management actions and decisions can explain a great deal of the presence or absence of criminal events at a particular facility, a finding that corroborates long-standing criminological research. Place management refers to the "care with which a person in charge of a facility takes in its upkeep and management" (Weisburd et al., 2016, p. 38; Eck and Wartell, 1997). Place managers can include a wide range of individuals such as sales clerks, front office workers, doormen, apartment managers, and business owners. Place managers are not the same as security managers. The latter are people who "manage security systems, policies, procedures. Security personnel can include the chief security officer (CSO), vice president of security, security director, chief of security, account manager, security supervisor and post commander" (ASIS International, 2009a, p. 33). Place managers are akin to guardians whereas security managers have specialized roles and delimited responsibilities that are typically regulated by local ordinances and state laws. Security managers or personnel implement, monitor, and maintain physical security measures. Several ASIS International documents address roles and responsibilities of security personnel. These documents include: ASIS CSO.1–2008, *Chief Security Officer (CSO) Organizational Standard*; *Chief Security Officer (CSO) Guideline*; *Workplace Violence Prevention and Intervention*; and *Private Security Officer (PSO) Selection and Training Guideline*.

Keeping commercial facilities safe and secure can be difficult without well-organized place management. Place management decision-making and business-related choices can create environments that suppress or facilitate crime. Madensen (2007) describes four basic features of place management: organization of space, regulation of conduct, control of access, and acquisitions of resources. These place management functions suggest several important reasons why some places are more criminogenic than others: poor organization of space, failed or inept regulation of conduct; lack of control of access or permitting access to the wrong clientele; mismanagement of resources (fraud); and the inability to garner resources to support general business operations.

Place management actions can influence, regulate, and control how offenders, targets, and others meet in time and space. As Weisburd and colleagues (2016, p. 50) note, place managers "often influence routines (e.g., opening and closing times) of places and the guardianship at places." Place managers' guardianship decisions can influence both the physical and social arrangements at places, provide incentives or disincentives for offender contact with targets, and influence offenders' risks of apprehension. CPTED can be particularly applicable to regulating the actions of offenders and potential targets because of its principles of natural surveillance, access control, and territoriality (i.e., sense of control over an environment) (Kennedy, 1993). That said, CPTED must be applied by place managers if its basic features are to be effective in reducing crime. That is, CPTED is less likely to be effective in the absence of place managers acting as capable guardians.

Place managers can play an important role in establishing a sense of ownership to assist legitimate occupants or users become vigilant observers and controllers of space. To quote the ASIS International (2009a, p. 7) *Facilities Physical Security Measures Guideline*, "the theory is that people will pay more attention to and defend a particular space or territory from trespass if they feel a form of 'psychological ownership' in the area. Thus, it is possible—through real or symbolic markers—to encourage tenants or employees to defend property from incursion." Criminal events can proliferate in spaces that occupants and users do not claim as members or guardians. CPTED suggests adding enticements and incentives to draw legitimate users to a space to engage in noncriminal activities. Legitimate activities can undermine or replace criminal activities by pushing out undesirable and illegitimate users of the space.

Place managers can be key agents in reducing opportunities for crime at places through changes in staff, training activities, and other business decisions. The criminological literature suggests that patron characteristics can increase or decrease the likelihood of violence at bars. The patrons that frequent particular bars are not attracted there by accident or happenstance. Rather, place management decisions shape and influence what kinds of patrons attend the bar. A college bar that offers cheap drinks, has a reputation for admitting underage patrons, and hosts a "hip hop" night with dancing will likely attract a large group of intoxicated young men. These conditions suggest that the bar may be at greater risk of violence when compared with a hybrid bar-restaurant that serves expensive food and drinks and caters to more mature patrons. Previous studies confirm the relationship between violence and staff, training, and security (Homel and Clark, 1994). Violence is more likely to occur in bars where the staff are aggressive or poorly trained (Homel et al., 1992), lack professional boundaries (Graham et al., 2006), or are mostly male (Quigley et al., 2003).

Several prominent researchers including Eck and Eck (2012), Felson (1995), Mazerolle and colleagues (1998), and Madensen and Eck (2008) have contributed insights on the role of place managers as potentially important elements in guardianship. Bar staff can discourage potential troublemakers from frequenting the establishment if staff are successful in effectively responding to problems and neutralizing potentially violent situations before they escalate. Responsible alcohol service training programs, bartender and doorman training, and an understanding of the pejorative influences of toxic environments (heat, noise, smoke, crowding) have all been helpful in reducing violence among bar patrons (Graham and Homel, 2008; Graham et al., 2006; Roberts, 2007; Graham, 1999; McManus and O'Toole, 1994; Roberts, 2009; Scott and Dedel, 2006). The finding that business choices, place management decisions, and policies of a commercial facility can affect the propensity of criminal events also resonates with other commercial environments and facilities, including schools (Gottfredson et al., 2002), convenience stores (White and Muldoon, 2015), and parks (Madensen, 2007).

ADMINISTRATIVE NEGLIGENCE, VICARIOUS LIABILITY, AND THE DOCTRINE OF *RESPONDEAT SUPERIOR*

8

INTRODUCTION

In this chapter, we examine expert witness reports in cases involving administrative negligence which is the liability of an employer for his or her own intentional or negligent conduct regarding the hiring, retaining, training, or supervising of an employee. Administrative negligence or direct liability follows a general rule that one is liable only for one's own actions and not for the actions of others. Vicarious liability, a form of secondary or indirect liability, refers to a situation where someone is held responsible for the actions or omissions of another person (Rottenstein Law Group LLP, 2018; Pastor, 2007, pp. 300–301). In a workplace context, an employer can be liable for the acts or omissions of his or her employees, provided it can be shown that these actions took place in the course of their employment. Courts often apply vicarious liability to an employer–employee relationship, but it can also apply to other situations where a superior is held responsible for the acts of a subordinate. The doctrine of vicarious liability has a long history in western jurisprudence and has been a major element in the U.S. tort system for decades (Epstein and Sharkey, 2016; Schwartz, 1996). Lawsuits initiated by third parties against employers for injuries caused by employees are among the most common civil lawsuits in the United States (Roszkowski and Roszkowski, 2005, p. 235).

One type of vicarious liability is *respondeat superior* which, in personal injury tort cases, means "let the master answer."[1] When respondeat superior applies, an employer may be liable for an employee's negligent actions or omissions that occur during employment. The test for respondeat superior liability is derived in most states from section 219(1) of the American Law Institute's Restatement (Second) of Agency: "A master is subject to liability for the torts of his servants committed while acting in the scope of their employment" (American Law Institute, 1965). The "scope of employment" standard typically includes "those acts which relate to the employee's duties according to his or her job description and those activities and methods used to carry out the objectives of the employment" (Camacho, 1993, p. 787). At the same time, "scope of employment" is an imprecise term and courts have usually resolved questions about its nature through an evaluation of factual details on a case-by-case basis (Roszkowski and Roszkowski, 2005, pp. 234–238).

---

[1]Respondeat superior is also known as the "master-servant" rule and U.S. courts have imported the doctrine from the English common law. See *Bosh v. Cherokee County Bldg. Authority*, 305 P. 3d 994—Okla: Supreme Court 2013 (noting that respondeat superior is a common law doctrine).

Over the decades, courts have expanded the reach of administrative negligence to permit employers to be held liable for third-party injuries resulting from the intentional acts of their employees. Courts may hold an employer responsible "even when the injurious acts are committed *outside* the scope of the employment relationship if a *special relationship* exists between the injured parties and the employer" (Camacho, 1993, p. 790, emphasis in original). Today, this relationship includes licensees, invitees, and customers. Whereas respondeat superior focuses upon the conduct of the employee, negligence actions, in contrast, focus on the action or inaction of the employer. "An employer can be held liable if an employee's actions are outside of the scope of employment if the employer, itself, committed negligence. In a negligence action, plaintiffs typically argue that there is a causal link between the employer's negligence in employment and the subsequent violence" (Whitten and Mosley, 2000, p. 516).

In short, the doctrine of respondeat superior is based on the theory that the employee is the agent of, or is acting for, the employer. "Therefore, the scope of employment limitation on liability which is a part of the respondeat superior doctrine is not implicit in the wrong of negligent hiring."[2] In addition, unlike claims brought under respondeat superior, suits for administrative negligence can "expose the employer to punitive damages if there was gross negligence or recklessness in hiring an employee" (Scott, 1987, p. 24; quoted in Camacho, 1993, p. 792, footnote 24). "Allegations must reveal a connection between the employment and the plaintiff sufficient to establish a legal duty on the part of the employer to the plaintiff or establish that the plaintiff was within the zone of foreseeable risks created by the employment. A special relationship will fulfill this duty requirement" (Camacho, 1993, p. 790, footnote 12).

The notion of administrative negligence directs the forensic criminologist to investigate whether the employer exercised due care when hiring, training, retaining, supervising, or entrusting an employee. Over the decades, courts have referred to Section 213 (Principal Negligence or Recklessness) of the American Law Institute's Restatement (Second) of Agency as authority for administrative negligence causes of action:

> A person conducting an activity through servants or other agents is subject to liability for harm resulting from his conduct if he is negligent or reckless: (a) in giving improper or ambiguous orders or in failing to make proper regulations; or (b) in the employment of improper persons or instrumentalities in work involving risk of harm to others; or (c) in the supervision of the activity; or (d) in permitting, or failing to prevent, negligent or other tortious conduct by persons, whether or not his servants or agents upon premises or with instrumentalities under his control.

Section 213 encompasses not only the doctrine of negligent hiring, but also the related negligent retention, negligent supervision and training, and negligent entrustment causes of action.

When determining whether an employer is liable for the acts of an employee, some states will consider whether the tortious act was: (1) primarily employment rooted, (2) reasonably incidental to the

---

[2]*Di Cosala v. Kay,* 450 A.2d 508, 515 (N.J. 1982). "Accordingly, the negligent hiring theory has been used to impose liability in cases where the employee commits an intentional tort, an action almost invariably outside the scope of employment, against the customer of a particular employer or other member of the public, where the employer either knew or should have known that the employee was violent or aggressive, or that the employee might engage in injurious conduct toward third persons" (*Hersh v. Kentfield Builders, Inc.,* 385*Mich.* 410, 189 *N.W.*2d 286, 288 (1971); *LaLone v. Smith,* 39 *Wash.*2d 167, 234*P.*2d 893 (1951); *Priest v. F.W. Woolworth Five & Ten Cent Store,* 228 *Mo. App.* 23, 62 *S.W.*2d 926 (1933)).

BOX 8.1 TYPES OF ADMINISTRATIVE NEGLIGENCE

Negligent Hiring: A claim for negligent hiring "is based on the principle that an employer is liable for the harm resulting from its employee's negligent acts in the employment of improper persons or instrumentalities in work involving risk of harm to other" (Kittling, 2010, p. 1). Employers have a duty of reasonable care in screening individuals who, when hired, may pose a threat of injury to fellow employees, members of the public, or the workplace in general. Negligent hiring claims against employers can stem from a variety of crimes and injuries caused by employees including murder, sexual assault, injury, and property loss.

Negligent Training: An employer can be liable to the public for the harmful acts of employees if the employer fails to use reasonable care in training and supervising employees. Negligent training claims can arise from cases of false arrest and use of force.

Negligent Assignment/Entrustment: Negligent assignment is assigning an employee to a job without ascertaining his or her competence or retaining an employee on a job who is known to be incapable of performing the job. Negligent entrustment involves the employer's failure to properly supervise or control an employee's custody, use, or supervision of equipment or facilities entrusted to him or her. Negligent entrustment goes beyond employee incompetence in carrying out his/her duties to incompetence in the use of equipment entrusted to the employee.

Negligent Retention: Negligent retention occurs when an existing employee behaves badly on the job and is inadequately disciplined, thus encouraging more bad behavior, or is not fired even though the gravity of his or her act clearly called for his or her termination. The major difference between negligent hiring and negligent retention "is the time at which the employer is charged with knowledge of the employee's unfitness. Negligent retention occurs when, during the course of employment, the employer becomes aware or should have become aware of problems with an employee that indicated his unfitness, and the employer fails to take further action, such as investigation, discharge, or reassignment" (Kittling, 2010, p. 7; Whitten and Mosley, 2000, p. 527; see also *Garcia v. Duffy*, 492 So. 2d 435, 438–439 (Fla. Dist. Ct. App. 2d Dist. 1986)).

Negligent Supervision: Negligent supervision encompasses an employer's failure to reasonably control or monitor the actions taken by his or her employees. In some states, negligent training is a variant of negligent supervision. In other states, the law recognizes negligent supervision as a separate and distinct theory in addition to theories of negligent hiring and negligent retention (*Anspach v. Tomkins Industries, Inc.*, 817 F. Supp. 1499, 1519–1520 (D. Kan. 1993); *Kansas State Bank & Tr. Co. v. Specialized Transportation Services, Inc.*, 249 Kan. 348, 819 P.2d 587 (1981)). In Kansas, for example, negligent supervision includes not only the failure to supervise but also the failure to control persons with whom the defendant has a special relationship, including the defendant's employees or persons with dangerous propensities (See *Nero v. Kansas State University*, 253 Kan. 567, 861 P.2d 768 (1993); *J. W. v. State*, 253 Kan. 1, 853 P.2d 4 (1993)).

Negligent Failure to Direct: involves the failure of an employer to establish and promulgate clear policies and procedures to guide the actions of employees.

Negligent Referral: Negligent referral occurs when an employer provides an employee with a good character reference in order to rid itself of her/him even though the employee may be dangerous to others.

Source: Kennedy, D.B., 2014. Evolving practice parameters of forensic criminology. In: Morewitz, S.J., Goldstein, M.L. (Eds.), Handbook of Forensic Sociology and Psychology. Springer, New York, NY, pp. 1–27; Whitten, A.D., Mosley, D.M., 2000. Caught in the crossfire: employers' liability for workplace violence. Mississippi L. J. 70, 505–555.

performance of the employee's duties, (3) occurred on the employer's premises, and (4) occurred during hours of employment (American Law Institute, 1965). "If the purpose of serving the employer's business actuates the employee to any appreciable extent, the employer is liable."[3] Box 8.1 provides a description of seven types of administrative negligence that a plaintiff might allege in an injury case: negligent hiring, training, assignment/entrustment, retention, supervision, failure to direct, and referral. These seven types are heterogeneous and are not inclusive of all the examples of administrative negligence.

---

[3]*Bourgeois v. Allstate Ins. Co.*, 820 So. 2d 1132, 1136 (La. App. 5 Cir. 2002).

As with all negligence claims, the claimant must prove four elements of a tort: (1) that the defendant (in this case, the employer) owed the plaintiff a duty of care, (2) that this duty was breached, (3) that there was a causal relationship between the harm suffered and the breach of the employer's duty, and (4) that the plaintiff suffered harm/damages. In evaluating proximate cause, the courts will consider whether injury to the plaintiff was a reasonably foreseeable consequence of the breach of duty.[4] Most states follow the rule set forth in the American Law Institute's Restatement (Second) of Agency Section 213 that liability for various types of administrative negligence (hiring, retention, supervision, etc.) "requires evidence that the employer knew or reasonably should have known of the employee's propensity to engage in the type of conduct that caused the plaintiff's injury."[5]

Importantly, foreseeability is a key element of any claim of administrative negligence and vicarious liability. "It is not necessary that the employer foresee the particular injury that occurred, but only that the employer reasonably foresee an appreciable risk of harm to others."[6] According to Connecticut courts, "defendants cannot be held liable for their alleged negligent hiring, training, supervision or retention of an employee accused of wrongful conduct unless they had notice of said employee's propensity for the type of behavior causing the plaintiff's harm."[7] In New York, a claim for negligent hiring or retention can arise when an employer places an employee in a position to cause foreseeable harm, that is, harm which the injured party most probably would have been spared had the employer taken reasonable care in supervising or retaining the employee. An essential element of these causes of action is the notion of constructive knowledge, that is, that the employer knew or should have known of the employee's propensity for the conduct that caused the injury.[8] As Massachusetts courts have argued, "[e]ssentially, the issue is one of foreseeability: is the information about the employee that is or should have been known to the employer of such a character that a reasonable person in the employer's shoes would have reasonably foreseen a risk of the general type of harm that ultimately did occur?" (Kittling, 2010, p. 14). To address a claim for administrative negligence and vicarious liability, courts may ask whether the employee's act was "foreseeable" in the sense that it was a predictable risk, was facilitated by employment, or was an outgrowth or outcome of the employment.

In the following sections, we analyze several expert witness reports to explain how a forensic criminologist might address issues related to breach of duty, violation of standards of care, and causation related to administrative negligence claims. In cases of administrative negligence, the forensic criminologist can focus analytical attention on whether an organization played a causal role in creating opportunities that may have facilitated or encouraged the criminal act. Thus, the starting point of the analysis of claims regarding administrative negligence and vicarious liability is the organization, rather than the individual actor or offender "a reflection of the fact that modern-day vicarious liability is

---

[4]*Cramer v. Housing Opportunities Com.*, 304 Md. 705, 712–713 (Md. 1985); *Sigler v. Kobinsky*, 2008 WI App 183 (Wis. Ct. App. 2008).

[5]*Herron v. Morton*, 155 Fed.Appx. 423, 425–426 (11th Cir. 2005); see also *Munroe v. Universal Health Servs., Inc.*, 596 S. E.2d. 604, 606 (Ga. 2004).

[6]*Saine v. Comcast Cablevision of Ark., Inc.*, 354 Ark. 492, 497 (Ark. 2003).

[7]*Cherniak v. Connecticut Post Newspaper Co.*, No.CV040412889, 2005 WL 3624208, at *3 (Conn. Super. Ct. Dec. 12, 2005).

[8]*Detone v. Bullit Courier Service, Inc.*, 140 A.D.2d 278, 279 (N.Y. App. Div. 1988); see also *Gallo v. Dugan*, 228 A.D.2d 376 (N.Y. App. Div. 1996).

centrally concerned with the liability of enterprises and institutions" (Chamallas, 2013, p. 157).[9] As we point out, administrative negligence cases are diverse and there is no universal blueprint to guide the forensic criminologist in the assessment of foreseeability, breach of standards of care, and causation. A wide variety of facts, topics, and issues characterize administrative negligence cases. The cases can range from work-related accidents, to breaches of physical security, to sexual assault and rape. Not surprisingly, each case will involve different forms of evidence, focus on different issues and policy considerations, and offer different explanations of the principal rationales underlying the vicarious liability of employers.

CASE EXAMPLE: NEGLIGENT TRAINING AND SUPERVISION INVOLVING A MURDER IN A HOTEL RESTAURANT

This case concerns the murder of two hotel restaurant managers, Jesus Magana and David Ortega (both pseudonyms) in the Well Done Steakhouse (a pseudonym) at a major hotel. One night, Antonio Santiago and former employee Jimmy Anaya (both pseudonyms) came to the restaurant's back door and buzzed to be let in. Even though no cleaning company personnel were expected at this time and these two men were not following the appropriate protocol for entry, they were allowed entry by dishwasher Michael Vacarro (pseudonym). Santiago and Anaya then herded the restaurant's employees into the freezer and shot and killed Magana and Ortega. Although none of the employees witnessed the murders, they described the shootings as being preceded by arguments and struggles. The murderers were later apprehended, pleaded guilty to the murders, and each was sentenced to more than 100 years in prison.

In this case, the mother and brothers of one of the victims sued the hotel, restaurant, and cleaning service. The forensic criminologist was asked by counsel for the defense to comment on issues relating to security and negligence. The following materials were reviewed: initial police reports, Well Done Steakhouse and hotel incident reports, employee statements, two plaintiff's expert witness reports, photographs, property diagrams, personnel records, security logs, several newspaper accounts of the murders, pleadings and other documents pertaining to hotel policies and procedures, and depositions of three people. In addition, the hotel and restaurant premises were inspected on two evenings.

Based on the investigation, the forensic criminological report opines that the "two murders were likely the result of either [Well Done] Restaurant's failure to train and supervise its employees properly or the result of its employees' failure to follow this training." Restaurant establishments open at night are vulnerable to robbers coming in through the back door. The National Fire Protection Association (2006, p. 50) specifically states at 16.4.1.2.3, "[m]any robberies occur through the back door." Miller's

---

[9]Chamallas (2013, p. 142) lists several oft-cited court cases on vicarious liability that shifted legal attention to the risks created by organizations. These cases include *Lisa M. v. Henry Mayo Newhall Memorial Hospital* 907 P.2d 358, 363 (Cal. 1995) (quoting *Carr v. Wm. C. Crowell Co.*, 171 P.2d 5, 8 (Cal. 1946)); *Fahrendorff ex rel. Fahrendorff v. N. Homes, Inc.*, 597 N.W.2d 905, 911 (Minn. 1999) (citing *Marston v. Minneapolis Clinic of Psychiatry & Neurology, Ltd.*, 329 N.W.2d 306, 311 (Minn. 1982)); *John R. v. Oakland Unified Sch. Dist.*, 769 P.2d 948, 964 (Cal. 1989) (citing *Martinez v. Hagopian*, 227 Cal. Rptr. 763, 767 (Cal. Ct. App. 1986)); *Mary M. v. City of Los Angeles*, 814 P.2d 1341, 1344 (Cal. 1991) (quoting *Perez v. Van Groningen & Sons, Inc.*, 719 P.2d 676, 678 (Cal. 1986)); *Rodgers v. Kemper Constr. Co.*, 124 Cal. Rptr. 143, 149 (Cal. Ct. App. 1975).

(1988, p. 95) oft-cited restaurant security guide notes that "[s]ince robbers often enter through back or kitchen doors, these doors require extra security."

As the forensic criminological report elaborates:

> Robbers targeting restaurants prefer a back-door entry where they can avoid being seen by customers and because these robbers expect to find cash in the "back of the house" where the manager's office is located. Robbers also like to hit around closing time because many customers have already left and the evening's cash receipts have been fully accumulated and gathered together for counting. For these reasons, all reputable restaurant chains with which I am familiar develop very strict protocols concerning opening of the back door, particularly at night. Basically, the back door is to be opened from the inside only under very special conditions and then by authorized personnel only.
>
> Also well known to the restaurant/hospitality industry is the fact that the vast majority of injuries occurring during armed robbery come about because of actual or perceived resistance on the part of the victim. Either because the robber is frightened or because he becomes angry, victim resistance often precipitates violence [citations to Faulkner et al., 2001; Indermaur, 1996]. Since most victims do not resist, the majority of armed robberies do not result in death or injury [citation to Karmen, 2006, Chapter 6].
>
> Based on these realities then, every restaurant of Well Done's type should develop a protocol for use of the back door, and every such restaurant should train its employees in the safest ways to act during a robbery. In the case of the Well Done Restaurant in the hotel, there was a specific protocol in place, but it does not appear that Mr. Vacarro followed this protocol; instead, he opened the back door to the two perpetrators of this violence.

In any administrative negligence case, a forensic criminologist should carefully investigate whether the premises owner and employees followed the organization's formal policies and procedures in the conduct of business activities. Back-door protocols and robbery training policies in the restaurant industry are discussed in Education Foundation of the National Restaurant Association's (1993) *Food Service Security: Manager Program*. Other organizations such as the Restaurant Loss Prevention and Security Association (formerly NFSSC) and local police departments also provide lists of security guidelines for restaurants to adopt to prevent injuries from robberies.

The forensic criminological report continues:

> With regard to training employees in appropriate responses to a robbery, I have not seen Well Done training materials which emphasize any of the following appropriate responses: stay calm, do not stare at the robber, avoid any continuous eye contact, cooperate with the robber, avoid surprises by telling the robber what you are about to do, keep your hands in plain sight where they can always be seen by the robber, tell the robber if someone is in a back room or if somebody could make an unexpected noise, if you do not understand what the robber is telling you to do, ask for clarification, above all, stay calm. Robbery training for employees at businesses dealing with the public and where money changes hands is somewhat consistent across industries (for similar recommendations directed at convenience store employees, see Alitzio and York, 2007).

In this case, plaintiffs alleged that CleanMan Cleaning services (a pseudonym) was responsible for the murders since one of the attackers was a former CleanMan employee and wore a CleanMan uniform during the robbery. Based on the evidence, the forensic criminological report opines that actions of CleanMan Cleaning Services were not a proximate cause of the murders. The established protocol was that the CleanMan supervisor would enter through the restaurant's main door using a key and an alarm code after the restaurant's employees had finished their shifts and left the premises. The supervisor would then go to the back door and let in the cleaning crew. All CleanMan employees were to arrive in a marked truck. Nobody but the supervisor would know the code, have the key, or allow CleanMan employees, wearing their shirts with company logos, to enter through the back door. Because the back door is located in a "blind spot" not seen by passersby or other onlookers, attendance to this back-door protocol was even more important. Furthermore, on the night of the incident, it appears that the hotel did nothing to prevent an unauthorized passenger vehicle from being parked in a commercial zone, where the cleaning truck was supposed to park. Another reason to strictly enforce the protocol was the proximity to the back door of the manager's office, which contained the safe. According to the report, "[e]ither Mr. Vacarro was not trained to honor this protocol, or he chose to ignore his training."

As the forensic criminological report continues:

> I have also considered the facts of this case as they may relate to CleanMan. Although one of the robbers, Jimmy Anaya, had at one time been an employee of CleanMan, he was not an employee at the time of these murders. Even though he had not been subjected to an extensive background check before being hired, there was nothing to be discovered by such a background check to prevent him from being hired anyway. I understand Mr. Anaya did not have a criminal record. I note also that entry-level positions such as his, particularly as such positions do not allow access to a vulnerable population, do not require criminal history checks. Nonsensitive entry-level positions, particularly where employees are highly fungible and anonymous to a client, do not call for notification every time someone quits or is fired from such a high-turnover position. Although an ex-employee's keys, proximity cards, full uniforms, and computer-access codes should be accounted for, I have not encountered any standards requiring a T-shirt bearing a company logo to be returned.
>
> Even so, I understand CleanMan required its T-shirts to be returned before issuing final paychecks, and Anaya signed for his last check. I also understand that a CleanMan employee has knowledge of Anaya returning his shirts after being discharged. Finally, a reasonable person could not foresee (as in proximate cause) that a T-shirt kept by a former employee with no known history of violence would be utilized as part of a robbery-murder. T-shirts with various company names on them are to be found virtually everywhere throughout the population (Coca Cola, Nike, Corona, etc.) and do not constitute an instrumentality commonly associated with harm to others [citation to Pastor, 2007, pp. 91–92].

In a case of administrative negligence, a crucial analytical task for the forensic criminologist is to assess whether the employer's actions or inactions were a proximate cause of the injury and that the harm was foreseeable. In the previous case, the plaintiffs claimed that the defendants—hotel, restaurant, and cleaning company—violated a standard of care by not providing security for contractors, visitors, and guests entering the hotel. Yet the forensic evidence suggests that an errant employee of the restaurant disobeyed back-door protocol and allowed the two murderers into the restaurant to commit the violence. That is, the actions of Mr. Vacarro were the proximate cause of the murders.

A major lesson of this case is that a forensic criminologist should understand and be able to explain the importance of adhering to principles of management in hierarchical organizations to maintain physical security and information security. Forensic criminologists should understand basic management terms such as unity of command (holds that an employee should only be answerable to one person), chain of command (refers to a company's hierarchy of reporting relationships), and span of control (refers to the number of subordinates under the manager's direct control). Forensic criminologists should also understand the importance of written records, formalized policies, bureaucratic procedures, and organizational rules to help inform a judge and jury in their decision-making. As one court has noted, "expert testimony is routinely required 'in negligence cases ... which involve issues of safety, security and crime prevention,'"[10] including allegations of "negligent 'hiring, training, and supervision of ... security personnel.'"[11] While expert testimony is central to any negligence case, whether a cause of injury is foreseeable is a question for the jury.[12]

CASE EXAMPLE: NEGLIGENT HIRING AND THEFT AT A CONDOMINIUM UNIT

This case involves the theft of several valuable items from a condominium unit owned and occupied by Carry McCloud (a pseudonym), an 85-year-old senior citizen. During 2003 and 2004, several other residents also reported to management that they were missing items, but to no avail. Eventually, a police investigation in April and May of 2006 revealed that the condominium manager, Mrs. Penelope Daniels (a pseudonym), had stolen from Mrs. McCloud's unit such valuables as china platters, cups and saucers, as well as a leather billfold. Also missing from the unit was jewelry valued at hundreds of thousands of dollars. These thefts left Mrs. McCloud so frightened that she had to leave her home of many years and suffered a significantly diminished quality of life. Due to her advancing age, Mrs. McCloud had come to trust and rely upon Mrs. Daniels and had allowed this building manager access into her home. This trust was violated in a criminal fashion and Mrs. McCloud initiated a lawsuit.

In this case, counsel for the plaintiff requested comment on any violations of standards of care regarding personnel security practices. The following documents were reviewed in preparation of a forensic criminological report for retaining counsel: formal complaint, official police investigation, correspondence from and to condominium management, a timeline of pertinent events, trial transcripts, depositions pertaining to a prior litigation case, and depositions given by Daniels, the condominium manager, and one other person. A physical inspection of the building was also conducted.

According to the forensic criminological report:

> The best way to approach the problem of insider crime is through careful screening and selection of potential employees. It is axiomatic in the security industry that the more sensitive a job, the more carefully an applicant for that job must be screened. Accordingly, the professional literature is replete with information extolling the need for careful hiring practices and detailing the various

---

[10]*Briggs,* 481 F.3d at 845-46 (quoting *Varner,* 891 A.2d at 267).

[11]*Farooq v. MDRB, Corp.,* 275 Fed.Appx. 11, 12 (D.C.Cir.2008) (quoting *Predzin v. DC Arena Ltd. P'ship,* No. 02CA 9582, at 5 (D.C.Super.Ct. Oct. 7, 2003)).

[12]See *O'Cain v. Harvey Freeman and Sons, Inc.,* 603 So. 2d 824 - Miss: Supreme Court 1991 at 830 ("the question of superseding intervening cause is so inextricably tied to causation, it is difficult to imagine a circumstance where such issue would not be one for the trier of fact.").

methodologies to be used in screening personnel [citations to DeMey and Flowers, 1999; Rosen, 2004; Fay, 2002, pp. 235–240; Nixon and Kerr, 2008; ASIS International, 2006].

These exhortations apply specifically to real estate management as well [citation to Griswold, 2001, pp. 249–254]. Mrs. Daniels' job as property manager at [condominium complex] was extremely sensitive for two primary reasons: She had access to the residents' units and knowledge of their patterns; and, notably in this case, a number of the residents of the building were vulnerable senior citizens, many of whom are susceptible to financial exploitation [citations to Brogden and Nijar, 2000; Payne, 2000; Reed, 2005; Wilber and Reynolds, 1996]. As will be explained more fully below, the defendants were negligent in failing to properly screen Mrs. Daniels before placing her in such a sensitive position as building manager. This constitutes negligent hiring.

Given that Mrs. Daniels was inadequately screened in the first place, she should have been supervised more carefully, especially when condominium board members began to receive reports of thefts. In addition to negligent supervision, failure to remove her from active employment (suspension with or without pay would have been appropriate) would constitute negligent retention and negligent entrustment [citation to Pastor, 2007, pp. 59–103].

It is axiomatic in the fields of personnel security and criminology that the "best predictor of future behavior is past behavior" (Gabor, 1986, p. 48; Morris and Miller, 1987). The close linkage between past and future behavior is precisely why responsible employers do background checks on potential employees who are being considered for sensitive positions. Since much human behavior occurs in patterns and routines, how one has performed in past jobs may be indicative of how one will perform in future jobs. Employers often use background checks as a means of judging a job candidate's character and abilities, and to identify potential hiring risks for security reasons.

Based on the analysis, the forensic investigation finds that condominium manager Mr. Robert Bernard (a pseudonym) and the Board of Directors should have done a background check on Mrs. Daniels before hiring her. Had they done so, they would have learned of her bankruptcy history, her past criminal charges for writing bad checks, and her termination from her prior property management position for dishonesty. It is also probable Bernard would have learned that Mrs. Daniels had not worked in real estate as she claimed on her resume.

According to the forensic criminological report:

Mr. Robert Bernard (condominium manager) admitted in his deposition at page 63 and again at page 139 that he did no comprehensive background check on Mrs. Daniels. In fact, he did not even take the basic step of contacting her prior employer. Had he done so, he could have learned of her dishonestly and, possibly, of her violation of the rules pertaining to the acceptance of cash. It is unknown at this writing whether or not Penelope Daniels even filled out an employment application form, the starting point for comprehensive employee screening.

Had Mr. Bernard contacted Betty Rosalyn [a pseudonym], Mrs. Daniels' prior employer ... the details of Daniels' discharge likely would have been made known to Bernard [and] ... it is likely he would at least have learned Rosalyn would not rehire Daniels. Often the simplest and most direct question to ask a former employer is, "Would you rehire?" Former employers can convey to the potential employer a great deal of information merely by the alacrity with which they respond to this question. Due to the sensitivity of the position to be filled, this information should have been enough to prompt Bernard to request a criminal history check of local police jurisdictions and also to request a credit report. Even a check with the University of Maryland may have revealed that Mrs. Daniels misrepresented her educational history.

Finally, had Mr. Bernard decided to submit Mrs. Daniels' application to the Board, notwithstanding this adverse information, a prudent property management executive should have supervised Mrs. Daniels more closely, particularly after reports of missing items began to make their way up the communications chain. Board member and current president Peter Billington [a pseudonym] testified in his deposition that Penelope Daniels' job was extremely sensitive (at pages 22 and 33) and that board members relied on Mr. Bernard to conduct a suitable background investigation on Mrs. Daniels (see pages 28, 30, and 43).

The issues of central concern in this case pertain to personnel security—the protection of an organization's assets from its own employees. Crimes committed by employees are particularly harmful to an organization and its employees because insiders can have privileged knowledge of the value and location of assets, access to these assets, and an intimate knowledge of systems set up to defend these assets (Hollinger and Clark, 1983; Schulman, 2005; Mars, 1982; Lipman and McGraw, 1988, pp. 51–59). Moreover, perpetrators may succeed to the extent they can "pass" as honest and trustworthy individuals.

Mrs. Daniels' position at the apartment was a sensitive position and she appears to have violated the trust of the residents and her employer. The Board of Directors of the condominium association expected and relied on Mr. Bernard to do an appropriate background check on Mrs. Daniels before presenting her to the board. He did not do so and, from a personnel security standpoint, was negligent for not having done so.

The previous case suggests at least two reasons why some organizational settings may become criminogenic: first, individuals that lack security awareness of insider threats may inadvertently help foster crime opportunities; and, second, without oversight and accountability individuals may take advantage of opportunities to misuse interpersonal ties and hide instances of misconduct within legitimate interactions. Research on white-collar crime and the sociology of fraud notes that insider crimes and the compromising of organizational assets are linked to issues involving trust, interaction, and opportunity (Baumer et al., 2017; Eaton and Korach, 2016; Fligstein and Roehrkasse, 2016; Harrington, 2012; Nash et al., 2013). An offender can commit insider theft when using misrepresentation or deception to secure unfair or unlawful gain, typically by creating and exploiting the appearance of a routine transaction. As Granovetter (1985, p. 681) has observed, "the trust engendered by personal relations presents, by its very existence, enhanced opportunity for malfeasance." Among other things, theft of personal valuables and fraud may be facilitated by the need and willingness of most people to believe that others are trustworthy until given reason for doubt (Fine, 2009). Similarly, fraudsters benefit from "accusatory reluctance" in which people may feel uncomfortable in voicing doubts about the honesty and motivations of others.

Small businesses are especially vulnerable to fraud, embezzlement, and internal theft because they have few resources to compensate for the losses. Nearly 30% of all business failures are caused by employee theft according to the Better Business Bureau. Corporate security experts estimate that 25%–40% of all employees steal from their employers (Catalano, 2014). According to the Association of Certified Fraud Examiners (ACFE) (2014), companies lose 5% of their revenues each year to employee fraud. Based on information gathered from the ACFE's 2014 Global Fraud Study, the median loss caused by a single case of occupational fraud is $145,000. The study also revealed that companies with less than 100 employees had 28% higher fraud losses than larger companies. Theft by more sophisticated employees can cause even greater damage as evidenced by the numerous corporate scandals that have plagued the United States over the last two decades: for example, Enron (2001), Worldcom (2002), Tyco (2002), Bernie Madoff's Ponzi scheme (2008), among others. Employee dishonesty has an insidious effect and can eventually destroy an organization, in this case a condominium community, because of the loss of assets and the irreplaceable loss of trust in an organization's ability to protect its members.

CASE EXAMPLE: CLAIMS OF NEGLIGENCE AND THE ACTIONS OF A SECURITY GUARD

This case concerns a fatal fire that occurred in May 2012 at an assisted living apartment complex for the elderly and disabled. Two people were killed: a three-year-old boy and his grandmother. Two other residents were injured in the fire. A lawsuit was brought against the apartment management company, security guard-on-duty Polly Fettweis (a pseudonym), building ownership, and DDD Security, Inc. (a pseudonym) which had contracted to secure the premises.

In this case, counsel for the defendant requested comment on claims of negligence and breach of duty. Among the documents reviewed were the complaints, answers to interrogatories, and responses to production of documents. Also reviewed were multiple fact witness depositions and plaintiffs' expert reports. An inspection of the property was conducted in 2015.

Following are excerpts from the forensic criminological report:

> The plaintiffs' expert reports of Messrs. Galliano, Zuna, Wallerstein, and East (all pseudonyms) reflect that these gentlemen believe that Polly Fettweis, the security guard on duty the evening of the fire, should not have been hired by DDD Security, Inc. because she misrepresented her educational and employment background. There are also claims that she was not adequately trained or supervised, that she failed to follow post orders, and that she did not adequately investigate the smoke conditions on the seventh floor which were reported to her. I address each of the previous opinions individually below.
>
> *Hiring of Security Officers*
>
> Under [state government] law, a security officer must be registered with the state police. Such a registrant must be eighteen years of age and free of any disqualifying convictions. There is no … state requirement for a GED or a high school diploma, but AAA (a pseudonym)—[training mandated for all contract security positions in the state]—applicants must be literate enough to pass the twenty-four hours of required training [citation to a deposition].
>
> DDD Security, Inc. waived their internal requirement for a GED since Ms. Fettweis had a valid AAA license and had provided proof of employment for one year [citation to a deposition]. She was placed at a client's site that did not contractually require a high school diploma or its equivalent. I also understand that Ms. Fettweis "puffed" and was inaccurate in her application regarding her dates of past employment and failed to reveal the full history of her termination from earlier employment.

While I cannot condone such misrepresentation during the employment application process, Fettweis's background, even if fully revealed, would not have precluded DDD Security, Inc. from hiring her. Ms. Fettweis was a mature individual who was validly trained and registered by AAA. She provided proof of employment for one year. She had no criminal background. She handled her employment interview competently. DDD Security's decision to hire her for the security officer position at this property would not have been unreasonable.

Training of Security Officers

All registrants under AAA must successfully pass a predetermined course of training involving twenty-four hours of instruction in order to be licensed. A minimum of two hours of instruction entails discussion of First Aid/CPR and any other subject areas the … State Police require. A review of reputable security officer basic training materials does not yield a particular emphasis on fire protection curricula although the subject is certainly touched upon [citation to ASIS International, 2011a]. Based on her valid registration with AAA, Polly Fettweis had the aforementioned required training. According to industry practices, if [the management company] wanted DDD security officers to have additional fire-related training, [management company] could have contracted DDD Security to provide further training. However, the [state government] qualified Ms. Fettweis to be a security guard at the time of this incident.

Bonny Moreno [a pseudonym] is an experienced "Lead Guard" at the property and trained Ms. Fettweis for her post on such duties as conducting tours, logbook maintenance, pull cord operations, fire extinguishers, incident reports, and use of keys for various parts of the building. Ms. Fettweis was trained for her post [citation to deposition of Bonny Moreno, pp. 56–57]. Ms. Fettweis was also given "on-the-job" training by another security officer when she began her duties [citation to Polly Fettweis deposition at pp. 71–73, 75–77]. Ms. Fettweis also received training from Randi Rousseau [a pseudonym] from [management company], which included instructions to investigate any reported emergency situation in order to verify circumstances before reporting it to building management or calling 911.

Supervision of Security Officers

Industry practices allow the supervision of a security officer through the use of a "lead guard" (a uniformed position held by an individual with the most authority/seniority assigned to a client post). Bonny Moreno filled that role. Standard practice of DDD Security, Inc. was also to have the post officer visited on a regular basis by a field supervisor who would visit several client locations during a given shift. This supervisor was Sam Michaels (a pseudonym) and, according to Ms. Fettweis, he would check in periodically to monitor guard activities [Fettweis deposition at p. 111]. Fettweis also had supervisory direction available to her by calling DDD's operations center. She could also receive direction from the client's office manager. DDD's supervisory practices reasonably comported with industry standards in this regard [citation to Canton, 1996, pp. 160–164].

In this case, an expert witness for the plaintiffs claimed that Polly Fettweis violated post orders by not calling 911 immediately after being informed that there was a smoke condition on the seventh floor. Upon studying the post orders for the apartment complex, we can see that orders actually refer to calling 911 in case of fire, not smoke. It is common practice for security officers to investigate and verify that an emergency situation exists before calling 911. Once a fire is verified, and simple extinguishment is impossible, then 911 is to be called (Purpura, 1991, p. 256; International Foundation for Protection Officers, 1998, p. 119; Fay, 2002, p. 256).

It is important for a forensic criminologist to understand industry practice and recognize that false alarms/nuisance alarms have long been a major problem for the protective services. For example, because the majority of burglar and robbery alarms are false, some sort of verification process is usually in place (e.g., a call back from the monitoring service or central station) (Cunningham and Taylor, 1985, p. 61; Sampson, 2001). In this case, no mechanical fire or smoke alarm had activated, and prior to 9:19 p.m., Ms. Fettweis had only a single phone call upon which to react. Nevertheless, she chose to take the proper action, which was to investigate and verify that a smoke condition did, in fact, exist before calling 911.

Aside from senior citizens injuring themselves should they decide to evacuate, each time a false alarm is raised, the likelihood increases that it will be ignored the next time (Sampson, 2004). The forensic criminological report notes that "[Ms. Fettweis] went to the seventh floor not once upon notification that the entire floor was full of smoke, but twice, in a reasonable attempt to detect smoke and its source before calling 911. Ms. Fettweis acted in accordance with her instructions from property management to investigate and verify that an emergent situation actually existed before calling 911" [citations to Polly Fettweis deposition at pp. 307–308, 310–311 and Randi Rousseau deposition at pp. 143, 153].

The forensic criminological report continues:

Failure to Investigate

Decision makers in public safety roles such as policing and security are expected to use their discretion in often ambiguous situations. They frequently must find a "satisficing" solution to a complex situation given time limitations, incomplete information, environmental pressures, and the cognitive limitations of the human mind. This is the "bounded rationality" which characterizes much of police and security decision-making, particularly under stressful conditions [citation to Snook and Cullen, 2009]. At about 7:44 p.m. on June 3, 2012, Polly Fettweis was *first* informed of a smoke condition "filling the hallway" of the seventh floor. Yet, when she went directly to the seventh floor to investigate at 7:45 p.m. and again (without prompting) at 7:59 p.m., this was not the case. No smoke alarms had activated. No smoke or any indicia of smoke was noticed by Ms. Fettweis on these two occasions.

Note also that various other individuals had entered and exited the seventh floor without reporting a smoke condition. I note also that plaintiff's fire origin and cause opinion acknowledges that the smoke of the apartment fire would have been contained by the apartment's fire door and that flame and smoke may have greatly intensified only when the apartment door was opened, leading to a sort of backdraft effect due to the sudden availability of oxygen [citation to expert report].

Thus, on the first two occasions of Fettweis's visit to the seventh floor, there was no heat, smoke, or smell (i.e., no indicia) of fire in the hallway. There was no evidence of a fire emergency to report. Thus, having no evidence of a fire in two visits to the seventh floor and, given her responsibility to supervise the building entrance, it was reasonable for her to thereafter return to her first floor post. Plaintiffs' experts also opine that Ms. Fettweis violated DDD's post orders because she (1) went to the bathroom and (2) used the elevator during her investigations. These opinions are based on a misreading of the post orders and industry standards.

On the occasion of Ms. Fettweis's third visit to the floor at about 9:19 p.m, when Scott Ramis [a pseudonym] approached her with information concerning noises coming from Apartment 7C and a smoke condition in Apartment 8C, she responded with alacrity by immediately calling the superintendent to gain entry to Apartment 7C for further investigation. It was not until Mr. Carl Roberto [a pseudonym] actually opened the door that a fire condition became apparent. Ms. Fettweis reacted immediately by pulling the fire alarm lever, calling 911, and alerting other residents. As far as attempting a rescue under the fire conditions as they developed once the door was opened, even fully trained, professional police officers are advised not to do so, given the likelihood of their own resulting injury [citation to International Association of Chiefs of Police, 2015, pp. 1–3). Ms. Fettweis complied with industry practice and post orders by conducting a third investigation at 9:19 p.m. and then, after verifying the emergency situation, notifying the fire department.

In this case, the forensic criminological report concludes that Ms. Fettweis was qualified in accordance with industry standards to serve as a security officer at the assisted living apartment complex at the time of the incident. Ms. Fettweis's training met state government requirements and DDD's supervision of Ms. Fettweis conformed to industry practices. Training beyond that required by the state government Security Officer Registration Act would have been provided by DDD Security, Inc. if the apartment management had contracted for it. Likewise, DDD Security, Inc. would have conducted a comprehensive risk analysis had apartment management requested and funded this project, which goes above and beyond the provision of guard services. If apartment management would have been willing to pay for an additional guard to be on duty to assist Ms. Fettweis in her job function, DDD Security, Inc. would have provided such a guard. Ms. Fettweis's actions in investigating reports of smoke on the evening of May 3, 2012, were consistent with her post orders. The apartment management's instructions for the security officers assigned to the assisted living complex were reasonable under security industry standards.

As in any action for negligence, a plaintiff asserting a cause of action for administrative negligence must prove duty, breach, causation, and damages. If we focus on the issue of negligent training, we can see that over the decades, courts have held that negligent training claims will fail as a matter of law without expert testimony establishing the standard of practice for training employees for the job at issue.[13] It is not enough to show the mistakes or errors of the employee; rather, to recover against the employer under a negligent training theory, evidence of a *specific* standard of care for training *and its breach* is required.[14]

---

[13]Judge Merrick Garland surveyed many such decisions in *Burke v. Air Serv International, Inc.*, 685 F.3d 1102, 1106-07 & n. 2 (D.C.Cir.2012) (affirming summary judgment dismissing negligent training claim based on the plaintiff's assertion that "lay jurors could have intuited the proper standard of care from their knowledge of old Westerns"). See also *Moore v. District of Columbia*, 79 F.Supp.3d 121, 144–45 (D.D.C.2015) (surveying authorities and granting summary judgment dismissing negligent-training claims).

[14]*See Carter v. Nat'l R.R. Passenger Corp.*, 63 F.Supp.3d 1118, 1156–57 (N.D. Cal. 2014) (granting summary judgment dismissing negligent training claim because "[p]laintiffs do not link any of the evidence [of the errors of an Amtrak train engineer] to any *specific* federal standard of care [for training] … or explain how the evidence, if credited by the jury, would establish a violation of such a standard"); *Wimer v. State*, 122 Idaho 923, 841 P.2d 453, 455 (Ct.App.1992) (affirming summary judgment dismissing claim that the state negligently trained game officers who charged elk hunters with criminal violations; concluding affidavit testimony that the "training and supervision must have been deficient because of the manner in which *this* investigation was conducted" was insufficient to support an inference based on a "single incident standing by itself" (quoting *Anderson v. City of Pocatello*, 112 Idaho 176, 731 P.2d 171, 181 (1986)).

Courts have generally looked upon allegations of negligent training with caution and skepticism due to varying and sometimes conflicting testimony concerning indictors and measures of "adequate" and "inadequate" training. Courts have ruled that summary judgment is appropriate if plaintiffs' conclusory allegations concerning inadequate training do not create genuine issues of material fact.[15] Claims are often made that employees either did not have enough training or had the wrong training for the specific job they were assigned. Since claims of administrative negligence are fraught with complexity and dispute, a forensic criminologist can identify the accepted industry standards and explain to a jury whether the employer failed to meet minimally adequate standards.

CONCLUSIONS

The notion of administrative negligence and the doctrine of respondeat superior can apply to torts in the realms of information security, physical security, and personnel security (Post et al., 1991). Information security concerns trade secrets, internal competitive documents, and information assurance (cybersecurity). Physical security deals with issues of access control, lighting, guard tours, sightlines, natural surveillance, and related matters. Personnel security generally involves matters of employee integrity and other internal threats to an organization (employee theft, fraud, embezzlement). Personnel security concerns the risk of workers (insiders) exploiting their legitimate access to an organization's assets for unauthorized and often illegal purposes. While any organization can expect to address external threats, place managers must pay attention to internal threats and crimes perpetuated by employees including theft, embezzlement, fraud, and workplace violence. These threats often lead to extensive corporate damage, human suffering, and economic ruin and bankruptcy.

The actions and decisions of place managers can have a major impact on the organization's ability to manage security risks and assess the internal and external context of potential threats. Not only might a commercial enterprise be sued for a criminal act occurring on its property, a lawsuit might arise out of the actions of its own employees. Should a salesperson assault a customer, or a contract security officer wrongfully detain a suspected shoplifter, liability may attach. In addition to crimes by employees, modern organizations must be concerned about crimes against employees. Accordingly, security and loss prevention professionals must be increasingly prepared to deal with forensic issues as they help guide their organizations in the assessment and management of different security risks including physical security risks, information security risks, and personnel security risks.

The case examples alleging administrative negligence we have discussed in this chapter are not static and all-inclusive. In recent decades, respected institutions—from the Catholic Church, to the Boy Scouts, to Penn State, Michigan State, and the BBC—have become entangled in scandals involving allegations of extensive sexual abuse of vulnerable children and young people. Behind these scandals is not only a story of abusive individuals who hurt large numbers of victims but also a story of administrative carelessness, blatant disregard of codes of ethical conduct, and improper supervision and oversight. "The story of widespread abuse and institutional failure is now so familiar it is hard

---

[15]*Barr v. County of Albany*, 50 NY 2d 247—NY: Court of Appeals 1980 at 258 (granting summary judgement because "[n]o attempt was made to demonstrate how such direct supervision could have altered the consequences of the Deputy Sheriffs' actions, nor do plaintiffs set forth any evidence that the Deputy Sheriffs lacked training in proper law enforcement techniques").

to keep track of even the high-profile cases," according to one legal scholar (Chamallas, 2013, p. 133). In response to these and other cases, some commentators claim that tort law has expanded over the decades to address abuse and exploitation cases under the doctrine of respondeat superior. At the same time, cases are often complicated and courts can often rule against vicarious liability in cases of sexual assault and misconduct (Schwartz, 1996; Weber, 1991; Chamallas, 2013).

Legal commentators expect new tort actions involving administrative negligence to evolve and become more diverse (for an overview, see Mann and Roberts, 2015). In recent decades, negligent firing, negligent referral, negligent undertaking, negligent credentialing, negligent licensing, negligent failure to evict, negligent eviction, negligent failure to warn, and negligent ejectment have become established causes of action and plaintiffs have filed many lawsuits utilizing these theories. Occasionally, companies may arbitrarily and capriciously fire employees who then extract workplace revenge on other workers (negligent firing). Negligent referral can occur when an individual serving as a reference for a candidate for employment intentionally lies about the candidate or intentionally withholds information he/she knows to be true that causes injury to a third party (Belknap, 2001). Allegations of negligent referral and misrepresentation have happened in cases of pedophilic school teachers and violent corporate administrators.[16] A landlord may be put on notice that tenants pose a danger to other tenants or to invitees if there is ongoing drug or gang activity, or the presence of a mentally disturbed or violent tenant. In facing a negligent eviction claim, a bar or tavern may have to respond to the issue of whether it owed an affirmative duty to ensure an intoxicated patron's safety after he or she was evicted from the property.[17] Also, the claim of negligent ejectment has emerged in recent years in which a plaintiff alleges a bar breached a duty to use reasonable care when ejecting an intoxicated customer.[18]

---

[16]"An employer electing to give a recommendation must do so with reasonable care and disclose enough information so that the recommendation is not misleading" (Whitten and Mosley, 2000, p. 537). In the landmark case of *Randi W. v. Muroc Joint Unified School District* 929 P.2d 582 (Cal. 1997), the court held that liability could be imposed upon an employer based upon the failure to use reasonable care in the recommendations of a former employee. The court deemed the glowing letters of recommendation, which failed to disclose information about disciplinary action taken against the former employee for sexual harassment and his resignation due to sexual misconduct charges, to be "affirmative misrepresentation" (*Randi W.*, 929 P.2d at 584). The prospective employer, another school district, relied upon the letters of recommendation in its decision to hire (*Id*). Subsequently, the employee sexually assaulted a student in the new school district (*Id*). In examining the issue of recommendations, the court in *Randi* determined that the person giving a letter of recommendation "owes to third persons a duty not to misrepresent the facts in describing the qualifications and character of a former employee, if making these misrepresentations would present a substantial, foreseeable risk of physical injury to the third persons" (*Id*. at 591). "Therefore, when the former employer elected to provide some information, it was then obligated to disclose all other facts materially qualifying the facts disclosed. Otherwise, 'half of the truth may obviously amount to a lie, if it is understood to be the whole'" (quoting Whitten and Mosley, 2000, p. 538).

[17]*Rodriguez v. Primadonna Company,* LLC., 216 P. 3d 793—Nev: Supreme Court 2009 (concluding that "a proprietor does not, as a matter of law, have an affirmative duty to prevent injury to an intoxicated patron subsequent to an eviction"); *Groh v. Westin Operator*, LLC, 352 P. 3d 472—Colo: Court of Appeals, 4th Div. 2013 (holding that "a hotel must evict a guest in a reasonable manner, which precludes ejecting a guest into foreseeably dangerous circumstances resulting from either the guest's condition or the environment").

[18]In *Doe v. O.C. Seacrets, Inc.*, et al., 2012 WL 3257581 (Md., 2012), plaintiff, a patron at Seacret's bar, in Ocean City, Maryland sued the bar for alleged failure to exercise reasonable care when bar staff ejected her for intoxication. Plaintiff Doe attempted to reenter the bar to retrieve her purse and be with her friends, but Seacrets staff allegedly would not let her reenter. Shortly after ejection, Doe was assaulted and raped in a nearby parking lot. The woman's assailant, Lorenzo Ivan Garcia-Moreno, pleaded guilty to first-degree rape, kidnapping and other crimes in March 2012 and was sentenced to 30 years in prison. The case against Seacrets bar proceeded to trial and a jury ultimately ruled in favor of the defendant.

As new forms of administrative negligence arise, forensic criminologists must be prepared to adapt and modify their theoretical and methodological skill sets to assist legal counsel in case evaluation, case development, and the preparation of forensic evidence. In previous chapters we have stressed that forensic criminologists should be thoroughly conversant with theories of crime and place including rational choice theory, routine activities theory, CPTED, situational crime prevention theory, crime pattern theory, social opportunity perspectives, and social disorganization perspectives on high-crime places. Given the increasing diversity of administrative negligence cases, we feel forensic criminologists would benefit by familiarizing themselves with theories of organizational behavior, social network analysis, and diffusion theories. Just as some places can be more crime prone than other places, research using "criminogenic tiers" theory has suggested that some organizations and industries can be more criminogenic than others. The degree of criminogenic propensity can depend on internal organizational characteristics, structure of social networks, and organizational connections to external agents (Baker and Faulkner, 2003; Denzin, 1977; Farberman, 1975; Simpson, 2010; Sutherland, 1945; Tillman, 2009). Organizations can be rigidly structured or loosely coupled and therefore have different impacts on pressures or strains linked to crime. Criminogenic processes may be crime coercive (illegal behavior is directly linked to corporate profits and desired by top managers) or crime facilitative (leaders allow structural conditions to encourage criminal activities to exist) (Simpson, 2010).

To investigate and analyze cases involving administrative negligence, a forensic criminologist can draw on a variety of theoretical resources to examine whether pressures and constraints that affect one level in an organization may nurture criminogenic motivations and opportunities at other levels. A forensic criminologist can use social network analysis, case study analysis, and organizational ethnographies, among other social science methods, to identify whether a certain type of administrative wrongdoing—for example, discrimination, harassment, covert sexual assault and abuse, and so on—is a predictable risk in an organization. Could it be that the 80–20 rule that applies to crime concentration in risky facilities and places could also apply to certain organizations or organizational cultures? That is, for any group of similar organizations, could it be that "a small proportion of the group accounts for the majority of crime experienced by the entire group?" (Eck et al., 2007, p. 226). Viewing places and organizations as key objects of criminological analysis is a radical proposition given the traditional focus of criminology on individuals (offenders and victims). Just as place matters in the study of crime, so too can organizations matter, especially when we consider cases involving allegations of administrative negligence and vicarious liability.

WORKPLACE VIOLENCE

INTRODUCTION

This chapter investigates the questions of foreseeability, standards of care, and causation in negligent security claims pertaining to workplace violence. "Workplace violence" is a broad category of diverse activities and impacts related to occupational exposure to violence. The Occupational Safety and Health Administration (OSHA) defines workplace violence as "any act or threat of physical violence, harassment, intimidation or other threatening or disruptive behavior that occurs at the work site" (U.S. Department of Labor, 2018). ASIS International, the world's largest membership organization for security management professionals, defines workplace violence as a "spectrum of behaviors— including overt acts of violence, threats and other conduct—that generates a reasonable concern for safety from violence" (ASIS International, 2011b, pp. 3, 5). This definition assumes "a nexus exists between the behavior and the physical safety of employees and others (such as customers, clients, and business associates), on-site, or off-site when related to the organization" (2011, pp. 3, 5). According to this definition, workplace violence is not limited to on-site physical attacks and can include threats of assault. Moreover, the victim or target of violence can be anyone, so long as a nexus exists to the workplace. The victim or target can be an employee, a visitor to the workplace, or an attendee at an organization-sponsored event.

Liability and legal issues related to workplace violence can be complicated and complex (Lies, 2008; Chappell and Di Martino, 2006). Federal and state laws and statutory considerations can intertwine with both criminal and civil remedies and rights depending on who is the offender and who is the victim (e.g., employer, coworker, contractor, or customer). Different states have different statutes related to workplace violence and federal regulations require employers to comply with occupational safety and health standards (ASIS International, 2011b, pp. 50–54). Under the General Duty Clause, Section 5(a)(1) of the Occupational Safety and Health Act of 1970, OSHA requires employers to provide their employees with a place of employment that is "free from recognized hazards that are causing or are likely to cause death or serious physical harm to … employees."[1] A 2011 Directive permits OSHA to investigate all incidents of workplace violence, whether they involve fatalities or not, including a determination of whether the employer used the most effective, feasible controls available to protect its employees from acts of workplace violence (U.S. Department of Labor, 2011). To cite an

---

[1] U.S. Department of Labor. Occupational Safety and Health Administration. Sec. 5 Duties. Available from: https://www.osha.gov/laws-regs/oshact/section5-duties. Accessed May 14, 2019.

Practicing Forensic Criminology. https://doi.org/10.1016/B978-0-12-815595-0.00009-2

employer for violating the General Duty Clause, the Secretary of the U.S. Department of Labor must prove all four of the following: (1) the employer failed to keep the workplace free from a hazard that employees were exposed to, (2) the hazard was recognized, (3) the hazard was likely to cause death or serious physical harm, and (4) there was a feasible and economically viable way to correct the hazard (American Bar Association, 2014).

An employer will be on notice of the risk of workplace violence if the workplace has experienced past acts of violence (actual notice) or the employer becomes aware of threats, intimidation, or other indicators showing that the potential for violence in the workplace exists (constructive notice) (Hargrave, 2001; Litwack and Schlesingerm, 1999). Employers are not strictly liable for workplace violence under the OSH Act and OSHA has not issued any formal standards on workplace violence. Whether an employer is liable under the General Duty Clause for an incident of workplace violence depends on the facts of the case.

As we point out in this chapter, liability of employers for violent criminal acts at the workplace is rapidly evolving as plaintiffs and defendants challenge traditional defenses to negligence, such as an unforeseeable event or superseding cause, in workplace violence cases. Sometimes, the employer, as opposed to the perpetrator, is the one that victims and their families may attempt to hold civilly responsible. In the context of workplace violence, employers as well as perpetrators potentially may be liable to employees and third parties. Liability may be direct or vicarious, and the price of liability can run high, since punitive damages may be allowable for the "willful, wanton, or reckless disregard for the safety of others."[2] Civil liability cases on workplace violence can include negligent hiring and retention. Premises owners that do not have a workplace violence and intervention program in place could be subject to liability. Even if an organization has a workplace violence program, plaintiff's attorneys and experts may attempt to attack the program if there is nonexistent employee training, orientation, and comprehension (Security Executive Council (SEC), 2018).

Moreover, since the 1980s, mass casualty events and domestic terroristic attacks have generated a considerable amount of litigation surrounding workplace violence. A series of shootings by U.S. postal workers during the late 1980s and early 1990s precipitated research on workplace violence and mass casualty events (U.S. Postal Service Commission on a Safe Secure Workplace, 2000). On August 20, 1986, postman Patrick Sherrill walked into his workplace, shot and killed 14 coworkers and injured six more people before shooting himself in the head. On October 10, 1991, a former U.S. postal worker, Joseph Harris, killed two employees at a post office in Ridgewood, New Jersey. These well-publicized events focused public and research attention on workplace violence, resulting in the widely used slang phrase, "going postal," which typically denotes an employee losing control over his or her emotions and engaging in violent acts against coworkers. Since the 1980s, there have been hundreds of people killed or injured in workplace violence and other mass casualty incidents. The October 2017 mass shooting at a country music concert in Las Vegas was the deadliest attack on U.S. soil since the September 11, 2001 attacks on New York and Washington, D.C. Other mass casualty events, such as Virginia Tech (2007), Columbine (1999), Sandy Hook (2012), Aurora movie theater (2012), and Parkland, FL (2018), have attracted much media attention and spawned protracted litigation.

---

[2]*Summers v. St. Andrew's Episcopal School, Inc.*, 759 So. 2d 1203 (Miss. 2000). *Doe ex rel. Doe v. Salvation Army*, 835 So. 2d 76 (Miss. 2003). *Warren v. Derivaux*, 996 So. 2d 729 (Miss. 2008).

Workplace violence litigation claims are heterogeneous and can involve a variety of claims and allegations, injuries, legal arguments, and legal obligations. Employees can inflict a considerable amount of violence on customers, patients, students, coworkers, or others with whom they come into contact. Unless a defendant employer can establish certain interactions are clearly "beyond the scope of employment," injured plaintiffs may sue employers when their employees attack a customer, sexually assault a student, patient, or guest, or misrepresent security levels at a property. Plaintiffs may sue an employer for the actions or inactions of independent contractor employees such as housekeeping personnel and security personnel under the notion of "nondelegable duty." Over the decades, victims of workplace violence have attempted to sue contract security companies for somehow failing to prevent an irate patient or armed student from entering the premises. Plaintiffs have accused security officers at government offices and manufacturing facilities of failing to prevent armed workers from entering and shooting ex-lovers, fellow workers, and former supervisors.[3] Just as the circumstances and targets of workplace violence vary, so do offender motivations and the collateral impacts and socio-spatial consequences of violent incidents in workplaces.

A broad range of negligent security lawsuits may be included under the general heading of workplace violence. In some cases, an employer may face liability for its own acts or omissions when the perpetrator of workplace violence is not an employee but the violence occurs at the employer's workplace. These claims can include claims of premises liability generally, or claims based on duties that arise when the employer has a "special relationship" with either the individual who is the perpetrator of violence or the person who is at risk from violence. If an employee commits an act of workplace violence then the courts may not hold the employer vicariously liable under the theory of respondeat superior, because the offending employee would not be acting on behalf of the employer within the scope of employment. In other cases, the employer may have liability for its own acts or omissions. Courts may hold an employer liable for negligence under the theories of negligent hiring or retention if the employer hired or retained an employee who was or should have been known by the employer to be dangerous. These theories of negligence may also apply if an employer could have learned of the employee's dangerous tendencies through a routine investigation but failed to do so.

Our discussion of workplace violence in this chapter is by no means exhaustive or comprehensive. Rather, our reportage of various cases and liability trends represents a partial and incomplete introduction to the vast area of workplace violence litigation that has changed dramatically over the decades (Dolan, 2000; Piccarello, 2005; Creed, 2007; Davis, 2000; Elzen, 2001). We first identify the various types of workplace violence and discuss current research on the extent, costs, and causes of workplace violence incidents. We then present a case of sexual assault in the workplace and describe the various challenges victims of workplace violence face in seeking compensation from employers. Next, we examine how a forensic criminologist would address issues involving foreseeability, standards of care, and causation in cases involving mass shootings. Public mass shootings, also known as "active shooter incidents" or "rampage shootings," are a particularly unusual type of workplace violence homicide. Mass shooters not only kill specific targets, but they also shoot random strangers or bystanders in workplaces that are also schools, theaters, malls, concerts, restaurants, or shopping centers

---

[3]In the case of the September 2013 Washington Navy Yard shooting, when Aaron Alexis fatally shot 12 people and injured three people, families of the deceased sued several defendants for failing to anticipate and prevent the mass shooting. *Jacobs v. The Experts, Inc.*, 212 F. Supp. 3d 55—Dist. Court, Dist. of Columbia 2016.

(Lankford, 2016a; Newman et al., 2004). These attacks tend to generate a great deal of media coverage, public fear, and political debate because, hypothetically, anyone could be the next victim (Duwe, 2007). We then discuss a case involving a mass shooting at an automobile plant in which the shooter committed suicide. Finally, we consider the evolving nature of terrorist threats and mass casualty events and explain their potential impact on foreseeability approaches, standards of care, and liability judgments.

TYPES OF WORKPLACE VIOLENCE

Over the last several decades, workplace violence has emerged as a major organizational, community, and societal problem. Estimates from OSHA suggest that every year, up to two million U.S. workers report having been victims of workplace violence (U.S. Department of Labor, 2018). While workplace violence can range from physical assault to robbery to homicide, the most common form of physical violence in the workplace is simple assault. The Bureau of Justice Statistics (2018) defines simple assault as an "attack without a weapon resulting either in no injury, minor injury (for example, bruises, black eyes, cuts, scratches or swelling) or in undetermined injury requiring less than 2 days of hospitalization."

According to the National Crime Victimization Survey (NCVS) administered by the Bureau of Justice Statistics, rates of simple assault and serious violent victimization (rape, robbery, and aggravated assault) are similar for unemployed individuals and employed individuals attacked outside the workplace. While individuals in many fields have a greater risk of victimization outside the workplace, individuals in some occupations are at a greater risk for violence in the workplace. Law enforcement officers have the highest rate of workplace violence, followed by mental health professionals (Harrell, 2011). Overall, compared to violence outside the workplace, workplace violence is rare; however, given the amount of time that Americans spend at work, it is an important subset of crime.

Over the past several decades, criminologists have realized that workplace violence is far too complex and diverse for researchers to analyze and investigate as a singular issue or homogeneous topic. Scholars, researchers, and practitioners tend to classify incidents of workplace violence into four broad categories based on the offender's relationship to the victim and workplace: Type I, criminal intent; Type II, customer/client; Type III, worker on worker; Type IV, personal relationship (Barling et al., 2009; ASIS International, 2011b). Fig. 9.1 provides a description of these different types, lists examples, and specifies various risk factors for each type of workplace violence.

Mass casualty events—mass shootings, bombings, vehicle ramming attacks, or other crimes with multiple fatalities—receive extensive media and policy attention due to the number of victims and the impact on their communities. While many agencies and organizations record and publish information on mass casualty events, measuring and reporting on these crimes is complicated by the absence of a commonly recognized definition. The Congressional Research Service (CRS) defines mass shootings as events where a killer murders more than four people with a firearm "within one event, and in one or more locations in close proximity" (Krouse and Richardson, 2015, p. 12). The U.S. Congress uses the term "mass killings" and describes these events as "three or more killings in a single incident" (P.L. 112–265). The FBI uses the term "Active Shooter," which it defines as "an individual actively engaged in killing or attempting to kill people in a populated area" (Federal Bureau of Investigation (FBI), 2018a; Blair and Schweit, 2014; Silver et al., 2018). Nongovernmental organizations, including

Type of Event	Description	Examples	Risk Factors for Targeted Violence
Type I	Offender has no relationship with the victim or workplace establishment. In these incidents, the motive is usually robbery or another type of crime such as an act of terrorism	Shoplifting, armed robbery, assault at small late-night retail establishments such as liquor stores, gas stations, convenience stores	Contact with the public, handling money, working alone or in small numbers
Type II	Offender currently receives services from the workplace, often as a customer, client, patient, student, or inmate. Violence against public safety personnel, bus or cab drivers, teachers and social workers, sales personnel and medical, psychiatric, and nursing care workers	A nurse who is assaulted by a patient in an emergency room, a teacher who is attacked by a student, a social worker who is victimized by a client in a community setting, and a police officer who is killed during a "routine" traffic stop	Employees who provide services, care, advice, or education
Type III	Offender is either a current or former employee who is acting out toward coworkers, managers, or supervisors	Employer-employee or employee-employee relationship; subordinate-supervisor violence	Situational factors such as job stress, perceptions of abusive and unfair supervision and surveillance by management; perception that management is over-controlling
Type IV	Offender is not employed at the workplace, but has a personal relationship with an employee. Often, these incidents are due to domestic disputes between employee and offender	Violence perpetuated against current or former spouse, relative, friend, or acquaintance; males stalking females; use of the workplace as an access point to confront the targeted victim and commit violence	People who have suffered tumultuous relationships with their husbands or boyfriends

FIG. 9.1

Classification of workplace violence events.

Source: ASIS International, 2011b. Workplace Violence Prevention and Intervention. American National Standard ASIS/SHRM WVPI.1-2011. ASIS International Alexandria, VA; Savard and Kennedy (2014, pp. 250–2); Kennedy, D. B., Homant, R. J., Homant, M. R., 2004. Perception of injustice as a determinant of support for workplace aggression, J. Bus. Psychol. 18, 323–336; Barling, J., Dupré, K.E., Kelloway, E.K., 2009. Predicting workplace aggression and violence. Annu. Rev. Psychol. 60, 671–692.

Mother Jones, USA Today, and the Stanford Mass Shootings in America (MSA) data project, use various combinations of these definitions.[4]

Much criminological research has focused on the interaction of individual-level variables and work-related stresses in predicting workplace violence (for an overview, see Barling et al., 2009). For example, case histories of Type III workplace mass murderers often include some accounting of how their perceived injustices resulted in a profound anger toward their employer, organization, or employees/supervisors. These disgruntled employees feel the organization or boss has unjustly threatened their job, stymied their career, or treated them unfairly (Baumeister, 2001; Cale and

---

[4]2018 NCVRW Resource Guide: Mass Casualty Shootings Fact Sheet. Available from: https://ovc.ncjrs.gov/ncvrw2018/info_flyers/fact_sheets/2018NCVRW_MassCasualty_508_QC.pdf. Accessed 4 May 2018.

Lillienfeld, 2006; Cartwright, 2002; Fox and Levin, 2007; Holmes and Holmes, 2000; Southerland et al., 1997). Some scholars point out that perceived injustice may generate hatred, anger, and a desire for revenge, though researchers disagree on whether perceptions of injustice are a function of socialization, unfulfilled cultural expectations, or psychological attributes (Kennedy et al., 2004; for an overview, see Hershcovis et al., 2007). Other research suggests that work-related stresses such as abusive supervision (Inness et al., 2005), poor leadership behaviors (Hershcovis et al., 2007), role conflict, role overload, role ambiguity, work constraints, and lack of job autonomy (Bowling and Beehr, 2006) are associated with workplace violence. While some perpetrators of workplace violence may suffer from psychosis, researchers know that having a mental illness is not necessarily an ingredient for violent criminal actions (Swanson, 2011).

Other research has examined the linkages among occupational context, job characteristics, and situational factors in determining workplace violence. Regarding occupational context, employees who provide service, care, advice, or education are at increased risk for assault, especially if clients, customers, inmates, or patients are experiencing frustration, insecurity, or stress (e.g., Barling et al., 2009, pp. 678–679; LeBlanc and Kelloway, 2002; Lamberg, 1996). High-risk industries include health care (especially mental health facilities), taxi service, and all-night retail (ASIS International, 2011b, p. 18). In fact, most workplace homicides involve Type I attacks associated with robbery. High-risk situational factors include employees working at night or home, workplace located in a high crime area, employees handling cash, workplace with valuable goods on hand, business open to the public, alcohol sales as part of the business, workplace that serves patients or holds prisoners, and a history of violence at the workplace (2011, p. 18). In their analysis of the predictors of workplace aggression, Homant and Kennedy (2003) suggest that a high level of organizational crisis proneness may interact with dispositional and contextual factors to exacerbate the conditions for Type III workplace violence. According to Homant and Kennedy (2003, p. 64), the crisis-prone organization is implicated in employee aggression in two ways: "by failing to attend to conflicts as they develop, so that they may evolve into aggressive behavior; and by fostering the stressful working conditions that create many of the frustrations that in turn eventually result in aggression."

CASE EXAMPLE: SEXUAL ASSAULT IN THE WORKPLACE

This case involves the sexual assault of Holly Bartman by Mr. Martin Naquin (both pseudonyms) in the parking lot of Beauty Product Innovation (BPI) (a pseudonym). Ms. Bartman and Mr. Naquin were both employees of Marketing and Diversification Services, Inc. (MDSI) (a pseudonym). BPI and MDSI were parties to a labor agreement under which MDSI provided staffing at the BPI facility (a cosmetic manufacturing plant). The agreement required MDSI to conduct background checks on all applicants before placing any employees at the BPI facility. The agreement also noted that BPI and MDSI shared the responsibility of ensuring that the facility provided a safe working environment. In 2001, BPI entered into a security agreement with MoonBeam LLC (a pseudonym), whereby MoonBeam would provide security for the BPI facility, including the parking lot. In this litigation, plaintiff Holly Bartman alleged that MoonBeam acted at the behest of BPI and MDSI, and that those two companies had control over how MoonBeam carried out its security obligations.

Beauty Product Innovation hired Naquin in 2009 shortly after Bartman was hired. At the time, Naquin was a registered sex offender, having been convicted of aggravated sexual battery of a child under the age of 13 in 2008. MDSI did not disclose Mr. Naquin's criminal history to Beauty Product

Innovation, even though MDSI had agreed to perform extensive employee background checks. In this case, plaintiff Bartman alleged that the defendants had a practice of hiring sex offenders and other convicted criminals because they provided a source of cheap labor. Bartman also claimed that the defendants knew or should have known that there was a significant history of crime near the facility. Additionally, plaintiff Bartman alleged that the parking lot was dimly lit and had poor visibility. She asserted that these conditions created an ongoing risk of sexual assault at the facility that BPI and MDSI knew of or should have known about.

Prior to the criminal incident, plaintiff Bartman complained to her floor supervisor about Naquin making vulgar comments and unwanted sexual advances to her. The supervisor told her that he would take care of the problem and he would try not to schedule the two to work together. Bartman claimed that she usually tried to have friends escort her out to her car after work because of concerns for her safety, particularly a fear of Naquin.

During one night in April 2009, Naquin assaulted and battered Bartman on multiple occasions by touching her leg, thigh, and groin area. After Bartman's shift ended that night, she waited to leave until Naquin clocked out and left the facility so she could avoid meeting him in the parking lot. After he left, she exited the building through a different door and proceeded to her car alone. As she approached her car, Naquin pulled up alongside her and engaged in a violent, sexual assault that lasted fifteen minutes. She repeatedly screamed for help in the parking lot, but no one came to her aid. MoonBeam was supposed to have at least three security officers on site and at least one stationed in the parking lot. Additionally, MoonBeam was to monitor the facility via closed circuit surveillance cameras. However, on the night of the incident, there were no guards in the parking lot, and no one came to offer help at any point during the assault.

The following day, Bartman called the police to report the assault, and the police arrested Naquin. He later pled guilty in state court to a charge of rape. Bartman attempted to return to work a week later but emotional distress resulting from the incident forced her to resign.

This workplace violence case concerns issues involving negligent hiring, negligent supervision, and negligent security. Counsel for the plaintiff requested comment on the actions of BPI and MDSI that led to the criminal event. Another security expert witness hired by attorneys for the plaintiff addressed concerns regarding physical security of the parking lot (lighting, lack of surveillance, nature of patrols by MoonBeam Security). The documents reviewed include the legal complaint, police report of the matter, other incident reports, criminal court files, answers to written discovery, witness statements, deposition transcripts and exhibits, BPI internal documents, and BPI/MDSI services agreement. Also examined were employment files, amended complaint, calls for service to the assembly plant, witness affidavits, scholarly journal articles and textbooks pertinent to negligent hiring and other examples of administrative negligence, and depositions given by seven individuals familiar with the crime. The plant facility and parking lot were inspected and a physical security survey of the general neighborhood of the BPI plant was conducted.

According to the forensic criminological report:

> [I]t is my opinion that Beauty Product Innovation (BPI) negligently placed Martin Naquin, a convicted sex offender, by failing to secure an adequate background check on him. Although Beauty Product Innovation had contracted with MDSI to do this background check, which it failed to do, security is a nondelegable duty. There is no evidence that Beauty Product Innovation performed periodic "quality checks" to make sure MDSI was performing its contracted duties. There is also

evidence that Beauty Product Innovation and MDSI failed to respond promptly to complaints involving the sexual harassment of Holly Bartman by Martin Naquin. Plaintiff testified she informed BPI managers Bailey and Stanford (both pseudonyms) of her sexual harassment by Naquin but both deny having been so informed.

Security managers have been well informed by the legal profession that it may be against public policy and EEOC rulings to *automatically* refuse to hire an ex-offender [emphasis in original]. Employers must take into consideration the nature of prior offenses, the nature of the job to be filled, passage of time since last offense, and any positive accomplishments attributable to the offender [citations to Hickox, 2010; Creed, 2007]. Given Naquin's record of assault even before his more recent conviction for Aggravated Sexual Battery and given judicial notice of a high rate of recidivism among convicted rapists,[5] *Naquin should not have been hired for a job involving close contact with women* [emphasis in original]. If placed in a job requiring prolonged contact with women, any reports of sexual harassment should have been acted on more quickly than they may have been in the instant case. According to an affidavit by Sam Adamson (a pseudonym), Naquin and Bartman were assigned to the same line on April 10, 2009. I do not know if management had even spoken to Naquin about his unacceptable harassing behavior toward Ms. Bartman, although no MDSI or BPI supervisory personnel testified to ever having done so.

Although MDSI was the actual employer of the people working at Beauty Product Innovation, it also acted in the capacity of a background screening company by virtue of its agreement with Beauty Product Innovation. As renowned security expert Charles Sennewald and others have written, "Employees don't do what you expect, they do what you inspect" [Sennewald, 2014, p. 31].

Security practitioners advise that preemployment screening companies and others who sell similar services to various industries should themselves be carefully screened and would, ideally, be members of the National Association of Professional Background Screeners (NAPBS) (Rosen, 2004, pp. 407–429). When choosing a background screening provider, due diligence should involve asking the company about its error rate and resolution rate (Shipp, 2012, p. 7). Companies that contract with screening organizations should also conduct spot checks on applicant folios to make sure complete background checks are being done. Such does not appear to have been the case with Martin Naquin.

As the forensic criminological report elaborates:

With regard to the negligence of MDSI, this defendant failed to investigate and inform Beauty Product Innovation of Martin Naquin's prior conviction for a sex offense, a fact readily available on a state-required sex offender registry website. Naquin's sexual aggressiveness was evident in his relatively recent prior conviction wherein he boldly grabbed a fourteen-year old girl, tried to sexually assault her in the bathroom of a private home and actually chased her down the street, eventually forcing his hand down her pants in order to grab her vagina and her buttocks. Her continued screaming eventually dissuaded him from continuing the attack which by then had been occurring in a church parking lot. There is nothing subtle in Mr. Naquin's Modus Operandi. It would also appear that MDSI blatantly violated other screening expectations detailed in the service contract. This,

---

[5]See *Mulloy v. United States*, 937 F. Supp. 1001, 1013 (D. Mass. Aug 30, 1996), n. 13. See also, Langevin, et al. 2004; Furby, et al. 1989.

> however, is clearly a jury question and requires little further comment from me other than to say the service agreement I read was quite clear in its expectations. Moreover, even without the contract, MDSI breached duties to properly screen new hires.
>
> MDSI, however, was the actual employer of the people it sent to work under the direction of BPI. Anything to be said about BPI's duty to screen employees would certainly apply to MDSI. In addition, given that MDSI would likely have known something more of the backgrounds of many of its employees, or at a minimum should have known more, there should have been far closer supervision of certain employees and an institutional predisposition to act immediately to discipline bad behavior. Mr. Naquin was not the only sex offender in the company's employ as several additional men with sex offense histories were also employed there. Also, because a supervisor reviewed Naquin's Department of Corrections document before hiring him in 2010, she had reason to inquire as to the nature of his conviction. Questions of negligent assignment, negligent retention, and negligent supervision could be added to any complaints about negligent hiring.

Over the decades, courts have refined and expanded general negligence principles to require an owner of a business catering to the public to maintain a reasonably safe environment to protect business invitees from foreseeable harm by employees and third persons. Both security and human resources professions emphasize the importance of a preemployment background investigation, proactive response to employee warning signs of potential violence (e.g., bullying and intimidation), and screening and responding to allegations of gender and racial discrimination, sexual assault, and sexual harassment in the workplace. Preemployment and postemployment background investigations can serve as an opportunity for an organization to reduce its exposure to the risk of workplace violence. There are numerous authoritative sources detailing the importance of protecting employees and the public from bad hires, and of the importance of preventing quid pro quo and hostile environment sexual harassment from harming all employees, male and female (see, e.g., ASIS International, 2009b, 2011b; Nixon and Kerr, 2008; Rosen, 2004; Schell and Lanteigne, 2000; Littler and Fastiff, 1995). As noted by the ASIS International (2009b, p. 8) Pre-Employment Background Screening Guideline:

> Appropriate due diligence is necessary that the applicant hired does not pose a foreseeable risk to others with whom he or she might interact while on the job. The failure to properly screen out dangerous applicants may give rise to a negligent hiring claim if the individual intentionally harms someone in the course of his or her employment.

Workplace sexual assault may have significant consequences for both victims and employers. According to Garrett (2011b, p. 20), "[s]exual assault is an opportunistic offense perpetrated by those who are more powerful than their victims and frequently occurs in locations that lack appropriate security." "[I]dentifying workplace security deficits and providing prevention programs are central to eliminating sexual assault in the workplace." Routine activity theory would view sexual assault through the lens of the convergence of a motivated offender, a suitable target/victim, and the absence of capable guardianship. Alternatively, "the lack of any one of these elements is sufficient to prevent the successful completion of a direct-contact predatory crime" (Cohen and Felson, 1979, p. 589). Eck (2003, p. 88) has restated routine activities theory in the following way: "a crime is highly likely when an offender and a target come together at the same place at the same time, and there is no one nearby to control the offender, protect the target, or regulate conduct at the place."

Characteristics of the organization may be predictors of sexual assault risk. These characteristics may include, among others, lack of autonomy, lack of opportunities for upward mobility in the organization, and perceptions of a sexualized workplace (Dekker and Barling, 1998; Harned et al., 2002; Leiter et al., 2001). Several researchers including Harned and colleagues (2002), Leiter and colleagues (2001), and Wassell (2009) note that work environments that have historically excluded women are at higher risk for workplace sexual assault. Researchers theorize that social exclusion and marginalization reflects and reinforces low sociocultural and organizational power for women that, in turn, puts them at greater risk of sexual assault victimization. Employers who fail to protect their employees from sexual violence in the workplace may be liable for damages.

SEXUAL ASSAULT CLAIMS, WORKERS' COMPENSATION BAR, AND THE PERSONAL-ANIMOSITY DOCTRINE

Courts have long barred sexual abuse victims from recovery in tort cases involving allegations of employer intentional or negligent conduct. Absent vicarious liability, courts have often dictated that sexual abuse victims seek compensation from the offenders themselves, "a notoriously unreliable source of funds given the fact that many offenders end up in jail and few individuals are able to satisfy large tort judgments in the absence of insurance" (Chamallas, 2013, p. 136). For decades, businesses have been relatively immune from lawsuits instituted against them by their own employees for injuries sustained while at work because in many jurisdictions workers' compensation has been their exclusive remedy. Even when a criminal assault causes the harm, the injured employee may not be able to pursue a lawsuit based on the negligence of the employer. This doctrine, otherwise known as the workers' compensation bar, dictates that plaintiffs may seek damages only through workers' compensation laws and cannot sue employers for negligence. According to Kennedy (2013, p. 239), "[u]nless plaintiff experts can establish that a robbery or injury was virtually certain to occur, and wholly inadequate preventive measures were nonetheless in place, a negligent security lawsuit is likely to fail due to worker compensation exclusions" (see also Savard and Kennedy, 2014, p. 257).

In recent decades, however, courts have begun to weaken this barrier to compensation and carved out exceptions to workers' compensation laws thus allowing increasing numbers of employees or their heirs to sue employers for crime-related injuries sustained at the workplace (Kennedy, 2006; Sakis and Kennedy, 2002). Fig. 9.2 provides an overview of the diversity of exceptions to the exclusive-remedy doctrine. These exceptions may allow injured workers and the survivors of deceased employees to pursue premises liability lawsuits for negligent and/or inadequate security. The case examples in Fig. 9.2 are illustrative of court and legislative attitudes toward exclusive remedy. The figure encompasses past and present attitudes, but we do not mean it to be an exhaustive inventory.

Over the decades, employee plaintiffs have filed workplace violence lawsuits under claims of violations of Title VII of the U.S. Civil Rights Act of 1964, a federal law that prohibits employers from discriminating against employees on the basis of sex, race, color, national origin, and religion. Plaintiffs have also filed suits alleging that defendants violated the Americans with Disabilities Act and the Rehabilitation Act. Plaintiffs have also sued for defamation, slander, invasion of privacy, harassment, employer's vicarious liability, and forms of negligence related to security, hiring, supervision, and retention (ASIS International, 2012a, pp. 362–363). Some victims have been able to establish that

Types of Exceptions	Description	Statutes and Oft-cited Court Cases
Statutory:		
Minimum Number of Employees	Workers' compensation statutes may not coverworkers employed by small businesses. Most state statutes apply only to businesses that employ more than a minimum number of employees—usually three to five. In some jurisdictions, employees of smaller establishments—such as convenience stores and gas stations—who are victimized in the workplace can assert traditional claims of inadequate/negligent security against their employers	*Ex parte A-O Mach. Co., Inc.*, 749 So. 2d 1268 (Alaska 1999); *Withers v. Black*, 53 S.E.2d 668 (N.C. 1949). But see *Huff v. Smith Trucking*, 6 S.W.3d 819 (Ky. 1999) (rejecting minimum-number requirements)
Opt-Out Statutes	A few states allow employees to exclude themselves from the workers' compensation system and pursue common law tort actions against their employers for negligence. In one jurisdiction, employees under age 18 are given the additional benefit of electing their favored remedy after suffering an assault, attack, or injury in the workplace	*Williams v. Razor Enters.*, 70 S.W.3d 274 (Tex. Ct. App. 2002); KY. REV. STAT. ANN. §342.395(1) (1996); N.J. STAT. ANN. §34:15-1 (2000); R.I. GEN. LAWS §28-29-17. (2002); N.J. STAT. ANN. §34:15-9; See *Pappano V. Shop Rite Of Pennington, Inc.*, 517 A.2d 178 (N.J. Super. Ct. App. Div. 1986); See *Patterson V. Martin Forest Prods.*, 774 So. 2d 1148 (La. Ct. App. 2000)
Employer's Failure to Maintain Insurance Coverage	Workers' compensation statutes require business owners to purchase and maintain insurance coverage for their employees. Under certain circumstances, however, the business owner can become a self-insured entity—that is, one with enough money in reserve to pay workers' compensation benefits, including lost wages, medical expenses, and vocational rehabilitation. A self-insured entity that fails to purchase workers' compensation insurance, maintain premiums, or keep adequate funds in reserve subjects itself to tort liability	Fla. Stat. Ch. 440.11(1) (2002); Minn. Stat. §176.031 (1993); S.C. Code Ann. §42-5-40 (1962); S.D. Codified Laws §62-3-11 (1977); See *Smeester V. Pub-N-Grub, Inc.*, 527 N.W.2d 5 (Mich. Ct. App. 1995)
Federal Employers' Liability Act and the Jones Act	The Federal Employers' Liability Act provides legal authority for railroad workers to avoid the exclusive-remedy doctrine, and the Jones Act does the same for seamen. Victims of workplace violence have used these statutes to recover substantial verdicts from their employers	*Smeester v. Pub-N-Grub, Inc.*, 527 N.W.2d 5 (Mich. Ct. App. 1995); 45 U.S.C. §51 (1986); 46 U.S.C. app. §688 (1975); No. 457, 900 (La., E. Baton Rouge Parish Dist. Ct. Feb. 17, 2000)
Intentional Torts	The exclusive-remedy doctrine does not immunize business owners against intentional torts. Most jurisdictions limit this exception to so-called true intentional torts—those committed by employers with a "specific intent and desire to injure." A few states define an intentional tort in broader terms and allow such claims whenever employers act with "knowledge that an injury was substantially certain to occur"	Idaho Code §72-209 (1971); Mont. Code Ann. §39-71-411 (1979); S.D. Codified Laws §62-3-2 (1978); *Taylor v. Transocean Terminal Operators, Inc.*, 785 So. 2d 860 (La. Ct. App. 2001); *Travis v. Dreis & Krump Mfg. Co.*, 551 N.W.2d 132 (Mich. 1996); *Lantz v. Nat'l Semiconductor Corp.*, 775 P.2d 937 (Utah Ct. App. 1989); 360 N.W.2d 214 (Mich. Ct. App. 1984); *Johnson v. BP Chems.*, Inc., 707 N.E.2d 1107 (Ohio 1999); *Eller v. Shova*, 630 So. 2d 537 (Fla. 1993); *Rovasio v. Wells Fargo Armored Services. Corp.*, 767 A.2d 1288, 47 Conn. S11pp. 30 (2001)
Exceptions Recognized by the Courts:	**Description**	**Oft-cited Court Cases**
Workplace harassment	Most jurisdictions recognize that workers who have been raped, assaulted, or murdered in the workplace because of their sex, race, religion, or national origin are not limited to the workers' compensation remedy. An employer is ordinarily liable for "hostile work environment" harassment if it fails to take prompt remedial action to protect a worker once it learns of the problem. Although most jurisdictions reject hostile-work-environment claims based on a single incident, several allow them if the incident was sufficiently severe, as in the case of rape. In some states, employers are held strictly liable for sexual assaults committed by their supervisors	*Slayton v. Mich. Host, Inc.*, 376 N.W.2d 664 (Mich. Ct. App. 1985); *Konstantopoulous v. Westvaco Corp.*, 690 A.2d 936 (Del. 1996). *Silkwood v. KerrMcGee Corp.*, 464 U.S. 238 (1984); *Sheridan v. Forest Hills Pub. Sch.*, 637 N.W.2d 536 (Mich. Ct. App. 2001); *Champion v. Nationwide Sec., Inc.*, 545 N.W.2d 596 (Mich. 1996); *Doe v. Capital Cities*, 58 Cal. Rptr. 2d 122 (Ct. App. 1996); *Ferris v. Delta Air Lines, Inc.*, 277 F.3d 128 (2d Cir. 2001); *Radtke v. Everett*, 501 N.W.2d 155 (Mich. 1993)

FIG. 9.2

Evolving approaches on exceptions to workers' compensation for workplace violence injuries.

Source: Sakis, J.R. and Kennedy, D.B., 2002. Violence at work. Trial 38 (13), 32–37.

Continued

Personal-animosity doctrine	Offenders sometimes attack co-workers for reasons unrelated to their employment. State laws usually preclude victims from recovering workers' compensation benefits because the injuries did not arise out of—and in the course of—employment. Courts may permit an employee to bring a traditional tort action against an employer if an offender victimized a worker for personal reasons. The courts commonly refer to this rule as the "personal-animosity doctrine" because the risk of physical assault has its roots in the victim's personal life and spills over into the workplace	*Security Ins. Co. v. Nasser*, 704 SW 2d 390 - Tex: Court of Appeals 1985; *Morris v. Soloway*, 428 NW 2d 43 (Mich: Court of Appeals 1988); *Peterson v. RTM Mid-America*, 434 SE 2d 521 (Ga: Court of Appeals 1993)
Independent claims of surviving relatives	Most workers' compensation statutes provide benefits to the relatives of deceased workers as an exclusive remedy. A few jurisdictions, however, recognize an exception to this rule, and permit surviving relatives to bring independent claims against the deceased worker's employer. Such jurisdictions have distinguished the surviving relatives' independent claims from those derived from the deceased worker, which are barred by the exclusive-remedy doctrine	45 F. Supp. 2d 1015 (D. Mont. 1999); *Johnson*, 707 N.E.2d 1107; *Ferriter v. Daniel O'Connell's Sons, Inc.*, 413 N.E.2d 690 (Mass. 1980); *Mullarkey v. Florida Feed Mills, Inc.*, 268 So. 2d 363 (Fla. 1972)
Off-hours assaults	Sometimes offenders assault employees on employers' premises before the employees begin work, after hours, or while visiting the workplace for pleasure. Many of these workers have avoided the exclusive-remedy doctrine by arguing that they were not engaged in the course of their employment when the assault occurred. Some states deny workers' compensation in instances when the visit is social or recreational, which means that workers and the surviving relatives of deceased employees in such cases can bring lawsuits against the employers	*Cremeans V. Maynard*, 246 S.E.2d 253 (W. Va. 1978); *Zepf V. Hilton Hotel & Casino*, 786 A.2d 154 (N.J. Super. Ct. App. Div. 2001); 403 N.W.2d 410 (S.D. 1987); Mich. Comp. Laws. Ann. §418.301 (3) (1999)
Employer's breach of duty to provide security	Workers have also argued that their employers breached a contractual or assumed duty to provide a safe workplace. Courts may rely on the employment procedures manual to support a decision that the employer had voluntarily assumed the duty to protect its workers	*Vaughn v. Granite City Steel Division of National Steel Corp*, 576 N.E.2d 874 (Ill. App. Ct. 1991)
Third-Party Exceptions:	**Description**	**Oft-cited Court Cases**
Labor Unions	Victims of workplace violence may sue labor unions for assaults committed by their members on temporary workers or those who decide not to strike or to cross picket lines. Federal law also regulates the conduct of labor unions. The Norris-LaGuardia Act, for example, imposes liability on unions when they authorize, ratify, or participate in assaults by their members	*United Brotherhood v. Humphreys*, 203 Va. 781, 127 S.E.2d 98 (1962); 32 29 U.S.C. §106 (1998); *Laborers' Int'l Union of N. Am. v. Rayburn*, 559 So. 2d 1219 (Fla. Dist. Ct. App. 1990)
Franchisor Liability	Courts may hold franchisors liable for negligently performing an assumed duty to provide security to employees of the franchisee. The outcome of cases often turns on the amount of control that the franchisor exercises over the franchisee's daily operations	*Martin v. McDonald's Corp.*, 572 N.E.2d 1073, 213 Ill. App. 3d 487, 157 Ill. Dec. 609 (App. Ct. 1991); *Decker v. Domino's Pizza*, Inc., 644 NE 2d 515 (Ill: Appellate Court, 5th Dist. 1994)
Contract Security Companies	Courts may hold security companies negligent if their actions result in harm to an employee	*Holshouser v. Shaner Hotel Group Properties*, 518 S.E.2d 17 (NC: Court of Appeals 1999); *Bonds v. Abbeville Gen. Hosp.*, 782 So. 2d 1188 (La. Ct. App. 2001)
Commercial Landlords or Management Companies	Victims of workplace violence have also asserted claims of negligence and inadequate security against commercial landlords and management companies	*Nickelson v. Mall of Am. Co.*, 593 N.W.2d 723, 726 (Minn. App. 1999); *Sharon P. v. Arman, Ltd.*, 989 P. 2d 121 (Cal: Supreme Court 1999)

FIG. 9.2, cont'd

employers were independently negligent for failing to screen, train, or monitor the offending employee. Respondeat superior imposes liability through the employer/employee relationship, whereas claims of negligent hiring/retention focus on the direct negligence of the employer.[6]

In a case of sexual assault in the workplace, a plaintiff has to prove that the offending employee had a propensity for violence. Moreover, the plaintiff has to prove that the employer knew or should have known of such propensity (e.g., actual and/or constructive knowledge). In addition, the plaintiff has to prove that the employer hired the employee negligently or with callous disregard for the rights of people with whom the employee could reasonably come into contact.[7] Feehan and Keller (2013, p. 18) suggest that plaintiffs and defendants need to answer four questions to determine whether a negligence claim against the injured party's employer is barred: was the injury accidental? Did the injury occur in the course of the employment? Did the injury arise out of the employment? Is there some other reason why the injury is not compensable under the Workers' Compensation Act?

In some jurisdictions, courts may allow an employee to sue an employer if an employee victimized another employee for personal reasons. The courts commonly refer to this rule as the "personal-animosity" or "personal-animus" doctrine because the risk of physical assault is rooted in the victim's personal life and spills over into the workplace (Savard and Kennedy, 2014; Sakis and Kennedy, 2002). The party asserting the personal animus exception must establish that the assailant had a preexisting relationship with or a preexisting animosity toward the employee and that he or she intended to injure the employee for reasons personal to the assailant.[8] In some jurisdictions, "the personal animus exception will rebut the presumption that an injury that occurs on the employer's premises is work-related."[9]

In the sexual assault case discussed before, attorneys for the defendants filed a separate motion to dismiss plaintiff Bartman's complaint under the theory that the state Workers' Compensation Act offered the exclusive remedy for her. The state Workers' Compensation Act provided, in part, that employees' sole remedy for injuries or death by accident arising out of and in the course of the employment existed under the workers' compensation law. The parties agreed that the incident in this case constituted an "accident" that occurred "in the course of employment." Where they disagreed, however, and the question the court addressed in the sexual assault litigation, was whether the incident also fell under the "arising out of" prong of the statute. The defendants argued that the criminal act did arise out of Bartman's employment. Thus, the exclusivity provisions of the state Workers' Compensation Act should bar her lawsuit.

---

[6]*Patterson v. Blair,* 172 S.W.3d 316, 369 (Ky. 2005)—citing *American Gen. Life and Accident Inc. Co. v. Hall,* 74 S.W.3d 688, 692 (Ky. 2002).

[7]In their discussion of Mississippi law pertaining to employers' liability for workplace violence, Whitten and Mosley (2000, p. 526) note that a "possibility of violence is not sufficient … [t]here must be evidence that the employee 'was a person of known vicious character or one whom the employer should have known had a vicious character'" (see *Offshore Logistics, Inc. v. Astro-Marine, Inc.,* 482 F. Supp. 1119, 1121 (E.D. La.1980); *Thatcher v. Brennan,* 657 F. Supp. 6—Dist. Court, SD Mississippi 1986 at 11 (citing *Schultz v. Evelyn Jewell, Inc.,* 476 F.2d 630, 631 (5th Cir. 1973)).

[8]*Butler v. Southern States Co-op., Inc.,* 270 Va. 459, 620 S.E.2d 768, 772–773 (2005) ("plaintiff's injuries from sexual assault did not arise from her employment because her assailant's 'actions were the result of his asserted personal attraction' to her and 'could not be fairly traced to her employment'"). Quoted from *Jones v. Kroger Ltd. Partnership I,* 80 F. Supp. 3d 719—Dist. Court, WD Virginia 2015.

[9]*Allegheny Ludlum Corp. v. Workers' Compensation Appeal Board (WCAB) (Hines),* 913 A. 2d 345—Pa: Commonwealth Court 2006.

In contrast, plaintiff Bartman asserted that the assault was of a purely personal nature that was completely unrelated to her employment, thus exempting her claim from the worker's compensation bar. According to Bartman, the Workers' Compensation Act did not apply to every injury that occurred at a workplace. The proper focus, she contended, was whether the injury was personal in nature and thus not part of the "actual risks" associated with the employment. As the court found, Naquin had a history of unwanted sexual advances directed toward Bartman. The attack appeared to be the result of his asserted personal attraction to her and not anything related to the conditions of her employment.

According to the court, even if the defendants had known or should have known that Naquin posed a danger to the plaintiff because of his history of sexual assault, this knowledge should not automatically transform his personal violent predilections and attraction to the plaintiff into a condition of employment for purposes of the state Workers' Compensation Act. The sexual assault against Bartman was not a random assault that resulted because of the conditions under which the employer requires an employee to do work. Rather, the attack was personal in nature between two individuals who happened to be coworkers. The personal nature of the attack thus removed the claim from the exclusivity provision of the state Workers' Compensation Act. That is, the criminal attack against Bartman was not an act in furtherance of the employers' business. Therefore, the court ruled that Bartman's employment was not a proximate cause of the criminal attack, as the defendants argued. The court also opined that to grant the defendant's view would be to grant tort immunity to employers who were negligent in screening applicants or investigating complaints.

FORENSIC CRIMINOLOGY AND WORKPLACE SHOOTINGS

Workplace shootings that involve shooter suicide, multiple injuries, and/or multiple fatalities pose unique investigative challenges for the forensic criminologist. The seeming randomness and unpredictability of mass shootings suggests that such events are foreseeable everywhere and yet perhaps unforeseeable at any specific time and place. A forensic criminologist would need to know the controlling case law and consider whether the jurisdiction adheres to a prior similar acts test, totality of circumstances test, balancing test, or a hybrid of these tests of foreseeability. A forensic criminologist would evaluate whether the security company or the employer was on notice of danger of a mass shooting. That is, did the shooter make any credible threats or otherwise warn others that she or he was going to shoot up the premises before the incident? Here a forensic criminologist would assess whether there is evidence that the defendant knew of the dangerous propensities of the individual responsible for the crime. In a jurisdiction following a prior similar acts test, a forensic criminologist would evaluate whether there is evidence of past acts of indiscriminate shootings on the premises. If not, then courts have held the criminal conduct is unforeseeable as a matter of law.[10] Under a totality of circumstances test, a plaintiff would need to demonstrate any demographic, situational, behavioral, or land-use characteristics that would suggest that the premises owner or manager should have foreseen the shooting.

---

[10]*Wilbert v. Metropolitan Parks District.*, 950 P. 2d 522—Wash: Court of Appeals, 2nd Div. 1998. According to the Washington Supreme Court, "[i]f the criminal act that injures the plaintiff is not sufficiently similar in nature and location to the prior act(s) of violence, sufficiently close in time to the act in question, and sufficiently numerous, then the act is likely unforeseeable as a matter of law under the prior similar incidents test" (*McKown v. Simon Property Group, Inc.*, 344 P. 3d 661—Wash: Supreme Court 2015).

Furthermore, a forensic criminologist would investigate whether the security practices followed by the organization and security firm were within the standard of care for premises security. In addition, a forensic criminologist would assess whether there was a causal relationship between the defendant's actions or inactions and the shooting that contributed to the plaintiff's injuries. A forensic criminologist would address causation in terms of cause-in-fact and proximate cause.

In commenting on the November 2005 Tacoma Mall shooting where a shooter wounded six people, the Washington State Court of Appeals concluded "an intervening [criminal] act is not foreseeable if it is 'so highly extraordinary or improbable as to be wholly beyond the range of expectability.'"[11] In this case, Dominick Maldonado entered the Tacoma Mall in possession of an assault rifle and another firearm. After firing off several rounds, he was told to drop his weapon by Brandon McKown, who had pulled his own handgun to stop Maldonado. Maldonado shot and paralyzed McKown and then entered a Sam Goody's store, where he kept several employees and customers hostage for over three hours. Maldonado eventually surrendered to police. McKown brought a negligence action in state court against the mall property owner (Simon Property Group Inc.), alleging, in part, that Simon failed to exercise reasonable care to protect him from foreseeable criminal harm. The Washington Supreme Court noted that it is not the "unusualness of the act that resulted in injury to [the] plaintiff that is the test of foreseeability, but whether the result of the act is within the ambit of the hazards covered by the duty imposed upon [the] defendant."[12]

The 2005 Tacoma Mall shooting is illustrative of the challenges facing forensic criminologists in their assessment of foreseeability of a mass shooting incident, especially in a shopping mall. As we pointed out in Chapter 7, shopping malls may attract criminals and spawn criminal events because of the millions of people that visit each year (Savard and Kennedy, 2014, p. 259; Kinney et al., 2008). "Large shopping centers with higher volumes of patrons tend to attract more crime compared to smaller shopping centers because there are more potential victims, but an individual's risk of becoming a crime victim does not necessarily increase" (Savard and Kennedy, 2014, p. 259). Moreover, for an individual the odds of becoming a victim of a mass shooting at a large regional mall are low given the large number of annual visitors that visit malls every year. One could conclude that a mass shooting at a regional mall is foreseeable, but this would be due in large part to the number of visitors and not reflective of a given individual's statistical risk of victimization. One could consider shopping centers as vulnerable places to crime because of their multiple entry points and permeable perimeters that allow people to freely enter and exit. Moreover, "[s]hopping centers face the dilemma of incursions by people who have intentions of committing criminal or terroristic acts, while at the same time facilitating entry for legitimate customers" (Savard and Kennedy, 2014, p. 265).

In the Tacoma Mall shooting case, plaintiff lawyers for McKown argued that consideration of the "place or character" of a business is a distinct, alternative method of establishing reasonable foreseeability of a criminal event. According to the court, however, McKown offered "no test, criteria, or parameters regarding how 'character' is to be established or assessed." Plaintiff attorneys described the Tacoma Mall as a "soft target" "whose 'place or character' made the harm reasonably foreseeable." Yet the court was not convinced. "But aside from this bald assertion," McKown "offers no explanation

---

[11]*Christen v. Lee*, 113 Wash.2d 479, 780 P.2d 1307 (1989); quoting *McLeod v. Grant Cnty. Sch. Dist. No. 128*, 42 Wash.2d 316, 255 P.2d 360, 364 (1953).

[12]Quoting from *Rikstad v. Holmberg*, 76 Wash.2d 265, 456 P.2d 355, 358 (1969); *McKown v. Simon Property Group, Inc.*, 689 F. 3d 1086—Court of Appeals, 9th Circuit 2012.

as to how or why the 'character' of the mall necessarily made the mass shooting in this case 'reasonably foreseeable.'"

The court also referred to an FBI study of active shooter incidents from 2000 to 2013 that implied that malls were not necessarily susceptible to mass shootings compared with other public spaces (Blair and Schweit, 2014). The FBI study showed that while 45.6% of mass shooting incidents occur in places of commerce, 27.5% occur in businesses open to the public, 14.4% occur in businesses closed to the public, and 3.8% occur in malls, which equals the number of incidents in houses of worship. Educational institutions accounted for 24.4% of active shooter incidents, with another 10.0% on government property, 9.4% in public spaces, 4.4% in residences, and 2.5% in health care facilities. As the court argued, "[i]n light of these statistics and without a concrete proposal for determining the parameters of a duty created by the 'character' of a business, we leave that question for another day."[13]

In the Tacoma Mall case, the district court granted summary judgment to the mall owner ruling that as a matter of law the shooting was not reasonably foreseeable. The district court held that McKown failed to present competent evidence of prior similar criminal incidents on the mall premises. Under this foreseeability test, a plaintiff must show that past acts of violence on the business premises were sufficiently similar in nature and location to the criminal act that injured the plaintiff. The plaintiff needed to show that past criminal acts were sufficiently close in time to the act in question, and sufficiently numerous to have put the business on notice that such a violent act (e.g., mass shooting) was likely to occur. In applying the prior similar acts test, the court considered evidence of six other shootings and three other gun-related incidents on the Tacoma Mall premises but concluded these were not prior similar acts. The court reasoned that these other incidents were significantly different in "nature, scale, and location" from the indiscriminate mass shooting inside the mall. The court also concluded that past criminal incidents were too distant and remote in time, occurring between 5 and 13 years before the attack that injured McKown.[14] The court determined that the shooting incident was not foreseeable as a matter of law and that, as a result, the mall owner owed no duty to protect plaintiff McKown from a third-party criminal incident (i.e., the criminal actions of the shooter).

CASE EXAMPLE: MASS SHOOTING-SUICIDE

This Type III workplace violence case concerns the shooting of three workers at an automobile plant. The shooter also shot himself and died at the scene. In this case, one of the wounded workers initiated a lawsuit claiming that the automobile company had actual knowledge of a dangerous condition, that is, the risk of the shooter's violent actions at the plant. The plaintiff also alleged that plant security was inadequate to protect against the threat posed by the shooter. In addition, plaintiff claimed defects in both the overall security arrangements and program, and negligence on the part of the defendant security company, with whom the automobile plant had contracted to provide security services inside and outside the plant. The plaintiff pointed to the lack of screening or similar measures to detect whether employees could enter the plant with firearms. He noted that neither the automobile plant management nor the security company monitored the video cameras at the employee entrances. Plaintiff also

---

[13]*McKown v. Simon Property Group, Inc.*, 344 P. 3d 661—Wash: Supreme Court 2015.
[14]*McKown*. Id. at 2–4.

asserted that the automobile plant's Workplace Violence Prevention Program (WVPP) was inadequate in both its design and implementation.

According to excerpts from the forensic criminological report:

> When attempting to assess suicide potential or homicide potential, one must consider both risk factors and protective factors. Protective factors (which disincline one toward violence) are also known in the threat assessment literature as "buffers" (see Corcoran and Cawood, 2004, p. 109). While plaintiff has pointed out several risk factors which he believes should have led [automobile plant] management to be substantially certain that [the shooter] would violently attack his colleagues, there has been no mention of why it was not substantially certain that [the shooter] would become violent. He was a long-term employee of over 20 years who had never attacked a fellow employee. According to police interviews, he was described as a good guy (or nice guy) by [three employees]. ... [The shooter] was not socially isolated and was living with his girlfriend. He still had contact with his family. In fact, he had dinner with his former wife and one of his sons on the evening of the shooting. Neither thought he was contemplating violence.
>
> There is no evidence of a history of psychiatric treatment. Nobody reported [the shooter] to be hallucinating, delusional, profoundly depressed, destroying objects, or suffering from acute and chronic intoxication. He was not particularly regarded as a "gun nut," made no recent specific threats of violence, and was not known by management to have a keen interest in workplace violence incidents around the country.
>
> Finally, there is no standard of care requiring body searches, the use of metal detection technology, or the presence of security officers at employee entry points. Manufacturing employees cannot be feasibly subjected to airport-style scrutiny each and every time they enter the workplace. While it is theoretically possible an employee may wish to bring a firearm to work, it is not generally foreseeable enough (reasonably likely to occur) to justify the enormous burden which would be imposed on employer and employee alike should such an access control system be implemented.

In conclusion, the forensic report suggests that "there was no reason that [the automobile plant] should have been or was substantially certain that [the shooter] would commit the violent acts ... [H]is behavior on the night in question could not have been anticipated by [the automobile company management]."

For courts to impose liability on a business owner for injuries a plaintiff sustained on the owner's premises, not only must the plaintiff prove foreseeability, but the plaintiff must also show that the premises owner had actual or constructive knowledge of the situation or condition that caused the injury. Even if the injured plaintiff can show that the premises owner or manager knew that the shooter posed a risk of harm, the plaintiff must show that the injuries she or he suffered were "substantially certain" to occur from the shooter's entry onto the premises.[15] That is, the employee is not likely to

---

[15]Some states require that the injured employee show that the employer had "actual knowledge of the *exact* dangers which ultimately caused" the injury (emphasis added) (*Hinton v. YMCA of Cent. Stark Cty.,* 2006 WL 1746111 (Ohio App.2006)). Also, some states require that the plaintiff provide evidence that the employer knew and was "substantially certain" that, if subjected to this danger—that is, mass shooting—in the workplace, the employee would be harmed (*Fyffe v. Jeno's Inc.,* 59 Ohio St.3d 115, 118, 570 N.E.2d 1108 (1991)). Even if a plaintiff shows that the employer had knowledge of a dangerous condition, "it does not follow that [the employer] knew that injury to its employees was certain, or substantially certain, to result" (*Mitchell v. Lawson Milk Co.,* 40 Ohio St.3d 190, 192–193, 532 N.E.2d 753 (1988)). An employer's "knowledge and appreciation of the risk of harm," without more, "is insufficient to impute knowledge with substantial certainty that [the] harm would befall its employees" (*Singleton v. Ohio Concrete Resurfacing, Inc.,* 2007 Ohio 2012 (Ct. App. 2007 at 34)).

recover on a claim of employer intentional tort absent proof that the injury was substantially certain to result from a known risk of harm.

Moreover, if the plaintiff sues the security firm, the plaintiff must present sufficient proof of actual knowledge that the security system and operations were deficient or that any deficiencies endangered the employees. Sometimes the defendant employer may file a cross-claim against the security company, essentially shifting any blame to the security company. Such a situation occurred in the Bartman sexual assault case that we discussed earlier. But a premises owner's responsibility for the security of invitees cannot be delegated to a contracted organization. Ultimate responsibility for the security of invitees remains with the premises owner.

In the case of the shooting at the automobile plant, the plaintiff's expert testified that the automobile plant's perimeter security for entering and exiting the plant was "consistent with the standard" of manufacturing plants in the United States. The expert also testified that the lack of guards to monitor ingress into the plant was consistent with the industry standard. Finally, plaintiff's expert stated it is not standard for auto assembly plants to have metal detectors at the entrances. In the end, the court ruled that although the shooter was able to enter the plant with a concealed weapon, this was not a substantially certain result of any alleged or actual defects in the automobile plant's security system.

Mass shootings at schools, concerts, and other workplaces can be horrific, and lawsuits initiated by injured plaintiffs face a high bar to prove foreseeability, breach of duty, and proximate causation. Criminologists, legal scholars, and security practitioners currently debate whether physical security upgrades (metal detectors), armed guards, or other security measures might have a deterrent effect on mass shooters. Did the security firm's execution of security duties entice or attract a shooter to the premises? That is, did a shooter choose the place because it had weak security? Or, did the shooter choose the place for other reasons such as a high concentration of people to shoot? Did the rampage shooter harbor "delusions of grandeur" and seek fame and glory through killing? (Lankford, 2016b). Pathological depression, paranoia, lack of insight, external attribution of blame, anger, and compensatory narcissism often characterize active shooters (also known as rage murderers, rampage shooters, berserkers, and amoks) (Hempel et al., 2000; Palermo, 1997).

In addition, much criminological research shows that many people who commit mass shootings are suicidal at the time of their attacks. Research suggests that some shooters intend to die by a self-inflicted gunshot wound or by a shootout with police (e.g., suicide by cop). Nearly half of the perpetrators of mass shootings carried out between 1982 and 2018 took their own lives at or near the scene of their crime, according to a mass shooting database maintained by Mother Jones magazine (Follman et al., 2018). Add in the individuals who were shot and killed during subsequent encounters with police and about 7 out of 10 mass shooters do not survive. Death appears to be no deterrent to mass shooters. Lankford (2015, p. 586) contends that "many mass murderers appear to care more about harming others than they do about protecting themselves, and they often commit suicide or refuse to surrender and are killed by police."

The theoretical variants of environmental criminology offer much insight to forensic criminologists involved in investigations of mass shootings and other workplace violence incidents. Rational choice theory would view a mass shooting as a rational act insofar as the decision-making process that preceded the shooting was deliberative and informed by information in the immediate environment. These points resonate with the classic criminological work of Clarke and Cornish (1985) who noted that the contemplation of crime and the carrying out of the criminal activity do not involve a single decision. Rather, "crime events have a beginning, middle and end, and across the crime commission process many separate decisions are required" (Sidebottom and Wortley, 2016, p. 165). Most offenders, even mass shooters, make decisions sequentially. They tend to use cost–benefit techniques and rational decision-making processes for achieving their crime goals, for evaluating targets, and assessing the presence or absence of capable guardians. These rational practices and sequences can include schema for framing situations and scripts for selecting particular kinds of criminal behavior.

The insights of environmental criminology can assist the forensic criminologist in investigating the impact of socio-spatial conditions and physical and social settings on the etiology of mass shootings. Criminologists know that situational characteristics and environmental conditions can provide motivations and constraints to criminal activity and make some types of offending easier. Exploring the "crime facilitators" (Clarke, 2009; Clarke and Eck, 2005) of mass shootings may help uncover the influence of the risks, efforts, rewards, provocations, or excuses associated with such heinous events. Cornish (1994) developed the concept of *crimes scripts* to explain the choices, decisions, and sequence of actions offenders adopt prior to, during, and after the commission of a crime. As the crime event unfolds, the offender needs to make rational choices to move from one action and achievement to the next. In examining active shooter events using rational choice theory and crime script analysis, Osborne and Capellan (2017) suggest that different decision-making processes are at work in the planning, execution, and conclusion stages of a shooting. Event characteristics can overlap with different scripts (autogenic, victim specific, and ideological) to influence the selection of the location and the time and day of the active shooter event.

FORESEEABLE AND/OR UNFORESEEABLE: TERRORISM AND MASS CASUALTY EVENTS

A mass shooting or other type of attack that leads to many casualties needs to meet several criteria for authorities to label it as an act of domestic terrorism and therefore prosecute it through the criminal justice system. Specifically, "domestic terrorism" refers to activities that (A) involve acts dangerous to human life that are a violation of the criminal laws of the United States or of any State; (B) appear to be intended—(i) to intimidate or coerce a civilian population; (ii) to influence the policy of a government by intimidation or coercion; or (iii) to affect the conduct of a government by mass destruction, assassination, or kidnapping; and (C) occur primarily within the territorial jurisdiction of the United States.[16] Drawing the line between mass murder and terrorism is not always clear and straightforward. Researchers and scholars suggest that authorities may label a mass killing as act of terrorism or an act of mass murder depending on the motivation (political and/or ideological) of the suspect, selection of the target site, and selection of the target population (see, e.g., Fox et al., 2016; Hamm, 2007; Bowie et al., 2012).

Criminologists and sociolegal researchers debate whether the rise and seeming proliferation of terrorist attacks and mass casualty events portend a major transformation in meanings and applications of foreseeability (Fox and DeLateur, 2014; La Fetra, 2006, pp. 426–428; Lewis, 2016; Perry, 2002; Dain and Brennan Jr, 2003; Vizzard, 2014). Each new mass causality event brings a new wave of litigation as injured plaintiffs and families of the deceased victims file suits against the property owner, manager, and security firm. On the one hand, one might argue that mass casualty events and domestic

---

[16]P.L. 102–572, title X, § 1003(a)(3), Oct. 29, 1992, 106 Stat. 4521; amended Pub. L. 107–156, title VIII, § 802(a), Oct. 26, 2001, 115 Stat. 376.

terrorist attacks are rare events, as are pandemic events or executive hostage situations. These low frequency yet high impact events are difficult to plan for, respond to, and mitigate. Finch (2017, p. 1) has noted that negligent security lawsuits seeking damages from property owners, operators, and security providers following a terrorist attack are "a fairly recent trend." Prior to the 1990s, "courts typically held that losses suffered as a result of terrorist attack were attributable to terrorists, not property." Courts generally found that a mass casualty event or terrorist attack was "so remote that as a matter of law no rational juror could find that a landowner should have known about it" (Budd, 2016, p. 1). Courts have long held that mass casualty events are not foreseeable since such attacks are so rare and "so unlikely to occur within the setting of modern life." Thus, "a reasonably prudent business enterprise would not consider its occurrence in attempting to satisfy its general obligation to protect invitees from reasonably foreseeable criminal conduct."[17]

Since the 1990s, however, plaintiff attorneys have increasingly challenged the long-standing notion that terrorist attacks and mass casualty events are rare, once-in-lifetime events that are unforeseeable. Terrorist bombings in Oklahoma City in 1995 and New York in 1993 as well as the September 11, 2001 disaster have generated much legal and policy discussion concerning whether a commercial landlord's duty to its tenants and invitees should include some duty to protect against terrorist attacks and mass casualty events (Piccarello, 2005; Homburger and Grant, 2003; Pastor, 2007, pp. 515–593). A New York court held that the Port Authority was liable for the 1993 World Trade Center bombings, finding that the terrorist strike would not have occurred but for inadequate provision of security at the World Trade Center. In particular, the court ruled that terrorist attacks are foreseeable and that venue owners and operators should take "reasonable measures" to defend against them.[18]

Litigation arising out of the September 11, 2001 attacks added to the momentum of holding business owners, property managers, and security providers liable for injuries from an act of terrorism (Dain and Brennan Jr, 2003; Finch, 2017). Following those attacks, families of the victims sued a variety of entities, including the manufacturers of the hijacked airplanes. In these cases, the defendants argued that because the events of September 11 were so extraordinary and rare, the airlines had no duty to the victims. For defendants, terrorists had not previously used a hijacked airplane as a suicidal weapon to destroy buildings and murder thousands. In refusing to dismiss one case, Judge Alvin K. Hellerstein disagreed with the defendants' arguments and noted:

> I conclude that the crash of the airplanes was within the class of foreseeable hazards resulting from negligently performed security screening. While it may be true that terrorists had not before deliberately flown airplanes into buildings, the airlines reasonably could foresee that crashes causing death and destruction on the ground was a hazard that would arise should hijackers take control of a plane. The intrusion by terrorists into the cockpit, coupled with the volatility of a hijacking situation, creates a foreseeable risk that hijacked airplanes might crash, jeopardizing innocent lives on the ground as well as in the airplane. While the crashes into the particular locations of the World Trade Center, Pentagon, and Shanksville field may not have been foreseen, the duty to screen passengers and items brought on board existed to prevent harms not only to passengers and crew, but also to the ground victims resulting from the crashes of hijacked planes, including the four planes hijacked on September 11.[19]

---

[17]*Lopez v. McDonald's Corp.*, 193 Cal. App. 3d 495, 509–510, 238 Cal. Rptr. 436 (Cal. Ct. App. 1987).

[18]*Nash v. Port Authority of New York and New Jersey* 856 N.Y.S.2d 583 (N.Y. App. Div. 2008).

[19]*September 11 Litigation*, 280 F. Supp. 2d 279—Dist. Court, SD New York 2003 (P. 296).

As Judge Hellerstein reasoned, although there had been no terrorist incidents before the ones of September 11, 2001 where terrorists combined both an airplane hijacking and a suicidal explosion, he could not say that the risk of crashes was not reasonably foreseeable to an airplane manufacturer. In this case, the plaintiffs alleged that it was reasonably foreseeable that a failure to design a secure cockpit could contribute to a takeover of a cockpit by hijackers or other unauthorized individuals. These actions could substantially increase the risk of injury and death to people and damage to property. These allegations, according to Judge Hellerstein, were sufficient to establish Boeing Airline's duty to exercise reasonable case.

In reviewing the changing nature of post-terror attack litigation, Finch (2017) suggests that with Hellerstein's decision, "plaintiffs can now argue that basically any terrorist attack is 'foreseeable,' thereby requiring venue owners and operators to take 'reasonable' security mitigation measures to deter, defeat or mitigate terrorist attacks." Thus, it may be that what was once in the past considered an unlikely and unpredictable event, such as a mass casualty event resulting from a terrorist attack or shooting, might not be considered unexpected or unforeseeable today. In comparing the September 11, 2001 attacks with the 1995 domestic terrorist truck bombing of the Alfred P. Murrah Federal Building in Oklahoma City, Homburger and Grant (2003, p. 681) contend that "[s]ociety has learned that what once was unthinkable is now not only imaginable but is likely foreseeable. Combining the willingness of religious extremists to commit suicide-missions with the devastation brought to America's Heartland by a home-grown terrorist leads one to the logical conclusion that anything can become foreseeable." As one attorney has put it: "After 9/11, just about anything is foreseeable; and therein lies the problem. Courts now have to grapple with the implications of imposing liability on private and public entities for catastrophic criminal acts" (Purcell, 2010, p. 3). According to another attorney:

> Based upon increased terrorist activity throughout the world, substantial security policies initiated and discussed by Congress, and the establishment of federal entities such as the Director of Homeland Security and the Transportation Security Administration, there is ample evidence that government officials and the industry itself acknowledges the likelihood of future attacks, thus making them a foreseeable risk. Therefore, information regarding potential or anticipated criminal or terrorist activity, general risk in the particular area of concern, and a failure to exercise reasonable care under these circumstances will likely support claims (Leighton, 2010, pp. 2–3).

Since the September 11, 2001 attacks and subsequent litigation, plaintiff lawyers have increasingly challenged defendants' reliance on a prior similar acts test to establish the foreseeability of a mass casualty event. Indeed, the absence of a history of similar accidents may not relieve a premises owner of the duty to protect patrons from injuries caused by a mass shooting or terrorist attack. The defendant business may have constructive knowledge of similar incidents that have happened at other similar locations. Constructive knowledge of these attacks may be sufficient to establish foreseeability.[20] In some cases and in some jurisdictions, courts may allow plaintiffs to submit evidence other than prior acts of similar events to establish foreseeability.

In the case of the mass shooting inside a movie theater in Aurora, Colorado in 2012, the district court considered factors such as (1) prior mass shootings in various settings since 1984; (2) other shooting incidents at other movie theaters prior to this incident; (3) additional security hired by 80 of Cinemark's

---

[20]*Springtree Properties, Inc. v. Hammond*, 692 So. 2d 164 (Fla: Supreme Court 1997).

approximately 300 theaters to patrol their theaters for the midnight premiere of the Dark Knight Rises film; (4) a Homeland Security bulletin dated May 17, 2012 entitled "Terrorist Interest in Attacking Theaters and Similar Mass Gatherings"; (5) a suicide bombing in April of 2012 in Mogadishu, Somalia; and (6) a communication from an al-Qa'ida-linked extremist advocating attacks on U.S. theaters.[21]

In denying summary judgment to the defendants in the Aurora, Colorado movie theatre shooting, the court stated that what was "so unlikely to occur within the setting of modern life to be unforeseeable in [the past] was not necessarily so unlikely in 2012."[22] Here the court disagreed that a shooting in a movie theatre was so unprecedented as to be unforeseeable as a matter of law. Just because a commercial establishment has not experienced a terrorist attack or mass casualty event does not mean that such an event is not foreseeable. According to the court:

> One such relevant fact in the setting of modern life is simply the changed landscape in which any school or base of business where large numbers of people congregate operated in July of 2012. Although theaters had theretofore been spared a mass shooting incident, the patrons of a movie theater are, perhaps even more so than students in a school or shoppers in a mall, "sitting ducks." One might reasonably believe that a mass shooting incident in a theater was likely enough (that is, not just a possibility) to be a foreseeable next step in the history of such acts by deranged individuals.[23]

In the end, the jury ruled the Cinemark theater chain not liable in the 2012 Aurora, Colorado movie massacre.

As mass casualty events and terrorist attacks continue, premises owners and managers are likely to face carefully crafted and cogent arguments from plaintiff attorneys that such incidents are foreseeable. Further, like all negligent security cases, the analysis of each case will be fact intensive and depend on factors such as prior similar incidents, the type of venue and location of the premises, and any actual or constructive knowledge of specific credible threats (Homburger and Grant, 2003; Piccarello, 2005). Other issues underling the assessment of premises owner liability for terrorist acts may include compliance with governmental regulations, compliance with the premises owner's own policies and procedures, and the "reasonableness" and effectiveness of any security protections she or he implemented. Finch (2017) argues that "following an act of terror, an owner, operator or provider facing liability can expect expensive and protracted litigation over the 'reasonableness' of their security measures." After September 11, 2001, according to Homburger and Grant (2003, p. 681), "owners of apartment buildings, shopping centers, office buildings and industrial sites must rethink whether their buildings now become foreseeable targets of terrorist crimes. The attack by religious extremists on an office building in lower Manhattan has put owners of all types of real estate on notice that terror can strike anywhere at any time." In describing the "post-September 11 conundrum," Dain and Brennan Jr (2003, p. 88) suggest that "[i]f a property owner hides his or her head in the sand" and fails to adopt security measures "the property owner risks not meeting the prescribed standard of care. On the flip side, by being proactive, the property owner may meet his or her standard of care, but expand the realm of foreseeable risks to his or her detriment."

---

[21]*Axelrod v. Cinemark Holdings, Inc. et al.*, 65 F. Supp. 3d 1093, 1099, 2014 (D. Co. 2014).

[22]*Axelrod v. Cinemark Holdings, Inc.*, 65 F. Supp. 3d 1093, 1099 (D. Colo. 2014).

[23]*Axelrod v. Cinemark Holdings, Inc.*, 65 F. Supp. 3d 1101 (D. Colo. 2014).

Issues involving the generality and geographical specificity of terrorist attacks will likely be prominent in defendants' arguments. That is, defendants may argue that while the occurrence of terrorist acts in general might be foreseeable, a premise owner can rarely foresee a specific terrorist act occurring in a specific place. Even if plaintiffs can develop a compelling and persuasive foreseeability argument and analysis, they will face the two challenges of demonstrating a violation of standards of care and proving causation. In denying defendants' motion for summary judgment in the Aurora movie theatre shooting, the judge asked, "what should a reasonable theater have done before July 20, 2012 even if it recognized that 'it could happen to us'?" Would any reasonable preventative measure or combination of measures have stopped the shooter? His assault was not a random event. He carefully planned and executed the shooting. Plaintiffs acknowledged that the Cinemark theatre had various security-oriented policies and procedures in effect in July 2012, both nationally and locally. "Whether the Cinemark reasonably could be expected to have implemented any specific additional security measure in light of what was known at the time and the realities of the theater business is not an easy question to answer," according to the judge.[24]

In short, an expanding area of forensic criminology involves the analysis of crime foreseeability and security standards of care as they relate to the question of liability for workplace violence incidents that may also involve active shooters and terrorist attacks. Attorneys and courts can utilize the expertise of forensic criminologists to investigate and address questions concerning the foreseeability of harm and the reasonableness of security in light of foreseeable harm connected with a mass casualty event. Ultimately, courts will address questions of the foreseeability of terrorist attacks and mass casualty events on a case-by-case basis, following different statutory and case law that bears upon security issues. Established precedent may include definitions and tests of foreseeability, observations on the reasonableness of security measures in a particular situation, and controlling opinions on causation.

---

[24]*Axelrod v. Cinemark Holdings, Inc.*, 65 F. Supp. 3d 1093, 1103 (Dist. Court, D. Colorado 2014).

WRONGFUL CONVICTION LITIGATION

INTRODUCTION

The last two decades or so have seen an explosion of litigation initiated by people wrongly convicted of crimes committed by others or for "crimes" that never occurred.[1] "Wrongful conviction" is a broad and heterogeneous concept that has several different thematic and topical meanings. The term can refer to the conviction of a factually or "actually" innocent person (Zalman, 2006), a conviction achieved in part through the violation of constitutional rights, or a conviction through the manipulation of legal procedures that render the court proceedings fundamentally illegal and unfair. Several scholars have labeled wrongful convictions as "miscarriages of justice" and distinguished between "errors of due process" and "errors of impunity" (for overviews, see Forst, 2010, 2004; Leo, 2005). The former can range from violations of a defendant's rights to the conviction of a factually innocent person. The latter can range from the failure to apprehend a criminal to the acquittal of a factually guilty defendant. Errors of impunity refer "to a lapse of justice that allows a culpable offender to remain at large" (Forst, 2004, p. 23) or in some other way escape justice, as may have happened in the acquittal of OJ Simpson in the criminal case.

Over the decades, advances in forensic science investigative techniques and the application of DNA technology have improved how researchers can investigate cases and interpret forensic evidence. In 1989, Gary Dotson was the first person to be exonerated of a criminal conviction by DNA evidence. For the first time, DNA technology had been successful in establishing the innocence of an individual wrongly convicted of a crime. Since then, according to the Innocence Project, a national litigation and public policy organization dedicated to exonerating wrongfully convicted individuals, DNA analysis has exonerated 385 people as of July 2018 (Innocence Project, 2018). In May 2012, Sam Gross and Rob Warden launched the National Registry of Exonerations (NRE), an online database of exonerations housed at the University of Michigan Law School. The Registry currently lists 1889 exonerations and has become an authoritative source on wrongful convictions, listing more than five times as many

---

[1]The research literature on wrongful conviction is vast and continues to expand and become more differentiated and specialized. For general overviews, see Westervelt and Humphrey (2001); Rossmo (2008); Huff and Killias (2013); Redlich and colleagues (2014); Zalman and Carrano (2013/2014); Cutler (2012). For coverage of comparative issues, see Lupária (2015). For coverage of more general sociolegal policy and regulatory interventions and impact, see Ogletree Jr. and Sarat (2009); Cooper (2014); Medwed (2017).

Practicing Forensic Criminology. https://doi.org/10.1016/B978-0-12-815595-0.00010-9

non-DNA exonerations as DNA exonerations, a ratio that continues to grow. As discussed by Leo (2017), the study of wrongful convictions has catalyzed a huge growth in the number of cases exposed to public and expert scrutiny. This growth has helped produce new specialized academic and scientific studies and writings about the negative consequences of erroneous convictions for exonerees, crime victims, and families (Irazola et al., 2014; Scott, 2010; Armour, 2004).

The phenomenon of wrongful convictions has sparked much public outrage concerning the incarceration of innocent people, harsh police interrogation methods, and failure of the criminal justice system to bring the guilty to justice (for an overview, see Medwed, 2017). Law professors, legal practitioners, psychologists, sociologists, and criminologists have identified several specific practices that they believe have contributed significantly to wrongful convictions (Huff, 2002; Huff and Killias, 2013; McMurtrie, 2005; Risinger and Risinger, 2011/2012; Turvey and Cooley, 2014; Simon, 2012). The standard list of wrongful conviction sources includes, among others, mistaken eyewitness identification, false confessions, forensic science error or fraud, ineffective assistance of counsel, prosecutorial misconduct (e.g., withholding exculpatory evidence), jailhouse snitch perjury, "tunnel vision," and other cognitive biases that can in combination result in erroneous decisions (Gross, 2008; Huff, 2002; Zalman, 2010/2011).

Yet at least two caveats are in order. First, as noted by Acker (2017, p. 12), "the catalog of the specific problems that recur in wrongful conviction cases does not demonstrate that their role is causal." Rather, the "same troubling factors that surface in cases of wrongful conviction might also be prevalent in cases that do not result in wrongful convictions, cases which instead are screened and eliminated short of prosecution or end with a not guilty verdict."

Second, some cases may involve several of these sources, and researchers and criminologists have argued that it is more valid to identify these activities as errors or correlates rather than causes of wrongful convictions (Gould et al., 2013; Gould and Leo, 2010; Medwed, 2017). Focusing on causes or causation is misplaced, according to Leo and Gould (2009, p. 16): "wrongful conviction scholarship tends to portray causation as unidimensional—one case illustrates the problem of eyewitness misidentification, another case demonstrates the problem of false confession, a third case exhibits the problem of junk science, etc.—even though we know that cases of wrongful conviction have multiple sources." "If we exclusively examine cases of wrongful conviction," according to Acker (2017, p. 12), "we can only be assured that we will have identified several *correlates* of erroneous verdicts" (emphasis in original).

While journalists and some legal scholars have expressed alarm at the huge growth in the number of exonerations, others have noted that data and trends on wrongful convictions are imprecise and inconsistent. Two points are worth mentioning. First, the study of wrongful convictions has a long history (for an overview, see Gould and Leo, 2010). They have occurred during the colonial period (e.g., the Salem witch trials) (Huff et al., 1996) and during the early 19th century (Davis and Leo, 2014; Center on Wrongful Convictions, 2016). As discussed by Leo and Gould (2009, pp. 11–14), Edward Borchard wrote about the subject in a 1913 article published in the *Journal of the American Institute of Criminal Law and Criminology* (continued by the *Journal of Criminal Law and Criminology* in 1931) and in a book titled *Convicting the Innocent* published in 1932. Indeed, Borchard identified the specific issues currently associated with wrongful convictions—eyewitness misidentification, forensic science errors, and false admissions—more than 80 years ago. In the late 1940s, Erle Stanley Gardner established "the Court of Last Resort," an unofficial body to investigate suspected cases of wrongful conviction. During the 1980s, the introduction of DNA testing in criminal cases galvanized public interest in wrongful convictions and catalyzed an explosion of media scrutiny of the legal system, legislative attention, and advocacy groups under the umbrella of the "innocence movement" (Medwed, 2008; Zalman, 2006).[2]

Second, researchers and scholars have pointed out that definitional ambiguities, inexact measures, and lack of a reliable quantitative methodology have confounded attempts to estimate the size, prevalence, and rate of wrongful convictions. Gross and O'Brien's (2008) study, which compared characteristics of 105 exonerated death row defendants with 137 executed capital defendants, demonstrated a 2.3% exoneration rate among death sentence cases (see also Gross, 2008). Rossmo's (2016, p. 213) review of the literature suggests that estimates of the frequency of wrongful convictions range from 0.5% of all felonies to 4.1% of death row inmates, and 5% and higher for murder and sexual assaults (see Huff et al., 1996; Roman et al., 2012).

Zalman (2012) used a qualitative methodology to estimate the incidence of wrongful convictions at between 0.5% and 2% of all felony convictions in the United States. Zalman's (2017, pp. 1–2) analysis notes that the few empirical studies of exoneree samples derived from known defendant universes demonstrate error rates in the range of 2%–5% for homicide, death sentences, and serious sexual conduct cases (Roman et al., 2012). We cannot extrapolate empirically derived rates to all crimes because base rate data do not exist. Nevertheless, Zalman (2017, p. 2) "suggests a plausible error felony-conviction rate of at least 1 percent annually" and proposes that there are about 10,000 wrongful convictions a year, of which about 4000 are imprisoned. "If this qualitative estimate were 2% or 3%, the numbers would be doubled or tripled. Innocence experts believe that America's prisons hold at least 50,000 innocent people" (p. 2).

In sum, we know that systems of justice can be susceptible to error and documented cases of wrongful conviction continue to grow. That said, we cannot confidently draw conclusions about the prevalence or dominant causes of wrongful convictions from the various exoneration databases or other studies en masse. Generalizations are difficult to make from the data contained in the exoneration databases maintained by the Innocence Project and the NRE because these are not likely to be representative of the presumably much larger universe of cases involving innocent persons convicted of crimes. Researchers have described the information currently available about wrongful convictions as the "tip of the iceberg" (Findley and Scott, 2006, p. 291; Garrett, 2011a, p. 11), "a drop in the bucket" (National Registry of Exonerations [NRE], 2016, p. 2), and "a tiny fraction" of the complete picture (Krajicek, 2015).

In this chapter, we examine three cases to illustrate the ways in which a forensic criminologist can use criminological methods and theories to assess evidence in a wrongful conviction lawsuit. We examine cases involving allegations of unlawful arrest and malicious prosecution without probable cause, fabrication of evidence, and false confession. As many scholars and researchers recognize, erroneous convictions involve complex investigations; multiple contributing factors; complicated juror decisions; and deviations from organizational rules, policies, and investigative practices that may have changed over time (for an overview, see Medwed, 2017). Our goal is

---

[2]The "innocence movement" is a constellation of advocacy groups comprised of lawyers, journalists, researchers, and activists who work to exonerate the wrongfully convicted and promote legal system and policy reforms to correct the known causes of wrongful convictions (Zalman, 2010/2011). Zalman's (2017) edited special issue of the *Journal of Contemporary Criminal Justice* focused on analysis of the innocence movement by several researchers and an innocence movement leader (See Acker, 2017; Norris, 2017; Konvisser and Werry, 2017; Leo, 2017; Findley, 2017).

to explain how and under what conditions criminological concepts and approaches can assist a fact finder in understanding the various sources and processes of error (e.g., tunnel vision, confirmation bias, eyewitness (mis)identification, false confession, coercive interrogation, forensic error and fraud, police and prosecutorial misconduct, among others). Criminological approaches and methods can explain how investigative and adjudicative breakdowns can occur in different types of cases that lead to erroneous convictions. Overall, we discuss several common causes of erroneous conviction and explain how a forensic criminologist can use available policing and criminological literature to inform a fact finder about the actions of police investigators in bringing a case forward and of a prosecutor in prosecuting it (Girod, 2014; Osterburg and Ward, 2010).

CASE EXAMPLE: EYEWITNESS (MIS)IDENTIFICATION

This case arises out of the (mis)identification of Plaintiff Larry James (a pseudonym), an elderly person allegedly responsible for numerous thefts in a major U.S. metropolitan area. The thefts had the same modus operandi. The suspect would allegedly knock on a victim's door and identify himself as a neighbor. He would then invite himself in for coffee and, after excusing himself to use the bathroom, he would steal money or personal items from the victim's home. Mr. James was eventually arrested by several police departments based on probable cause to believe he had faked a friendship with several different senior citizens, insinuated himself into their homes, and then stole from them. The arrests garnered media attention from several news stations that broadcast Mr. James's name and photograph throughout the area. In one municipality, police department detectives arrested Mr. James for larceny in a building after he victimized two senior couples, Bill and Mary Tempesta (pseudonyms) and Lenny and Victoria Westerfield (pseudonyms). These couples identified Mr. James after detectives showed them several photospreads. Ultimately, the county prosecutor's office declined to prosecute Mr. James. Several factors may have influenced the prosecutor's decision not to prosecute including a negative polygraph finding and the commission of a similar crime by another unknown person, or report of same while Mr. James was on an electronic tether.

Mr. James sued six police departments and individual officers alleging unlawful arrest, use of unduly suggestive identification procedures, and malicious prosecution without probable cause in violation of the Fourth and Fourteenth Amendments. Probable cause is "reasonable grounds for belief, supported by less than prima facie proof but more than mere suspicion."[3] To determine whether probable cause exists, a court will examine the totality of the circumstances and assess whether the facts and circumstances known to the arresting police officer were sufficient to believe that the individual committed the offense. That is, a police officer has probable cause for an arrest when the facts and circumstances known to him or her would warrant a prudent person to conclude that an offense has been committed and that the subject committed it.[4] In a malicious-prosecution lawsuit, a plaintiff must prove by a preponderance of evidence that the police detectives "knowingly and deliberately, or with a reckless disregard for the truth, made false statements or omissions

---

[3]*Sykes v. Anderson*, 625 F.3d 294, 306 (6th Cir. 2010); *United States v. McClain*, 444 F.3d 556, 562 (6th Cir. 2005); *United States v. Ferguson*, 8 F.3d 385, 392 (6th Cir. 1993).
[4]*Hinchman v. Moore*, 312 F.3d 198, 205-06 (6th Cir. 2002); *Green v. Throckmorton*, 681 F.3d 853, 865 (6th Cir. 2012).

that create[d] a falsehood and such statements or omissions were material, or necessary, to the finding of probable cause."[5]

In this case, Mr. James made four allegations that he claimed undermined the officers' claims of probable cause. First, he alleged that local police department detectives Steven McMillian (a pseudonym) and William Matlock (a pseudonym) "rigged" the photo lineup process to secure a false identification.[6] Regarding the photo array, James asserted it was unduly suggestive because his photo contained a blue background that stood out from the other five "fillers" (foils, distractors), thus arguably creating an unduly suggestive photo array. Second, James claimed the black and white array was suggestive based on the dress of all subjects. Third, he alleged that the eyewitnesses had strikingly different descriptions of the perpetrator. Fourth, he argued that detectives provided post-identification feedback, thereby biasing the identification process and tainting the case.

In this case, several witnesses separately identified Mr. James and stated that they were "100% positive" that he had stolen from their house. The identification occurred mere days after the thefts, and at least two victims spent several minutes with Mr. James while he drank his coffee. These eyewitnesses were able to observe him closely under good conditions during daylight hours. The court also noted that the witnesses' description of the suspect as being an elderly man with gray hair, approximately 5'7" tall, and weighing 170 pounds, closely conformed to Mr. James' actual height and weight. "Under these circumstances," according to the court, "even if the photo array was flawed … there is no reason to doubt the [witnesses'] identifications. They were reliable."

In the end, the court concluded that the police officers had probable cause to seek an arrest warrant and did not influence the decision to prosecute. The court could not say it was clearly established that there was no probable cause for arrest given the strength of the multiple witness identifications. The court also held that there were minimal grounds on which Mr. James' photograph differed from the others. The court also rejected James' malicious prosecution claim. That is, the court found no evidence that the officers turned over untruthful materials or that they showed reckless disregard for the truth to establish probable cause. These findings and conclusions reflect the results of the forensic criminological investigation.

According to the forensic criminologist's report:

> A photo lineup which may have been conducted in a suggestive manner can be "cured," per the U.S. Supreme Court, provided certain other mitigating identification conditions are present. According to *Manson v. Braithwaite*, 432 U.S. 98 (1977) and *Neil v. Biggers* 409 U.S. 188 (1972), a suggestive lineup could still be admissible if other conditions were favorable for identification purposes. For example, the … victims had an opportunity to focus their attention on the perpetrator's face. They spent considerable time with him under good lighting conditions and were quite confident in the

---

[5]*Sykes*, 625 F.3d at 305; *Hinchman v. Moore*, 312 F.3d 198, 205-06 (6th Cir. 2002).

[6]Police departments generally use three types of identification procedures: photo arrays, live lineups, and show-ups (National Research Council, 2014; Police Executive Research Forum, 2013). During a photo array, a detective presents a number of photographs—one suspect and usually five or more known innocent fillers—either all at once (simultaneous presentation) or one at a time (sequential presentation). According to a 2013 survey of randomly selected police departments by the Police Executive Research Forum (2013), 69% of photo-arrays are conducted by a nonblind administrator. This survey had a sample size of 1377 with 619 completed surveys, resulting in a response rate of 45%.

> accuracy of their positive identification. Furthermore, their description of [Mr. James] before the photo lineup was consistent with his photo image, and the lineup was conducted just weeks after, rather than several months or even years after the crime [citation to Wrightsman and Fulero, 2005, pp. 230–231]. No disguises were involved, this was not a cross-racial identification, and the perpetrator was seen up close rather than at a distance. These last three conditions are conducive to accurate identifications … [citation to Brewer and Wells, 2011]. I might add that at least five other … victims also identified [Mr. James] in cases filed with [four police departments].

The previous excerpt from the forensic criminological report cites the famous U.S. Supreme Court decision *Manson v. Braithwaite* (1977) to buttress the investigative findings that eyewitness identifications obtained from photo arrays must be subjected to additional scrutiny to determine whether the identifications are reliable.[7] Essentially, courts are concerned with the integrity of the eyewitness evidence and the impartiality of the witness's memory of the criminal event and of the actions of the offender. Identifications should be based on the independent recollection of the witness and not be the result of unduly suggestive police procedures. The *Manson* case suggested five key points that trial courts should use in deciding whether the identification was so unreliable that it should be excluded at trial:

1. The eyewitness's opportunity to view the perpetrator at the crime scene.
2. The degree of attention the eyewitness focused on the perpetrator.
3. The accuracy of the witness's description of the perpetrator.
4. The time elapsed between the witness's identification of the suspect and witnessing the crime.
5. The certainty of the witness's identification of the suspect.

The forensic criminological report points out that several academic psychologists may disagree with the Supreme Court concerning the impact of these variables in "curing" a potentially suggestive lineup. Box 10.1 provides a list of court cases showing that numerous courts have held that photo arrays containing the defendant's picture with a different background are not suggestive and do not taint probable cause. Importantly, while scholars might have much to say about suggestive lineups, forensic criminologists should remember that the courts establish case law concerning these constitutional issues and not academic researchers (Wells and Quinlivan, 2009). The forensic report neither disputes nor supports the criticisms offered by forensic psychologists. Rather, police investigators must look to the courts for guidance.

A major issue raised by the plaintiff's expert witness was that the simultaneous photo lineup procedures used by the detectives significantly increased the likelihood of an identification error. According to the plaintiff's expert, the detectives should have conducted a photo lineup using a double-blind sequential viewing protocol. The sequential lineup shows lineup members to the witness one at a time and asks the witness to decide on each one before showing the next one. In contrast, the traditional simultaneous lineup shows the witness all lineup members at once. A double-blind procedure is one in which the law enforcement official administering the lineup has not been told which person

---

[7]See also, *Neil v. Biggers*, 409 U.S. 188, 93 S. Ct. 375, 34 L. Ed. 2d 401 (1972); *Perry v. New Hampshire*, 132 S. Ct. 716, 565 U.S. 228, 181 L. Ed. 2d 694 (2012).

BOX 10.1 COURT CASES ON RELATIONSHIP AMONG PHOTO ARRAYS, BACKGROUND, AND PROBABLE CAUSE

United States v. Gay, 423 F. App'x 873, 877 (11th Cir. 2011)—finding that a photo array was not unduly suggestive even though the defendant's photo and complexion were darker than the other photos and the defendant was wearing a different type of shirt.

United States v. Knight, 382 F. App'x 905, 907 (11th Cir. 2010)—holding an array was not unduly suggestive where the background differed slightly and the defendant had a slightly different complexion.

United States v. Gonzalez, 2011 WL 766580 (E.D.N.Y. 2011)—holding that a photo array was not suggestive where defendant's picture had the only blue background and defendant was only person wearing orange prison shirt.

United States v. Harris, 636 F. 3d 1026 (Court of Appeals, 8th Cir. 2011)—finding of "no evidence in the record that the identifying witnesses were influenced by the slight color variation." A "darker hue or different colored background does not in [itself] create an impermissible suggestion that the defendant is the offender," where the defendant was in front of a green-colored background while the other photos used a blue background.

United States v. Brennick, 405 F.3d 96, 99–100 (1st Cir. 2005)—holding that a photo identification was not suggestive although the defendant's photo had a darker background than the other photos.

United States v. Soto, 124 F. App'x 956, 965 (6th Cir. 2005)—holding that a photograph was not suggestive because the background was lighter, and the defendant was wearing a white shirt while the others wore dark clothing.

United States v. Mathis, 264 F.3d 321, 333 (3d Cir. 2001)—holding that a "slightly darker" background "did not significantly contribute to the array's unnecessary suggestiveness."

United States v. Burdeau, 168 F.3d 352, 357 (9th Cir. 1999)—holding that a photo was not suggestive even though it was "darker than the rest" and the defendant had his eyes closed.

---

is a suspect. Thus the term "double-blind" means that neither the administrator nor the eyewitness knows which individual in the lineup is the suspect. On the question of whether "blind" administrators should conduct lineups, a National Institute of Justice (1999, n.p.) report noted that "unintentional cues (e.g., body language, tone of voice) may negatively impact the reliability of eyewitness evidence," and that "psychology researchers have noted that such influences could be avoided if 'blind' identification procedures were employed" (see also Loftus, 2013). A number of research studies have produced evidence that if the person conducting a lineup knows which individual in the lineup is the suspect, he or she may inadvertently and unknowingly give nonverbal cues to the eyewitness. The effect of these cues could then compromise the validity of the process (Phillips et al., 1999; Garrioch and Brimacombe, 2001; Greathouse and Kovera, 2009; Kovera and Evelo, 2017; for an overview, see Gould and Leo, 2010, pp. 841–843).

The double-blind sequential viewing protocol advocated by some criminologists and academic psychologists is not a settled matter and remains a source of controversy (Mecklenburg et al., 2008; Wells et al., 2015, 2011; Wogalter et al., 2004; Charman and Quiroz, 2016). An oft-cited study by Mecklenburg and colleagues (2008) found that based on a series of yearlong multijurisdictional field experiments, the sequential double-blind method resulted in a loss of accurate identifications when compared to the simultaneous method. Kovera and Evelo (2017, p. 432) have noted that double-blind lineup administration "remains the least studied reform of eyewitness identification procedures." Some studies have failed to support the superiority of the sequential procedure over the more common simultaneous approach given that the size of the administrator-influence effect varies considerably (Clark, 2012b). For example, some studies find a strong administrator-influence effect with simultaneous lineups (e.g., Charman and Quiroz, 2016; Greathouse and Kovera, 2009; Haw and Fisher, 2004) whereas others find it with sequential lineups (e.g., Charman and Quiroz, 2016; Phillips et al., 1999). In an oft-cited experimental test of a sequential versus simultaneous lineup procedure, Wells and colleagues (2015, p. 12) expressed doubts:

> Although we launched this work [i.e., double-blind photo lineups using actual eyewitnesses] to find out if a sequential procedure used in many jurisdictions around the country reduces errors when compared with a simultaneous procedure, we found the performance of these witnesses to be quite poor regardless of the procedure used … Regardless of the explanation for the meager performance of these actual eyewitnesses, it is obvious that the sequential procedure is not the silver bullet. Whereas the current set of reforms proposed in psychological science (e.g., prelineup admonition instructions, double-blind administration, proper filler selection, sequential presentation) can help reduce identification errors, there is a long way to go.

Neither the National Research Council (2014, p. 3) nor the National Institute of Justice (1999) endorse sequential presentations in lineups and photo arrays. Norris and colleagues (2017, p. 7) assert that "[t]his lack of an official recommendation is largely based on the debate surrounding the potential for the sequential lineup procedure to negatively affect accurate identifications, and in particular of increasing the risk of false negatives, or a witness's failure to identify the true perpetrator" (Clark, 2012a; Wells, 2014). In a study using a policy analysis model based on decision theory to examine the utility of simultaneous and sequential lineups, Malpass (2006) found simultaneous lineups to be superior to sequential lineups. While psychologists have reported that certain eyewitness reforms are likely to reduce mistaken identifications, Clark (2012a) has pointed out that some of the same reforms have the potential to reduce accurate identifications as well. Moreover, studies that point to problems of eyewitness testimony and advocate for various reforms are based on the results of experimental controlled laboratory studies where guilt and innocence are known with certainty (for an overview, see Wells et al., 2015).

While some scholars and researchers advocate for the use of the double-blind, sequential protocol over the simultaneous lineup protocol, the majority of U.S. law enforcement agencies use single-blind procedures. A National Institute of Justice (NIJ) Guide published in 1999 did not recommend the adoption of blind lineup procedures, saying that such procedures "may be impractical for some jurisdictions to implement" because law enforcement agencies may not have sufficient personnel to ensure that a "blind" administrator could be available at all times in all police facilities (NIJ, 1999, p. 9). Through 2013, according to a national survey of police departments by the Police Executive Research Forum (2013), the most commonly reported procedure in use for administration of photo lineups (69%) and live lineups (92.1%) was a nonblind administrator. "This is consistently the most common method used by more than half of agencies regardless of agency size" (2013, p. x). Regarding sequential vs. simultaneous procedures, the Police Executive Research Forum (2013) survey found that that 68% of responding agencies used a simultaneous presentation of photographs for the administration of a photo lineup. Some jurisdictions have been reluctant to adopt double-blind sequential administration because of the constraints of preexisting rules, lack of financing, prosecutor discretion, and pragmatic concerns about implementation.

The suggestiveness of the interview process is only one issue of many in a long train of activities. Eyewitness investigations are complex and involve several discrete areas including identification procedures, interrogation, and the handling of informants. Police officers and detectives do not have total discretion and freedom to choose which investigative practices to follow in an eyewitness case. Police departments are likely to follow the evidentiary practices preferred by the local prosecutors who will take these cases to court. Detectives will follow the prosecutor's lead and direction. Also, a police department is not a research laboratory with abundant amounts of time and generous resources to assess and test whether different practices and procedures produce different results and outcomes. Practical difficulties combined with time pressures tend to constrain the options of police detectives and can make it difficult for some police departments to find officers to conduct sequential double-blind lineups.

CASE EXAMPLE: EVALUATING CLAIMS OF TUNNEL VISION AND CONFIRMATION BIAS

This case involves claims by Plaintiff Vincent Cipolla (a pseudonym) that Jan Michaels (a pseudonym), a police sergeant and certified fire investigator, deliberately fabricated evidence at a fire scene, engaged in malicious prosecution, and withheld exculpatory evidence. The case begins one night when firefighters from two different departments arrived at the scene of a fire at the home of Victoria Nicole (a pseudonym). Ms. Nicole and her children lived at this address along with Ms. Nicole's boyfriend, Vincent Cipolla, whose children would also live there from time to time. Although the fire was initially reported as a chimney fire, some responding firefighters were suspicious as to the nature of the fire and notified the local sheriff's office, which eventually involved state police sergeant Jan Michaels in an arson investigation of this fire. A year later, Mr. Cipolla was convicted of arson and sent to prison. He was released several years later after an investigation by a university-affiliated Innocence Clinic raised some issues about photographs which may not have been turned over to the defense under *Brady* requirements.[8] Because an Alcohol, Tobacco, and Firearm (ATF) arson expert had not had time to assess the impact of these photos on his initial opinions, a judge set aside the conviction, and a special prosecutor appointed by the state government decided not to reprosecute. Given the efforts involved in a new trial and the usual uncertainty about testimony, the assistant attorney general decided to dismiss the case with prejudice.

After his release, Mr. Cipolla initiated a lawsuit against the state government, county sheriff's office, and several law enforcement investigators for violations of his Fourth Amendment rights and Fourteenth Amendment rights. Specifically, he alleged that defendants failed to disclose exculpatory evidence to the prosecutor in violation of *Brady v. Maryland*, 373 U.S. 83 (1963). Cipolla also argued that defendants influenced or participated in the initiation of criminal prosecution by either supplying false information or omitting material information. In addition, he claimed that the county created policies, practices, and customs that failed to provide adequate training to its police officers. Cipolla argued that these actions caused him to be wrongfully detained without probable cause, charged with crimes he did not commit, wrongfully convicted and imprisoned, and deprived of liberty.

One of the core issues in this case was whether tunnel vision and confirmation bias tainted the sheriff's office examination of the arson evidence. Tunnel vision implies premature focusing on a particular

---

[8]In 1963, the U.S. Supreme Court ruled in *Brady v. Maryland* that the government has a duty to disclose material evidence to the defense which could change the outcome of a trial. This exculpatory evidence, often referred to as "Brady Material," could prove that the accused party is innocent or cast doubt on their guilt (see Rothlein, 2007).

suspect such that the "more law enforcement practitioners become convinced of a conclusion—in this case, a suspect's guilt—the less likely they are to consider alternative scenarios that conflict with this conclusion" (Gould and Leo, 2010, p. 851). Confirmation bias is the tendency to selectively search for or interpret information that validates one's initial preconceptions or hypotheses. Confirmation bias is usually not associated with deliberate manipulation or conscious intent to deceive. Rather, confirmation bias refers to the process of providing more emphasis or weight to evidence supporting a preexisting theory while discounting contradictory or disconfirming evidence.

The National Academy of Sciences (2009), the National Commission on Forensic Science (2015), and the President's Council of Advisors on Science and Technology (2016) have identified confirmation bias as a contributing source of forensic science error, noting that such errors are prevalent in DNA exoneration cases. In a recent survey of 403 forensic scientists from 21 countries, Kukucka and colleagues (2017, p. 452) found that "examiners regarded their judgments as nearly infallible and showed only a limited understanding and appreciation of cognitive bias." Most examiners believed they were immune to bias or could reduce bias through conscious intent and willpower. Furthermore, many examiners acknowledged bias in other domains but not their own and in other examiners but not themselves. Kassin and colleagues (2013) have coined the term *forensic confirmation bias* to describe and summarize the various ways in which one's beliefs, motives, and situational context can affect the collection and evaluation of evidence during the investigation of a criminal case.

In this case, the expert witness for plaintiff Cipolla criticized Jan Michaels' arson investigation as biased due to tunnel vision. This expert also claimed that Michaels "knowingly wrote the report" so as to "manufacture probable cause for arson..." As we have stated throughout this book, the role of the expert witness is to assist the trier of fact to understand the evidence or to determine a fact at issue. In this case, the proper subject for an expert witness to address is whether Michaels conducted an objectively reasonable criminal investigation, without bias and/or a preconceived notion of guilt not supported by evidence.

According to the forensic criminological investigation conducted by the expert witness for the defense:

> In my opinion, [Michaels] took proper steps to avoid "tunnel vision," and, thus, his investigation did not suffer from confirmation bias. Furthermore, there is no evidence whatsoever to support the egregious claim that [Michaels] purposefully or otherwise manufactured evidence or consciously disregarded exculpatory evidence. Even in instances where confirmation bias has been identified, it is more likely to have been an unconscious process rather than a deliberate process [citation to Simon, 2012, p. 25; Findley and Scott, 2006, p. 292].

To avoid tunnel vision and confirmation bias, forensic investigators should employ critical thinking and a field version of the scientific method to seek information that disconfirms their initial theories (Snook and Cullen, 2009, p. 90). In other words, if initial evidence points to a specific culprit for specific reasons, the wise investigator considers whether she or he can disconfirm this theory of the case. These points suggest that the investigator should avoid coming to conclusions early in the investigation. Rather, the investigator should begin the investigation without preconceived beliefs or impressions about the causes of the criminal event and wait to review all of the evidence before developing a hypothesis. The investigator should consider alternative causes and other explanations as to why the hypothesis may be incorrect (Blake, 2017, p. 13).

A forensic criminologist can investigate allegations of confirmation bias by asking several questions: First, is there evidence that investigators unconsciously correlated ambiguous or even contradictory information with the preferred direction of a case? Second, is there evidence that confirmation bias could have caused an experienced investigator to seek out information that positively correlated with the preferred direction of the case, thereby discounting alterative information sources that could challenge the findings and conclusions? Third, did the investigator miss any ignored leads, fail to pursue alternative lines of inquiry, or neglect to analyze evidence? Finally, was there any biased treatment of post-judgment evidence such as evidence that the investigator disregarded, downplayed, distorted, or illogically considered? (Rossmo, 2016, p. 217). A forensic criminologist can test for confirmation bias by considering what would happen if she or he changed the order of evidential discovery. The conclusions reached by the police detectives should not depend on the particular sequence in which they discovered the evidence. "If altering the evidential order changes the case conclusion, there is likely a problem with the investigative logic" (Rossmo, 2016, p. 217; Rossmo, 2008).

The forensic criminological report goes on to explain that Michaels attempted to disprove that the fire was intentionally set and that Cipolla was the culprit. Since none of these attempts to disprove intentionally were successful, there was probable cause to believe Cipolla had committed arson.

According to the forensic criminologist's report:

> Sgt. Michaels did not assume arson had been committed for over two weeks after his initial visit to the crime scene. He waited until electrical circuitry had been ruled out as a possible cause of the fire. Sgt. Michaels testified that he usually tests his theories with specialist colleagues; in this case with [one person] during their mutual visit to the fire scene and with [two other police sergeants] … Furthermore, in his deposition at pages 320–321, it is evident that Sgt. Michaels is aware of the importance of excluding alternative hypotheses, just as he is familiar with the need to avoid confirmation bias or expectation bias (a form of confirmation bias). In an attempt to disconfirm his notion that Mr. Cipolla was being untruthful about the events, Sgt. Michaels had Mr. Cipolla take a polygraph exam, which did not invalidate Sgt. Michaels' developing theory that Cipolla was criminally involved.

In short, the forensic investigation finds that Sgt. Jan Michaels' decision to focus on Mr. Cipolla at the beginning was not due to any premature judgment or confirmation bias. Rather, it was due to the various fire fighters' suspicions about the nature of the fire, which was reported as a chimney fire even though they found the stove to be lukewarm and its contents scarcely burned. Sgt. Michaels also testified that he took "with a grain of salt" the statements from Ms. Nicole's stepfather that Cipolla had set the fire.

Another method of combating confirmation bias is to avoid premature exclusion of suspects. A person with motive, means, and opportunity to commit the crime in question could be a viable suspect (Beveridge, 2011, p. 81).

As the forensic criminological report describes:

> In the instant case, Mr. Cipolla was the only person known to the authorities to possess all three [means, motive, and opportunity]. According to Victoria Nicole, she had asked him to move out the night before the morning of the fire, whereas he was hoping to build an extension onto her house in order to make more room for his children [citation to Nicole testimony at preliminary exam, pp. 15–16]. A fire would provide a reason for him to remain in order to rebuild, now with the

insurance funds. He, Cipolla, had the means (abilities) because of his firefighting experience. In fact, the record reflects an indication that Cipolla had boasted about his ability to set a fire without being caught. In fact, making "off-the-cuff" remarks or jokes about burning a structure can be used as evidence of planning or pre-knowledge [citation to Lyman, 1993, p. 373]. Mr. Cipolla also had the opportunity as he was the only adult present in the home when the fire started. Although there were children present, nobody has suggested any of them could be viable suspects or would have had motive, means, or opportunity. In other words, once it was determined the fire was set by human actions, Mr. Cipolla became the proper focus of attention.

In the end, the court found that the plaintiff failed to show that Michaels had acted recklessly in his investigation of the fire. To paraphrase the court's findings and conclusions, Michaels spent multiple hours at the site, produced an eight-page report of his findings, and took 115 photographs. At the scene, he spoke with the fire chief who stated that he was skeptical of Cipolla's claim that the fire originated as a small chimney fire. Michaels' analysis and conclusions supported the fire chief's doubts. During his follow-up investigation, Michaels took an additional twenty photographs and wrote a brief supplemental report. By this point, he had considered and eliminated other potential causes of the fire, such as natural and electrical causes. The testimony in this case supported Michaels' position that he did not deliberately fabricate evidence, and Cipolla offered no testimony or affirmative evidence to the contrary. Finally, the plaintiff's expert witness acknowledged that fire investigators viewing the same body of evidence sometimes reach different conclusions. This expert witness found no evidence that Michaels removed evidence from the scene, planted evidence at the scene, or fabricated evidence. Through the photographs, reports, and deposition testimony, the court noted that the evidence supports Michaels' claim that he attempted to investigate the fire scene thoroughly.

We can draw several lessons from the previous case on the problems of offering speculative opinions on the presence of cognitive bias to decide case-specific factual issues. First, expert witness claims about the presence of cognitive bias may not qualify as expert testimony according to Rule 702 unless the claims are relevant to the case at hand, supported with evidentiary proof, and based on a reliable method. Expert opinions must be products of "facts or data" and of "reliable principles and methods." Moreover, an expert's report must "assist the trier of fact to understand the evidence or to determine a fact in issue."

Second, while decades of psychological research have established that perception and decision-making are vulnerable to a host of cognitive biases, any allegation of cognitive bias must go beyond summarizing general scientific evidence and make case-specific descriptive and causal claims using a reliable method for doing so. We cannot simply assume that general social science research on cognitive bias will support a case-specific claim. Rather, an expert witness must establish empirically the fit between general research findings on cognitive bias, the particulars of a wrongful conviction case, and case-based evidence of cognitive bias. Reliable descriptive and causal claims about the presence of confirmation bias require reliable methods of descriptive observation and causal inference.

A third lesson from the previous case is that forensic criminologists should conduct a systematic and thorough forensic examination before arriving at any conclusions about a case. The forensic criminologist should remain objective, use a rational investigative research design, and carefully avoid the interjection of prejudgment. Some experts might cite vivid testimony or anecdotes that supposedly illustrate cognitive bias at work and then opine that the materials they have reviewed are "consistent" with the conclusion that bias was at work. Yet it is crucial that these experts disclose what methods they followed to measure "consistency." Experts must also state what methods they used to determine whether and how a forensic science investigation (e.g., arson) was "vulnerable" to bias in cases of wrongful conviction. A thorough investigation involves checking all leads, checking key leads to ensure consistency, pursuing disconfirming or counterfactual evidence forthrightly, and corroborating important data sources using other data sources.

CASE EXAMPLE: EVALUATING ALLEGATIONS OF FALSE CONFESSION

This case surrounds the wrongful conviction of James Jackson (a pseudonym) who was exonerated by DNA evidence in the rape and murder of Melinda Kaminski (a pseudonym). She had been raped, strangled, mutilated, doused with gasoline, and set afire. Months after the incident, the local police department arrested Jackson and he gave a court-reported statement implicating himself and two other men, William Danielson and William Dercher (both pseudonyms). The police later confirmed that Dercher was incarcerated at the county jail on the day of Kaminiski's rape and murder. The court held separate juries because the confessions of Danielson and Jackson were inadmissible against the other. The juries found both defendants guilty and the judge sentenced them to life in prison without parole. Later, after the court of appeals affirmed the convictions, DNA tests established that hairs found at the murder scene and cellular material found under Kaminski's fingernails could not have come from either Jackson or Danielson. Prosecutors dismissed the charges and released Jackson and Danielson from custody. Jackson then sued the city for various damages from his conviction that he claimed resulted from a forcibly extracted confession.

As we have stressed throughout this book, at the outset of each case, a forensic criminologist should conduct a thorough analysis including a comprehensive and exhaustive review of all case-related information and evidence (Turvey, 2008, pp. 190–193). In a case of allegations of false and coerced confession, a forensic criminologist should comment on issues from an academic research perspective and not draw conclusions about the veracity of a confession. Forensic criminologists are not lie detectors. It is up to the jury to resolve factual issues and decide whether the evidence supports claims of coerced confession. As McCann (1998, p. 16) puts it, "the truth or falsity of the confession are actually legal issues for the trier of fact to determine; they are not issues that behavioral science experts can definitively determine." Drawing on criminological methods and theories, forensic criminologists can make linkages between general social science research findings and specific case questions. Where appropriate, judge and jurors may then apply criminological knowledge, methods, and theories to the facts of the case at hand.

Faigman and colleagues (2014) offer an approach that forensic criminologists may find useful in criminological expert testimony relating to wrongful conviction litigation cases. Specifically, they make a distinction between social framework evidence that describes general scientific propositions and diagnostic evidence that uses general propositions to understand individual cases. Social framework evidence provides jurors with background information helpful to them in understanding and processing wrongful conviction allegations related to tunnel vision, confirmation bias, eyewitness (mis) identification, false confession, coercive interrogation, forensic error and fraud, police and prosecutorial misconduct, among others. Also known as "educational" testimony," social framework testimony offers an analytical lens through which criminologists and forensic experts typically view cases.

Diagnostic evidence is particularized expert evidence that addresses the specific facts of a case. According to Faigman and colleagues (2014, p. 418), "[j]udicial analysis of 'fit,' expert qualifications, testability, error rates, peer review, general acceptance, helpfulness, and other traditional admissibility criteria for expert evidence will often vary, sometimes significantly," based on the distinction between social framework evidence and diagnostic evidence. Social scientists and criminologists routinely testify in criminal and civil matters but generally limit their contributions to general principles that would be relevant when applied to the unique factual circumstances of any given case. The jury must decide precisely how to apply the general principles to the facts at hand and decide the ultimate issues (Kennedy, 2013; Monahan and Walker, 2014; Monahan et al., 2008; Mulkey, 2009).

A basic question in this case is whether James Jackson, William Danielson, and William Dercher gave their confessions voluntarily or whether investigators used force, the threat of force, or police-directed rehearsal and scripting to extract the confessions. Here the forensic criminologist would investigate whether the suspects made their statements knowingly and intelligently. The forensic criminologist would also want to know the types of interrogation methods the investigators used to solicit a confession. If investigators used violence to extract a confession, then the police and courts cannot use the confessions as evidence of guilt. Over the decades, the U.S. Supreme Court has ruled that a confession is inadmissible when police use coercive techniques or subject the suspect to abusive conditions.[9]

In the following excerpt, the forensic criminological report provides a description of the Reid Technique, a method of questioning suspects developed by consultant and polygraph expert John Reid.

> Over many years, a technique known as the Reid Technique has been developed by investigators and is the most common technique used in interrogation across the U.S [citations to Inbau et al., 2001; Wrightsman and Kassin, 1993, pp. 59–83]. Essentially, this technique involves helping a criminal to rationalize his crime as an understandable human error, which will not lead to harsh punishment due to his remorse. There is also an implication that things will go worse for the subject in terms of sentencing if he does not confess. Detectives may also appear to want to act on behalf of the suspect and to have his best interests at heart, and there is subtle pressure on the suspect to see it that way. This approach is professionally permissible, taught in police training sessions around the country, and is generally effective. Unfortunately, some individuals subjected to this technique will confess to a crime they have not committed. Hence, this technique has its detractors [See, for example, Leo, 2008] … The courts, however, seem to acknowledge the difficulties inherent in getting criminals to confess and allow the police a certain leeway. Please note police interrogation techniques also have supporters [See, for example, Cassell, 1998].

---

[9]According to the U.S. Supreme Court "[s]tatements compelled by police interrogations of course may not be used against a defendant at trial" (see *Brown v. Mississippi*, 297 U.S. 278, 286, 56 S.Ct. 461, 80 L.Ed. 682 (1936); *Chavez*, 538 U.S. at 767 (citing United States v. *Verdugo-Urquidez*, 494 U.S. 259, 264, 110 S.Ct. 1056, 108 L.Ed.2d 222 (1990)); see also *Bram v. United States*, 168 U.S. 532, 542, 18 S.Ct. 183, 42 L.Ed. 568 (1897); "a reasonable public official interrogating a criminal suspect would have recognized that coercing a confession by abusive language and physical contact, along with coaching the suspect as to the details of the confession, clearly violates the suspect's constitutional right against self-incrimination." See *Anderson v. Creighton*, 483 U.S. 635, 640, 107 S.Ct. 3034, 97 L.Ed.2d 523 (1987). See Perez (2010, p. 62) for a listing of relevant U.S. Supreme Court cases.

Supporters argue that the Reid Technique is useful in extracting information from otherwise unwilling suspects, while critics have charged the technique can elicit false confessions from innocent people (Davis and Leo, 2014). On one hand, Perez (2010, p. 710) suggests that the evidence that accusatory interrogations create false confessions "is considerably weak given the relatively few false confessions this tactic produces in comparison to the other two outcomes: the production of either no confession or a truthful confession." On the other hand, Leo (2018, p. 5) contends that from the 1990s to the present, police interrogation methods and practices have become controversial because of police-induced false confessions that often lead to the wrongful conviction of the innocent, as documented by DNA and non-DNA exonerations (Kassin et al., 2009; Drizin and Leo, 2003). This last point is not surprising given that the Reid Technique is designed to "persuade a rational guilty person who knows he is guilty to rethink his initial decision to deny culpability and choose instead to confess" (Davis and Leo, 2014, p. 49; Leo, 2018, p. 19). Police are trained to deal with opposition, pressure, and denial by the suspect. The purpose of interrogation techniques is to convince the guilty person to confess to the crime. When these same techniques are used on innocent suspects, "they carry a heightened risk that they will elicit false statements, admissions, and/or confessions" (p. 19).

To add nuance and complexity, some police investigators may believe they can identify a false confession when given but research suggests they may not be much better at detecting lies than private citizens (Hartwig et al., 2004; DePaulo and Pfeifer, 1986; Vrij, 2000). The point is that false confessions may occur as a result of the interrogation process even though police officers will not know that this has happened in a particular case. The fact a confession later proved to be false does not mean that investigators knew this at the time. Thus, according to Perez (2010, p. 27), false confessions are "difficult to detect because they are usually unintended and unrecognized by the interrogators" (see also Ofshe and Leo, 1996, p. 999). "The phenomenon of false confession is difficult to identify and prove," according to Leo (2018, p. 12), because they "often mimic true confessions: they are typically vivid, detailed, and contain unique non-public details that are said to reveal inside knowledge but instead are the product of police contamination (i.e., leaking or feeding of non-public case facts)."

As described by Kennedy (2015, p. 43):

> A [common] scenario presented by plaintiffs involves a youthful or otherwise suggestible suspect who is prematurely judged to be guilty by police investigators. He or she is then placed under stressful interrogation conditions that include direct or implied threats of conviction or promises of leniency. In an effort to escape these unpleasant pressures, the innocent subject will confess to a crime, certain details of which have been leaked by the interrogator during the interrogation process, known as "contamination error," and these details are subsequently recounted during the confession.

Over the decades, criminologists have developed a three-part classification scheme or taxonomy that distinguishes among various types of false or unreliable confessions that can find their way into criminal cases: Voluntary False Confession, Compliant False Confession, and the Internalized False Confession (Kassin, 2005; Kassin and Gudjonsson, 2004). In the case of a "Voluntary False Confession," the subject consciously chooses, on his or her own, to confess to a crime for some ulterior motive. She or he may wish to protect someone or to be the subject of much attention. She or he may also issue a false confession simply to mislead police out of animosity toward them or even to set up an alibi to avoid prosecution for a more serious crime (Conti, 1999). A false confessor may also experience what criminologists refer to as "duping delight," or simply the joy of manipulating others. A Compliant False Confession can be coerced and is offered by the suspect to avoid external pressure or to obtain a reward. Finally, Internalized False Confessions otherwise known as coerced or persuaded false confessions "are those in which an innocent person—tired, confused, and subjected to highly suggestive proce-dures—comes to believe that he or she committed the crime, sometimes forming a false memory in the process" (Kassin, 2005, p. 221). Thus, a forensic criminologist may draw on this classification scheme to assist courts in understanding "how" and "why" questions concerning a false confession.

According to the forensic criminological report:

> Assistant State's Attorney Mark Richards [a pseudonym] testified at his deposition that William Danielson told him he confessed to being present at the murder because he, Danielson, thought Richards was looking for a witness to identify Dercher and Jackson as the murderers. Danielson may have thought these services would buy him leniency relative to his involvement in the murder of Benny Tipton [a pseudonym] [citation to Mark Richards deposition at pp.121–2]. Assuming Mr. Danielson's confession in the Melinda Kaminski case was false, it may have been a "Compliant False Confession," wherein he believed he would be treated more leniently if he confessed or more puni-tively if he did not. Another form of compliant false confession, somewhat more rare, occurs when a subject dislikes the emotional stress of the interrogation process and simply wants to make it stop by confessing to the crime. The confession also may have been a "Persuaded False Confession," where a subject with a bad memory of a certain time period (sometimes due to drug abuse or intoxication) may come to believe he committed the crime. He comes to believe in the evidence and the explanations offered by the interrogators. I note in the Amended Complaint Mr. Danielson is quoted as saying "by the time [the Defendant officers] were through, I actually thought I did it." I don't see how Mr. Danielson would have said that if he confessed primarily in order to avoid being further beaten.

The previous excerpt illustrates how expert testimony can educate and teach a fact finder about the role and importance of criminological theories and approaches in understanding the different types of false confessions. The excerpt blends case-specific evidence with the different typologies of false confes-sions to assist the fact finder in understanding suspect–interrogator interactions for the purpose of re-solving questions of fact in the case. The three typologies link police tactics to different types of confessions and can help the fact finder interpret the evidence and reach a conclusion (verdict). The discussion suggests that different kinds of errors, situational pressures, and decision-making can influence the interrogation process and outcome (i.e., did the process produce a false, involuntary, or unreliable confession?). What is important is that the expert testimony not only focuses on the dif-ferent typologies but makes explicit connections between the evidence and criminological knowledge. Not all expert knowledge is equally influential and persuasive. Rather, according to Cutler and Kovera (2011, p. 55), "[e]xpert testimony that is concretely linked to trial evidence is more influential than testimony that leaves the link implicit."

Forensic criminologists can testify about various factors associated with false confession, character-istics of the interrogation process, and the procedures used to elicit a confession. They are not allowed, however, to opine about the validity of the confession itself, for it is the jury's responsibility to determine whether the statement is accurate. In the following excerpt, the forensic report introduces the reader to the method of Content-Based Criteria Analysis, a forensic procedure used in many countries to evaluate whether statements (e.g., of sexual abuse) are based on experienced or fabricated events.

According to the forensic criminological report:

> With regard to the March 1992 confessions of Jackson, Danielson, and Dercher, there is nothing inherent in the written words which would lead an observer to question their face validity. Not unexpectedly, the confessors each identify one of the other participants as the murderer. There is sufficiently rich detail to suggest that actual rather than contrived memories are at work. Content-Based Criteria Analysis is a technique for assessing the veracity of written statements. This technique regards as indicators of truthfulness such things as unusual details, quantity of details, descriptions of interactions, and accounts of subjective mental state [citation to Vrij, 2000; Lamb et al., 1997; Pezdek et al., 2004]. For example, in Jackson's confession of March 22, 1992, he described Melinda Kaminski's physical positioning during Danielson's sexual attack as "the crab," wherein her legs were on top of Danielson's shoulders. In Dercher's confession, he described how William Danielson put the murdered woman's panties up to his nose, smelled them, declared that the victim was a "funky bitch," and then threw the panties on the sidewalk. Danielson seems to describe Melinda Kaminski's death rattle when he said she made a "weird noise" as the stick was shoved "way up into Melinda's asshole." Unique sensory details such as those described above have been determined by FBI researchers to be reasonable indicators of the veracity of written statements [citation to Adams and Jarvis, 2006].

The previous excerpt from the forensic criminological report suggests that the confessions of Jackson, Danielson, and Dercher were sufficiently consistent with each other, yet not so consistent and patterned as to imply rehearsal. In conclusion, the forensic report notes that the case detectives had at that time what they considered solid confessions that forensic evidence was to corroborate at trial. To fail to pursue the prosecution of the perpetrators of such a crime, against whom probable cause then existed, would have put the community at risk of further victimization.

Criminologists, researchers, and police officers themselves recognize that false confessions are consistently one of the leading sources of error in the American legal system and one of the most prejudicial sources of false evidence that lead to wrongful convictions (Davis and Leo, 2014; Leo, 2008; Kassin, 2015). A police interrogation that induces a false confession not only may result in a wrongful incarceration or conviction, but it may also allow the true perpetrator to go free and commit additional violent crimes. Forensic criminologists can be important in cases involving a disputed interrogation and/or confession evidence since they can employ criminological theory and methods to educate triers of fact about the general findings from criminological research on interrogation and confession. When applied to case-specific matters, criminological theory and method can help a fact finder understand the practices and processes of modern interrogation to evaluate reliable and unreliable confession evidence.

CONCLUSIONS

This chapter has described some of the different ways in which a forensic criminologist can serve the criminal justice system relative to assessing evidence related to wrongful convictions. Expert witness investigation is akin to "translational criminology" in which a forensic criminologist can bring criminological knowledge to police and legal practitioners to help them deal with the copious litigation issues swirling around wrongful litigation. There are abundant opportunities for forensic criminologists to contribute their expertise to the court system when dealing with cases involving wrongful conviction. A forensic criminologist can review evidence, police investigations, and court proceedings to help the court determine whether police detectives missed any important data or evidence in building their case against a suspect. A forensic criminologist can investigate whether detectives followed the appropriate protocol and formal practices of their department in conducting an eyewitness investigation. Related, a forensic criminologist can evaluate the evidence to see whether, how, and under what conditions detectives may have created a false identification of a suspect. More broadly, a forensic criminologist can delve deeply or systematically into the multivariable, interactive, and complex nature of human action and institutional context to evaluate the multiple sources of causation in wrongful conviction cases. Here a forensic criminologist can make use of theories and methods in organizational behavior to identify how organizational tasks, processes, and structures can generate adverse outcomes including the prosecution of an innocent person or the release of a guilty person.

While some cases of wrongful conviction may involve overzealous, unethical, and even illegal behavior of individual actors, a forensic criminologist will need to be sensitive to situating these individual actions in a broader structural and organizational framework (Doyle, 2014, 2010; Huff, 2002). A forensic criminologist can investigate the ways in which large-scale structural and contextual factors can influence the perceptions, attitudes, and behaviors of actors within the criminal justice system. As rational agents, police detectives may face limits in formulating and solving complex investigative problems and in processing (receiving, storing, retrieving, transmitting) information.

Scholars refer to this view of the investigative process as "bounded rationality" and it represents a real-world approach to justice taken by police, prosecutors, defense attorneys, and judges (Snook and Cullen, 2009). Bounded rationality implies that when people are faced with complex decisions, they may take reasoning shortcuts that can then lead to suboptimal decision-making. Various kinds of reasoning shortcuts unfold within complex institutional and social environments that constrain some actions, enable other actions, influence decision-making, and help shape the rules that are most immediately responsible for producing wrongful convictions. Like other organizations, police departments can be affected by bureaucratic inertia, limited resources, competing demands, low information levels, weak lines of communication within and between administrative levels, and pressures to obtain quick results. These factors can influence the pace, trajectory, and outcome of an investigation.

While it may be easy in retrospect to criticize the past actions of police, reasonable explanations often exist for what may appear to be obvious errors that contributed to wrongful convictions or errors that convinced judges to set aside verdicts. For example, bite mark evidence and hair analysis may seem today to involve flawed forensics, but at the time of an original conviction, the forensic odontology and forensic pattern identification communities may have viewed them far more favorably (Collins and Jarvis, 2009; Pyrek, 2007; Cole, 2012). Kennedy (2015, p. 67) suggests that "[j]ail house informants may have been psychopaths who could have just as easily persuaded defense attorneys as they did original prosecutors and detectives due to their manipulation skills" (Kennedy, 2015, p. 67). Acker (2017, p. 15) provides another example:

> [R]ather than focusing only on a prosecutor's breach of duty in a case that produces a wrongful conviction, we might ask whether the job advancement criteria employed in a district attorney's office—or, more fundamentally, whether the incentives intrinsic to the adversarial system itself—place undue emphasis on securing convictions at the expense of doing justice.

Overall, a forensic criminologist should understand that police departments will gather criminal evidence following the procedures and processes outlined by prosecutors. Yet prosecutors enjoy absolute immunity when working within their official capacities. Therefore, other actors within the criminal justice system—for example, police and city governments—have been and will continue to be targets of wrongful conviction litigation.

Finally, the analysis presented in this chapter resonates with recent criminological debates over the various trade-offs associated with proposed reform measures for addressing wrongful convictions. In discussing remedies to address eyewitness misidentification, Cassell (2017, p. 5) contends that "many of the reform measures … appear to carry with them not only the prospect of avoiding misidentifications but also the possibility of discouraging accurate identifications." More broadly, as Slobogin (2014, p.) has noted, "[m]ost reformist energy has understandably been focused on reducing wrongful convictions, through improved interrogation techniques, and identification procedures, defense involvement in the investigative process, and the like. Most of these reforms, however, could also increase wrongful acquittals." Risinger and Risinger (2011/2012, p. 898) suggest that limitations and problems with eyewitness misidentification are hard to address and solve because they are "inherent in the phenomenon." In noting that "[w]rongful convictions do not appear to have a simple explanation of cause and effect," Leo and Gould (2009, p. 18) warn that many of the same factors found in wrongful convictions—for example, eyewitness misidentifications, false confessions, informant perjury, junk science, tunnel vision, police and prosecutorial error, and so on—"are found in other cases that do not end in erroneous convictions."

These debates suggest that changes in criminal investigation and interrogation techniques, while important, may not address what Cassell (2017) argues is the "root cause" of wrongful convictions: insufficient resources devoted to the criminal justice system. While devoting more resources to the criminal justice system will not solve all the problems, more resources could help defense counsel (and police and prosecuting agencies) to locate persuasive evidence of guilt or innocence in particular cases and could lessen the incidence of future wrongful convictions overall.

CIVIL LITIGATION INVOLVING POLICE AND CORRECTIONS

INTRODUCTION

Over the decades, municipal police departments and correction facilities have been subjected to a variety of lawsuits alleging violations of constitutional rights and federal statutes. Plaintiffs sue in federal court primarily for Fourth, Eighth, and Fourteenth Amendment violations and in state courts for tortious actions. The Fourth Amendment protects citizens' right to be free from illegal search and seizure and establishes that government can conduct a search based upon probable cause (i.e., reasonable expectation, based on evidence, that someone has perpetrated an illegal act). The Eighth Amendment protects citizens' right to be free from excessive bail and government infliction of cruel or unusual punishment. The Fourteenth Amendment addresses citizenship rights, defines national citizenship, and forbids states from restricting the rights of citizens or other persons. Historically, lawsuits against police or correction officers have been limited and generally confined to charges of brutality. In contemporary times, however, issues of liability have expanded beyond these kinds of delimited allegations to "include virtually every task performed by criminal justice personnel" (Ross, 2018, p. 27).

Lawsuits against police officers and corrections facilities are inevitable and recurring for two major reasons: "criminals do not wish to be interfered with, and they do not want to be in jail" (Kennedy, 2014, p. 11). Hence, conflict with police and corrections officers will ensue, and this conflict is at the heart of litigation. Ryan (2007) has identified twelve high-risk, critical police tasks that are frequently linked to litigation against police departments and sheriffs' offices. These include use of force; pursuit and emergency vehicle operations; search and seizure including arrest; care, custody, and control of prisoners; domestic violence; property and evidence; off-duty conduct and off-duty paid details; sexual harassment/misconduct; selection and hiring; complaints and internal investigations; special operations (SWAT, narcotics, high risk warrants service); and dealing with the mentally ill or emotionally disturbed persons (see also Ross, 2000, p. 171). Corrections activities that are at high risk for litigation include strip searches; identity verification; classification errors and mistakes; duty to protect from assault; grievances; medical (e.g., delay in medical care, jail officer failure to follow doctor's orders, dental needs); suicide; use of force; nutrition; religious meals/materials/worship; among other activities (Ryan, 2009).

People can sue the government for civil rights violations based on Title 42, Section 1983 of the 1871 Civil Rights Act. Section 1983 applies when someone acting "under color of" state level or local law has deprived a person of rights created by the U.S. Constitution or federal statutes. Section 1983 is intended to provide citizens with the ability to hold government legally accountable for violations

Practicing Forensic Criminology. https://doi.org/10.1016/B978-0-12-815595-0.00011-0

of civil rights and to safeguard them against abuses by law enforcement and corrections officers (Turvey and Torres, 2010, pp. 288–289). Section 1983 "serves the important role of reminding government agents that they are subordinate to law just like everyone else" (p. 289). The U.S. Supreme Court established in *Cooper v. Pate* (1964) that state prisoners can bring lawsuits against correction officers under Section 1983. Under *Monell v. New York City Department of Social Services* (436 U. S. 658 (1978)), a municipal government can be held liable for a Section 1983 violation if a plaintiff can demonstrate that a deprivation of a federal right occurred as a result of a local government policy. Municipalities, however, cannot be held liable under Section 1983 for constitutional torts on a notion of *respondeat superior,* which imposes liability on an employer for wrongful actions of an employee regardless of the absence of fault by the employer. The implication is that "municipal policy makers may be liable for acts of their police officers when those acts are directed by either an official policy or departmental custom" (Ross, 2000, p. 172).

One of the most important standards that courts have applied to civil litigation involving police and corrections is the "deliberate indifference" standard, established in the famous case of *Estelle v. Gamble* (1976). In this case, the U.S. Supreme Court ruled that deliberate indifference to a prisoner's serious illness, medical needs, or injury states a cause of action under Section 1983. "Deliberate indifference is not easily defined, is difficult to apply, and difficult for a prisoner to meet" (Ross, 2018, p. 352). That said, according to Ross (p. 352), "'[d]eliberate' means that a particular course of action has been chosen from among various alternatives, and 'indifference' means that there has been some conscious disregard for a person's rights." To establish deliberate indifference, a court must first find that the plaintiff suffered from an objectively serious medical condition.[1] The court will then investigate whether the defendant knew of and disregarded a substantial risk to the prisoner's health. "Even objective recklessness—failing to act in the face of an unjustifiably high risk that is so obvious that it should be known— is insufficient to support an Eighth Amendment violation" (Sweeney, 2017, p. 64). Ross (2018, p. 352) points to several ways that defendants can bring a Section 1983 claim:

> The refusal of correctional or medical personnel to provide care, or delay in providing care may be actionable under the deliberate indifference standard. A series of incidents that, if viewed in isolation, appear to involve only negligence may give rise to deliberate indifference. Problems caused by understaffing, a lack of or deficient equipment, substandard facilities, and a lack of procedures may be so egregious that the ensuing inability to render adequate medical care is so evident that the failure to redress these problems is tantamount to "deliberate indifference."

Over the decades, the U.S. Supreme Court has expanded the standard of deliberate indifference to cover not only health care services but other prison claims including condition of confinement, failure to protect, failure to train, and detainee suicides.

In this chapter, we address three high litigation risks associated with police and correctional operations: (1) detainee suicide, (2) allegations of deliberate indifference to the medical needs of a mentally ill and emotionally disturbed person, and (3) use of force in law enforcement actions. We first discuss a case of detainee suicide and describe how a forensic criminologist would investigate and gather

---

[1]*Farmer v. Brennan*, 511 U.S. 825, 834 (1994).

evidence in such a case. Suicides and attempted suicides of arrestees taken into custody present a significant problem for police and corrections personnel. These actions normally allege the agency and its employees failed to take steps to prevent a suicide. Under Section 1983, plaintiffs may allege a city violated the constitutional rights of a self-injured person by failing to protect him or her from self-inflicted injuries.

Next, we examine a case involving allegations of violations of constitutional rights and violations of federal and state law for injuries a young woman incurred after she was released from police custody. This case addresses the question of whether government has a duty to protect individuals not in custody from harm by private persons. Section 1983 claims emerging from a failure to protect may assert that a police officer's action or inaction caused harm to the plaintiff. The plaintiff may allege that the police department as a whole was intentionally negligent, grossly negligent, or deliberately indifferent to the needs of the plaintiff. The lawsuit generally will assert that the department's custom, policy, and procedures (or lack thereof) were the "proximate cause" of the injury. The plaintiff will attempt to show that the police department ignored industry standards, historically ignored problems in the department, and failed to correct constitutional deficiencies. As we show, expert testimony from a forensic criminologist can be relevant and helpful to a jury in understanding whether the conduct of the officers and aides in responding to the young woman's medical needs was reasonable.

Finally, we analyze two cases of police use of force, a critical topic in civil liability. In the first case, we examine the response of a police officer to a late-night traffic stop. We address issues relating to fundamental attribution error, perceptions of the dangers of traffic stops, the nature of early morning/weekend traffic stops, police officer fatalities, and the "use-of-force" continuum. A use-of-force continuum is a standard with guidelines that specify how much force a police officer may use against a resisting subject in a given situation. In the second case, we examine a police officer's decision to use force during an arrest in a poor, high crime neighborhood. Our goal is to show how a forensic criminologist would investigate the intersection of police officer actions, situational constraints, and the totality of circumstances in an encounter with an offender. Overall, we address the ways in which a forensic criminologist can draw on extant criminological research to assist a jury in understanding questions that may arise in claims of excessive force: for example, what constitutes excessive force? What is reasonable force? Was the amount or type of force used by the officer appropriate and necessary? What is the appropriate standard with which to evaluate the use of force?

Because issues in tort litigation may involve the actions of police and corrections personnel, the insights provided by forensic criminology in the form of expert reports and testimony can be of crucial assistance to judicial and jury decision-making. A forensic criminologist may draw on criminological theories and methods to help a fact finder understand the actions or inactions of criminal justice system personnel in cases alleging police brutality, false arrest, and negligent training of officers. A forensic criminologist may explain how individual, contextual, and socio-spatial factors interact to explain behaviors associated with deaths in detention due to suicide, police misconduct, negligent operation of police vehicles, failure to arrest drunk drivers, malicious prosecution, police pursuits, among many other case examples. That said, we stress that our cases represent only a small segment of the vast and wide-ranging litigation in these areas. Each year, many hundreds if not thousands of lawsuits are filed against police and correctional personnel. Forensic criminological knowledge can be instrumental in varying degrees in the prosecution and defense of virtually all these cases.

CASE EXAMPLE: DETAINEE SUICIDE

This case arises out of the suicide of pretrial detainee Philip Davis (a pseudonym) while in custody at a county jail. During the early morning hours of November 13, 2013, Mr. Davis cut himself repeatedly with a shaving razor as corrections officers struggled with him to stop his violent, suicidal actions. Mr. Davis had been in custody since January 4, 2013. Upon admittance to the jail, he was evaluated for possible suicidality by jail mental health worker Stephen Sachs (a pseudonym) and cleared for general population on January 7, 2013. On October 16, family members reported to jail staff that Mr. Davis had threatened suicide if his case was to go forward to trial.

In response to this conditional threat, Mr. Sachs implemented a plan for future precautionary measures. Under the plan, Davis was to be placed on suicide watch 24 hours before any scheduled court appearances, the first of which was scheduled for November 19, 2013. While under suicide watch, Davis would be housed in an isolation cell with at least 30-minute checks lasting until a mental health assessment was completed. The next day, on October 17, notes in the jail inmate activity log reflect that Sachs was aware of a sergeant's concern regarding whether Davis should be interviewed more immediately due to the alleged suicide threats. Sachs determined, however, the plan need not change.

Shaving razors were passed out Sunday through Thursday after lockdown to any inmate who requested a razor. All inmates were entitled to request a razor, except those on suicide watch. On November 12, 2013, Davis put his name on the razor request sheet. At this time, Davis was not on suicide watch. At approximately 11:22 p.m. on November 12, a corrections officer distributed a razor to Davis. At approximately 12:09 a.m., the corrections officer went to collect the razor from Davis' cell and discovered Davis in the act of harming himself with the razor. A call went out and several individuals responded to Davis' cell, where he had to be restrained and disarmed by jail staff. He was transported to a hospital, where attempts to resuscitate him failed. Davis was pronounced dead due to multiple lacerations to the jugular vessel caused by the razor.

In this case, Philip Davis' mother sued on behalf of her decedent son pursuant to 42 U.S.C. Section 1983, alleging deliberate indifference to his medical needs in violation of the U.S. Constitution. In a deliberate indifference case involving detainee suicide, the plaintiff must demonstrate that a prison official's state of mind must evince "deliberateness tantamount to intent to punish."[2] Deliberate indifference includes both objective and subjective components.[3] The objective component requires proof that the detainee's medical need is "sufficiently serious" and courts have established "that suicidal tendencies are considered 'serious medical needs.'"[4] For the subjective component, a plaintiff must show: "(1) the prison official subjectively perceived facts from which to infer a substantial risk to the prisoner; (2) the official did in fact draw the inference; and (3) the official disregarded that risk." The subjective component may be satisfied if there is proof "that a prison official drew an inference from the available facts that there was a 'strong likelihood' of prisoner suicide, but then disregarded that risk by failing to take adequate precautions to mitigate the risk."[5] There is no right, however, ensuring that detainees will

---

[2]*Horn by Parks v. Madison Cty. Fiscal Ct.,* 22 F.3d 653, 660 (6th Cir. 1994).
[3]*Mantell v. Health Professionals Ltd.,* No. 13-4257 (6th Cir. 2015).
[4]*Bonner-Turner v. City of Ecorse,* No. 14-2337 (6th Cir. Sept. 14, 2015).
[5]*Mantell v. Health Professionals Ltd.,* No. 13-4257 (6th Cir. 2015).

be correctly screened for suicidal tendencies.[6] "Prison officials need only take reasonable precautions to prevent inmate suicide; they do not insure or guarantee the life of a prisoner."[7]

In this case, counsel for the defendant asked the forensic criminologist to evaluate whether Mr. Sachs's discretionary actions were within reasonable parameters of custody-related mental health practices. The following materials were reviewed: the Complaint, current court decisions concerning custody suicide, jail activity logs, corrections officers' incident reports, booking and screening documents, mental health notes concerning the detainee, correspondence and letters to and from Mr. Davis, court documents concerning the case, and other miscellaneous documents. Also reviewed were appropriate current professional literature on detainee suicide and five depositions. The jail was visited and interviews were conducted with a police captain and police lieutenant.

According to the forensic criminological investigation:

> Health care, including mental health care, is quite different in a custody setting than it is in a "free-world" setting. Inmates of all stripes have been described as "difficult, manipulative, aggressive, and demanding" [citation to Flanagan and Flanagan, 2001]. Malingering is used for secondary gain and, in fact, the DSM-IV-TR and the DSM-V both discuss the possibilities of malingering in a forensic setting (i.e., jail or prison) [citation to American Psychiatric Association, 2013, pp. 726–727]. Notwithstanding the possibility of inmate malingering for secondary benefit (e.g., hospitalization in a more comfortable setting with improved chances of escape) and the inherent impossibility of predicting suicide on an individual level even in a free-world population, skilled mental health workers do not dismiss the possibility that malingerers can, in fact, be suicidal as well [citations to Pokorny, 1983; Maris, 1992; Hughes, 1995].
>
> Due to the low base rate of suicide and the problem of false positives, it is generally not possible to effectively predict suicide at the individual level. This is a widely known conclusion … Hence, mental health workers must not dismiss an inmate's possible suicidality as mere malingering.
>
> Note that Stephen Sachs did no such thing and, in fact, laid out a detailed monitoring plan centered around Mr. Davis's three upcoming court dates, along with a plan to conduct separate mental health assessments prior to each of those court dates [citation to local county Jail Contact Note dated October 16, 2013, prepared by Stephen Sachs]. Thus, it would be completely erroneous to argue that Stephen Sachs consciously disregarded a serious medical need, putting Mr. Davis at risk. He did not. Plaintiff can only argue that Mr. Sachs's response and prevention plan was virtually no response at all. Neither is this the case.

There are a number of points to consider in understanding the nature of Mr. Sachs's response to future possibilities of self-injury by Mr. Davis, particularly given the totality of circumstances in this detainee suicide. Mr. Davis is reputed to have threatened suicide if his case went to trial. This type of threat is known as a "conditional" threat and is often employed to manipulate people into taking some action deemed beneficial by the threatener (Reccoppa, 2009, p. 110). According to Blasko and colleagues (2008, p. 70), "[s]ome inmates may feign or malinger suicidal intent or behavior in an attempt to

---

[6]*Davis v. Fentress Cty. Tenn.,* 6 Fed. App'x 243, 249 (6th Cir. 2001).
[7]*Galloway v. Anuszkiewicz,* 518 Fed. App'x 330, 334 (6th Cir. 2013).

manipulate their environment or derive secondary gains, making it difficult to identify genuine disorders from feigned disorders." A conditional threat is distinguished from a direct threat, an indirect threat, and a veiled threat (O'Toole, 2000). Importantly, individuals who are "contingently" suicidal (i.e., make conditional threats) are far less likely to commit suicide than those who are truly suicidal (Lambert, 2002, pp. 92–94).

As the forensic criminological report continues:

> Also, please note that corrections officers reported no signs of suicidality had been manifested by Mr. Davis since his initial screening some ten months prior to his death. In one Texas study, two-thirds of jail suicides took place within a month of admission to the jail [citation to Dillon, 2013]. Clearly, the greatest risk of inmate suicide is within the first days and weeks of incarceration, and Philip Davis had long since passed through that period with no obvious adverse effects.
>
> Given the above circumstances, there is no reason to believe that Mr. Davis was at imminent risk for suicide at the time of his death. He had not been abandoned by his family and was being emotionally supported by his mother and brother (protective factors). He displayed no signs or symptoms of suicidality to corrections officers or other inmates that we know of. To place him in a suicide cell because of a hearsay conditional threat, given the circumstances cited above, could actually have been perceived as more likely to be harmful than helpful to Mr. Davis. Inmates on suicide watch are confined to a bare cell, made to remain naked except for a suicide gown, in front of a camera, denied recreational activities, and deprived of social contact with other prisoners. These segregation conditions are believed to be detrimental to an inmate's mental health and have been cautioned against by at least one judicial commentator [citations to Felthous, 1997]. Federal District Court Judge Sharp wrote in *Strickler v. McCord* (2004) that "a duty to take the maximum precautions for all inmates with any level of suicide risk would make life miserable for any persons at a low level of risk for suicide."[8]

For a plaintiff to prevail in a Section 1983 suit, he or she must prove that the defendant displayed deliberate indifference to "strong likelihood" of suicide rather than a mere chance or possibility. According to Ross (2018, p. 480), deliberate indifference is more than making a mistake. Rather, it means "(1) officials knew or should have known that the prisoner was a suicide risk and steps were not taken to prevent it; and/or (2) the officers and agency were deliberately indifferent to the prisoner's serious medical or mental health needs."[9]

A key issue in this suit is whether a jury could conclude that there was a "strong likelihood" of Davis committing suicide. Here a forensic criminologist would address whether Sachs had actual knowledge or constructive knowledge that Davis was suicidal. Davis had not been on suicide watch for over nine months when Sachs learned of Davis' alleged statement. Moreover, Sachs had never previously determined Davis was suicidal or placed him on suicide watch. Sachs conducted an evaluation of Davis in January 2013 and determined he was not suicidal. According to Sachs, he understood through

---

[8]*Strickler v. McCord*, 306 F. Supp. 2d 818 (N.D. Ind. 2004).

[9]For controlling cases where courts apply a "strong likelihood" test of deliberate indifference in detainee suicides, see *Strickler v. McCord*, 306 F. Supp. 2d 818 (N.D. Ind. 2004); *Bell v. Stigers*, 937 F.2d 1340 (8th Cir. 1991); *Sanders v. Howze*, 177 F.3d 1245 (11th Cir. 1999).

information received in October that Davis might be a suicide risk "potentially in the future." Sachs stated he did not treat conditional threats based on an event happening the same way as if someone makes a direct threat of suicide. Sachs testified that he did not believe Davis was immediately suicidal on October 16. When questioned whether Davis should be interviewed sooner, Sachs decided to keep the plan as initially proposed—demonstrating that he did not perceive a "strong likelihood" of an immediate risk of suicide.

As the forensic criminological report concludes:

> Finally, I address two other matters pertaining to proximate cause. Had Mr. Sachs responded to Mr. Davis's conditional threat with a direct rather than an indirect assessment, would Davis have admitted to suicidal ideation and/or intent knowing this would result in being placed on suicide watch in a specially designated suicide-resistant cell? Given the obvious commitment Mr. Davis had to ending his life, it is likely he would have denied any intention of harming himself just as he had done ten months prior during his first assessment … Recall how the corrections officers had to struggle with Mr. Davis to try to stop him from slashing at his neck as he implored them to "let him go." … This denial of suicide ideation and planning is common among suicidal inmates who know the results of admitting to suicidality [citation to Tartaro, 2015]. In one study of veterans who had committed suicide, 85 percent had denied suicidality when formally assessed between 0–7 days prior to death by suicide [citation to Smith et al., 2013].
>
> Secondly, criticism has been directed at sheriff's personnel because Mr. Davis was allowed use of a razor with which to shave. Had Mr. Davis been denied access to a razor, in spite of the fact he was not on suicide watch, he likely would have simply used some form of ligature fashioned from clothing or bedding. In fact, the overwhelming majority (93 percent) of inmates who committed suicide chose asphyxiation by hanging as the method [citation to Hayes, 2012]. Keeping a razor from Mr. Davis would not have prevented him from killing himself.

In *Taylor v. Barkes* (2015), the U.S. Supreme Court ruled that there is no statutory, constitutional, or judicially created right to the proper implementation of suicide prevention polices.[10] Citing a number of cases, the Supreme Court noted that "the right to medical care for serious medical needs does not encompass the right to be screened correctly for suicidal tendencies"[11]; that alleged "weaknesses in the [suicide] screening process, the training of deputies[,] and the supervision of prisoners" did not "amount to a showing of deliberate indifference toward the rights of prisoners"[12]; that the "general right of pretrial detainees to receive basic medical care does not place upon jail officials the responsibility to screen every detainee for suicidal tendencies"[13]; and that "the right of detainees to adequate medical care" does not include "an absolute right to psychological screening."[14]

Explanations for detainee suicides range from a focus on characteristics of the inmate population to consideration of the conditions of imprisonment itself (Bowkar, 1980; Drapkin, 1976; Kennedy and Homant, 1988; Irwin, 1980; Sykes, 1966; Toch, 1975). Although not all inmates

---

[10]*Taylor v. Barkes*, 135 S. Ct. 2042, 575 U.S., 192 L. Ed. 2d 78 (2015).
[11]*Comstock v. McCrary*, 273 F. 3d 693—Court of Appeals (6th Circuit 2001).
[12]*Tittle v. Jefferson County Commission*, 10 F. 3d 1535—Court of Appeals (11th Circuit 1994).
[13]*Belcher v. Oliver*, 898 F. 2d 32—Court of Appeals (4th Circuit 1990).
[14]*Burns v. Galveston*, 905 F. 2d 100—Court of Appeals (5th Circuit 1990).

are devastated by the consequences of incarceration (Bukstel and Kilmann, 1980), research has shown that when entering a "total institution" (Goffman, 1961) like a prison, a person goes through a "mortification process" that strips him or her of individual and collective identities, imposes a stigmatized identity as a prisoner, removes personal autonomy, and limits or prohibits communication with the outside world (Abram et al., 2008; Marzano et al., 2011). Criminologists have found that occupation of a single cell, detainee status, and serving a life sentence are major correlates of detainee suicide. Other risk factors include recent suicidal ideation, history of attempted suicide, having a current psychiatric diagnosis, receiving psychotropic medication, and having a history of alcohol use problems (Fazel and Seewald, 2012; Fazel et al., 2008; Rudd et al., 2006).

Despite decades of scholarship and study on the causes of detainee suicide, researchers recognize that suicide is not possible to predict (Large, 2010; Murphy, 1984; Pokorny, 1983). Early research by Hayes (1983) called national attention to the problem and was followed by several attempts at further delineating characteristics of the suicidal inmate (Kennedy and Homant, 1988; Knoll, 2010; Lester and Danto, 1993). Notwithstanding booking and screening interviews designed to identify suicide potential, some newly admitted prisoners who had denied suicidality will kill themselves. Others with significant psychiatric histories pass their time in custody without incident. Because suicide watch can be stressful and possibly iatrogenic, mental health workers may eventually take an inmate off suicide precautions. In fact, many inmates tire of the boredom, lack of activity, and constant surveillance and will plead to be returned to general population. Some eventually kill themselves there and, even though the decision to return them to a normalized routine may have been right at the time, their ultimate death could still lead to litigation.

CASE EXAMPLE: LAWSUIT INVOLVING INJURIES INCURRED AFTER RELEASE FROM POLICE CUSTODY

This case concerns a suit initiated by Plaintiff Polly Kendal (a pseudonym), as guardian of the estate of Eileen Christine (a pseudonym), against a city government and various members of the city police department, alleging violations of Christine's constitutional rights and violations of federal and state law. Kendal sued on behalf of Christine, her daughter, for injuries that Christine incurred after the police department released her from custody. In this case, the plaintiff makes a Section 1983 complaint against the police for deliberate indifference to her daughter's medical needs and a Section 1983 claim against the city government.

Police officers arrested Eileen Christine one afternoon at an airport transit authority station. She had been creating a disturbance and using obscenities. Earlier, she had created a scene at the airport gate, from where she had hoped to depart for a return trip to her home. After her arrest for criminal trespass, Christine was processed at a local police station, where a report of her behavior prompted a watch commander to instruct a police sergeant to observe her behavior as well as conduct an interview. The sergeant conducted an interview that lasted about 35 minutes. At some point, the police called both parents. The stepfather returned the call and expressed concern for her well-being. Because the police sergeant did not believe she constituted a threat to herself or others and did not believe she was unable to provide for her basic physical needs, Christine was then transferred to the female holding cells at another police station without incident.

While at the station's female lockup area, similar to many detainees, Christine was occasionally uncooperative and continued to behave somewhat erratically. However, she did not threaten her own life nor did she threaten to harm others. She did not appear to be unable to provide for her basic physical needs in that she nourished herself and was aware of her surroundings, at least insofar as police officers were able to determine. The police department duly released Christine on a personal recognizance bond on a Monday evening. She chose not to board any city buses or trains but, instead, patronized a local restaurant wherein she eventually socialized with some neighborhood residents. She then went voluntarily to a nearby housing project where she continued to socialize with several young, male residents. About 5 hours after Christine left the police station, she was assaulted by a person who lived in the area. She was severely injured when she was pushed or jumped from a seventh-floor apartment window.

The counsel for the defendants asked the forensic criminologist to review the file and to comment on prisoner policies. The following materials were reviewed: the internal investigative statements and depositions of dozens of local police officers, including those having direct contact with Eileen Christine; depositions of police detainees, friends and family of Christine, her treating doctor, and her psychologists. Also reviewed were current mental health and criminological literature, newspaper coverage of the crime, local police department general orders, and the police investigation of this assault committed against Christine, as well as pertinent legal motions and opinions (correspondence from defendants' counsel). The forensic criminologist also read and analyzed the expert reports provided by three expert witnesses.

According to the forensic criminological report:

> Central to this litigation is the argument that Eileen Christine should not have been released from police custody at all or should have been released in some other way. Polly Kendal asserts, through her attorneys, that Eileen was acting in such a bizarre fashion throughout her detention that she should have been taken instead to a mental health facility for her own protection. While it may be that Ms. Christine could have benefited from long-term psychiatric care, it was not acceptable police practice to detain her, once she was bonded out, in order to convey her to a behavioral emergency service. By operation of constitutional case law, unless she was a danger to herself, a danger to others, or was unable to provide for her basic physical needs, she could not be deprived of her liberty. Our courts have decided that homeless people have a right to be homeless, and schizophrenics have a right to wander aimlessly down the sidewalk talking to themselves. Accordingly, even someone with a bipolar illness cannot be detained by police simply because he or she may be deemed by observers to be mentally ill. Indeed, police officers are sued for taking people involuntarily for emergency psychiatric evaluations.

The previous excerpt suggests that a "right to be detained" doctrine would put police in a catch-22, damned-if-you-do, damned-if-you-don't situation. Police officers are not social workers or psychiatrists, and it can be difficult and challenging for them to separate persons who need mental health care (or other medical care) from persons who are pretending and playacting. Sending even a few arrested persons out for mental health evaluation from each lock up or jail could overwhelm medical facilities. In some U.S. cities, police make tens of thousands of arrests annually, many for minor infractions (such as Christine's) that ordinarily are followed by prompt release. Police cannot commit individuals for involuntary psychiatric evaluations merely because those individuals seem to have a mental disorder

(Conroy and Murrie, 2007, pp. 155–161). Police administrators must consider the U.S. Supreme Court decision in *O'Connor v. Donaldson* (1975) when formulating policies for encounters with mentally ill individuals. A key ruling in this case was that "a State cannot constitutionally confine ... a nondangerous individual who is capable of surviving safely in freedom by himself or with the help of willing and responsible family members or friends."[15] Likewise, the U.S. Supreme Court in *Addington v. Texas* (1979) raised the level of proof required for civil commitment from a "preponderance of evidence" to "clear and convincing evidence."

As the forensic criminological report continues:

> Thus, regardless of Eileen Christine's mental status, unless [local] police officers reasonably believed she was a danger to herself or others or she was unable to provide for her basic physical needs, she could not properly be detained against her will. [According to] *Elizabeth McN* (2006), "[s]uch weakness (as a member of society) does not warrant preemptive confinement whereby potential victims would be incarcerated in the interest of preventing criminals from preying upon them."[16] Given Eileen's hostile attitude toward the police, her wish to be released, and her denial that she was under medical care, there is no reason to believe she would have gone voluntarily to a hospital for a psychiatric evaluation.
>
> Police officers know they will encounter people with mental illness in the course of their work [citations to Watson et al., 2004; Cordner, 2006]. In fact, most criminal justice professionals know that many of the problems of the mentally ill have now been transferred to the criminal justice system from the state mental health system [citations to Whitmer, 1980; Lamb and Weinberger, 2005]. Police officers must be allowed the discretion they need in their attempts to assess the appropriate course of action when dealing with the mentally ill [citation to Teplin, 2000]. Law enforcement must strive to balance an individual's right to be free from state interference against society's right to be protected from an aggressive individual and, perhaps, an individual's need to be protected from himself. If even society's most learned mental health professionals disagree about how best to strike this balance, we must certainly give law enforcement discretion in their decision-making [citations to Torrey, 2008; Bloom, 2004; Tanay, 2007; Brooks, 2007]. Social workers, psychologists, and psychiatrists find it difficult to predict suicide and dangerous behavior [citations to Monahan, 1981; Rudd et al., 2006; Schopp and Quattrocchi, 1995]. Such a task is certainly no easier for police officers.

In any litigation case, the development of expert witness testimony takes place not only through engagement with the facts of a case but also through engagement with other experts' interpretations of the facts. During the litigation proceedings, retaining counsel may ask an expert witness to provide a rebuttal analysis to challenge and contest the opinions reached by an opposing expert witness. A rebuttal analysis can play different roles. It can call into question the position of the opposing expert, or suggest problems in the credibility and accuracy of the opposing expert's methods and analysis. A rebuttal analysis can also establish and support the opinions and conclusions initially offered, and provide alternatives to areas believed to be incorrect. In the following quotes, we describe how a forensic criminologist

---

[15]*O'Connor v. Donaldson*, 422 U.S. 576, U.S. Supreme Court (1975).
[16]*Elizabeth McN*, 855 N.E.2d 588, 367 Ill. App. 3d 786, 305 Ill. Dec. 421 (App. Ct. 2006).

would critically engage an opposing expert's report to identify contradictions or inconsistencies with an eye toward assisting a fact finder understand the underlying facts of the case.

> I read with great interest Dr. Dennis Jenicke's [a pseudonym] report ... Dr. Jenicke speaks in terms of psychiatric hospital, jail, and prison standards of care. This case refers to arrests, pre-trial detainees, and temporary holding facilities such as police lockups. In my opinion, Dr. Jenicke's report poses the question: Was Eileen "gravely disabled?" In [this jurisdiction], the appropriate question is: Was Eileen able to provide for her basic physical needs? In my opinion, she was. While she may have been experiencing mood swings and was emotionally unstable, she was able to meet her physical needs for clothing, sustenance, and shelter. She took nourishment while in custody, did not appear malodorous or disheveled, had no open wounds, and was aware of her surroundings. There is no clear evidence she suffered from hallucinations or delusions.
>
> Having poor social judgment does not constitute being unable to care for one's basic physical needs. If her detention had been extended beyond 48 hours because one or more of the defendants committed her, they would have violated her constitutional rights and would have been subject to suit [citation to *County of Riverside v. McLaughlin* (1991)]. Officers are required to minimize the time a presumptively innocent person spends in jail. Eileen's detention could only be extended for extraordinary, emergency circumstances. Any unreasonable delay violates the 4th Amendment. Imagine the consequences for a free society if police and medical personnel were allowed to take people into custody for having "poor social judgment." Please note also that an involuntary visit to an ER for a psychiatric evaluation can be quite degrading and stressful and can be utilized punitively [citation to Stefan, 2006, pp. 3–9].

The forensic criminological report also provides a rebuttal to another expert witness for the plaintiffs in this case, Sheriff Ken James (a pseudonym). James questions why it took so long to release Eileen Christine on bond but acknowledges that her lack of cooperation may have played a role in any delays. In his report, Sheriff Ken James also implies that several local police officers were less than forthcoming in their recollections about the Christine case and cites contradictory testimony by lockup arrestees as part of his reason for this belief. Courts have long opined that credibility issues are for the jury to decide. Box 11.1 lists the different circuit courts that have ruled on the inadmissibility of expert testimony regarding the credibility of a witness.

According to the forensic criminological report:

> Sheriff James also believes that ... police personnel violated lockup procedures, ... and, perhaps, Guidelines for Arrestee Screening. Article IV states, in part, that a lockup is not meant for those with symptoms of a severe mental disorder ... hallucinations or delusions. There is no evidence Eileen suffered from either. As for lockup screening guidelines, Eileen never threatened suicide or implied she was suicidal. There is also no evidence she was unaware of her surroundings or was unable to follow simple commands. Moreover, Eileen's ultimate injuries were caused by a third-party criminal act, not by Eileen's failure to care for her basic physical needs.
>
> Once again, I do not suggest that Eileen was not emotionally disturbed or otherwise afflicted with some form of psychiatric disorder. However, unless she was suicidal, a physical threat to others or was unable to provide for her basic physical needs, a [local] police officer would not have had sufficient cause to detain her for the purposes of psychiatric evaluation. It is this very same treatment

limitation which explains why so many schizophrenics remain free in our communities today. Regardless of how badly they may seem to be in need of treatment, such treatment cannot be forced upon them unless they are unable to care for themselves or pose a threat to themselves or others. Even then, there remains an issue concerning the permissibility of forced medication and the right to refuse treatment [citations to Mayman and Guyer, 2007; Winick, 1997; Appelbaum, 1988; Simon, 2003] ... While there may be a lack of societal consensus over how to resolve these difficult issues, the legal requirements of police officers are perfectly clear: involuntary commitment is legally and constitutionally prohibited without clear and convincing evidence that a person is a threat to herself or others, or is unable to provide for her basic needs as spelled out in the [state government] statutes.

BOX 11.1 CIRCUIT COURT RULINGS ON THE ADMISSIBILITY OF EXPERT TESTIMONY REGARDING CREDIBILITY OF OTHER WITNESSES

- First Circuit: *United States v. Gonzalez-Maldonado*, 115 F.3d 9, 16 (1st Cir. 1997). "An expert's opinion that another witness is lying or telling the truth is ordinarily inadmissible pursuant to Rule 702 because the opinion exceeds the scope of the expert's specialized knowledge and therefore merely informs the jury that it should reach a particular conclusion."
- Second Circuit: *Nimely v. City of New York*, 414 F.3d 381, 398 (2d Cir. 2005). "[T]his court, ... has consistently held that expert opinions that constitute evaluations of witness credibility, even when such evaluations are rooted in scientific or technical expertise, are inadmissible under Rule 702."
- Fourth Circuit: *United States v. Dorsey*, 45 F.3d 809, 815 (4th Cir. 1995). "[E]xpert testimony can be properly excluded if it is introduced merely to cast doubt on the credibility of other eyewitnesses, since the evaluation of a witness's credibility is a determination usually within the jury's exclusive purview."
- Seventh Circuit: *United States v. Vest*, 116 F.3d 1179, 1185 (7th Cir. 1997). "Credibility is not a proper subject for expert testimony; the jury does not need an expert to tell it whom to believe, and the expert's stamp of approval on a particular witness' testimony may unduly influence the jury."
- Eighth Circuit: *Engesser v. Dooley*, 457 F.3d 731, 736 (8th Cir. 2006). "An expert may not opine on another witness's credibility."
- Ninth Circuit: *United States v. Rivera*, 43 F.3d 1291, 1295 (9th Cir. 1995). "[A]n expert witness is not permitted to testify specifically to a witness' credibility or to testify in such a manner as to improperly buttress a witness' credibility."
- Tenth Circuit: *United States v. Hill*, 749 F.3d 1250 (10th Cir. 2014) and *United States v. Toledo*, "[T]he credibility of witnesses is generally not an appropriate subject for expert testimony" because it (1) "usurps a critical function of the jury"; (2) "is not helpful to the jury, which can make its own determination of credibility"; and (3) when provided by "impressively qualified experts on the credibility of other witnesses is prejudicial and unduly influences the jury."
- Eleventh Circuit: *United States v. Beasley*, 72 F.3d 1518, 1528 (11th Cir. 1996). "Absent unusual circumstances, expert medical testimony concerning the truthfulness or credibility of a witness is inadmissible ... because it invades the jury's province to make credibility determinations."

Source: U.S. v. Hill, 749 F.3d 1250 (10th Cir. 2014); United States v. Toledo 985 F.2d 1462, 1470 (10th Cir. 1993); Circuit Consensus: Excluding Expert Opinion Testimony on Witness Credibility. Federal Evidence Review. Editors Blog. May 2, 2014. Available from: https://federalevidence.com/blog/2014/may/circuit-consensus-excluding-expert-opinion-testimony-witness-veracity (Accessed 18 August 2018).

In this case, plaintiffs raised three theories related to allegations of negligence: (1) that the state violated Christine's constitutional right to medical care while in custody; (2) that Christine should have been kept in custody longer to facilitate medical care; and (3) that defendants put Christine in danger by releasing her where and when they did, and in a mental state that left her unable to protect herself. Concerning the first two theories, the duty to provide mental health care is a source of much debate and controversy. In this case, while Christine was in custody, some officers thought that she was just being difficult, some thought that she was on drugs, and some thought that she was no worse than the run of loud and uncooperative people who do not want to be in custody. The third theory, known as the state-created danger doctrine, contends that state actors who create or increase danger to an individual can be held liable for violation of the Fourteenth Amendment. To make out a proper danger creation claim, a plaintiff must demonstrate that:

(1) the charged state entity and the charged individual actors created the danger or increased plaintiff's vulnerability to the danger in some way;
(2) plaintiff was a member of a limited and specifically definable group;
(3) defendants' conduct put plaintiff at substantial risk of serious, immediate, and proximate harm;
(4) the risk was obvious or known;
(5) defendant acted recklessly in conscious disregard of that risk; and
(6) such conduct, when viewed in total, is conscience shocking.[17]

These six factors create a high bar for plaintiffs in cases alleging Section 1983 violations of constitutional rights. Over the years, various court decisions have ruled that police do not have a duty to detain someone for treatment or protect persons from injury caused by private persons.[18] *DeShaney v. Winnebago County Department of Social Services* (1989) holds that the U.S. Constitution does not create a right to be protected from criminal predators. The Justices held in *DeShaney* that neither a potential victim's helplessness nor the state's knowledge that failure to intervene exposes a vulnerable person to a risk of crime requires the state to offer protection. A lesson of the *DeShaney* case is that a Section 1983 action cannot succeed when the injury comes from a third person.[19] Moreover, researchers and scholars have debated how large a role the state must play in the creation of danger and in the creation of vulnerability before it assumes a corresponding constitutional duty to protect (Eisenhauer, 2015; Zhang, 2011).

CASE EXAMPLE: EARLY MORNING TRAFFIC STOP

This case concerns William Yoakum (a pseudonym) who was stopped for speeding 73 mph in a 55-mph zone by Deputy Sheriff Brian Baade (a pseudonym). This violation occurred at approximately 1:09 a.m. on a Saturday morning. Because of the appearance of Mr. Yoakum's blood shot eyes and

---

[17]*McClendon v. City of Columbia*, 258 F.3d 432 (5th Cir. 2001); *Currier v. Doran*, 242 F.3d 905 (10th Cir. N.M. 2001).
[18]*Stevens v. Green Bay*, 105 F.3d 1169 (7th Cir.1997); *King v. East St. Louis School District* 189, 496 F.3d 812 (7th Cir.2007) (school not required to detain a pupil to prevent her from walking through a high-crime neighborhood).
[19]*DeShaney v. Winnebago County Department of Social Services*, 489 U.S. 189, 109 S.Ct. 998, 103 L.Ed.2d 249 (1989). As discussed by Davenport (1999), Chief Justice Rehnquist, writing for a 6-3 majority in the DeShaney case, stated that the due process clause of the Fourteenth Amendment, the basis of Section 1983 actions, is a constraint and limitation on a state power, "not an imposition of an affirmative obligation on the part of a state to provide services" (p. 246). "The Court reasoned that because the due process clause does not require the state to provide protective services, the state bears no liability for injuries that could have been prevented had it chosen to furnish them" (p. 246). Therefore, the state was not liable for its failure to provide protective services to a child injured by a beating from his father. With this decision, "the Court drew a rigid line between an action of a state which deprives an individual of rights and a failure of a state to act which has the same result" (p. 246). In dissenting, Justice Brennan questioned the drawing of this line and the failure of the majority to focus on the actions taken by the state to aid the abused child.

slurred words as well as an odor of alcoholic beverages, Deputy Baade asked for his driver's license. Mr. Yoakum answered that he did not have one in his possession and subsequently failed to pass field sobriety tests. Until Mr. Yoakum learned he was to be arrested, he cooperated fully with Deputy Baade. Upon being advised of his arrest, however, Mr. Yoakum disregarded the officer's request to turn around and place his hands behind his back. Instead, he dropped to the ground and began crying and moaning something to the effect of "not again." Mr. Yoakum actively resisted the officer's attempt to control his arms, and the ensuing struggle led to Deputy Baade punching him about the head several times. Back-up deputies arrived on the scene with a police dog. Mr. Yoakum struck the police dog, an action that resulted in Deputy Baade striking Mr. Yoakum again to deter further assault on the police dog. The dog then engaged in a "bite and hold" attempt to bring Mr. Yoakum under control. Afterwards, Mr. Yoakum sued the sheriff's department and Deputy Brian Baade.

Counsel for the defense asked the forensic criminologist to review the case and indicate whether he could contribute to a jury's understanding and evaluation of the issues in this suit. The following materials were reviewed: the 402-page State Police investigation of this matter; internal documents of the sheriff's department, including the Captain's Board report; jail booking records; a use of force report from the Police Department; a report issued by the Police Department concerning an earlier operating while intoxicated (OWI) and resisting arrest incident concerning Mr. Yoakum; and four depositions.

According to the forensic criminological investigation:

> My first opinion is that the officers' actions must be understood in light of the "fundamental attribution error" (FAE) [citation to Bartol and Bartol, 2004, p. 61]. The FAE refers to the human tendency to view the actions of police officers as motivated primarily by personal predispositions rather than taking sufficiently into account the situational pressures under which the officers were acting at the moment. When we assess our own actions, however, we often explain our actions by these situational pressures and minimize our personal predispositions as explanations for our behaviors. In this case, we must understand the situational pressures under which Deputy Baade and the other officers were operating when they brought Mr. Yoakum physically under control.

When considering actions of the police, fundamental attribution error refers to the human tendency to view police officer behaviors and decision-making as motivated primarily by individual choices. Yet, decades of scholarship and research has shown that forensic investigators need to understand police actions as taking place in a socio-spatial context that shapes and constrains behavior, creates some kinds of opportunities rather than others, and guides decision-making (Gaines and Kappeler, 2014; Ross, 2018; Rossmo, 2008). That is, the forensic criminologist needs to take sufficiently into account the situational pressures under which the officers were acting.

Fundamental attribution error attributes the actor's behavior to his or her personality, to something "in" the actor rather than to the circumstances that are "outside" or "external" to the actor. A major indicator of fundamental attribution error is the tendency to provide causal explanations for the behavior of others in largely dispositional or personal terms (Stephan and Stephan, 1990, p. 23; Feigenson, 2000, pp. 62–65; Robbennolt, 2000; Dripps, 2003).

In this case, we must understand the situational pressures under which police officers were operating when they brought Mr. Yoakum physically under control.

As the forensic criminological report continues:

> Second, this was a late night, early morning traffic stop by a lone officer on a weekend. Thus, in addition to the risks inherent in any late night stop, the likelihood a driver would have been under the influence, because this was a weekend, substantially increases. As we know, alcohol is involved in some way or another in most violent crimes. Under these circumstances, police officers must be particularly alert and must insist on protocol. Studies of officers who were murdered or assaulted reveal that victim officers were those who used force only at the last moment, were "laid back" and "easy going" and did not follow operational rules at traffic stops, and had a tendency to "drop their guard" [citation to Pinizzotto and Davis, 1992, p. 32].

In the U.S. Supreme Court decision *Rodriguez v. United States* (2015), the Court noted that "[t]raffic stops are especially fraught with danger to police officers." In another U.S. Supreme Court case, *Arizona v. Johnson* (2009), the Court acknowledged that, in traffic stops, police may minimize the risk of harm by exercising "unquestioned command of the situation." In fact, criminologists have found vehicle pullovers to be the third most dangerous law enforcement activity a patrol officer can encounter (Martin, 2016). In *Graham v. Connor* (1989), the U.S. Supreme Court noted "not every push or shove, even if it may later seem unnecessary in the peace of a judge's chamber, violates the Fourth Amendment."

As the forensic criminological report elaborates:

> My third opinion concerns the behavior of Mr. Yoakum during his interaction with Deputy Baade. Although Yoakum was initially quite cooperative, his entire demeanor changed suddenly when he learned he was about to be arrested. He dropped to the ground, began crying and wailing, and actively resisted Baade's attempts to control his hands. Yoakum refused to take his hands out of his pockets, and later in the struggle, he lay prone with his hands hidden under his body and resisted the deputy's attempts to pull his hands behind his back as both men struggled on the ground.

Criminologists and law enforcement officers know about the problem of "hidden hands," including hidden hands tucked under a prone subject. A subject with hidden hands at his waistband, where a weapon is often kept, can suddenly shoot or stab an officer before the officer can possibly react (known as action-reaction gap concerning timing or the reactionary gap concerning distance) (Lewinski et al., 2016, pp. 70–83; Miller, 2015). Lewinski and colleagues (2016) discuss how a prone subject can produce and fire a weapon in little over half a second. In a related scenario, "an unsecured suspect lying prostrate and spread-eagled on the ground, ten feet from an officer, head facing away, can be on top of that officer's chest in less than three seconds." The forensic criminologist opines that "[b]ecause it is the subject's behavior which determines the police officer's behaviors in response, it is my opinion that Mr. Yoakum's refusal to show his hands and his resistance to Deputy Baade's attempts to control them, led to the head strikes delivered to Yoakum."

The forensic criminological report continues:

> My fourth opinion concerns head strikes. While they should normally be avoided, they are not prohibited as a rule if they can be justified under the circumstances. Yoakum's continued resistance put

Baade in a position where he could reasonably anticipate an immediate attack. Baade's duty was to control the situation and not just to wait to see what would happen next. According to research by Dr. Richard Johnson at the University of Toledo, a former Indiana State Trooper: "The findings here suggest that when a police officer contacts an angry person during an official police-citizen encounter, if the person places his or her hands in his or her pockets, the officer will likely become very concerned about the safety of the situation. The officer may sharply order the citizen to remove his hands from his pockets and may even draw a weapon in response to this perceived serious danger. In the eyes of the officer, this behavior is akin in seriousness to assuming a boxer's stance and moving toward the officer" [citation to Johnson, 2017, p. 297].

Given the circumstances of the struggle with Yoakum, Deputy Baade may not have believed he could disengage from Mr. Yoakum long enough to safely draw and engage his CEW [conducted energy weapon, a.k.a. Taser] or that it would take effect. Head strikes were more timely and, please note, they were empty-hand and did not involve the use of a baton or other instrument. Note also that Training Sergeant Matt Richardson [a pseudonym] seemed initially not to object to the head strikes per se, but rather to the fact that Baade did not transition to another technique when head strikes did not produce a prompt effect [reference to state police report, p. 17]. According to Deputy Baade, Mr. Yoakum was imbued with considerable strength. He was determined not to comply with Deputy Baade just as he had not complied with and then fought with police while under the influence of alcohol and driving [according to a prior arrest]. Given all the above, Deputy Baade's attempts to control Mr. Yoakum and defend himself at the same time do not seem unreasonable.

My fifth and final opinion (as of this writing) is that reasonable officers could disagree as to the propriety or impropriety of Deputy Brian Baade's actions in attempting to control and arrest Mr. William Yoakum. Indeed, there could be a fair and reasonable debate as to the propriety of delivering empty-hand head strikes to a subject refusing to show his hands and resisting arrest. For example, ... Deputy Baade ... testified that [the] Police Department chief ... and ... County Corporal believe his actions were reasonable. Deputy Baade's acts were not prohibited by any settled law, at least as far as I know [citation to AELE Law Journal, 2018].

The forensic report concludes that "Mr. Yoakum engaged in three of the above warning behaviors, in addition to refusing to show his hands. Deputy Baade ceased any and all empty-hand head strikes the instant Mr. Yoakum was brought under control and then summoned medical attention for him. This does not bespeak a punitive use of force."

During any struggle with a subject, a law enforcement officer must protect his or her sidearm from possible attempts to grab it. Police estimate that slightly over 10% of murdered officers are killed by their own guns in "weapon takeaway" shootings. Deputy Baade was forced to engage in ground fighting with Mr. Yoakum, exacerbating the dangers of a weapon takeaway and further exhausting the officer, another dangerous situation. Mr. Yoakum also demonstrated significant emotional lability as his mental state suddenly changed dramatically, a situation not unknown in "sudden ambush" attacks on officers as noted by Schonten and Brennan (2016) and Dvorak and colleagues (2013).

When assessing the appropriateness of an officer's use of force, it is customary to apply a "use-of-force continuum" to the facts at hand. According to the continuum used in many state law enforcement academy physical tactics basic training, an officer may use soft, empty-hand control over a person who disregards verbal direction. Importantly, the citizen controls the level of force in an encounter. A police officer escalates his use of force in order to control the situation as the citizen requires more force to be used by increasing his or her level of resistance (even to that of active aggression) (Crawford and Burns, 2008; Klahm and Tillyer, 2010; Lee et al., 2014; Terrill and Reisig, 2003).

The U.S. Supreme Court has ruled that courts should review a police officer's use of force in accordance with the Fourth Amendment and the objective reasonableness test or standard. That is, "the question is whether the officers' actions are 'objectively reasonable' in light of the facts and circumstances confronting them, without regard to their underlying intent or motivation."[20] The controlling case for police officer use of force is *Graham v. Connor* (1989). Ross (2018, pp. 292, 307), paraphrasing the *Graham v. Connor* (1989) decision, points to several factors courts may apply in a court's review of a claim of excessive force: the severity of the crime at issue; whether the suspect is actively resisting arrest; whether the suspect is an immediate threat to the officer(s) or others; whether the suspect is attempting to evade arrest. As the Court in the *Graham* case noted, the "calculus of reasonableness must embody allowance for the fact that police officers are often forced to make split-second judgments—in circumstances that are tense, uncertain, and rapidly evolving—about the amount of force that is necessary in a particular situation."[21] Courts will evaluate the evidence and determine "reasonableness" of police actions based on the perception of the officer and not through hindsight. Since reasonableness is flexible and malleable, there can be no immutable and unchanging definition and standard. Like all cases, the courts will determine the reasonableness of the use of force on a case-by-case basis.

CASE EXAMPLE: USE OF FORCE IN A HIGH CRIME AREA

On June 13, 2014, police were dispatched in response to a citizen who called 911, identified herself, and expressed that a group of youths, one of whom was in possession of a gun, were walking north on a neighborhood street. As the police approached a group of youths fitting the description given by the caller, Dan Boswell (a pseudonym) broke from the group and began running between the houses on the street. Officer Sean Cannon (a pseudonym) eventually joined the search, spotted Boswell, and began a foot pursuit. Officers at the scene reported Boswell moving his hand into his waistband (as if to secure a weapon). Officer Cannon was aware that Officer Melton (a pseudonym) reported Boswell was "grabbing his waistband" and took this to mean he may have had a handgun tucked into his pants. Notably, Beat CCC (a pseudonym) was known for gun violence, weapons offenses, drug activity, and gang activity. Officer Cannon caught up as Boswell leaped a fence and fell into a residential back yard. Boswell then assumed a prone position and repeatedly refused commands to remove his hands from beneath his torso. Fearing he may be shot, Officer Cannon struck Boswell on the back of his head with his right fist as it held a flashlight. Boswell was eventually cuffed and received treatment for lacerations. A handgun was retrieved along the route of Boswell's flight.

---

[20]*Graham v. Connor*, 490 US 397—U.S. Supreme Court (1989); *Scott v. United States*, 436 U. S. 128, 137-139 (1978).
[21]*Graham v. Connor*, 490 US 397—U.S. Supreme Court (1989).

In this case, plaintiff Boswell asserts a Fourth Amendment claim against Officer Cannon for (1) unreasonable stop, seizure, and arrest; (2) unreasonable and excessive force; and (3) assault and battery. Courts recognize three categories of seizure and each indicates a different level of scrutiny.[22] An investigatory stop requires reasonable suspicion that criminal activity is afoot; a frisk requires reasonable suspicion that the suspect stopped is armed and dangerous; and an arrest requires probable cause that a crime has occurred.[23] An officer may conduct a stop if the officer "possesses a particularized and objective basis for suspecting the particular person of criminal activity based on specific and articulable facts."[24] In other words, "[a]n investigatory stop must be justified by some objective manifestation that the person stopped is, or is about to be, engaged in criminal activity."[25] Courts generally permit the "use of force … to effect a stop when such a show of force is reasonable under the circumstances of the stop."[26]

Courts analyze excessive force claims under the Fourth Amendment's reasonableness standard, which looks to "whether the officers' actions are 'objectively reasonable' in light of the facts and circumstances confronting them, without regard to their underlying intent or motivation."[27] "The operative question in such cases is 'whether the totality of the circumstances justifie[s] a particular sort of search or seizure,'"[28] in this case, Officer Cannon's application of force. "The reasonableness of the use of force is evaluated under an 'objective' inquiry that pays 'careful attention to the facts and circumstances of each particular case.'" Importantly, "[t]he 'reasonableness' of a particular use of force must be judged from the perspective of a reasonable officer on the scene, rather than with the 20/20 vision of hindsight."[29] "Excessive force claims … are evaluated for objective reasonableness based upon the information the officers had when the conduct occurred."[30]

The forensic criminologist was asked by counsel for the defense to review the case and to comment on the various factors that may explain Officer Sean Cannon's decision to use force during the arrest of Dan Boswell. The following materials were reviewed: police arrest and use of force records, criminal trial transcripts, socioeconomic census data, criminal statistics for the city and surrounding neighborhood, Rule 26 disclosures and EMT reports, police training materials, training records, the Manual of Procedure, daily activity logs, professional literature on hazards of policing, and reports by two expert witnesses. The forensic criminologist also met with four other witnesses, a crime analyst of the local police department, and Officer Sean Cannon. The chase route and the surrounding neighborhood were also investigated.

---

[22]*Smoak v. Hall*, 460 F. 3d 779-81—Court of Appeals, 6th Circuit 2006; *Arizona v. Johnson*, 555 U.S. 323, 326-27, 129 S.Ct. 781, 172 L.Ed.2d 694 (2009).

[23]*Johnson*, 555 U.S. at 326-27, 129 S.Ct. 781 (2009).

[24]*Smoak v. Hall*, 460 F.3d 778 (6th Circuit 2006).

[25]*United States v. Cortez*, 449 U.S. 411, 417, 101 S.Ct. 690, 66 L.Ed.2d 621 (1981).

[26]*United States v. Heath*, 259 F.3d 522, 530 (6th Cir. 2001); *United States v. Lindsey*, 114 Fed.Appx. 718, 721 (6th Cir. 2004); *United States v. Merritt*, 695 F.2d 1263, 1273 (10th Cir. 1982).

[27]*Graham v. Connor*, 490 U.S. 386, 397, 109 S.Ct. 1865, 104 L.Ed.2d 443 (1989).

[28]*County of Los Angeles, Calif. v. Mendez*, 137 S.Ct. 1539, 1542, 198 L.Ed.2d 52 (2017) (quoting *Tennessee v. Garner*, 471 U.S. 1, 8-9, 105 S.Ct. 1694, 85 L.Ed.2d 1 (1985)).

[29]Quoting *Graham*, 490 U.S. at 396, 109 S.Ct. 1865.

[30]*Saucier v. Katz*, 533 U.S. 194, 207, 121 S.Ct. 2151, 150 L.Ed.2d 272 (2001).

Generally, forensic criminologists find it helpful to understand the nature of the neighborhood to address how and why questions concerning an officer's actions when arresting a suspect. The nexus of individual action and socio-spatial context is a fundamental theoretical component of environmental criminology, as we have stressed throughout this book. Proponents of environmental criminology study crime, criminality, and victimization as they relate to time and place (Bottoms and Wiles, 2002, p. 621). Over the decades, much criminological research has found that neighborhoods of concentrated poverty tend to have higher rates of violence and theft than more affluent neighborhoods (Agnew and Brezina, 2011; Bjerk, 2007; Krivo and Peterson, 1996). For example, several studies find that persistent poverty and unemployment are strongly related to such crimes (Aaltonen et al., 2011; Farnworth et al., 1994; Jarjoura et al., 2002; Thornberry and Christenson, 1984; Bushway, 2011; Carlson and Michalowski, 1997; Colvin, 2000; Gould et al., 2002; Rosenfeld and Messner, 2009; Yearwood and Koinis, 2011). High crime rates in a neighborhood often translate to a higher risk of firearms assaults against police (Kuhns et al., 2016, p. 21). Therefore, a first step in evaluating a police action is to understand the nature of the neighborhood.

According to the forensic criminological report:

> The area in which Mr. Boswell was spotted, pursued, and apprehended was in Johnson County [a pseudonym] Census Tract 0032, Blockgroup 1. The median household income for 2009–2013 was $25,662 compared to the … county median income of $51,667 and the [city] median income of $39,227. About 45 percent of the residents of this blockgroup are below the poverty level, almost double the percentage for the city [reference to data collected by demographers at BonData]. Data such as these tend to correlate with crime, so a higher crime rate than the city average is to be expected [citation to Ellis et al., 2009, p. 60]. This assumption proved to be true.
>
> Mr. Boswell was apprehended in the yard at 9913 Marty Street [a pseudonym], not far from where the chase began. This address is located in Beat CCC [a compilation of several Beats], which has one of the highest crime rates. The robbery rate for CCC (668 per 100,000) and the aggravated assault rate (1,294 per 100,000) approximated those rates for the [city] (682 and 1,256). By way of comparison, the robbery rate for [the city] in 2013 was 246 per 100,000, and the aggravated assault rate was 395 per 100,000. In fact, Beat C5 reports more aggravated assaults per square mile than any area of the city (155 per square mile).
>
> During my interview with police department crime analyst Molly Angelica [a pseudonym] she indicated to me there was gang activity in the area (the "Baxter Boys") [a pseudonym] and her data showed that Beats C4, C5, and C6 had the highest numbers of gun-related incidents in the city. Just down the street from where Mr. Boswell was apprehended sits Pocket Park [a pseudonym], where three people were struck by gunfire in 2013 alone. Finally, again based on crime analyst Molly Angelica's data, Beat C5 had the second highest rate of drug law violations in the city (Beat W8 appeared to have a higher rate, possibly due to its central downtown location where a lot of transients gather). In my opinion, these facts about Beat C5 made the report of a potential gun crime even more credible, in addition to the fact that it was reported by a citizen whose willingness to give her name made her concerns all the more important to investigate actively. This "citizen-informant doctrine" is introduced and labeled in J. Thompson and G. Starkman, "The Citizen Informant Doctrine," Journal of Criminal Law and Criminology 64 (1973): 163–173.

Another topic that a forensic criminologist might address in a case involving use of force is the danger to officers in policing high crime areas. Decades of research shows that policing is one of the most dangerous careers as 10% of all officers are assaulted each year, and more than one quarter will be injured (Bierie, 2017). From 1999 to 2009, approximately 600 police officers were feloniously killed, and more than 700 died as the result of accidents across the United States (Kachurik, 2013).

According to the forensic criminological investigation:

> Current criminological thinking identifies areas where there are drug activities, gang activities, problem buildings, property foreclosures, and spotty lighting as areas of high risk for assaults against police officers [citation to Caplan et al., 2014; Maretta and Caplan, 2013]. These descriptors all apply to the area where Officer Cannon pursued Mr. Boswell. Add to this the fact that ambushes of police officers have increased in recent years and that foot pursuits in possible arrest situations are inherently dangerous, and we can see why Officer Cannon should have been on high alert [citations to McAllister, 2015; Bohrer, 2000, pp. 10–15].

A third topic that a forensic criminologist may address is the danger to the officer if there is a struggle with the suspect. Courts have ruled that police officers who put themselves in danger to keep communities safe "are often forced to make split-second judgments—in circumstances that are tense, uncertain, and rapidly evolving—about the amount of force that is necessary in a particular situation."[31] "[W]hether the use of deadly force at a particular moment is reasonable depends primarily on objective assessment of the danger a suspect poses at that moment."[32]

As the forensic criminological report notes:

> What immediately prompted Cannon's use of force against Boswell was Boswell's refusal to show his hands by removing them from beneath his prone body. Applied research has shown that a prone suspect with "hidden hands" can produce and fire a weapon in various directions in about one-half to three-quarters of a second (0.52 to 0.77 seconds) [citation to Lewinski et al., 2016]. The reactionary gap is such that no police officer could respond to this movement fast enough to save his life or the life of another officer or citizen. Mr. Boswell's youth did not diminish the threat of firearm violence reasonably perceived by Officer Cannon. Considerable evidence indicates that youthful access to firearms increases the risk of homicide, suicide, and unintentional gun injury in the home and in the community [citations to Duke et al., 2005; Braga, 2004].

Although some causes of action will tend to come and go, generic use-of-force issues are likely to remain a common cause of action because the use of force is so central to police officer roles and actions (Bittner, 1970). Criminologists have contributed much to the academic study of police use of force (Alpert and Fridell, 1992; Fyfe, 1988; Geller and Toch, 1995) and they can make a forensic contribution as well. Police are expected to overcome unlawful resistance to their legitimate actions but must do so within the boundaries of reasonableness. As a measure of what is reasonable, criminologists utilize various versions of a "use-of-force continuum" wherein legitimate police responses to subjects' levels of resistance are graphically detailed in many publications (Gillespie et al., 1998; Hemmens and Atherton, 1999; Kinnaird, 2003; Patrick and Hall, 2005). Guidance in when to use what level of force is provided by the continuum although the placement of intermediate levels of force can vary from one

---

[31]*Graham v. Connor*, 490 U.S. 386, 396-97, 109 S.Ct. 1865, 104 L.Ed.2d 443 (1989).
[32]*Bouggess v. Mattingly*, 482 F.3d 889 (6th Cir. 2007).

tactical expert to another. Criminologists are not necessarily expected to detail the precise mechanics of force, as there are defense and control tactics experts who will do that. Rather, the criminologist can search for agency patterns, or their absence, and can provide comparative, historical, and contemporary perspectives on the force-related policies and practices of the department or agency involved in litigation.

CONCLUSION

This chapter has examined several cases related to civil litigation concerning police and correctional facilities. Like other cases we have covered in past chapters, the examples we draw on represent only a limited selection from a vast area of litigation that is continually changing.

Over the decades, new court decisions have paved the way for police officers, police departments, and corrections officers and agencies to be held liable under Section 1983. There are many areas of negligence in the criminal justice system including wrongful death, failure to protect, false arrest and imprisonment, malicious prosecution, arrest and battery, and so on. Ross (2018, p. 497) notes that even though Section 1983 was enacted in 1871, it lay dormant and relatively unused until the 1960s. Today, Section 1983 is not only used against police and corrections officers but also against public officials. "Regardless of position or rank, criminal justice practitioners remain vulnerable to civil litigation and, based on past trends of Section 1983 lawsuits, nothing indicates that its use will decline in the future" (p. 497). "If the past can predict the future," according to Ross (2018, p. 497), "more shifts and expansions in areas already litigated should be expected alongside new decisions in emerging areas."

Lawsuits involving police actions and corrections practices are fertile areas of forensic criminological investigation since these personnel are operationally available 24 hours a day and 7 days a week and encounter a variety of different kinds of justice-involved individuals. At times, courts will need social science input to understand the behavioral antecedents or consequences pertinent to police and corrections actions and decision-making. Civil liability continues to evolve and develop particularly in areas of administrative negligence and supervision.

Like other areas of forensic criminology that we have covered in previous chapters, the area of police and corrections litigation requires that the expert witness understand the legal aspects of the case, the scope of the discovery process and analysis, and his or her role in litigation. Forensic criminologists should understand the distinction between *social framework evidence* that describes general scientific propositions, theories, and concepts (e.g., fundamental attribution error, routine activity theory, etc.) and *diagnostic evidence* that applies the general propositions to individual cases (Faigman et al., 2014). That is, a forensic criminologist should understand whether he or she is expected to proffer social framework evidence or diagnostic evidence. This can be a challenge because sometimes courts may limit a forensic criminologist to testifying to general group-level phenomena, leaving application and conclusions regarding specific cases to jurors. Other times, courts may permit a forensic criminologist to apply his or her knowledge to an individual case and offer opinions on whether it is an instance of the more general phenomenon. Whether forensic criminological testimony is sufficiently reliable to be admissible may vary depending on whether the testimony reports general scientific findings or whether the testimony seeks to use specific data and evidence to address the case at hand.

CONCLUSIONS AND ADDITIONAL PRACTICE CONSIDERATIONS

12

INTRODUCTION

In our book, we have drawn on examples from actual court cases and expert witness reports and testimony to demonstrate the different uses of criminological knowledge in the civil court system. One of our goals has been to show the usefulness of forensic criminology as a distinctive *practice* of research that can generate criminological knowledge to assist the courts in understanding the evidence presented at trial. This practice requires not only an understanding of how the legal system operates, but a working familiarity with statutes and case law that are relevant to the particular issue(s) at hand. In addition, the practice of forensic criminology requires knowledge and familiarity with a diversity of social science methods, theories, and analytical techniques to address problems posed by the legal system.

Our chapters have included excerpts from forensic criminological reports, in-depth discussions of the methodological and analytical bases of these investigations, and important lessons learned from actual litigation cases. Using diverse case examples, we have demonstrated how criminological expert witness research and testimony can be useful to the courts in understanding crime foreseeability, breach of duty, and causation. The engagement, integration, and synthesis of forensic evidence with criminological knowledge provides the foundation of expert witness reports and the arguments made by attorneys. As we have pointed out, criminological knowledge plays a central role in the ongoing expansion of legal liability generated by criminal events and the actions and inactions of police, corrections officers, business owners, place managers, and other formal and informal agents of social control. In this final chapter, we discuss the contributions and lessons of our book. We offer some guidelines to forensic criminologists for managing their roles in litigation to maximize the likelihood that sound and relevant scientific knowledge will be effective in resolving legal issues and problems presented to the courts.

VARIETY AND DIVERSITY OF FORENSIC CRIMINOLOGY

One of our major contributions has been to reveal the variety and diversity of forensic criminology in the setting of the courts and the civil litigation process. The social sciences offer many investigative sources, research findings, theoretical perspectives, methodological approaches, and data analytical techniques that can inform forensic criminological work. In our book, we have covered only a small segment of a rich and vast array of forensic criminology. Box 12.1 provides a list of examples of

Practicing Forensic Criminology. https://doi.org/10.1016/B978-0-12-815595-0.00012-2
241

BOX 12.1 EXAMPLES OF FORENSIC APPLICATIONS OF SUBSTANTIVE CRIMINOLOGY TO CIVIL AND CRIMINAL MATTERS

- ADHD and crime
- Adult entertainment and the sex trade
- Arson typologies (e.g., crime concealment)
- Character contests and assaults
- Club drugs
- Collective behavior, crowd control, and social contagion
- Crime Prevention Through Environmental Design
- Criminal profiling and serial criminals
- Criminal recidivism
- Deterrence theories
- Environmental criminology
- Expressive versus instrumental violence and deterrability
- False accusations of rape
- False confessions
- Fundamental attribution error
- Gang behavior
- Geographic profiling
- Hate crimes against gay bars
- Homelessness, mental illness, and crime
- Journey to crime
- Murder-suicide typologies
- Native American suicidology and suicidology of indigenous peoples
- Obedience to authority and social engineering
- Pedophiles and child molesters
- Personality disorders and criminal behavior
- Principles of threat and risk assessment
- Profiles and syndromes as character evidence
- Rapist typologies
- Rational choice theory and situational crime prevention
- Robbery typologies and robbery prevention
- Routine activities theory and lifestyle/exposure theory
- School bullying and school security needs
- Selective enforcement versus selective involvement theories
- Spouse abuse etiology and the police response
- Stalking behavior and management
- Tattoos and criminal behavior
- Theories of prejudice and discrimination in hiring, including reverse discrimination
- Theories of repeat victimization
- Theories of sexual harassment
- Tourist victimology
- Violence and drugs nexus
- Violence as catharsis or aggression enhancement
- Violence prediction
- Witness factors
- Workplace violence Types I–IV and crimes by employees

forensic applications of substantive criminology to civil and criminal matters. The Box shows the wide range of topics and subjects of litigation cases that connect with forensic criminology. Some of the topics and themes listed in Box 12.1 reflect and link to the examples and cases we have discussed in previous chapters. The topics we have focused on constitute a small sampling rather than the universe of criminological knowledge available to the courts in their efforts to render criminal justice.

Given the immense diversity and heterogeneity of the field, our treatment and analysis of the practice of forensic criminology has been deliberately selective and delimited. We have introduced only a diminutive number of issues including those related to premises liability for negligent security, administrative negligence, vicarious liability, sexual assault, workplace violence, wrongful conviction litigation, and the actions of police and corrections officers. Importantly, it is impossible to be exhaustive and comprehensive, and we wish to inform the reader that our book is only an introduction to an extensive field that is evolving, developing, and transforming. While American courts' reliance on criminological research and knowledge is well established, there is no universal blueprint to guide the forensic criminologist in the assessment of foreseeability, breach of duty, and causation. A multiplicity of facts, topics, and issues characterize many of the cases we have addressed. Not surprisingly, each case will involve different forms of evidence, substantive issues and policy considerations, and competing explanations of the principal rationales underlying allegations of negligence.

Importantly, courts now rely extensively on social science and criminological research to create a general empirical context for determining factual issues specific to particular cases, as in testimony on eyewitness identification, negligent security, workplace violence, police and corrections litigation, among other areas. Social science and criminological methods including surveys, crime foreseeability analyses, experiments, statistics, participant observation, interviews, focus groups, content analysis, and ethnography can be found in many factual cases. At times, their absence occasions a judicial rebuke. According to Monahan and Walker's (2011, p. 80) review of the continuities and changes that have occurred in the application of social science research to American law over the last 25 years: "it has become more difficult to find a Supreme Court constitutional decision implicating an empirical question in which at least one side did not *cite* to social science research than it has been to find a decision in which at least one side cited such research—a practice now as common among conservative as among liberal Justices" (emphasis in original).

Decades ago, courts' reliance on social science was often confused and always contested. Today, however, debates no longer take place on whether to rely on social science to create general contexts for resolving issues specific to a case but how best to present social science information and criminological knowledge to a fact finder.

A forensic criminologist can address damages in addition to the traditional tort concerns of establishing or challenging notions of duty, breach of duty, and causation. There are different notions of damage and damage assessment. On the one hand, in a wrongful death lawsuit, a criminologist may evaluate the prospects for long-term gainful employment of a person had he not been shot in self-defense by a police officer or a security officer. On the other hand, a person who suffers a legally recognized harm is often entitled to an award of damages in the form of money. The primary purpose of damages is compensatory, that is, to make up to the plaintiff for what he or she has lost due to the actions or inactions of a defendant. Social science research can determine the amount of loss and damage. Lonsway (2005) and Ellison (2005) discuss how, in civil cases, criminologists can help to establish damages resulting from a sexual assault through clinical assessment and diagnosis. Although psychologists, physicians, and economists can address injury and damage assessments, a forensic criminologist can discuss the impact of a crime on the victim, educate a jury on victimology and/or posttraumatic stress disorder (PTSD), and provide insights into secondary and indirect victimization.

Because a forensic criminologist can draw on different social science methods and theoretical orientations, there are numerous areas and litigation cases in which she or he can apply forensic criminological knowledge to help the courts resolve legal issues. Whereas academic criminologists almost invariably study crime at the group level and aim to make supra-individual generalizations, trial courts typically need expert knowledge to decide cases at the individual level. Faigman and colleagues (2014) describe the group to individual (G2i) challenge of reasoning from group data to decisions about individuals. Forensic criminologists testify to such matters as the conditions likely to lead to false confessions, factors that contribute to eyewitness misidentification, and the criminogenic propensities of people, places, and situations. These are all general population-based statements about the empirical world. They are the "G" of G2i and represent the ordinary perspective of traditional criminological research and expertise. However, in the courtroom, the operative questions pertain to the particular case at hand, the "i" of G2i: Did the suspect falsely confess? Was the witness's eyewitness identification accurate? Did the place managers breach a duty of care? According to Faigman and colleagues (2014, p. 420), "[i]n terms of scientific inference, reasoning from the group to an individual case presents considerable challenges and, simply put, is rarely a focus of the basic scientific enterprise. In the courtroom, it is the enterprise." Although it is the jury or fact finder that ultimately makes a decision or determines findings of fact, such a decision or finding can be influenced by the research investigation and testimony of a forensic criminologist.

In our chapters, we have provided examples from various cases on how a forensic criminologist may bridge the divide between the general and specific by applying extant criminological research to case-specific evidence to educate a jury in rendering a decision. Our chapters highlight different strategies that forensic criminologists can use to undertake research and provide testimony that can fit the case both legally (as mandated by the relevant substantive law) and empirically (as indicated by an assessment of criminological literature). Research by Faigman and colleagues (2014), Monahan and colleagues (2009, 2008), Mitchell and colleagues (2010; 2011), and King and colleagues (2012) note that forensic social scientists face daunting challenges in using scholarship that can meet scientific standards and that has peer acceptance in the social science community. Some of these challenges dovetail with the G2i dilemma and include difficulties of linking general social science theories to specific cases; using case-specific research to produce social facts; deriving case-specific evidence from social science principles; and employing reliable methods to formulate case-specific opinions while avoiding the use of subjective judgments to derive opinions.

As we have demonstrated in our chapters, the social science and criminological scholarship on the criminology of place has substantial external validity. Moreover, in the litigation context, this scholarship can provide a sound basis for analyzing the criminogenic features of places, organizational policies, and informal and formal actions that are alleged to have contributed to a crime. In our chapters, we have documented how a criminologist can use situational opportunity theories to understand individual victimization, employ theory and research to link situational opportunity and high crime places, and point to the kinds of workplace policies and practices that provide fertile ground for the emergence of criminogenic behaviors and actions.

For instance, a forensic criminologist may use a "crime foreseeability" model to examine whether a criminal act is reasonably foreseeable due to inadequate security, evidence of past similar offenses on or near a premises, or the nature and profile of the offender. As liability experts, forensic criminologists may opine on questions of standards of care in light of this foreseeability. They may also address the causal relationship between any alleged breach of standards and the damages suffered by a plaintiff. In an apartment setting, security standards may entail some combination of access control, sufficient lighting, effective locks, foliage control, tenant selection and retention, key control, courtesy patrols, and other property-specific measures. Here a forensic criminologist could explain to a jury exactly which security measures should have been in place given the level of foreseeability that a crime would occur. The criminologist may rely on ethnographic field observations and interviews to explain the actions of criminals in the circumstances. Conversely, a criminologist may also interpret the literature in such a way as to challenge a causal relationship between property conditions and a criminal's actions. The important point we wish to make is that criminologists have a rich reservoir of heterogeneous methods, theories, and perspectives from which to draw on when undertaking forensic criminological research.

THEORY AND METHOD IN THE PRACTICE OF FORENSIC CRIMINOLOGY

In our chapters, we have examined the ways in which forensic criminologists use social science methods and theories to determine adjudicative or case-specific facts and provide general contextual information to assist the courts in determining the facts of a case. As many of our cases show, the forensic criminologist works in a bottom-up fashion using different theories and concepts to address a research problem related to duty, breach of duty, and causation. Foreseeability is the key because it is an element both of duty and of causation. As we have pointed out in our chapters, in negligent security cases, foreseeability is a factor in the analysis of (1) whether the property owner had a duty to the injured person, and (2) whether the alleged failures of the property owner to provide adequate protection caused the injury.

In analyzing the foreseeability of a criminal event, a forensic criminologist may review testimony, documents, and other quantitative and qualitative information about a case. She or he would then assess how extant criminological and social science theory and research would apply to the specific circumstances of the socio-spatial context or organizational setting where a crime event occurred. Next, she or he would analyze the specific features of the sociophysical environment and the organization's policies and practices. She or he would evaluate these against what social science scholarship has shown to be factors that create criminogenic places and those that mitigate against crime.

Most criminological theories have been concerned with explaining why certain individuals or groups, exposed to particular psychological or social influences, or with particular inherited traits, are more likely to become involved in delinquency or crime. "Thus, theories of crime tend to be theories of motivation, which assume that variations in motivation or controls on motivations explain variations in criminal behavior, whether through individual or ecological differences" (Wilcox and Cullen, 2018, p. 124). This motivation-centric orientation focuses on why a particular individual committed a particular type of offense. But this orientation does not sufficiently answer why or how a crime event occurs. The commission of a crime requires not just the existence of a motivated offender but an opportunity to offend. That is, a criminal event cannot be explained simply by referring to criminal dispositions or the psychological traits of the offender.

As we have pointed out throughout our book, a crime is an event that happens because of the intersection of two factors in time and space: an offender's propensity or motivation to commit a crime and the opportunity to carry out the desired action (Wilcox and Cullen, 2018, p. 124). The criminologist can show how personal dispositions or psychological traits interact with socio-spatial (environmental), opportunity, and situational factors favoring crime to produce a criminal act at a particular place and time. The theoretical foundations of this evolving perspective derive primarily from seminal work in defensible space theory, crime prevention through environmental design (CPTED), situational crime prevention, routine activities theory, rational choice theory, place management theory, criminology of place, and crime pattern theory (for overviews and paradigmatic statements, see Wortley and Mazerolle, 2008; Lersch, 2004; Weisburd et al., 2016; Wilcox and Cullen, 2018).

Situational opportunity approaches have a close connection to environmental criminology theories because of the shared focus on (1) the study of crime events themselves and (2) the ways in which the structure of the physical and social environment affects the availability of criminal opportunities. "This line of study is also referred to as crime-event criminology, which explicitly denotes the focus on incidents, rather than using traditional criminology's focus on the causes of criminal behavior" (Wilcox and Cullen, 2018, p. 124). The relevance of situational opportunity within forensic criminology and mainstream criminology is obvious today. Much research has shown extensive empirical support for the earlier theories. Indeed, according to Wilcox and Cullen's (2018, p. 124) comprehensive review of the field, criminological scholarship is moving toward theoretical fusion and synthesis as scholars increasingly integrate the notion of situational opportunity into theories of criminal offending, "further eroding the once-stark divide between studies of situational opportunity and mainstream criminology."

One of our concerns in this book has been to demonstrate to the reader the limitations of both "grand theory" and "abstracted empiricism" when it comes to engaging case material and deriving case-specific opinions. Grand theory is a term coined by the American sociologist C. Wright Mills (1959) in *The Sociological Imagination* to refer to the form of highly abstract theorizing in which the formal organization and arrangement of concepts takes priority over data collection and empirical analysis. Grand theorizing seeks to formulate abstract theoretical systems and totalizing conceptualizations of the social world. Abstracted empiricism is an approach that focuses solely on the collection of data without any attention to criminological theory. Neither judges nor juries are likely to understand or appreciate the jargon of abstracted empiricism or grand theory.

A lesson of our book is that forensic criminological investigations should begin with what Robert Merton (1968, p. 39) famously referred to as middle-range theorizing, that is, the use of "theories that lie between the minor but necessary working hypotheses that evolve in abundance during day-to-day research and the all-inclusive systematic efforts to develop a unified theory that will explain all the observed uniformities of social behavior, social organization and social change." Middle-range theorizing begins with the delineation of clear concepts, propositions, and heuristic devices that are firmly backed up by observed data. As the research and analysis proceeds, middle-range theorizing moves progressively toward the elaboration of substantive theories and ad hoc (case-specific) explanations that can help a jury understand the context, framework, or nested nature of the criminal event under scrutiny. Importantly, juries are lay people and neither juries nor judges are likely to be familiar with professional jargon, sophisticated theories, or complex statistical techniques. In addition, it may be difficult for juries and judges to relate abstract academic concepts presented in court to real world cases and legal problems. Therefore, a forensic criminologist should approach juries and judges in a manner appropriate for an introductory survey course rather than as one might teach a graduate seminar for aspiring sociologists and criminologists.

ADVOCACY RESEARCH, EMOTIVE STATISTICS, AND JUNK SCIENCE

A major lesson of our book is that forensic criminologists and other experts should be aware and beware of the perils of advocacy research, emotive statistics, and junk science. Advocacy research is research that is one-sided, ideologically based, and plagued by confirmation bias. Criminologists that embrace advocacy research are driven by explicit commitment to advancing their notions of social and legal justice, what Belknap (2015, p. 1) calls "criminology activism." Emotive statistics is the presentation of statistical findings and figures to startle the audience and shock them out of their complacency using feel-good messages, embellished stores, and highly dramatic and emotionally charged interpretations of reality. The use of both advocacy research and emotive statistics reflects the agenda and intention of providing evidence and arguments to support a particular cause or narrow partisan viewpoint or position. Junk science is a term used to refer to spurious or fraudulent claims, or untested or unproven theories presented as scientific facts. As discussed by Burns (2008), junk science is a stigma, a negative label applied by opposing counsel to exclude the testimony of an expert witness. Claims may be made that an expert is not widely accepted as such by others in the relevant field and/or presents opinions that are biased or scientifically flawed (Lynch and Cole, 2005; Peyrot and Burns, 2001).

One lesson we hope the reader will learn from our book is that the forensic criminologist's role is to present evidence relevant to his or her expertise in a dispassionate and objective manner and not to advocate for a given verdict. "Forensic criminologists are, first and foremost, social and behavioral scientists whose true clients are the courts and not the agencies or attorneys who have retained their services" (Kennedy, 2014, p. 11). We recognize that researchers and scholars have long undertaken research projects to influence social change, ameliorate social problems, and reform public policy using scientific methods and procedures (Gilbert, 1997). Criminologists of diverse theoretical and methodological backgrounds have been interested in changing society and improving responses to perceived social injustices. In the court system, judges are not likely to allow testimony or admit evidence that is biased or prejudiced.

We believe it is centrally important for the forensic criminologist to understand that she or he should apply scientific principles and methods to case-specific data in the same way that she or he would use scientific principles and methods to analyze data outside the litigation context. Experts must not make guesses or sweeping conclusions or they risk a *Daubert* challenge. Over a decade ago, Wivell (2003) advised attorneys that "from the moment you retain an expert, you must understand that 'the day of the expert who merely opines and does so on the basis of vague notions of experience is over'."[1] According to *For the Defense*, published by the Defense Research Institute, a *Daubert* challenge to the admissibility of expert evidence "is a potent weapon of growing importance to the corporate defendant's arsenal in civil litigation" and "a standard part of the development of the defense" (Frederico et al., 2000). To meet such a challenge, an expert's methodology must be consistent with the research methods and procedures of science rather than based on subjective belief or unsupported speculation, as in ipse dixit testimony.

In our book, we have offered examples of scientifically informed criminological investigations and we have stressed the importance of reviewing the criminological literature and undertaking research

---

[1] *Kemp v. Tyson Seafood Group, Inc.*, No. 20000 WL 1062105, at *7 (D. Minn. July 19, 2000).

before drawing any conclusions to pass on to the legal community. Evidentiary and procedural matters will differentially constrain the efforts of a forensic criminologist depending on the type of case. Although the nature and quality of criminological analysis should not vary, the scope of the opinions a forensic criminologist will offer will depend not only on the pertinent law but also on the trial judge's interpretation of this law. Forensic criminologists should expect to be grilled about whether their forensic criminological report has accurately characterized the extant criminological scholarship and scientific research relied upon in the investigation; whether that scholarship does indeed meet scientific standards and has peer acceptance in the field of criminology; and whether the forensic criminologist's analysis accurately assesses the case materials. A forensic criminological investigation and analysis that is inadequate in any of these dimensions may not assist the trier of fact and may be vulnerable to a challenge to its admissibility. The forensic criminologist should be prepared to defend the accuracy and reliability of the analysis of case materials and, just as importantly, the relevance of the body of criminological scholarship and social science research applied to those facts.

Explicit, transparent, and task-appropriate methods for analyzing data from the case are building blocks of expert opinions. Mitchell and colleagues (2011, pp. 674–675) argue that experts should "provide a candid assessment of the inferences or understandings that may be drawn from these results in light of data and method constraints." That is, data collection and analysis should be made clear and the results of the investigation should be independent of the expert's subjective beliefs. For Mitchell and colleagues (2011, p. 676), explicitness and transparency "work together to guard against unreliable opinions. When an expert clearly discloses what data were analyzed, how they were analyzed, and the conclusions from this analysis, the court (perhaps with the aid of an opposing expert) can assess the appropriateness of the data and methods to answering the question at issue."

TOWARD A TRANSLATIONAL CRIMINOLOGY

Throughout our book, we have sought to nurture and advance "translational criminology"—that is, the translation of knowledge from criminological theory and research to forensic practice—to build strong connections among criminologists, social scientists, and policy makers. The goal of translational criminology, according to the National Institute of Justice (2011, p. 1) "is to break down barriers between basic and applied research by creating a dynamic interface between research and practice." Building a dynamic interface depends on cooperation, interaction, exchange, and reciprocity. On the one hand, practitioners in the fields of criminology and law enforcement face challenges in controlling and reducing crime. On the other hand, academic criminologists and social scientists develop new tools and ideas to overcome these challenges and evaluate their impact. Importantly, translational criminology is not just about bridging the "research-to-practice" gap. Rather, translational criminology is a blending or synthesis of research and practice "through a systematic study of the process of knowledge dissemination, recognizing that successful dissemination of research findings may require multiple strategies" (2011, p. 1). Successful dissemination requires that criminologists implement evidence correctly to figure out why it works and how to implement the evidence in real-world settings. Moreover, translational criminology prioritizes applicability, that is, the creation of criminological knowledge for real-world implementation.

To achieve our goal of a translational criminology, we have described the different roles and activities of the practicing forensic criminologist in the legal system with an eye toward improving the translation of forensic knowledge, theory, and methods into policy and practice. As we have shown in our chapters, practicing forensic criminology can be an effective mechanism for (1) translating academic criminological theories into concrete applications in the legal realm, (2) strengthening the scientific foundation of criminological research, and (3) improving the quality of forensic social scientific research in the legal system. Using examples of expert witness investigations and testimony, we have demonstrated the diverse ways in which forensic criminological research can be an effective agent of sociolegal change and policy transformation. We have illustrated, using actual case studies, the value of substantive knowledge a forensic criminologist can offer a judge, jury, and attorneys in deciding cases. A distinctive feature of our book is that we have revealed how criminological theories, knowledge, and methods can inform the decision-making of judges and juries and assist attorneys in developing their arguments.

Over the decades, forensic criminological testimony has contributed to court decisions that have, in turn, generated a host of security reforms and improvements. Ellis (2006) and Leighton (2000) argue that jury awards in the millions of dollars have been directly responsible for the development of new preventive security measures in hospitality, retail, multihousing, and academic settings. "Holding property owners and possessors liable for failure to protect guests has produced a safer society," according to Leighton (2000). Schools, shopping malls, hotels and motels, apartment complexes, and many entertainment venues routinely use security guards. Hotels now employ better key controls, like changing the code on key cards after each checkout, and security cameras are in place in many commercial areas and public places to surveil and record criminal activities. "Were it not for inadequate security litigation," Leighton maintains, "it is reasonable to assume these increased security measures that protect the public would not exist" (p. 3). Premises liability litigation is a driving force behind the continued improvement of security and safety for people invited onto commercial land uses. According to the National Center for Victims of Crime (2018), "the exposure to civil liability is a powerful incentive for landlords, businessmen, and other proprietors to enact the security measures necessary to prevent future victimizations."

Over the decades, legal remedies for premises liability have been provided by common law (judge-created law developed through private lawsuits). Common law provides remedies including compensation to victims injured by another's negligence. Common law countries have been converging toward a similar system of victim compensation for premises liability, although there is some diversity and unevenness due to national differences in terms of insurance, financing mechanisms, and systems of law. Continental European systems may allow a crime victim to recover, but only from the perpetrator, and in much smaller amounts. Importantly, even if other countries do not allow sufficient compensation in a court of law, there is still the court of public opinion which can punish business landholders and government agencies with negative publicity. Negative publicity can also bring down police and corrections chiefs by exerting political pressures on them should their agents violate the public trust. Our common law system of victim compensation for people who are injured by tortious actions or inactions is based on a system of shared moral codes and sentiments that undergird and provide the foundation for the legal system. People around the world share moral revulsion against a landlord who knowingly and uncaringly subjects a tenant to unnecessary criminal risk. In the United States, victims of an assault at a workplace might sue the owner and receive compensation while in other countries the results could be a boycott of a business or the removal of politicians/police or corrections chiefs.

In short, forensic criminology is a vast and expanding field that has evolved and continues to evolve as the forms and types of litigation expand and diversify. Social science and criminological research have now become central in many areas of legal practice, including negligent security, workplace violence, administrative negligence, wrongful conviction litigation, and litigation involving the actions of police and corrections officials. Forensic criminologists should anticipate new litigation cases as laws, regulations, and markets change. As such, we end with several questions. Given public concern with safety and security in the context of mass shootings, will hotels and schools adopt metal detectors at their entry points to control access? Is such a measure even reasonable? With terrorist attacks and mass casualty incidents seemingly on the rise, will courts embrace more flexible tests of foreseeability than in the past? Will we see increases in new forms of civil litigation as a potential remedy for behaviors typically associated with the criminal justice system (e.g., rape and sexual assault)? Will we see a widening of scope of legal responsibility for sexual assault? How will juries respond to allegations of administrative negligence by plaintiffs seeking to hold organizations and corporations liable for sexual injuries? Will these decisions be similar to or different from nonsexual injuries? The alternatives to criminal court are increasing for rape victims and the perceived social responsibility of sexual assault prevention is affecting more institutions than in the past. In turn, corporations are finding themselves in contentious civil suits over liability issues of sexual assault that were minor legal concerns decades earlier (Lippert et al., 2018).

We offer these questions not because we have the answers but because we wish to illustrate the evolving nature of litigation. In the end, we have only touched on a few of the many liability issues that currently preoccupy the courts or may do so in the future. As society changes and new forms of negligent and intentional torts arise, courts will need the research expertise and testifying skills of forensic criminologists in different areas. Going from the classroom to the courtroom should be a welcome opportunity for forensic criminologists to bring scientific evidence and research to bear on legal issues that impact society.

References

Aaltonen, M., Kivivuori, J., Martikainen, P., 2011. Social determinants of crime in a welfare state: do they still matter? Acta Sociol. 54 (2), 161–181.

Abram, K.M., Choe, J.Y., Washburn, J.J., Teplin, L.A., King, D.C., Dulcan, M.K., 2008. Suicidal ideation and behaviors among youths in juvenile detention. J. Am. Acad. Child Adolesc. Psych. 47 (3), 291–300.

Acker, J.R., 2017. Taking stock of innocence: movements, mountains, and wrongful convictions. J. Contemp. Crim. Justice 33 (1), 8–25.

Adams, T., 1988. Police Field Operations, fourth ed. Prentice-Hall, Upper Saddle River, NJ.

Adams, S.H., Jarvis, J., 2006. Indicators of veracity and deception: an analysis of written statements made to police, speech. Lang. L. 13 (1), 1–22.

Adams, A., Osborne, D., 2001. Victims' rights and services: a historical perspective and goals for the twenty-first century. McGeorge L. Rev. 33, 673–698.

Addicott, J.F., 2017. Enhancing cybersecurity in the private sector by means of civil liability lawsuits–the Connie Francis effect. U. Rich. L. Rev. 51, 857–895.

Adolf, D., 2012. Legal issues with security on higher education campuses: rethinking campus security liability. J. App. Secur. Res. 7 (2), 253–267.

AELE Law Journal, 2018. U.S. Supreme Court revisits the basics of probable cause and qualified immunity. AELE L. J. 101–112.

Agnew, R., Brezina, T., 2011. Juvenile Delinquency: Causes and Control. Oxford University Press, New York, NY.

Albright, L., Derickson, E.S., Massey, D.S., 2013. Do affordable housing projects harm suburban communities? Crime, property values, and taxes in Mount Laurel, NJ. City Community 12 (2), 89–112.

Alitzio, A., York, D., 2007. Robbery of Convenience Stores. U.S. Department of Justice, Washington, DC.

Alpert, G., Dunham, R., 1990. Police Pursuit Driving. Greenwood Press, New York, NY.

Alpert, G., Fridell, L., 1992. Police Vehicles and Firearms. Waveland Press, Prospect Heights, IL.

American Bar Association, 2014. Workplace Violence by PLC Labor and Employment. Workplace Violence, Practical Law Practice Note 7-505-7511. Available from: https://www.americanbar.org/content/dam/aba/events/labor_law/am/2014/1g_workplace_violence2.authcheckdam.pdf (Accessed 3 May 2018).

American Law Institute, 1965. Restatement (Second) of Torts. American Law Institute Publishers, Saint Paul, MN.

American Law Institute, 1977. Restatement of the Law (Second). Property (Landlord and Tenant). § 5. American Law Institute, Philadelphia, PA, p. 1.

American Psychiatric Association (Ed.), 2013. Diagnostic and Statistical Manual of Mental Disorders, fifth ed. American Psychiatric Association, Washington, DC.

Anderson, T., 2002. Laying down the law: a review of trends in liability lawsuits. Secur. Manag. 46 (10), 42–51.

Anderson, P.R., Winfree, L.T. (Eds.), 1987. Expert Witnesses: Criminologists in the Courtroom. State University of New York (SUNY) Press, Albany, NY.

Andresen, M., Farrell, G. (Eds.), 2015. The Criminal Act: The Role and Influence of Routine Activity Theory. Springer, New York, NY.

Angel, S., 1968. Discouraging Crime Through City Planning. Working Paper No. 75. Center for Planning and Development Research, University of California, Berkeley, CA.

Appelbaum, P., 1988. The right to refuse treatment with antipsychotic medications. Am. J. Psychiatr. 32, 251–255.

Archea, J.C., 1985. The use of architectural props in the conduct of criminal acts. J. Archit. Plan. Res. 2, 245–259.

Armour, S., 2004. Wrongly convicted walk away with scars. USA Today, October 13, 2004, 1A.

Armstrong, T.A., Katz, C.M., Schnebly, S.M., 2015. The relationship between citizen perceptions of collective efficacy and neighborhood violent crime. Crime Delinq. 61 (1), 121–142.

ASIS International, 2003. General Security Risk Assessment Guideline. ASIS International, Alexandria, VA.

ASIS International, 2009a. Facilities Physical Security Measures Guideline. ASIS GDL FLSM-2009. ASIS International, Alexandria, VA.

ASIS International, 2009b. Pre-Employment Background Screening. ASIS International, Alexandria, VA.

ASIS International, 2011a. Protection of Assets (POA): Security Officer Operations. ASIS International, Alexandria, VA.

ASIS International, 2011b. Workplace Violence Prevention and Intervention. American National Standard ASIS/SHRM WVPI.1-2011. ASIS International, Alexandria, VA.

ASIS International, 2012a. Protection of Assets (POA): Security Management. ASIS International, Alexandria, VA.

ASIS International, 2012b. Protection of Assets (POA): Physical Security. ASIS International, Alexandria, VA.

Association of Certified Fraud Examiners (ACFE), 2014. Cost of Fraud. Available from: http://www.acfe.com/rttn/images/cost-of-fraud-infographic.pdf (Accessed 8 April 2014).

Atlas, R.I., 2013. 21st Century Security and CPTED: Designing for Critical Infrastructure Protection and Crime Prevention. CRC Press, Boca Raton, FL.

Baer, G., 2003. Life: The Odds. Gotham Books, New York, NY.

Baker, P., Benny, D., 2013. The Complete Guide to Physical Security. CRC Press, New York, NY.

Baker, W.E., Faulkner, R.R., 2003. Diffusion of fraud: intermediate economic crime and investor dynamics. Criminology 41 (4), 1173–1206.

Baker, N.L., Vasquez, M.J., Shullman, S.L., 2013. Assessing employment discrimination and harassment. In: Handbook of Psychology, second ed. John Wiley and Sons, New York, NY, pp. 225–245.

Balko, R., 2017. The emperor of junk science forensics has died. Washington Post, August 31, 2017.

Barling, J., Dupré, K.E., Kelloway, E.K., 2009. Predicting workplace aggression and violence. Annu. Rev. Psychol. 60, 671–692.

Barocas, H., 1974. Iatrogenic and preventive intervention in police-family crisis situations. Int. J. Soc. Psychiatry 20 (1–2), 113–121.

Bartol, C., Bartol, A., 2004. Psychology and Law: Theory, Research and Application. Wadsworth, Belmont, CA.

Bates, N.D., 2004. Major Developments in Premises Security Liability III. Liability Consultants, Sudbury, MA.

Bates, N.D., 2007. Premises security liability. In: Vellani, K.H. (Ed.), Strategic Security Management: A Risk Assessment Guide for Decision Makers. Butterworth-Heinemann, New York, NY, pp. 265–283.

Bates, N.D., Frank, D.A., 2010. Premises security experts and admissibility considerations under *Daubert* and *Kumho*: a revised standard. Suffolk J. Trial App. Adv. 15, 179–347.

Baumeister, R., 2001. Violent pride. Sci. Am., 96–101.

Baumer, E.P., Lauritsen, J.L., Rosenfeld, R., Wright, R., 1998. The influence of crack cocaine on robbery, burglary, and homicide rates: a cross-city, longitudinal analysis. J. Res. Crime Delinq. 35, 316–340.

Baumer, E.P., Ranson, J.A., Arnio, A.N., Fulmer, A., De Zilwa, S., 2017. Illuminating a dark side of the American dream: assessing the prevalence and predictors of mortgage fraud across US counties. Am. J. Sociol. 123 (2), 549–603.

Bayley, D., 1994. Police for the Future New York. Oxford University Press, Oxford, UK.

Bazyler, M., 1979. Landowners' liability for failure to protect patrons from criminal attack. Ariz. L. Rev. 21, 727–754.

Beaudry, M., 1996. Contemporary Lodging Security. Butterworth-Heinemann, Boston, MA.

Becker, G.S., 1968. Crime and punishment: an economic approach. In: Fielding, N.G., Clarke, A., Witt, R. (Eds.), The Economic Dimensions of Crime. Palgrave Macmillan, London, pp. 13–69.

Belknap, J.W., 2001. Defamation, negligent referral, and the world of employment references. J. Small Emerging Bus. L. 5, 113–145.

Belknap, J., 2015. Activist criminology: criminologists' responsibility to advocate for social and legal justice. Criminology 53 (1), 1–22.

Beloof, D.E., 2005. The third wave of crime victims' rights: standing, remedy, and review. BYU L. Rev. 2005, 256–350.

Bennett, T., Wright, R., 1984. Burglars on Burglary: Prevention and the Offender. Averbury Publishing Co., Brookfield, VT.

Benson, M.L., Simpson, S.S., 2015. Understanding White-Collar Crime—An Opportunity Perspective. Routledge, New York, NY.

Berkley, B., 1997. Preventing customer altercations in nightclubs. Cornell Hotel Restaur. Admin. Q. 37, 82–94.

Bernasco, W., Block, R., 2011. Robberies in Chicago: a block-level analysis of the influence of crime generators, crime attractors, and offender anchor points. J. Res. Crime Delinq. 48 (1), 33–57.

Bernasco, W., Nieuwbeerta, P., 2005. How do residential burglars select target areas? Br. J. Criminol. 45, 296–315.

Beveridge, A., 2011. Forensic Investigation of Explosions, second ed. CRC Press, Boca Raton, FL.

Bielby, W., Coukos, P., 2007. Statistical dueling with unconventional weapons: what courts should know about experts in employment discrimination class actions. Emory Law J. 56, 1563–1612.

Bierie, D.M., 2017. Assault of police. Crime Delinq. 63 (8), 899–925.

Bittner, E., 1970. Function of the Police in Modern Society. U.S. Department of Health, Education and Welfare, Washington, DC.

Bjerk, D., 2007. Measuring the relationship between youth criminal participation and household economic resources. J. Quant. Criminol. 23 (1), 23–39.

Black, H.C., Garner, B.A., McDaniel, B.R., 2009. Black's Law Dictionary, vol. 126. West Group, St. Paul, MN.

Blackman, N., et al., 1963. The sudden murderer. Arch. Gen. Psychiatry 8 (1963), 101–106.

Blaikie, N., 2000. Designing Social Research. Policy Press, Cambridge, MA.

Blair, J.P., Schweit, K.W., 2014. A Study of Active Shooter Incidents, 2000–2013. Texas State University and Federal Bureau of Investigation, U.S. Department of Justice, Washington, DC. Available from: http://www.fbi.gov/news/stories/2014/september/fbi-releases-study-on-active-shooter-incidents/pdfs/a-study-of-active-shooter-incidents-in-the-u.s.-between-2000-and-2013 (Accessed 18 May 2018).

Blair, L., Wilcox, P., Eck, J., 2017. Facilities, opportunity, and crime: an exploratory analysis of places in two urban neighborhoods. Crime Prevent. Commun. Saf. 191, 61–81.

Blake, D.M., 2017. Cognitive bias and use of force investigations. Invest. Sci. J. 9(3).

Blake, W.F., Bradley, W.F., 1999. Premises Security: A Guide for Security Professionals and Attorneys. Butterworth-Heinemann, Wadsworth, MA.

Blasko, B.L., Jeglic, E.L., Malkin, S., 2008. Suicide risk assessment in jails. J. Foren. Psychol. Pract. 8 (1), 67–76.

Block, R.L., Block, C.R., 1995. Space, place and crime: hot spot areas and hot places of liquor-related crime. Crime Place 4, 145–184.

Bloom, J., 2004. Thirty-five years of working with civil commitment statutes. J. Am. Acad. Psychiat. Law 32, 430–439.

Blumstein, A., Wallman, J., 2006. The crime drop and beyond. Annu. Rev. L. Soc. Sci. 2, 125–146.

Boba, R., 2004. Interpreting crime data and statistics. In: Bruce, C., et al. (Eds.), Exploring Crime Analysis. International Association of Crime Analysts, Overland Park, KS, pp. 199–207.

Boba, R., 2009. Crime Analysis with Crime Mapping, second ed. Sage Publications, Los Angeles, CA.

Boggs, S., 1965. Urban crime patterns. Am. Sociol. Rev. 30, 899–908.

Bohrer, S., 2000. Establishing a foot pursuit policy: running into danger. FBI Law Enforc. Bull., 10–15.

Boss, D., Zajic, A., 2011. Casino Security and Gaming Surveillance. CRC Press, New York, NY.

Bottoms, A.E., Wiles, W., 2002. Environmental criminology. In: Maguire, M., Morgan, R., Reiner, R. (Eds.), Oxford Handbook of Criminology. Oxford University Press, Oxford, UK, pp. 620–656.

Bourgeois, L., 1979. Toward a method of middle-range theorizing. Acad. Manag. Rev. 4 (3), 443–447.

Bowers, K.J., Johnson, S.D., 2004. Who commits near repeats? A test of the boost explanation. West. Criminol. Rev. 5 (3), 12–24.

Bowie, V., Fisher, B.S., Cooper, C. (Eds.), 2012. Workplace Violence. Routledge, New York, NY.

Bowkar, L., 1980. Prison Victimization. Elsevier, New York, NY.

Bowling, N.A., Beehr, T.A., 2006. Workplace harassment from the victim's perspective: a theoretical model and meta-analysis. J. Appl. Psychol. 91 (5), 998–1012.

Boyatzis, R., 1981. Who should drink what, when and where if looking for a fight. In: Gottheil, E. (Ed.), Alcohol, Drug Abuse and Aggression. Charles C. Thomas, Springfield, IL, pp. 314–329.

Braga, A., 2004. Gun Violence Among Serious Young Offenders. U.S. Department of Justice, Washington, DC.

Braithwaite, A., Johnson, S.D., 2012. Space-time modeling of insurgency and counterinsurgency in Iraq. J. Quant. Criminol. 28, 31–48.

Brantingham, P.J., Brantingham, P.L. (Eds.), 1981. Environmental Criminology. Sage Publications, Beverly Hills, CA.

Brantingham, P.J., Brantingham, P.L., 1984. Patterns in Crime. Macmillan, New York, NY.

Brantingham, P.J., Brantingham, P.L., 1991. Introduction to the 1991 reissue: notes on environmental criminology. In: Brantingham, P.J., Brantingham, P.L. (Eds.), Environmental Criminology, second ed. Waveland Press, Prospect Heights, IL, pp. 1–6.

Brantingham, P.L., Brantingham, P.J., 1993. Nodes, paths, and edges: considerations on the complexity of crime and the physical environment. J. Environ. Psychol. 13, 3–28.

Brantingham, P., Brantingham, P., 1995. Criminality of place: crime generators and crime attractors. Eur. J. Crim. Pol. Res. 3 (3), 5–26.

Brantingham, P.L., Brantingham, P.J., 1999. A theoretical model of crime hot spot generation. Stud. Crime Crime Prevent. 8 (1), 7–26.

Brantingham, P.L., Brantingham, P.J., Wong, P., 1990. Malls and crime: a first look. Secur. J. 1, 175–181.

Brewer, N., Wells, G., 2011. Eyewitness identification. Curr. Dir. Psychol. Sci. 20 (1), 24–27.

Brodsky, S., 2012. Testifying in Court: Guidelines and Maxims for the Expert Witness. American Psychological Association, Washington, DC.

Brodsky, S.L., Gutheil, T.G., 2015. The Expert Expert Witness: More Maxims and Guidelines for Testifying in Court, second ed. American Psychological Association, Washington, DC.

Brogden, M., Nijar, P., 2000. Crime Abuse and the Elderly. Willan Publishing, Portland, OR.

Brooks, R., 2007. Psychiatrists' opinions about involuntary civil commitment: results of a national survey. J. Am. Acad. Psychiat. Law 35, 219–228.

Brower, M.A., 2010. The backlash of the implied warranty of habitability: theory versus analysis. DePaul L. Rev. 60, 849–894.

Brumback, K., 2018. Georgia Jury Awards $1 Billion After Guard Rapes Teen. Associated Press, May 23, 2018.

Bryson, D., Youmans, R., 1990. Crime, drugs and subsidized housing. Clear. Rev. 24, 435–447.

Bublick, E.M., 2006. Tort suits filed by rape and sexual assault victims in civil courts: lessons for courts, classrooms and constituencies. SMU L. Rev. 59, 55–122.

Buchman, J., 2007. The effects of ideology on federal trial judges' decision to admit scientific expert testimony. Am. Politics Res. 35, 671–693.

Budd, E., 2016. Foreseeing the unforeseeable- premises security litigation and mass casualty events. Mondaq Bus. Brief.

Buell, M.P., 1995. Liability for inadequate security. FLA. B.J. 69.

Bukstel, L.H., Kilmann, P.R., 1980. Psychological effects of imprisonment on confined individuals. Psychol. Bull. 88 (2), 469–493.

Bureau of Justice Statistics, 2016. Criminal Victimization in the United States. Bureau of Justice Statistics, New York, NY.

Bureau of Justice Statistics, 2018. Assault. Bureau of Justice Statistics, Washington, DC. Available from: https://www.bjs.gov/index.cfm?ty=tp&tid=316 (Accessed 15 May 2018).

Burns, S.L., 2008. Demonstrating "Reasonable Fear" at trial: is it science or junk science? Hum. Stud. 31 (2), 107–131.

Bursik Jr., R.J., Grasmick, H.G., 1993. Neighborhoods and Crime: The Dimensions of Effective Community Control. Lexington Books, New York, NY.

Burstein, H., 2001. Hotel and Motel Loss Prevention. Prentice-Hall, New York, NY.

Bushway, S., 2011. Labor markets and crime. In: Wilson, J.Q., Petersilia, J. (Eds.), Crime and Public Policy. Oxford University Press, Oxford, UK, pp. 183–209.

Calder, J.D., Sipes, D.D., 1992. Crime, security and premises liability: toward precision in security expert testimony. Secur. J. 3 (2), 1–16.

Caldwell, R.A., 2014. Gender matters! Socio-legal studies, courts-martial, and the US Military. In: Morewitz, S.J., Goldstein, M.L. (Eds.), Handbook of Forensic Sociology and Psychology. Springer, New York, NY, pp. 445–453.

Cale, E., Lillienfeld, S., 2006. Psychopathy factors and risk for aggressive behavior. Law Hum. Behav. 30, 51–74.

Camacho, R.A., 1993. How to avoid negligent hiring litigation. Whittier L. Rev. 14, 787–807.

Campbell, J., 2000. Keeping Illegal Activity Out of Rental Property: A Police Guide for Establishing Landlord Training Programs. Bureau of Justice Assistance, NCJ 148656, March 2000. Washington, DC: U.S. Department of Justice. Available from: http://safetampa.org/publications/landlordtraining.pdf (Accessed 3 January 2018).

Canton, L., 1996. Guard Force Management. Butterworth-Heinemann, Boston, MA.

Caplan, J.M., Marotta, P.L., Piza, E.L., Kennedy, W.L., 2014. Spatial risk factors of felonious battery to police officers. Policing 37 (4), 823–838.

Carlson, S.M., Michalowski, R.J., 1997. Crime, unemployment, and social structures of accumulation. Justice Q. 14 (2), 209–241.

Carrington, F., Rapp, J., 1991. Victims' Rights: Law and Litigation. Matthew Bender, London, UK.

Cartwright, D., 2002. Psychoanalysis, Violence and Rage-Type Murder. Routledge, New York, NY.

Cassell, P., 1998. Protecting the innocent from false confessions and lost confessions—and from Miranda. J. Crim. L. Criminol. 88 (1998), 497–556.

Cassell, P.G., 2017. Can we protect the innocent without freeing the guilty? Thoughts on innocence reforms that avoid harmful tradeoffs. In: Medwed, D. (Ed.), Wrongful Convictions and the DNA Revolution: Twenty-Five Years of Freeing the Innocent. Cambridge University Press, Cambridge, MA.

Catalano, T., 2014. 30% of Business Failures Are Caused by Employee Theft. Old Republic Surety. ORSC Blog. Available from: https://www.orsurety.com/blog/30-percent-of-business-failures-are-caused-by-employee-theft (Accessed 13 April 2018).

Center on Wrongful Convictions, 2016. First Wrongful Conviction: Jesse Boorn and Stephen Boorn. Available from: http://www.law.northwestern.edu/legalclinic/wrongfulconvictions/exonerations/vt/boorn-brothers.html (Accessed 11 July 2018).

Chaiken, J., Chaiken, M., 1990. Drugs and predatory crime. In: Tonry, M., Wilson, J. (Eds.), Drugs and Predatory Crime. University of Chicago Press, Chicago, IL.

Chainey, S., Tompson, L., Uhlig, S., 2008. The utility of hotspot mapping for predicting spatial patterns of crime. Secur. J. 21, 4–28.

Chamallas, M., 2011. Gaining some perspective in tort law: a new take on third-party criminal attack cases. Lewis Clark L. Rev. 14, 1351–1400.

Chamallas, M., 2013. Vicarious liability in torts: the sex exception. Valparaiso U. L. Rev. 48 (1), 133–192.

Chambliss, W., 1967. Types of deviance and the effectiveness of legal sanctions. Wis. L. Rev., 703–719.

Chappell, D., Di Martino, V., 2006. Violence at Work, third ed. International Labor Organization, New York, NY.

Charman, S.D., Quiroz, V., 2016. Blind sequential lineup administration reduces both false identifications and confidence in those false identifications. Law Hum. Behav. 40 (5), 477–487.

Chock, V.M., Kondo, L.H., 1989. *Knodle v. Waikiki Gateway Hotel, Inc.*: imposing a duty to protect against third party criminal conduct on the premises. U. Hawaii Law Rev. 11, 231–251.

Ciaccio, S., 1993. Comment, business owners' duty to protect patrons from the criminal acts of third parties in Louisiana. La. L. Rev. 53 (6), 1847–1878.

Cicchini, M.D., White, L.T., 2008. An empirical basis for the admission of expert testimony on false confessions. Ariz. St. LJ 40, 1–45.

Cicchini, M.D., White, L.T., 2015. Truth or doubt: an empirical test of criminal jury instructions. U. Rich. L. Rev. 50, 1139–1167.

Cicchini, M.D., White, L.T., 2017. Educating judges and lawyers in behavioral research: a case study. Gonzaga Law Rev. 53, 159–185.

Clark, S.E., 2012a. Costs and benefits of eyewitness identification reform: psychological science and public policy. Perspect. Psychol. Sci. 7, 238–259.

Clark, S.E., 2012b. Eyewitness identification reform: data, theory, and due process. Perspect. Psychol. Sci. 7 (3), 279–283.

Clark, K., Clark, M., 1947. Racial Identification and Preference in Negro Children. Bobbs-Merrill Company, Indianapolis, IN.

Clarke, R.V., 1980. Situational crime prevention: theory and practice. Brit. J. Criminol. 20 (2), 136–147.

Clarke, R.V., 1983. Situational crime prevention: its theoretical basis and practical scope. Crime Justice 4, 225–256.

Clarke, R.V.G. (Ed.), 1997. Situational Crime Prevention: Successful Case Studies. Harrow and Heston, Guilderland, New York, NY.

Clarke, R.V., 2005. Closing Streets and Alleys to Reduce Crime: Should You Go Down That Road. U.S. Department of Justice, Office of Community Oriented Policing Services, Washington, DC.

Clarke, R.V., 2008. Improving street lighting to reduce crime in residential areas. In: Community Oriented Polic. Serv. US Dep. Justice, Washington, DC.

Clarke, R.V., 2009. Situational crime prevention: theoretical background and current practice. In: Handbook on Crime and Deviance. Springer, New York, NY, pp. 259–276.

Clarke, R.V., Bichler-Robertson, G., 1998. Place managers, slumlords and crime in low rent apartment buildings. Secur. J. 11 (1), 11–19.

Clarke, R.V., Cornish, D.B., 1985. Modeling offenders' decisions: a framework for research and policy. Crime Justice 6, 147–185.

Clarke, R.V., Cornish, D.B., 2001. Rational choice. In: Paternoster, R., Bachman, R. (Eds.), Explaining Criminals and Crime. Roxbury, Los Angeles, CA.

Clarke, R.V., Eck, J.E., 2005. Crime Analysis for Problem Solvers in 60 Small Steps. Office of Community Oriented Policing Services, U.S. Department of Justice, Washington, DC.

Clarke, R., Eck, J., 2007. Understanding Risky Facilities. U.S. Department of Justice, Office of Community Oriented Policing Services, Washington, DC.

Clarke, R.V.G., Felson, M. (Eds.), 1993. Routine Activity and Rational Choice: Advances in Criminological Theory. 5. Transaction Publishers, New York, NY.

Clifton, D., 2012. Hospitality Security: Managing Security in Today's Hotel, Lodging, Entertainment, and Tourism Environment. CRC Press, New York, NY.

Coble, S., Scott, M.S., 2017. Problem-oriented policing as a form of translational criminology. Trans. Criminol. 12 (Spring 2017), 20–21.

Cohen, L.E., Felson, M., 1979. Social change and crime rate trends: a routine activity approach. Am. Sociol. Rev. 44, 588–608.

Cohn, M., 2014. Board Resigns From Forensic Accounting Credential Group. Accounting Today. Published March 13, 2014.

Cole, S.A., 2008a. Comment on scientific validation of fingerprint evidence under Daubert. Law Prob. Risk 7 (2), 119–126.

Cole, S.A., 2008b. The "Opinionization" of fingerprint evidence. BioSocieties 3 (1), 105–113.

Cole, S.A., 2009. Forensics without uniqueness, conclusions without individualization: the new epistemology of forensic identification. Law Prob. Risk 8 (3), 233–255.

Cole, S.A., 2012. Forensic science and wrongful convictions: from exposer to contributor to corrector. N. Engl. Law Rev. 46, 711–736.

Cole, S.A., 2013. Forensic culture as epistemic culture: the sociology of forensic science. Stud. Hist. Philos. Biol. Biomed. Sci. 44 (1), 36–46.

Collins, J.M., Jarvis, J., 2009. The wrongful conviction of forensic science. Foren. Sci. Pol. Manage. 1 (1), 17–31.

Collins, C.R., Neal, Z.P., Neal, J.W., 2017. Transforming social cohesion into informal social control: deconstructing collective efficacy and the moderating role of neighborhood racial homogeneity. J. Urban Aff. 39 (3), 307–322.

Colvin, M., 2000. Crime and Coercion. St. Martin's Press, New York, NY.

Connolly, D.A., Price, H.L., Read, J.D., 2006. Predicting expert social science testimony in criminal prosecutions of historic child sexual abuse. Leg. Criminol. Psychol. 11 (1), 55–74.

Conroy, M., Murrie, D., 2007. Forensic Assessment of Violence Risk. John Wiley and Sons, Hoboken, NJ.

Conti, R.P., 1999. The psychology of false confessions. J. Credibil. Assess. Witn. Psychol. 2 (1), 14–36.

Cooper, S.L. (Ed.), 2014. Controversies in Innocence Cases in America. Ashgate, Farnham, UK.

Corcoran, M., Cawood, J., 2004. Violence Assessment and Intervention. CRC Press, Boca Raton, FL.

Cordner, G., 2006. People With Mental Illness. U.S. Department of Justice, Washington, DC.

Cornish, D., 1994. The procedural analysis of offending and its relevance for situational prevention. In: Clarke, R.V. (Ed.), Crime Prevention Studies, vol. 3. Criminal Justice Press, Lynne Rienner Publishers, Monsey, New York, NY.

Cornish, D.B., Clarke, R.V., 2003. Opportunities, precipitators and criminal decisions: a reply to Wortley's critique of situational crime prevention. Crime Prevention Studies 16, 41–96.

Cornish, D.B., Clarke, R.V. (Eds.), 2014. The Reasoning Criminal: Rational Choice Perspectives on Offending. Transaction Publishers, Piscataway, NJ.

Costanzo, M., Krauss, D., 2010. Forensic and Legal Psychology. Macmillan, New York, NY.

Courtney, J., Wann, D., 2010. The relationship between sport fan dysfunction and bullying behaviors. N. Am. J. Psychol. 12 (1), 191–198.

Cozens, P., 2014. Think Crime! Using Evidence Theory and Crime Prevention Through Environmental Design for Planning Safer Cities. Praxis Education, Quinns Rock Perth, WA.

Cozens, P., Love, T., 2015. A review and current status of crime prevention through environmental design (CPTED). J. Plan. Lit. 30 (4), 393–412.

Cozens, P.M., Saville, G., Hillier, D., 2005. Crime prevention through environmental design (CPTED): a review and modern bibliography. Prop. Manage. 23 (5), 328–356.

Craighead, G., 2003. High-Rise Security and Fire Life Safety, second ed. Butterworth-Heinemann, Wadsworth, MA.

Crawford, C., Burns, R., 2008. Police use of force: assessing the impact of time and space. Polic. Soc. 18 (3), 322–335.

Creed, T.L., 2007. Negligent hiring and criminal rehabilitation: employing ex-convicts yet avoiding liability. Thomas L. Rev. 20, 183–234.

Cromwell, P.F., Olson, J.N., Avary, D.W., 1991. Breaking and Entering: An Ethnographic Analysis of Burglary. Sage, Newbury Park, CA.

Crowe, T., 1991. Crime Prevention Through Environmental Design. Buttherworth-Heinemann, Stoneham, MA.

Cui, L., Walsh, R., 2015. Foreclosure, vacancy and crime. J. Urban Econ. 87, 72–84.

Cullen, F., Agnew, R., 2006. Criminological Theory: Past to Present: Essential Readings. Oxford University Press, Oxford, UK.

Cunningham, W., Taylor, T., 1985. The Hallcrest Report: Private Security and Police in America. Chancellor Press, London, UK.

Cutler, B.L., 2012. Conviction of the Innocent: Lessons from Psychological Research. American Psychological Association, Washington, DC.

Cutler, B.L., Kovera, M.B., 2011. Expert psychological testimony. Curr. Dir. Psychol. Sci. 20 (1), 53–57.

Dain, D.P., Brennan Jr., R.L., 2003. Negligent security law in the commonwealth of Massachusetts in the post-September 11 era. N. Engl. Law Rev. 38, 73–96.

Davenport, K.L., 1999. DeShaney v. Winnebago County Department of Social Services, 489 U.S. 189 (1989), 19 Fla. St. U. L. Rev. 243–253.

Davis, J.M., 2000. Potential violence to the bottom line-expanding employer liability for acts of workplace violence in North Carolina. North Carolina L. Rev. 78 (6), 2053–2082.

Davis, R., 2001. Access to justice for immigrants who are victimized. Crim. Justice Pol. Rev. 12 (2001), 183–196.

Davis, R.C., Erez, E., 1998. Immigrant populations as victims: toward a multicultural criminal justice system. Research in Brief. National Institute of Justice, pp. 1–7. Available from: https://www.ncjrs.gov/pdffiles/167571.pdf (Accessed 27 August 2018).

Davis, R.C., Henderson, N.J., 2003. Willingness to report crimes: the role of ethnic group membership and community efficacy. Crime Delinq. 49 (4), 564–580.

Davis, D., Leo, R.A., 2014. The problem of interrogation-induced false confession: sources of failure in prevention and detection. In: Morewitz, S.J., Goldstein, M.L. (Eds.), Handbook of Forensic Sociology and Psychology. Springer, New York, NY, pp. 47–75.

Dawid, A.P., Faigman, D.L., Fienberg, S.E., 2014. Fitting science into legal contexts: assessing effects of causes or causes of effects? Sociol. Method. Res. 43 (3), 359–390.

de Treville, R., 2004. Time to check out liability trends. Secur. Manag. 48 (2), 61–65.

DeForest, P.R., Gaensslen, R.E., Lee, H.C., 1983. Forensic Science: An Introduction to Criminalistics. McGraw-Hill, New York, NY.

DeFrances, C.J., Smith, S.K., 1998. Perceptions of Neighborhood Crime, 1995. US Department of Justice, Office of Justice Programs, Bureau of Justice Statistics, Washington, DC.

DeKeseredy, W.S., Schwartz, M.D., Alvi, S., Tomaszewski, E.A., 2003. Crime victimization, alcohol consumption, and drug use in Canadian public housing. J. Crim. Just. 31 (4), 383–396.

Dekker, I., Barling, J., 1998. Personal and organizational predictors of workplace sexual harassment of women by men. J. Occup. Health Psychol. 3 (1), 7–18.

Delisi, M., 2016. Psychopathy as Unified Theory of Crime. Palgrave Macmillan, New York, NY.

DeMey, D., Flowers, J., 1999. Don't Hire a Crook. Facts on Demand Press, Tempe, AZ.

Denzin, N.K., 1977. Notes on the criminogenic hypothesis: a case study of the American liquor industry. Am. Sociol. Rev. 42 (6), 905–920.

Department of Housing and Urban Development (HUD), Office of Policy Development and Research (PD&R), 2016. Housing, inclusion, and public safety. In: Levitt, R. (Ed.), Evidence Matters. Available from: https://www.huduser.gov/portal/periodicals/em/summer16/index.html (Accessed 21 December 2017).

DePaulo, B., Pfeifer, R.L., 1986. On-the-job experience and skill at detecting deception. J. Appl. Soc. Psychol. 16 (3), 249–267.

Deryol, R., Wilcox, P., Logan, M., Wooldredge, J., 2016. Crime places in context: an illustration of the multilevel nature of hot spot development. J. Quant. Criminol. 32 (2), 305–325.

Di Tella, R., Schargrodsky, E., 2004. Do police reduce crime? Estimates using the allocation of police forces after a terrorist attack. Am. Econ. Rev. 94 (1), 115–133.

Dillman, K.N., Horn, K.M., Verrilli, A., 2017. The what, where, and when of place-based housing policy's neighborhood effects. Housing Policy Debate 27 (2), 282–305.

Dillon, D., 2013. A portrait of suicides in Texas jails: who is at risk and how do we stop it? LBJ J. Public Aff. 21, 51–67.

Doerner, W., Lab, S., 2002. Victimology, third ed. Anderson Publishing Co., Cincinnati, OH.

Dolan, J.B., 2000. Workplace violence: the universe of legal issues. Def. Couns. J. 67, 332–341.

Domanico, A.J., Cicchini, M.D., White, L.T., 2012. Overcoming Miranda: a content analysis of the Miranda portion of police interrogations. Idaho L. Rev. 49, 1–22.

Donnelly, P., 1988. Individual and neighborhood influences on fear of crime. Sociol. Focus 22 (1), 69–85.

Doyle, J.M., 2010. Learning from error in the American criminal justice system. J. Crim. L. Criminol. 100 (1), 109–147.

Doyle, J.M., 2014. An etiology of wrongful convictions: error, safety, and forward-looking accountability in criminal justice. In: Zalman, M., Carrano, J. (Eds.), Wrongful Conviction and Criminal Justice Reform: Making Justice. Routledge, New York, NY, pp. 56–72.

Drapkin, I., 1976. The prison inmate as victim. Victimology 1 (Spring), 98–106.

Dripps, D.A., 2003. Fundamental retribution error: criminal justice and the social psychology of blame. Vanderbilt L. Rev. 56 (5), 1338–1362.

Drizin, S.A., Leo, R.A., 2003. The problem of false confessions in the post-DNA world. NCL Rev. 82 (3), 891–1008.

Dror, I.E., Charlton, D., 2006. Why experts make errors. J. Forensic. Identif. 56 (4), 600–616.

Dror, I.E., Charlton, D., Péron, A.E., 2006. Contextual information renders experts vulnerable to making erroneous identifications. Forensic Sci. Int. 156 (1), 74–78.

Duke, N., Resnick, M.D., Borowsky, I.W., 2005. Adolescent firearm violence: position paper of the society for adolescent medicine. J. Adolesc. Health 37 (2), 171–174.

Duwe, G., 2007. Mass Murder in the United States: A History. McFarland, Jefferson, NC.

Dvorak, R.D., Pearson, M.R., Kuvaas, N.J., 2013. The five-factor model of impulsivity-like traits in an aggressive behavior. Aggress. Behav. 39 (3), 222–228.

Dvoskin, J.A., Guy, L.S., 2008. On being an expert witness: it's not about you. Psychiat. Psychol. Law 15 (2), 202–212.

Eaton, T.V., Korach, S., 2016. A criminological profile of white-collar crime. J. Appl. Bus. Res. 32 (1), 129–142.

Eck, J.E., 2003. Police problems: the complexity of problem theory, research and evaluation. Crime Prev. Stud. 15, 79–114.

Eck, J.E., 2006. Preventing crime at places. In: Sherman, L.W., Farrington, D.P., Welsh, B.C., MacKenzie, D.L. (Eds.), Evidence-Based Crime Prevention, revised ed. Routledge, New York, NY, pp. 241–294.

Eck, J.E., Eck, E.B., 2012. Crime place and pollution. Criminol. Public Policy 11 (2), 281–316.

Eck, J.E., Madensen, T.D., 2015. Meaningfully and artfully reinterpreting crime for useful science: an essay on the value of building with simple theory. In: Andresen, M., Farrell, G. (Eds.), The Criminal Act. Springer, New York, NY, pp. 5–18.

Eck, J.E., Wartell, J., 1997. Reducing Crime and Drug Dealing by Improving Place Management: A Randomized Experiment. US Department of Justice, Office of Justice Programs, National Institute of Justice, Washington, DC.

Eck, J.E., Weisburd, D., 1995. Crime places in crime theory. In: Eck, J.E., Weisburd, D. (Eds.), Crime and Place. Criminal Justice Press, New York, NY, pp. 1–33.

Eck, J.E., Clarke, R., Guerette, R., 2007. Risky facilities: crime concentration in homogeneous sets of establishments and facilities. Crime Prev. Stud. 21, 225–264.

Edenhofer, C.R., 1998. Investigating Inadequate Security Cases: The Key to Successful Litigation Is an Exhaustive Investigation. The Free Library. American Association for Justice. Available from: https://www.thefreelibrary.

com/Investigating+inadequate+security+cases%3b+the+key+to+successful...-a020409865 (Accessed 25 August 2018).

Edmond, G., 2007. Supersizing Daubert science for litigation and its implications for legal practice and scientific research. Vill. L. Rev. 52, 857–924.

Edmond, G., Mercer, D., 2004. Daubert and the exclusionary ethos: the convergence of corporate and judicial attitudes towards the admissibility of expert evidence in tort litigation. Law Pol. 26 (2), 231–257.

Edmond, G., Mercer, D., 2013. Conjectures and exhumations: citations of history, philosophy and sociology of science in US Federal Courts. Law Lit. 14 (2), 309–366.

Eisenhauer, C.M., 2015. Police action and the state-created danger doctrine: a proposed uniform test. Penn. St. L. Rev. 120 (3), 893–923.

Ellen, I.G., Lacoe, J., Sharygin, C.A., 2013. Do foreclosures cause crime? J. Urban Econ. 74, 59–70.

Ellis, Z., 2006. Avoiding Liability in Premises Security, sixth ed. Strafford Publications, Atlanta, GA.

Ellis, L., Beaver, K.M., Wright, J., 2009. Handbook of Crime Correlates. Academic Press, New York, NY.

Ellison, L., 2005. Closing the credibility gap: the prosecutorial use of expert witness testimony in sexual assault cases. Int. J. Evidence Proof 9 (4), 239–268.

Elzen, W.L., 2001. Workplace violence: vicarious liability and negligence theories as a two-fisted approach to employer liability. Is Louisiana clinging to an outmoded theory. Louisiana L. Rev. 62, 897–928.

Emison, B.A., 2013. Premises Liability; Vacations Gone Wrong; When Safety Is Ignored. Trial. 49.-Aug. Trial 19.

Engstad, P., 1975. Environmental opportunities and the ecology of crime. In: Silverman, R., Teevan Jr., J. (Eds.), Crime in Canadian Society. Butterworths, Toronto, CA, pp. 193–211.

Epstein, R.A., Sharkey, C.M., 2016. Cases and Materials on Torts. Wolters Kluwer Law & Business, Alphen aan den Rijn, South Holland, Netherlands.

Erickson, R.J., 1996. Armed Robbers and Their Crimes. Athena Research Corporation, Seattle, WA.

Erickson, R.J., 2003. Teenage Robbers: How and Why They Rob. Athena Research Corporation, San Diego, CA.

Erickson, R.J., Erickson, S.J., 2014. Target selection by criminal groups and gangs. In: Morewitz, S.J., Goldstein, M.L. (Eds.), Handbook of Forensic Sociology and Psychology. Springer, New York, NY, pp. 87–102.

Esper, D.A., Keating, G.C., 2006. Abusing duty. South. Calif. Law Rev. 79, 265–328.

Faigman, D.L., Monahan, J., 2005. Psychological evidence at the dawn of the law's scientific age. Annu. Rev. Psychol. 56, 631–659.

Faigman, D.L., Monahan, J., Slobogin, C., 2014. Group to individual (G2i) inference in scientific expert testimony. Univ. Chicago Law Rev. 81 (2), 417–480.

Farberman, H.A., 1975. A criminogenic market structure: the automobile industry. Sociol. Q. 18 (4), 438–457.

Farnworth, M., Thornberry, T., Krohn, M., Lizotte, A., 1994. Measurement in the study of class and delinquency. J. Res. Crime Delinq. 31 (1), 32–61.

Faulkner, K.A., Landsittel, D.P., Hendricks, S.A., 2001. Robbery characteristics and employee injuries in convenience stores. Am. J. Ind. Med. 40 (6), 703–709.

Fay, J., 2002. Contemporary Security Management. Butterworth-Heinemann, Boston, MA.

Fazel, S., Seewald, K., 2012. Severe mental illness in 33,588 prisoners worldwide: systematic review and meta-regression analysis. Br. J. Psychiatry 200 (5), 364–373.

Fazel, S., Cartwright, J., Norman-Nott, A., Hawton, K., 2008. Suicide in prisoners: a systematic review of risk factors. J. Clin. Psychiat. 69 (11), 1721–1731.

Federal Bureau of Investigation (FBI), 2018a. Active Shooter Resources. Office of Partner Engagement, Department of Justice, Washington, DC. Available from: https://www.fbi.gov/about/partnerships/office-of-partnerengagement/active-shooter-resources (Accessed 31 May 2018).

Federal Bureau of Investigation (FBI), 2018b. National Incident-Based Reporting System (NIBRS). Federal Bureau of Investigation (FBI). Criminal Justice Information Services (CFIS). https://www.fbi.gov/services/cjis/ucr/nibrs (Accessed 4 January 2019).

Feehan, J.G., Keller, B.W., 2013. Corporate liability for criminal acts of third parties. In: Heyl, Royster, Voelker & Allen, 28th Annual Claims Handling Seminar, Stay One Step Ahead, May 22, 2013, Bloomington, IL.

Feigenson, N., 2000. Legal Blame: How Jurors Think and Talk About Accidents. American Psychological Association, Washington, DC.

Felson, M., 1987. Routine activities and crime prevention in the developing metropolis. Criminology 25 (4), 911–932.

Felson, M., 1994. Crime and Everyday Life. Pine Forge Press, Thousand Oaks, CA.

Felson, M., 1995. Those who discourage crime. In: Eck, J.E., Weisburd, D. (Eds.), Crime and Place, vol. 4, Criminal Justice Press, Monsey, NY, pp. 53–66.

Felson, M., 2002. Crime and Everyday Life, second ed. Sage, Thousand Oaks, CA.

Felson, M., 2006. Crime and Nature. Sage Publications, London, UK.

Felson, R.B., Staff, J., 2010. The effects of alcohol intoxication on violent versus other offending. Crim. Justice Behav. 37 (12), 1343–1360.

Felson, R.B., Steadman, H.J., 1983. Situational factors in disputes leading to criminal violence. Criminology 21 (1), 59–74.

Felthous, A.R., 1997. Does isolation cause jail suicides? J. Am. Acad. Psychiatry Law 25 (3), 285–294.

Fennelly, L., Lombardi, J., 1997. Spotlight on Security for Real Estate Managers. Institute for Real Estate Management, Chicago, IL.

Field, D., 2010. The nature and role of expert forensic testimony. In: Petherick, W.A., Turvey, B.E., Ferguson, C.E. (Eds.), Forensic Criminology. Elsevier Academic Press, Burlington, MA (Chapter 17).

Finch, B., 2017. If It Happens Here: Facing Post-Terror Attack Litigation. Law 360. June 7, 2017.

Findley, K.A., 2017. The federal role in the innocence movement in America. J. Contemp. Crim. Justice 33 (1), 61–81.

Findley, K., Scott, M., 2006. The multiple dimensions of tunnel vision in criminal cases. Wisc. L. Rev. 2, 291–398.

Fine, G., 2009. Does rumor lie? In: Harrington, B. (Ed.), Deception: From Ancient Empires to Internet Dating. Stanford University Press, Stanford, CA, pp. 183–200.

Finkelhor, D., Asdigian, N.L., 1996. Risk factors for youth victimization beyond a lifestyle/routine activities theory approach. Violence Vict. 11, 3–19.

Fisher, B.S., Nasar, J.L., 1992. Fear of crime in relation to three exterior site features: prospect, refuge, and escape. Environ. Behav. 24 (1), 35–65.

Fisher, B.S., Sloan, J.J., Cullen, F.T., Lu, C., 1998. Crime in the ivory tower: the level and sources of student victimization. Criminology 36 (3), 671–710.

Fiske, S.T., Bersoff, D.N., Borgida, E., Deaux, K., Heilman, M.E., 1991. Social science research on trial: use of sex stereotyping research in *price waterhouse v. Hopkins*. Am. Psychol. 46 (10), 1049–1060.

Flanagan, N., Flanagan, T., 2001. Correctional nurses' perceptions of their role, training requirements, and prisoner health care needs. J. Correctional Health Care 8 (1), 75–76.

Fligstein, N., Roehrkasse, A.F., 2016. The causes of fraud in the financial crisis of 2007 to 2009: evidence from the mortgage-backed securities industry. Am. Sociol. Rev. 81 (4), 617–643.

Follman, M., Aronsen, G., Pan, D. 2018. US mass shootings, 1982–2018: data from Mother Jones' investigation. Mother Jones. Available from: https://www.motherjones.com/politics/2012/12/mass-shootings-mother-jones-full-data/ (Accessed 4 July 2018).

Foote, W.E., Lareau, C.R., 2013. Psychological evaluation of emotional damages in tort cases. In: Otto, R.K., Weiner, I.B. (Eds.), Handbook of Psychology: Forensic Psychology, second ed. John Wiley and Sons, Hoboken, NJ, pp. 172–200.

Ford, R.H., 2011. Negligent security: when is crime your problem? In: Premises and Security Liability Section Federation of Defense and Corporate Counsel. FDCC Winter Meeting, Hyatt Grand Champions Resort, Indian Wells, CA, February 26–March 5.

Forst, B., 2004. Errors of Justice. Cambridge University Press, Cambridge, UK.

Forst, B., 2010. Managing miscarriages of justice from victimization to reintegration. Albany L. Rev. 74 (3), 1209–1275.

Forsyth, C.J., 2014. The work of the sociologist as mitigation expert in cases of violent crime. In: Morewitz, S.J., Goldstein, M.L. (Eds.), Handbook of Forensic Sociology and Psychology. Springer, New York, NY, pp. 21–27.

Forsyth, C.J., 2017. The sociologist as story teller: the broken foster care system used as mitigation at criminal trial. Am. J. Crim. Justice 42 (1), 134–147.

Fox, J.A., DeLateur, M.J., 2014. Mass shootings in America: moving beyond Newtown. Homicide Stud. 18 (1), 125–145.

Fox, J., Levin, J., 2007. The Will to Kill: Making Sense of Senseless Murder, third ed. Allyn and Bacon, Boston, MA.

Fox, K.A., Nobles, M.R., Piquero, A.R., 2009. Gender, crime victimization and fear of crime. Secur. J. 22 (1), 24–39.

Fox, J.A., Levin, J., Fridel, E.E., 2016. Extreme Killing: Understanding Serial and Mass Murder. Sage Publications, Thousand Oaks, CA.

Fradella, H.F., et al., 2003. The impact of Daubert on the admissibility of behavioral science testimony. Pepperdine Law Rev. 30, 403–444.

Frederico, D.R., Weiner, R.A., 2000. Owning daubert: challenging expert testimony as a defense strategy. For the Defense 42 (11), 12–13, 47–48.

French, G., 1997. Government-Assisted Housing: Professional Strategies for Site Managers. Institute of Real Estate Management, Chicago, IL.

Fuller, S.S., 2013. The Trillion Dollar Apartment Industry: How the Apartment Industry and its 35 Million Residents Drove a Trillion Dollar Contribution to The National Economy. Analysis by National Multi Housing Council and National Apartment Association. Available from: https://www.nmhc.org/uploadedFiles/Articles/Research/FullerReportFinal.pdf (Accessed 4 December 2017).

Fyfe, J., 1988. Police use of deadly force: research and reform. Justice Q. 5, 165–205.

Gabbidon, S., 2003. Racial profiling by store clerks and security personnel in retail establishments. J. Contemp. Crim. Justice 19 (3), 345–364.

Gabor, T., 1981. The crime displacement hypothesis: an empirical examination. Crime Delinq. 27, 390–404.

Gabor, T., 1986. The Prediction of Criminal Behavior. University of Toronto Press, Toronto, CA.

Gaines, L.K., Kappeler, V.E., 2014. Policing in America. Routledge, New York, NY.

Gale Encyclopedia of Everyday Law, 2013. Hotel liability. In: Gale Encyclopedia of Everyday Law, third ed. Farmington, Gale.

Galster, G., Pettit, K., Santiago, A., Tatian, P., 2002. The impact of supportive housing on neighborhood crime rates. J. Urban Aff. 24 (3), 289–315.

Garrett, B., 2011a. Convicting the Innocent. Harvard University Press, Harvard, CT.

Garrett, L.H., 2011b. Sexual assault in the workplace. AAOHN J. 59 (1), 15–22.

Garrioch, L., Brimacombe, C.E., 2001. Lineup administrators' expectations: their impact on eyewitness confidence. Law Hum. Behav. 253, 299–315.

Geller, W., Toch, H., 1995. And Justice for All: Understanding and Controlling Police Abuse of Force. Police Executive Research Forum, Washington, DC.

Gerson, P.M., Schwartz, E.S., 2002. When Negligence Leads to Crime: Many Courts Have Expanded the Potential Liability of Property Owners, Possessors, and Managers for Negligent Security. Thorough Cases Analysis Means Rounding Up the Usual Suspects, Trial, December 2002.

Giannelli, P.C., 2017. Forensic Science *Daubert's* Failure. Case Western Reserve Law Review, Case Legal Studies Research Paper No. 2017-16. Available at: SSRN: https://ssrn.com/abstract=3031227.

Gilbert, J., 1986. Criminal Investigation, second ed. Charles E. Merrill Publishing Company, Columbus, OH.

Gilbert, N., 1997. Advocacy research and social policy. Crime Justice 22, 101–148.

Gill, M., Bryan, J., Allen, J., 2007. Public perceptions of CCTV in residential areas: "it is not as good as we thought it would be". Int. Crim. Justice Rev. 17 (4), 304–324.

Gillespie, T., Hart, D., Boren, J., 1998. Police Use of Force. Varro Press, Kansas City, MO.

Gilliam Jr., F.D., Iyengar, S., 2000. Prime suspects: the influence of local television news on the viewing public. Am. J. Political Sci. 44 (3), 560–573.

Girod, R.J., 2014. Logical Investigative Methods: Critical Thinking and Reasoning for Successful Investigations. CRC Press, Boca Raton, FL.

Glesner, B.A., 1992. Landlords as cops: tort, nuisance and forfeiture standards imposing liability on landlords for crime on the premises. Case West. Reserv. Law Rev. 42, 679–791.

Goffman, E., 1961. Asylums: Essays on the Social Situation of Mental Patients and Other Inmates. Anchor Books, New York, NY.

Goffman, E., 1979. Relations in Public: Micro Studies of the Public Order. Harper & Row, New York, NY.

Goldstein, P.J., 1985. The drugs/violence nexus: a tripartite conceptual framework. J. Drug Issues 15 (4), 493–506.

Gotham, K.F., 2000. Urban space, restrictive covenants and the origins of racial residential segregation in a US city, 1900–50. Int. J. Urban Reg. Res. 24 (3), 616–633.

Gotham, K.F., 2014. Race, Real Estate, and Uneven Development: The Kansas City Experience, 1900–2010, second ed. State University of New York (SUNY) Press, Albany, NY.

Gottfredson, D.C., Wilson, D.B., Najaka, S.S., 2002. School-based crime prevention. In: Sherman, L., Farrington, D., Welsh, B., Mackenzie, D.L. (Eds.), Evidence-Based Crime Prevention. Routledge, New York, NY, pp. 56–164.

Gould, B., 2006. Open to all? Regulating open street CCTV and the case for "symmetrical surveillance". Crim. Justice Ethics 25 (1), 3–17.

Gould, J.B., Leo, R.A., 2010. One hundred years later: wrongful convictions after a century of research. J. Crim. L. Criminol. 100 (3), 825–868.

Gould, J., Martindale, A., 2013. Child custody evaluations: current literature and practical applications. In: Otto, R.K., Weiner, I.B. (Eds.), Handbook of Psychology: Forensic Psychology, second ed. John Wiley and Sons, Hoboken, NJ, pp. 101–138.

Gould, E.D., Weinberg, B.A., Mustard, D.B., 2002. Crime rates and local labor market opportunities in the United States: 1977–1997. Rev. Econ. Stat. 84 (1), 45–61.

Gould, J.B., Carrano, J., Leo, R., Young, J., 2013. Predicting Erroneous Convictions: A Social Science Approach to Miscarriages of Justice, Final Technical Report, NCJ 241839. U.S. Department of Justice, Office of Justice Programs, National Institute of Justice, Washington, DC.

Graham, K., 1999. Safer Bars: Assessing and Reducing Risks of Violence. Center for Addiction and Mental Health, Toronto, ON.

Graham, K., Homel, R., 2008. Raising the Bar: Preventing Aggression in and Around Bars, Pubs and Clubs. Willan Publishing, Portland, OR.

Graham, K., La Rocque, L., Yetman, R., Ross, T.J., Guistra, E., 1980. Aggression and barroom environments. J. Stud. Alcohol 41 (3), 277–292.

Graham, K., Schmidt, G., Gillis, K., 1996. Circumstances when drinking leads to aggression: an overview of research findings. Contemp. Drug Probl. 23 (3), 493–557.

Graham, K., Bernards, S., Osgood, D.W., Homel, R., Purcell, J., 2005. Guardians and handlers: the role of bar staff in preventing and managing aggression. Addiction 100 (6), 755–766.

Graham, K., Bernards, S., Osgood, D., Wells, S., 2006. Bad nights or bad bars? Multilevel analysis of environmental predictors of aggression in late-night, large-capacity bars and clubs. Addiction 101 (11), 1569–1580.

Granovetter, M., 1985. Economic action and social structure: the problem of embeddedness. Am. J. Sociol. 91 (3), 481–510.

Greathouse, S.M., Kovera, M.B., 2009. Instruction bias and lineup presentation moderate the effects of administrator knowledge on eyewitness identification. Law Hum. Behav. 33 (1), 70–82.

Greenberg, S.A., 2003. Personal injury examinations in torts for emotional distress. In: Goldstein, A.M. (Ed.), Handbook of Psychology, vol. 11: Forensic Psychology. John Wiley & Sons, Inc., New York, NY.

Greene, E., Heilbrun, K., 2014. Psychology and the Legal System. Wadsworth, New York, NY.

Greenfield, L., 1998. Alcohol and Crime. U.S. Department of Justice, Washington, DC.

Griffiths, E., Tita, G., 2009. Homicide in and around public housing: is public housing a hotbed, a magnet, or a generator of violence for the surrounding community? Soc. Probl. 56 (3), 474–493.

Griswold, R., 2001. Property Management for Dummies. Hungry Minds, Inc., New York, NY.

Gross, S.R., 2008. Convicting the innocent. Annu. Rev. L. S.S. 4, 173–192.

Gross, S.R., O'Brien, B., 2008. Frequency and predictors of false conviction: why we know so little, and new data on capital cases. J. Empir. Leg. Stud. 5 (4), 927–962.

Gutmacher, N., 2016. Are your clients exposed to premises liability for third-party criminal acts? A top-10 list to reduce risks. Probate Property Mag. 30(5).

Haack, S., 2009. Irreconcilable differences? The troubled marriage of science and law. Law Contemp. Probl. 72 (1), 1–23.

Hamm, M.S., 2007. Terrorism as Crime: From Oklahoma City to Al-Qaeda and Beyond. New York University (NYU) Press, New York, NY.

Hannah, M., Bichler, G., Welter, J., 2007. Fraudulent online hotel booking. FBI Law Enforcement Bull. 76 (5), 1–8.

Hargrave, G., 2001. Risk assessment of workplace violence: ethical and procedural issues in evaluating employees. J. Threat. Assess. 1 (2001), 1–20.

Harned, M.S., Ormerod, A.J., Palmieri, P.A., Collinsworth, L.L., Reed, M., 2002. Sexual assault and other types of sexual harassment by workplace personnel: a comparison of antecedents and consequences. J. Occup. Health Psychol. 7 (2), 174–188.

Harrell, E., 2011. Workplace Violence 1993–2009, National Crime Victimization Survey and the Census of Fatal Occupational Injuries, Special Report. U.S. Department of Justice, Office of Justice Programs, Bureau of Justice Statistics, Washington, DC. Available from: www.bjs.gov/content/pub/pdf/wv09.pdf (Accessed 7 September 2018).

Harries, K., 1990. Geographic Factors in Policing. Police Executive Research Forum, Washington, DC.

Harrington, B., 2012. The sociology of financial fraud. In: Cetina, K.K., Preda, A. (Eds.), The Oxford Handbook of the Sociology of Finance. Oxford University Press, Oxford, UK, pp. 393–410.

Harris, J.A., 2002. Finding a remedy for renters. Trial 38 (13), 38–43.

Hart, T.C., Miethe, T.D., 2014. Street robbery and public bus stops: a case study of activity nodes and situational risk. Secur. J. 272, 180–193.

Hart, S.D., Storey, J.E., 2013. Clinical and forensic issues in the assessment of psychopathy. In: Otto, R.K., Weiner, I.B. (Eds.), Handbook of Psychology: Forensic Psychology, second ed. John Wiley and Sons, Hoboken, NJ, pp. 556–578.

Hartley, E., Swanson, G. (Eds.), 1952. Readings in Social Psychology. Holt, Rinehart and Winston, New York, NY, pp. 169–178.

Hartwig, M., et al., 2004. Police officers' lie detection accuracy: interrogating freely versus observing video. Police Q. 7 (4), 429–456.

Haw, R.M., Fisher, R.P., 2004. Effects of administrator-witness contact on eyewitness identification accuracy. J. Appl. Psychol. 89 (6), 1106–1112.

Hayes, L.M., 1983. And darkness closes in… A national study of jail suicides. Crim. Just. Behav. 10 (4), 461–484.

Hayes, L., 2012. National study of jail suicide: 20 years later. J. Correct. Health Care 18 (3), 233–245.

Hazan, F., 1998. Introduction to Criminology, fourth ed. Nelson-Hall, New York, NY.

Hemmens, C., Atherton, E., 1999. Use of Force. American Correctional Association, Lanham, MD.

Hempel, A.G., et al., 2000. A cross-cultural review of sudden mass assault by a single individual in the oriental and occidental cultures. J. Forensic Sci. 45, 582–588.

Henning, K., Stewart, G., 2015. Improving academic-police partnerships: observations and suggestions from a long-term partnership in Portland, Oregon. Trans. Criminol. 9, 17–19.

Hepenstal, S., Johnson, S.D., 2010. The concentration of cash-in-transit robbery. Crime Prevent. Commu. Saf. 12 (4), 263–282.

Hershcovis, M.S., Turner, N., Barling, J., Arnold, K.A., Dupré, K.E., Inness, M., LeBlanc, M.M., Sivanathan, N., 2007. Predicting workplace aggression: a meta-analysis. J. Appl. Psychol. 92 (1), 228–238.

Hewitt, M., 2004. Prove Notice With Standards and Statistics. 40-Dec Trial 26.

Hickox, S.A., 2010. Employer liability of negligent hiring of ex-offenders. Saint Louis Univ. School Law. 55, 1001–1046.

Hipp, J.R., 2007. Income inequality, race, and place: does the distribution of race and class within neighborhoods affect crime rates? Criminology 45 (3), 665–697.

Hipp, J.R., 2016. Collective efficacy: how is it conceptualized, how is it measured, and does it really matter for understanding perceived neighborhood crime and disorder? J. Crim. Just. 46, 32–44.

Hirsch, M.L., Quartaroli, T.A., 2011. If it please the court: sociologist as expert witness in a civil rights case. J. Appl. Soc. Sci. 5 (2), 33–39.

Hochstetler, A., 2001. Opportunities and decisions: interactional dynamics in robbery and burglary groups. Criminology 39 (3), 737–764.

Hochstetler, A., 2002. Sprees and runs: opportunity construction and criminal episodes. Deviant Behav. 23 (1), 45–73.

Holcomb, W., Daniel, A., 1988. Homicide without an apparent motive. Behav. Sci. Law 6 (3), 429–437.

Hollinger, R., Clark, J., 1983. Theft by Employees. Lexington Books, Lexington, MA.

Holmes, R., Holmes, S., 2000. Mass Murder in the United States. Prentice Hall, Upper Saddle River, NY.

Holzman, H.R., Hyatt, R.A., Dempster, J.M., 2001. Patterns of aggravated assault in public housing: mapping the nexus of offense, place, gender, and race. Violence Against Women 7 (6), 662–684.

Homant, R.B., Kennedy, D.B., 1997. Foreseeability of crime as a factor in premises liability for negligent security. In: Mattman, J.W., Kaufer, S., Chaney, J. (Eds.), Premises Security and Liability: A Comprehensive Guide From the Experts. vol. 1. Workplace Violence Research Institute, Laguna Beach, CA, pp. 1–13 (Chapter 2).

Homant, R., Kennedy, D., 2003. The crisis-prone organization as a factor in workplace aggression. Secur. J. 16 (4), 63–76.

Homburger, T.C., Grant, T.J., 2003. A changing world: a commercial landlord's duty to prevent terrorist attacks in post-September 11th America. John Marshall L. Rev. 36 (3), 669–686.

Homel, R., Clark, J., 1994. The prediction and prevention of violence in pubs and clubs. Crime Prev. Stud. 3 (1), 1–46.

Homel, R., Tomsen, S., Thommeny, J., 1992. Public drinking and violence: not just an alcohol problem. J. Drug Issues 22 (3), 679–697.

Hsieh, C.C., Pugh, M.D., 1993. Poverty, income inequality, and violent crime: a meta-analysis of recent aggregate data studies. Crim. Justice Rev. 18 (2), 182–202.

Huff, C.R., 2002. Wrongful conviction and public policy: the American Society of Criminology 2001 presidential address. Criminology 40 (1), 1–18.

Huff, C.R., Killias, M. (Eds.), 2013. Wrongful Convictions and Miscarriages of Justice: Causes and Remedies in North American and European Criminal Justice Systems. Routledge, New York, NY.

Huff, C.R., Rattner, A., Sagarin, E., 1996. Convicted but Innocent: Wrongful Conviction and Public Policy. Sage Publications, Thousand Oaks, CA.

Hughes, D., 1995. Can the clinician predict suicide? Psychiatr. Serv. 46 (5), 449–451.

Hughes, K., Anderson, Z., Morleo, M., Bellis, M.A., 2008. Alcohol, nightlife and violence: the relative contributions of drinking before and during nights out to negative health and criminal justice outcomes. Addiction 103 (1), 60–65.

Iacono, W.G., Lykken, D.T., Faigman, D.L., Kaye, D.H., Saks, M.J., Sanders, J., 2002. Modern Scientific Evidence: The Law and Science of Expert Testimony. West Publishing Company, New York, NY.

Immergluck, D., 2006. The impact of single-family mortgage foreclosures on neighborhood crime. Hous. Stud. 21 (6), 851–866.

Inbau, F., Reid, J., Buckley, J., Jayne, B., 2001. Criminal Interrogation and Confessions, fourth ed. Aspen Publishers, Inc., Gaithersburg, MD.

Indermaur, D., 1996. Reducing the opportunities for violence in robbery and property crime: the perspectives of offenders and victims. In: Homel, R. (Ed.), The Politics and Practice of Situational Crime Prevention. Willow Tree Press, Monsey, NY, pp. 133–157.

Inness, M., Barling, J., Turner, N., 2005. Understanding supervisor-targeted aggression: a within-person, between-jobs design. J. Appl. Psychol. 90, 731–739.

Innocence Project, 2018. Exonerate the Innocent. Innocence Project. Available from: https://www.innocenceproject.org/exonerate/ (Accessed 4 July 2018).

Institute of Management and Administration (IOMA), 2004. A New Look at How to Prevent Security-Related Lawsuits. IOMA's Security Director's Report, Institute of Management and Administration (IOMA), New York, NY, No. 04–5, 6–7.

Institute of Real Estate Management (IREM), 2014. Best Practices: Real Estate Management Service. Institute of Real Estate Management, Chicago, IL.

International Association of Chiefs of Police (IACP), 2015. Law Enforcement Fire Response: Concepts and Issues Paper. IACP Law Enforcement Policy Center, Alexandria, VA.

International Association of Professional Security Consultants (IAPSC), 2014. Forensic Methodology: Best Practices. IAPSC, San Francisco, CA.

International Council of Shopping Centers (ISCS), 2018. Shopping Center Definitions. International Council of Shopping Centers (ISCS). Available from: https://www.icsc.org/news-and-views/research/shopping-center-definitions (Accessed 15 February 2018).

International Foundation for Protection Officers, (Ed.), 1998. Protection Officer Training Manual, sixth ed. Butterworth-Heinemann, Boston, MA.

Irazola, S., Williamson, E., Stricker, J., Niedzwiecki, E., 2014. Addressing the impact of wrongful convictions on crime victims. NIJ J. 274, 34–38. Available from: http://nij.gov/journals/274/pages/victim-impact-wrongfulconvictions.aspx (Accessed 12 March 2019).

Irwin, J., 1980. Prisons in Turmoil. Little Brown, Boston, MA.

Jackson, K., 1985. Crabgrass Frontier: The Suburbanization of America. Oxford University Press, New York, NY.

Jacobs, J., 1961. The Death and Life of Great American Cities. Vintage, New York, NY.

Jacobs, B.A., 2004. The undeterrable offender and your clients liability. For the Defense 46(4).

Jacobs, B.A., 2005. When is crime foreseeable?'. For the Defense 47 (6), 57–58.

Jacobs, B.A., 2006. Foreseeability and Duty of Care in Third-Party Premises Liability. 35 Brief 54 Winter. 2005–2006.

Jacobs, B.A., 2010. Serendipity in robbery target selection. Br. J. Criminol. 50 (3), 514–529.

Jacobs, B.A., Cherbonneau, M., 2018. Perceived sanction threats and projective risk sensitivity: auto theft, carjacking, and the channeling effect. Justice Q. 35 (2), 191–222.

James, S., Nordby, J. (Eds.), 2003. Forensic Science: An Introduction to Scientific and Investigative Techniques. CRC Press, Boca Raton, FL.

Jarjoura, G.R., Triplett, R.A., Brinker, G.P., 2002. Growing up poor: examining the link between persistent childhood poverty and delinquency. J. Quant. Criminol. 18 (2), 159–187.

Jasanoff, S., 1992. What judges should know about the sociology of science. Jurimetric J. 32, 345–359.

Jasanoff, S., 2002. Science and the statistical victim: modernizing knowledge in breast implant litigation. Soc. Stud. Sci. 32 (1), 37–69.

Jasanoff, S., 2009. Science at the Bar: Law, Science, and Technology in America. Harvard University Press, Cambridge, MA.

Jeffery, C.R., 1971. Crime Prevention through Environmental Design. Sage, Beverly Hills, CA.

Jenkins, P., Kroll-Smith, J.S. (Eds.), 1996. Witnessing for Sociology: Sociologists in Court. Greenwood Publishing Group, New York, NY.

Johnson, R.R., 2017. Show me your hands! Police and public perceptions of violent interpersonal cues. J. Police Crim. Psychol. 32 (4), 289–299.

Johnson, S.D., Bowers, K.J., 2004a. The burglary as clue to the future: the beginnings of prospective hot-spotting. Eur. J. Criminol. 1 (2), 237–255.

Johnson, S.D., Bowers, K.J., 2004b. The stability of space-time clusters of burglary. Br. J. Criminol. 44 (1), 55–65.

Johnson, S.D., Bowers, K.J., Hirschfield, A.F.G., 1997. New insights into the spatial and temporal distribution of repeat victimization. Br. J. Criminol. 37 (2), 224–241.

Kachurik, S., 2013. Police officers killed on duty: a different view. Int. J. Police Sci. Manag. 15 (2), 114–124.

Kaminsky, A., 2008. A Complete Guide to Premises Security Litigation, third ed. American Bar Association Publishing, Chicago, IL.

Karmen, A., 2006. Crime Victims: An Introduction to Victimology, sixth ed. Wadsworth, Belmont, CA.

Kassin, S.M., 2005. On the psychology of confessions: does innocence put innocents at risk? Am. Psychol. 60 (3), 215–228.

Kassin, S.M., 2015. The social psychology of false confessions. Soc. Issues Pol. Rev. 9 (1), 25–51.

Kassin, S., Gudjonsson, G., 2004. The psychology of confessions: a review of the literature and issues. Psychol. Sci. Public Interest 5 (2), 33–67.

Kassin, S.M., Drizin, S.A., Grisso, T., Gudjonsson, G.H., Leo, R.A., Redlich, A.D., 2009. Police-induced confessions: risk factors and recommendations July 15, 2009. Law Hum. Behav., Univ. of San Francisco Law Research Paper No. 2010–13, Available from SSRN: https://ssrn.com/abstract=1483878 (Accessed 12 March 2019).

Kassin, S.M., Dror, I.E., Kukucka, J., 2013. The forensic confirmation bias: problems, perspectives, and proposed solutions. J. Appl. Res. Memory Cognition 2 (1), 42–52.

Keller, K.S., 2004. Securing security expert testimony: overcoming the Daubert challenge to reach the witness stand. Secur. J. 17 (3), 21–29.

Kelley, E., 2009. Practical Apartment Management, sixth ed. Institute of Real Estate Management, Chicago, IL.

Kelling, G., et al., 1974. The Kansas City Preventive Patrol Experiment. Police Foundation, Washington, DC.

Kennedy, D.B., 1990. Facility site selection and analysis through environmental criminology. J. Crim. Just. 18, 239–252.

Kennedy, D.B., 1993. Architectural concerns regarding security and premises liability. J. Archit. Plan. Res. 10 (2), 105–129.

Kennedy, D.B., 2006. Forensic security and the law. In: Gill, M. (Ed.), The Handbook of Security. Palgrave Macmillan, New York, NY, pp. 118–145.

Kennedy, D.B., 2010. Foreword. In: Peterick, W.A., Turvey, B.E., Ferguson, C.E. (Eds.), Forensic Criminology. Elsevier Academic Press, Burlington, MA, pp. xv–xvii.

Kennedy, D.B., 2013. Applications of forensic sociology and criminology to civil litigation. J. Appl. Social Sci. 7 (2), 233–247.

Kennedy, D.B., 2014. Evolving practice parameters of forensic criminology. In: Morewitz, S.J., Goldstein, M.L. (Eds.), Handbook of Forensic Sociology and Psychology. Springer, New York, NY, pp. 1–27.

Kennedy, D.B., July 2015. Wrongful conviction litigation: a criminological perspective. For the Defense (67), 42–43.

Kennedy, D.B., Homant, R.J., 1988. Predicting custodial suicides: problems with the use of profiles. Justice Q. 5 (3), 441–456.

Kennedy, D., Hupp, R., 1998. Apartment security and litigation: key issues. Secur. J. 11 (1), 21–28.

Kennedy, D., Sakis, J., 2008. From crime to tort: criminal acts, civil liability and the behavioral science. In: Canter, D., Zukauskiene, R. (Eds.), Psychology and Law. Ashgate Publishing, Aldershot, UK, pp. 119–142.

Kennedy, D.B., Homant, R.J., Homant, M.R., 2004. Perception of injustice as a determinant of support for workplace aggression. J. Bus. Psychol. 18, 323–336.

King, A.G., Klein, J.S., Mitchell, G., 2012. Effective use and presentation of social science evidence. Emp. Rel. L. J. 37 (4), 3–22.

Kinnaird, B., 2003. Use of Force. Looseleaf Law Publications, Flushing, NY.

Kinney, J.B., Brantingham, P.L., Wuschke, K., Kirk, M.G., Brantingham, P.J., 2008. Crime attractors, generators and detractors: land use and urban crime opportunities. Built Environ. 34 (1), 62–74.

Kirkland, K., 2011. Texas and the restatement third of torts: liability for physical and emotional harm. Texas Bar J. 74, 292–297.

Kittling, N.M., 2010. Negligent hiring and negligent retention: a state by state analysis. In: American Bar Association. 4th Annual Section of Labor and Employment Law Conference. November 6, 2010, Chicago, IL. Fundamentals Track—Statutory Claims: Everything Old is New Again. Available from: https://www.americanbar.org/content/dam/aba/administrative/labor_law/meetings/2010/annualconference/087.authcheck dam.pdf (Accessed 30 March 2018).

Klahm, C.F., Tillyer, R., 2010. Understanding police use of force: a review of the evidence. Southwest J. Crim. Justice 7 (2), 214–239.

Kling, J.R., Liebman, J.B., Katz, L.F., 2005. Bullets don't got no name: consequences of fear in the ghetto. In: Weisner, T.S. (Ed.), Discovering Successful Pathways in Children's Development: Mixed Methods in the Study of Childhood and Family Life. University of Chicago Press, Chicago, IL, pp. 243–281.

Klinger, D., Bridges, G., 1997. Measurement error in calls-for-service as an indicator of crime. Criminology 35, 705–726.

Knoll, J., 2010. Suicide in correctional settings: assessment, prevention, and professional liability. J. Correct. Health Care 16 (3), 188–204.

Kohr, R., 1991. Mastering the challenge of securing a budget motel. Secur. Manag. 33–34, 39–40.

Konvisser, Z.D., Werry, A., 2017. Exoneree engagement in policy reform work: an exploratory study of the innocence movement policy reform process. J. Contemp. Crim. Justice 33 (1), 43–60.

Kovera, M.B., Evelo, A.J., 2017. The case for double-blind lineup administration. Psychol. Public Policy Law 23 (4), 421–437.

Krajicek, D.J., 2015. America's Guilt Mill. The Crime Report. Available from: http://www.thecrimereport.org/news/inside-criminal-justice/2015-02-americas-guilt-mill (Accessed 17 July 2018).

Krivo, L.J., Peterson, R.D., 1996. Extremely disadvantaged neighborhoods and urban crime. Soc. Forces 75 (2), 619–648.

Krouse, W.J., Richardson, D.J., 2015. Mass Murder with Firearms: Incidents and Victims, 1999–2013. Congressional Research Service, Library of Congress, Washington, DC.

Kubrin, C.E., Weitzer, R., 2003. New directions in social disorganization theory. J. Res. Crime Delinq. 40 (4), 374–402.

Kubrin, C.E., Wo, J.C., 2016. Social disorganization theory's greatest challenge: linking structural characteristics to crime in socially disorganized communities. In: Piquero, A.R. (Ed.), The Handbook of Criminological Theory. John Wiley and Sons, New York, NY, pp. 121–136.

Kuhns, J.B., Dolliver, D., Bent, E., Maguire, E.R., 2016. Understanding Firearms Assaults Against Law Enforcement Officers in the United States. Office of Community Oriented Policing Services, US Department of Justice, Washington, DC.

Kukucka, J., Kassin, S.M., Zapf, P.A., Dror, I.E., 2017. Cognitive bias and blindness: a global survey of forensic science examiners. J. Appl. Res. Mem. Cogn. 6 (4), 452–459.

Kurtz, E.M., Koons, B.A., Taylor, R.B., 1998. Land use, physical deterioration, resident-based control, and calls for service on urban streetblocks. Justice Q 15, 121–149.

La Fetra, D.J., 2006. A moving target: property owners' duty to prevent criminal acts on the premises. Whittier L. Rev. 28, 409–462.

La Vigne, N.G., Samantha, S.L., 2011. Evaluation of Cameras to Prevent Crime in Commuter Parking Facilities: A Summary. Justice Policy Center, Urban Institute, Washington, DC.

Lab, S., 2007. Crime Prevention: Approaches, Practices and Evaluations, sixth ed. Anderson Publishing, Cincinnati, OH.

Lamb, H.R., Weinberger, L.E., 2005. The shift of psychiatric inpatient care from hospitals to jails and prisons. J. Am. Acad. Psychiatry Law 33 (4), 529–534.

Lamb, M.E., Sternberg, K.J., Esplin, P.W., Hershkowitz, I., Orbach, Y., Hovav, M., 1997. Criterion-based content analysis: a field validation study. Child Abuse Negl. 21 (3), 255–264.

Lamberg, L., 1996. Don't ignore patients' threats, psychiatrists told. J. Am. Med. Assoc. 275, 1715–1716.

Lambert, M.T., 2002. Seven-year outcomes of patients evaluated for suicidality. Psychiatr. Serv. 53 (1), 92–94.

Landoll, D.J., Landoll, D., 2016. The Security Risk Assessment Handbook: A Complete Guide for Performing Security Risk Assessments, second ed. CRC Press, New York, NY.

Lang, E., et al., 1995. Drinking settings and problems of intoxication. Addict. Res. 3 (2), 141–149.

Lankford, A., 2015. Mass murderers in the United States: predictors of offender deaths. J. Foren. Psychi. Psych. 26 (5), 586–600.

Lankford, A., 2016a. Are America's public mass shooters unique? A comparative analysis of offenders in the United States and other countries. Int. J. Comp. Appl. Crim. Just. 40 (2), 171–183.

Lankford, A., 2016b. Fame-seeking rampage shooters: initial findings and empirical predictions. Aggress. Violent Behav. 27, 122–129.

Large, M.M., 2010. No evidence for improvement in the accuracy of suicide risk assessment. J. Nerv. Ment. Dis. 198 (8), 604.

LeBlanc, M.M., Kelloway, E.K., 2002. Predictors and outcomes of workplace violence and aggression. J. Appl. Psychol. 87 (3), 444–453.

Lee, H., Vaughn, M.S., Lim, H., 2014. The impact of neighborhood crime levels on police use of force: an examination at micro and meso levels. J. Crim. Just. 42 (6), 491–499.

Leesfield, I.H., Peltz, R.D., 2013. Premises Liability: Vacations Gone Wrong. 49-Aug Trial 14.

Leighton, J.E., 2000. Fighting New Defenses in Inadequate Security Cases. 36-Apr Trial 20. April 2000.

Leighton, J.E., 2009. Sex, drugs and violence: inadequate premises security litigation in Florida. In: Daily Business Review Seminar, Miami, FL, October 2009. Available from: https://leightonlaw.com/sex-drugs-violence-publication-nov-2009/ (Accessed 14 December 2017).

Leighton, J.E., 2010. Terrorism as an inadequate security case. In: Paper Presentation at the AAJ Annual Convention. Vancouver, British Columbia, July 2010. Available from: http://leightonlaw.com/wp-content/uploads/files/Terrorism%20as%20an%20Inadequate%20Security%20case%20-%20AAJ%20Vancouver1280876352.pdf (Accessed 8 September 2018).

Leiter, M., Frizzell, C., Harvie, P., Churchill, L., 2001. Abusive interactions and burnout: examining occupation, gender, and the mediating role of community. Psychol. Health 16 (5), 547–563.

Lens, M.C., 2013. Subsidized housing and crime: theory, mechanisms, and evidence. J. Plan. Lit. 28 (4), 352–363.

Leo, R., 2005. Rethinking the study of miscarriages of justice: developing a criminology of wrongful conviction. J. Contemp. Crim. Justice 21 (3), 201–223.

Leo, R., 2008. Police Interrogation and American Justice. Harvard University Press, Cambridge, MA.

Leo, R.A., 2017. The criminology of wrongful conviction: a decade later. J. Contemp. Crim. Justice 33 (1), 82–106.

Leo, R.A., 2018. Police Interrogation and Suspect Confessions. Law Research Paper. No. 2018-09. University of San Francisco School of Law, University of San Francisco, San Francisco, CA.

Leo, R., Gould, J., 2009. Studying wrongful convictions: learning from social science. Ohio State J. Crim. Just. 7 (7), 7–30.

Lersch, K.M., 2004. Space, Time, and Crime. Carolina Academic Press, Durham, NC.

Lester, D., Danto, B., 1993. Suicide Behind Bars: Prediction and Prevention. The Charles Press, Philadelphia, PA.

Levi, M.D., Nussbaum, D.S., Rich, J.B., 2010. Neuropsychological and personality characteristics of predatory, irritable, and nonviolent offenders: support for a typology of criminal human aggression. Crim. Justice Behav. 37 (6), 633–655.

Lewinski, W., Dawn, A., Seefeldt, C.R., Gonin, M., Sargent, S., Dysterheft, J., Thiem, P., 2016. The speed of a prone subject. Law Enforce. Exec. Forum 16 (2016), 70–83.

Lewis, S.K., 2016. The cost of raising a killer-parental liability for the parents of adult mass murderers. Villanova L. Rev. 61.

Lewis, D., Salem, G., 1986. Fear of Crime. Transaction Books, New Brunswick, NJ.

Lies, M.A., 2008. Preventing and Managing Workplace Violence: Legal and Strategic Guidelines. American Bar Association, Chicago, IL.

Lipman, M., McGraw, W.R., 1988. Employee theft: a $40 billion industry. Annals 498 (1988), 51–59.

Lippert, A., Golding, J., Lynch, K., Haak, E., 2018. When a corporation rapes: perceptions of rape in civil court for corporate defendants. Psychol. Crime Law 24 (7), 703–726.

Littler, M., Fastiff, T., 1995. Terror and Violence in the Workplace. M. Lee Smith Publishers & Printers, New York, NY.

Litwack, T., Schlesingerm, L., 1999. Dangerousness risk assessments: research, legal, and clinical considerations. In: Hess, A., Weiner, I. (Eds.), The Handbook of Forensic Psychology, second ed. John Wiley, New York, NY, pp. 171–217.

Loftus, E.F., 2013. 25 Years of eyewitness science … finally pays off. Perspect. Psychol. Sci. 85, 556–557.

Loftus, E.F., et al., 2013. Eyewitness Testimony: Civil and Criminal. Matthew Bender and Co., New York, NY.

Lonsway, K.A., 2005. The use of expert witnesses in cases involving sexual assault. In: Violence Against Women, pp. 2–21. Available from: http://ncdsv.org/images/UseExpertWitnessesSexAssaultCases.pdf (Accessed 24 September 2018).

Lopez, P., 2000. Foreseeable zone of risk: an analysis of Florida's off-premises liability standard. U. Miami L. Rev. 55, 397–417.

Luckenbill, D., 1977. Criminal homicide as a situated transaction. Soc. Probl. 25 (2), 176–186.

Lupária, L. (Ed.), 2015. Understanding Wrongful Conviction: The Protection of the Innocent Across Europe and America. Wolters Kluwer, Alphen aan den Rijn, Netherlands.

Lyman, M., 1993. Criminal Investigation. Prentice Hall, Upper Saddle River, NJ.

Lynch, J.P., Cantor, D., 1992. Ecological and behavioral influences on property victimization at home: implications for opportunity theory. J. Res. Crime Delinq. 29 (3), 335–362.

Lynch, M., Cole, S., 2005. Science and technology studies on trial: dilemmas of expertise. Soc. Stud. Sci. 35 (2), 269–311.

Macdonald, E., 1999. The making of an expert witness: it's definitely in the credentials. Wall Street Journal, February 8, 1999.

Madensen, T.D., 2007. Bar Management and Crime: Toward A Dynamic Theory of Place Management and Crime Hotspots. Doctoral Dissertation, University of Cincinnati, Cincinnati, OH.

Madensen, T., Eck, J., 2008. Violence in bars: exploring the impact of place manager decision-making. Crime Prev. Community Safety 10 (2), 111–125.

Malleson, N., Andresen, M.A., 2016. Exploring the impact of ambient population measures on London crime hotspots. J. Crim. Just. 46, 52–63.

Malpass, R.S., 2006. A policy evaluation of simultaneous and sequential lineups. Psychol. Public Policy Law 12 (4), 394–418.

Mann, R.A., Roberts, B.S., 2015. Business Law and the Regulation of Business. Nelson Education, New York, NY.

Marchione, E., Johnson, S.D., 2013. Spatial, temporal and spatio-temporal patterns of maritime piracy. J. Res. Crime Delinq. 50, 504–524.

Maretta, P., Caplan, J., 2013. Felonious Assault and Injury to Law Enforcement: Epidemiology and Spatial Risk Factors. Rutgers Center on Public Security Policy Brief, Rutgers, The State University of New Jersey, School of Criminal Justice, Newark, NJ, pp. 1–18.

Maris, R., 1992. Forensic suicidology: litigation of suicide cases and equivocal deaths. In: Bongar, B. (Ed.), Suicide: Guidelines for Assessment, Management, and Treatment. Oxford University Press, Oxford, UK, pp. 235–252.

Mark, M., 1999. Social science evidence in the courtroom: Daubert and beyond? Psychol. Public Pol. Law 5, 175–193.

Marlow, C., 2013. Premises Liability: Focus on the Facts. 49-Aug Trial 42.

Mars, G., 1982. Cheats at Work. Unwin Paperbacks, Boston, MA.

Martin, J., 2016. Science, experience, and the law support changing traditional vehicle-stop tactics. Law Enforce. Exec. Forum 16 (1), 58–69.

Martinez, R., Valenzuela, A. (Eds.), 2006. Race, Ethnicity and Violence. New York University Press, New York, NY.

Martinez, N.N., Lee, Y., Eck, J.E., Soo Hyun, O., 2017. Ravenous wolves revisited: a systematic review of offending concentration. Crime Sci. 6 (1), 2–26.

Marzano, L., Hawton, K., Rivlin, A., Fazel, S., 2011. Psychosocial influences on prisoner suicide: a case-control study of near-lethal self-harm in women prisoners. Soc. Sci. Med. 72 (6), 874–883.

Massey, J.L., Krohn, M.D., Bonati, L.M., 1989. Property crime and the routine activities of individuals. J. Res. Crime Delinq. 26 (4), 378–400.

Mayman, D., Guyer, M., 2007. Defendant's constitutional right against forced medication in "Sell" hearings. J. Am. Acad. Psychiatry Law 35 (1), 118–120.

Mazerolle, L., Roehl, J., Kadleck, C., 1998. Controlling social disorder using civil remedies: results from a randomized field experiment in Oakland, California. In: Mazerolle, L., Roehl, J. (Eds.), Civil Remedies and Crime Prevention. In: Crime Prevention Studies, vol. 9. Lynne Rienner Publishers, Boulder, CO, pp. 141–159.

Mazerolle, L.G., Ready, J., Terrill, W., Waring, E., 2000. Problem-oriented policing in public housing: the Jersey City evaluation. Justice Q. 17 (1), 129–158.

McAllister, B., 2015. Foot pursuits: keeping officers safe. FBI Law Enforce. Bull. July (2015), 14–17.

McCabe, M., Wauchope, M., 2005. Behavioral characteristics of men accused of rape: evidence for different types of rapists. Arch. Sex. Behav. 34 (2), 241–253.

McCann, J.T., 1998. A conceptual framework for identifying various types of confessions. Behav. Sci. Law 16 (4), 441–453.

McManus, R., O'Toole, S., 1994. The Nightclub, Bar and Restaurant Security Handbook, third ed. Locksley Publishing, Swampscott, MA.

McMurtrie, J., 2005. The role of the social sciences in preventing wrongful convictions. Am. Crim. L. Rev. 42 (4), 1271–1288.

McNeeley, S., 2015. Lifestyle-routine activities and crime events. J. Contemp. Crim. Justice 31 (1), 30–52.

McNulty, T.L., Holloway, S.R., 2000. Race, crime, and public housing in Atlanta: testing a conditional effect hypothesis. Soc. Forces 79 (2), 707–729.

Mecklenburg, S.H., Bailey, P.J., Larson, M.R., 2008. The Illinois field study: a significant contribution to understanding real world eyewitness identification issues. Law Hum. Behav. 32 (1), 22–27.

Medwed, D.S., 2008. Innocentrism. Univ. Ill. L. Rev. 5, 1549–1572.

Medwed, D.S. (Ed.), 2017. Wrongful Convictions and the DNA Revolution: Twenty-Five Years of Freeing the Innocent. Cambridge University Press, Cambridge, MA.

Menard, A., 2001. Domestic violence and housing. Violence Against Women 7 (6), 707–720.

Merry, S.E., 1981. Defensible space undefended: social factors in crime control through environmental design. Urban Aff. Q. 16 (4), 397–422.

Merton, R., 1968. Social Theory and Social Structure. Free Press, New York, NY.

Merton, R.K., 1973. The Sociology of Science. The University of Chicago Press, Chicago, IL and London, UK.

Michael, K., Ellis, Z., 2003. Avoiding Liability in Premises Security, fifth ed. Strafford Publications, Atlanta, GA.

Miethe, T.D., McDowall, D., 1993. Contextual effects in models of criminal victimization. Soc. Forces 71 (3), 741–759.

Miethe, T.D., Meier, R.F., 1990. Opportunity, choice, and criminal victimization: a test of a theoretical model. J. Res. Crime Delinq. 27 (3), 243–266.

Miller, W., 1958. Lower class culture as a generating milieu of gang delinquency. J. Soc. Issues 14 (3), 5–19.

Miller, S.G., 1988. Protecting Restaurant Profits: Managing Security. Lebhar Friedman Books, New York, NY.

Miller, J., 1998. Up it up: gender and the accomplishment of street robbery. Criminology 36, 37–66.

Miller, L., 2015. Why cops kill: the psychology of police deadly force encounters. Aggress. Violent Behav. 22, 97–111.

Mills, C.W., 1959. The Sociological Imagination. Oxford University Press, New York, NY.

Mitchell, G., Walker, L., Monahan, J., 2010. Beyond context: social facts as case-specific evidence. Emory L. J. 60, 1109–1155.

Mitchell, G., Monahan, J., Walker, L., 2011. The ASA's missed opportunity to promote sound science in court. Sociol. Methods Res. 40 (4), 605–620.

Monahan, J., 1981. Predicting Violent Behavior: An Assessment of Clinical Techniques. Sage, Beverly Hills, CA.

Monahan, J., 2006. A jurisprudence of risk assessment: forecasting harm among prisoners, predators, and patients. Virginia L. Rev. 92, 391–435.

Monahan, J., Walker, L., 2011. Twenty-five years of social science in law. Law Hum. Behav. 35, 72–82.

Monahan, J., Walker, L., 2014. Social Science in Law: Cases and Materials, eighth ed. Foundation Press, New York, NY.

Monahan, J., Walker, L., Mitchell, G., 2008. Contextual evidence of gender discrimination: the ascendance of "Social Frameworks." Va. L. Rev. 94 (7), 1715–1749.

Monahan, J., Walker, L., Mitchell, G., 2009. The limits of social framework evidence. Law Probab. Risk 8 (4), 307–321.

Moore, M.M., 1984. The landlord's liability to his tenants for injuries criminally inflicted by third persons. Akron L. Rev. 17 (3), 395–411.

Moore, H.A., Friedman, J., 1993. Courtroom observation and applied litigation research: a case history of jury decision making. Clin. Sociol. Rev. 11 (1).

Morenoff, J.D., Sampson, R.J., Raudenbush, S.W., 2001. Neighborhood inequality, collective efficacy, and the spatial dynamics of urban violence. Criminology 39 (3), 517–559.

Morewitz, S., Goldstein, M. (Eds.), 2014. Handbook of Forensic Sociology and Psychology. Springer, New York, NY.

Morgenstern, M., 2017. Daubert V. Frye—A State-By-State Comparison. Expert Institute. Available from: https://www.theexpertinstitute.com/daubert-v-frye-a-state-by-state-comparison/ (Accessed 20 July 2017).

Morris, N., Miller, M., 1987. Predictions of Dangerousness in the Criminal Law. National Institute of Justice, Washington, DC, pp. 1–8. Research in Brief.

Mostafa, C., 2006. The implied warranty of habitability, foreseeability, and landlord liability for third-party criminal acts against tenants. U. Calif. Los Angeles Law Rev. 54, 971–997.

Mulkey, L.M., 2009. The sociologist as expert witness: a resource for resolving injustice in the case of personal injury. J. Appl. Soc. Sci. 3 (1), 27–35.

Murphy, G.E., 1984. The prediction of suicide: why is it so difficult? Am. J. Psychother. 38 (3), 341–349.

Murray, C., 1983. The physical environment and community control of crime. In: Wilson, J. (Ed.), Crime and Public Policy. ICS Press, Washington, DC, pp. 107–122.

Musheno, M.C., Levine, J.P., Palumbo, D.J., 1978. Television surveillance and crime prevention: evaluating an attempt to create defensible space in public housing. Soc. Sci. Q. 58 (4), 647–656.

Mustaine, E.E., Tewksbury, R., 1998. Predicting risks of larceny theft victimization: a routine activity analysis using refined lifestyle measures. Criminology 36 (4), 829–858.

Nash, R., Bouchard, M., Malm, A., 2013. Investing in people: the role of social networks in the diffusion of a large-scale fraud. Soc. Netw. 35 (4), 686–698.

Natarajan, M. (Ed.), 2017. Crime Opportunity Theories: Routine Activity, Rational Choice and Their Variants. Routledge, New York, NY.

National Academy of Sciences, 2009. Strengthening Forensic Science in the United States: A Path Forward. National Academies Press, Washington, DC.

National Center for Victims of Crime, 2018. Civil justice for victims of crime any crime victim may be able to file a civil lawsuit against a perpetrator or other responsible party. Available from: http://victimsofcrime.org/help-for-crime-victims/get-help-bulletins-for-crime-victims/civil-justice-for-victims-of-crime (Accessed 24 September 2018).

National Commission on Forensic Science, 2015. Ensuring that forensic analysis is based upon task-relevant information. Available from: https://www.justice.gov/ncfs/file/818196/download.

National Fire Prevention Association (NFPA), 2006. Guide for Premises Security. National Fire Prevention Association, Quincy, MA.

National Fire Protection Association (NFPA), 2018. NFPA 730: Guide for Premises Security. National Fire Protection Association, Washington, DC.

National Institute of Justice (NIJ), 1999. Eyewitness Evidence: A Guide for Law Enforcement NIJ Guide. National Institute of Justice. Available from: https://www.ncjrs.gov/pdffiles1/nij/178240.pdf (Accessed 2 June 2018).

National Institute of Justice, 2011. What is translational criminology? NIJ J. 268, Available from: https://www.nij.gov/journals/268/Pages/criminology.aspx (Accessed 26 August 2018).

National Registry of Exonerations [NRE], 2016. Exonerations in 2015. The National Registry of Exonerations. University of Michigan Law School, Ann Arbor, MI. Available from: http://www.law.umich.edu/special/exoneration/Documents/Exonerations_in_2015.pdf (Accessed 17 July 2018).

National Research Council, 2009. Strengthening Forensic Science in the United States: A Path Forward. National Academies Press, Washington, DC.

National Research Council, 2014. Identifying the Culprit: Assessing Eyewitness Identification. The National Academies Press, Washington, DC. Available from: https://www.nap.edu/catalog/18891/identifying-the-culprit-assessing-eyewitness-identification (Accessed 2 June 2018).

National Restaurant Association, 1993. Food Service Security: Manager Program. Educational Foundation of the National Restaurant Association, Chicago, IL.

Nelson, T., Weschler, H., 2001. An introduction to spectator aggression. In: Wann, D. et al. (Ed.), Sport Fans: The Psychology and Social Impact of Spectators. Routledge, New York, NY.

Nelson, T., Weschler, H., 2003. School spirits: alcohol and collegiate sports fans. Addict. Behav. 28 (1), 1–11.

Nettler, G., 1989. Criminology Lessons. Anderson, Cincinnati, OH.

Newland, L., 1997. Hotel Protection Management Spokane. TNZ Publishers, New York, NY.

Newman, O., 1973. Defensible Space: Crime Prevention Through Urban Design. Macmillan, New York, NY.

Newman, O., 1995. Defensible space: a new physical planning tool for urban revitalization. J. Am. Plan. Assoc. 61 (2), 149–155.

Newman, O., 1996. Creating Defensible Space. U.S. Department of Housing and Urban Development, Office of Policy Development and Research, Washington, DC.

Newman, G., Clarke, R.V., 2016. Rational Choice and Situational Crime Prevention: Theoretical Foundations. Routledge, New York, NY.

Newman, K., Fox, C., Roth, W., Mehta, J., Harding, D., 2004. Rampage: The Social Roots of School Shootings. Basic Books, New York, NY.

Nixon, W.B., Kerr, K., 2008. Background Screening and Investigations: Managing Hiring Risk from the HR and Security Perspectives. Butterworth-Heinemann, Boston, MA.

Nolan, J., Connolly, M., 1983. Black's Law Dictionary, Abridged fifth ed. West, St. Paul, MN.

Norris, R.J., 2017. Framing DNA: social movement theory and the foundations of the innocence movement. J. Contemp. Crim. Justice 33 (1), 26–42.

Norris, R.J., Bonventre, C.L., Redlich, A.D., Acker, J.R., Low, C., 2017. Preventing wrongful convictions: an analysis of state investigation reforms. Crim. Justice Policy Rev. 1–30.

O'Toole, M.E., 2000. The School Shooter: A Threat Assessment Perspective. Diane Publishing, Quantico, VA.

Ofshe, R.J., Leo, R.A., 1996. The decision to confess falsely: rational choice and irrational action. Denver U. L. Rev. 74 (4), 979–1122.

Ogletree Jr., C.J., Sarat, A. (Eds.), 2009. When Law Fails: Making Sense of Miscarriages of Justice. New York University Press, New York, NY.

Osborne, J.R., Capellan, J.A., 2017. Examining active shooter events through the rational choice perspective and crime script analysis. Secur. J. 30 (3), 880–902.

Osterburg, J.W., Ward, R.H., 2010. Criminal Investigation: A Method for Reconstructing the Past. Routledge, New York, NY.

Otto, R.K., Goldstein, A.M., 2013. Overview of forensic psychology. In: Weiner, I.B., Otto, R.K. (Eds.), Handbook of Psychology, vol. 11: Forensic Psychology, second ed. John Wiley and Sons, Hoboken, NJ, pp. 3–15.

Otto, R.K., Weiner, I.B. (Eds.), 2013. Handbook of Psychology: Forensic Psychology, second ed. John Wiley and Sons, Hoboken, NJ.

Palermo, G., 1997. The Berserk syndrome: a review of mass murder. Aggress. Violent Behav. 2, 1–8.

Palmer, R.A., 1989. The hospitality customer as crime victim: recent legal research. J. Hosp. Tour. Res. 133, 225–229.

Parillo, V., 1985. Strangers to These Shores, second ed. John Wiley and Sons, New York, NY.

Pastor, J., 2007. Security Law and Methods. Butterworth-Heinemann, Boston, MA.

Patrick, U., Hall, J., 2005. In defense of self and others. Carolina Academic Press, Durhman, NC.

Payne, B.K., 2000. Crime and Elder Abuse. Charles C. Thomas, Springfield, IL.

PBS Frontline, 2012. Real CSI. Season 30. Episode 10. April 17, 2012. Https://Www.Pbs.Org/Wgbh/Frontline/Film/Real-Csi/.

Peguero, A.A., Popp, A.M., 2012. Youth violence at school and the intersection of gender, race, and ethnicity. J. Crim. Just. 40 (1), 1–9.

Peguero, A.A., Popp, A.M., Koo, D.J., 2015. Race, ethnicity, and school-based adolescent victimization. Crime Delinq. 61 (3), 323–349.

Perez, D.A., 2010. The (in)admissibility of false confession expert testimony. Touro L. Rev. 26 (1), 23–74.

Perry, A.M., 2002. Guilt by saturation: media liability for third-party violence and the availability heuristic. Nw. U.L. Rev. 97, 1045.

Petherick, W., Ferguson, C., 2017. Forensic criminology as a research problem: using traditional processes in a forensic context. In: Jacobsen, M.H., Walklate, S. (Eds.), Liquid Criminology: Doing Imaginative Criminological Research. Routledge, New York, NY, pp. 77–90.

Petherick, W., Turvey, B.E., Ferguson, C.E. (Eds.), 2010. Forensic Criminology. Academic Press, Cambridge, MA.

Peyrot, M., Burns, S.L., 2001. Sociologists on trial: theoretical competition and juror reasoning. Am. Sociol. 32 (4), 42–69.

Pezdek, K., Morrow, A., Blandon-Gitlin, I., Goodman, G.S., Quas, J.A., Saywitz, K.J., Bidrose, S., Pipe, M.E., Rogers, M., Brodie, L., 2004. Detecting deception in children: event familiarity affects criterion-based content analysis ratings. J. Appl. Psychol. 89 (1), 119–126.

Phillips, M.R., McAuliff, B.D., Kovera, M.B., Cutler, B.L., 1999. Double-blind photoarray administration as a safeguard against investigator bias. J. Appl. Psychol. 84 (6), 940–951.

Piccarello, C.M., 2005. Terrorism, tourism, and torts: liability in the event of a terrorist attack on a sports or entertainment venue, 12 Jeffrey S. Moorad. Sports L. J. 365 (2005), 365–392.

Piliavin, I., Gartner, R., Thornton, C., Matsueda, R.L., 1986. Crime, deterrence, and rational choice. Am. Sociol. Rev. 51 (1), 101–119.

Pinizzotto, A., Davis, E., 1992. Killed in the Line of Duty: A Study of Selected Felonious Killings of Law Enforcement Officers. U.S. Department of Justice, Washington, DC.

Piquero, A.R. (Ed.), 2015. The Handbook of Criminological Theory. John Wiley and Sons, New York, NY.

Pokorny, A., 1983. Prediction of suicide in psychiatric patients. Arch. Gen. Psychiatry 40 (3), 249–257.

Police Executive Research Forum, 2013. A National Survey of Eyewitness Identification Procedures in Law Enforcement Agencies. Police Executive Research Forum. Available from: http://www.policeforum.org/assets/docs/Free_Online_Documents/Eyewitness_Identification/a%20national%20survey%20of%20eyewitness%20identification%20procedures%20in%20law%20enforcement%20agencies%202013.pdf (Accessed 2 June 2018).

Popkin, S.J., Gwiasda, V.E., Rosenbaum, D.P., Amendolia, J.M., Johnson, W.A., Olson, L.M., 1999. Combating crime in public housing: a qualitative and quantitative longitudinal analysis of the Chicago Housing Authority's anti-drug initiative. Justice Q. 16 (3), 519–557.

Popkin, S.J., Gwiasda, V.E., Olson, L.M., Rosenbaum, D.P., Buron, L., 2000. The Hidden War: Crime and the Tragedy of Public Housing in Chicago. Rutgers University Press, New Brunswick, NJ.

Post, R., Kingsbury, A., Schachtsiek, D., 1991. Security Administration: An Introduction to the Protective Services. Butterworth-Heineman, Boston, MA.

Poyner, B., 1983. Design Against Crime: Beyond Defensible Space. Butterworth, London, UK.

Pratt, T.C., Cullen, F.T., 2005. Assessing macro-level predictors and theories of crime: a meta-analysis. Crime Justice 32, 373–450.

President's Council of Advisors on Science and Technology, 2016. Report to the President, Forensic Science in Criminal Courts: Ensuring Scientific Validity of Feature-Comparison Methods. Executive Office of the President of the United States, President's Council of Advisors on Science and Technology, Washington, DC.

Purcell, B., 2010. Liability for criminal acts of third parties: targets, liability theories and defenses. In: Wisconsin Defense Counsel Summer Conference, 5–6 August 2010, Purcell and Wardrope Chtd. Available from: http://www.wdc-online.org/application/files/4014/8027/4536/Purcell_Outline.pdf (Accessed 9 August 2018).

Purpura, P., 1991. The Security Handbook. Delmar Publishers, New York, NY.

Pyrek, K.M., 2007. Forensic Science Under Siege. Elsevier Academic Press, New York, NY.

Quigley, B., Leonard, K., 2004/2005. Alcohol use and violence among young adults. Alcohol Res. Health 28, 191–194.

Quigley, B.M., Leonard, K.E., Collins, R.L., 2003. Characteristics of violent bars and bar patrons. J. Stud. Alcohol 64 (6), 765–772.

Rajan, A., Haider, D., Hearn, A.S., 2015. What's a shopkeeper to do now? For the Defense, Feb. 1, 2015, 54–58.

Rand, G., 1983. Crime and Environment: An Approach for Los Angeles. University of California, Los Angeles (UCLA). Urban Innovations Group, Los Angeles, CA.

Rand, G., 1984. Crime and environment: a review of the literature and its implications for urban architecture and planning. J. Archit. Plan. Res. 1, 3–19.

Raphael, J., 2001. Public housing and domestic violence. Violence Against Women 7 (6), 699–706.

Ratcliffe, J.H., 2006. Video surveillance of public places. Problem-Oriented Guides, Police Response Guides Ser. In: No. 4, Off. Community Oriented Polic. Serv. US Dep. Justice, Washington, DC.

Ratcliffe, J., 2010. Crime mapping: spatial and temporal challenges. In: Piquero, A., Weisburd, D. (Eds.), Handbook of Quantitative Criminology. Springer, New York, NY, pp. 5–24.

Ratcliffe, J.H., Taniguchi, T., Taylor, R.B., 2009. The crime reduction effects of public CCTV cameras: a multimethod spatial approach. Justice Q. 26 (4), 746–770.

Reccoppa, L., 2009. Mentally ill or malingering? 3 clues cast doubt. Curr. Psychiatr. Ther. 8 (12), 110.

Redlich, A.D., Acker, J.R., Norris, R.J., Bonventre, C.L. (Eds.), 2014. Examining Wrongful Convictions: Stepping Back, Moving Forward. Carolina Academic Press, Durham, NC.

Reed, K., 2005. When elders lose their cents: financial abuse of the elderly. Clin. Geriatr. Med. 21, 365–382.

Reid, R.N., 2005. Facility Manager's Guide to Security: Protecting Your Assets. Fairmont Press, Lilburn, GA.

Research and Forecasts, 1980. The Figgie Report on Fear of Crime: America Afraid. A-T-O, Inc., Willoughby, OH.

Richardson, J.T., Swain, K.G., Codega, J., Bazzell, K., 1987. Forensic sociology: some cautions and recommendations. Am. Sociol. 18 (4), 385–393.

Risinger, D.M., Risinger, L.C., 2011/2012. Innocence is different: taking innocence into account in reforming criminal procedure. NY L. School L. Rev. 56 (3), 869–910.

Ritzer, G., 2005. Enchanting a Disenchanted World: Revolutionizing the Means of Consumption. Pine Forge Press, Thousand Oaks, CA.

Robbennolt, J.K., 2000. Outcome severity and judgments of "Responsibility": a meta-analytic review 1. J. Appl. Soc. Psychol. 30 (12), 2575–2609.

Roberts, J.C., 2007. Barroom aggression in Hoboken, New Jersey: don't blame the bouncers! J. Drug Educ. 37 (4), 429–445.

Roberts, J.C., 2009. Bouncers and barroom aggression: a review of the research. Aggress. Violent Behav. 14 (1), 59–68.

Roberts, P., 2013. Renegotiating forensic cultures: between law, science and criminal justice. Stud. Hist. Philos. Biol. Biomed. Sci. 44 (1), 47–59.

Roland, D.L., 1989. Progress in the victim reform movement: no longer the forgotten victim. Pepperdine L. Rev. 17, 35–58.

Roman, J., Walsh, K., Lachman, P., Yahner, J., 2012. Post-Conviction DNA Testing and Wrongful Conviction. Urban Institute, Justice Policy Center, Washington, DC.

Roncek, D.W., Bell, R., 1981. Bars, blocks, and crimes. J. Environ. Syst. 11 (1), 35–47.

Roncek, D.W., Faggiani, D., 1985. High schools and crime: a replication. Sociol. Q 26 (4), 491–505.

Roncek, D.W., LoBosco, A., 1983. The effect of high schools on crime in their neighborhoods. Social Sci. Q 64 (3), 598–613.

Roncek, D.W., Maier, P.A., 1991. Bars, blocks, and crimes revisited: linking the theory of routine activities to the empiricism of "Hot Spots". Criminology 29 (4), 725–753.

Roncek, D.W., Bell, R., Francik, J.M., 1981. Housing projects and crime: testing a proximity hypothesis. Soc. Probl. 29 (2), 151–166.

Rondeau, M.B., Brantingham, P.L., Brantingham, P.J., 2005. The value of environmental criminology for the design professions of architecture, landscape architecture and planning. J. Archit. Plan. Res. 22, 294–304.

Rooney, M.J., 1995. Liability of a premises owner for the provision of security: the Massachusetts experience. Suffolk U. L. Rev. 29, 51–83.

Rosen, L., 2004. The Safe Hiring Manual. Facts on Demand Press, Tempe, AZ.

Rosenfeld, R., Messner, S.F., 2009. The crime drop in comparative perspective: the impact of the economy and imprisonment on American and European burglary rates. Br. J. Sociol. 60 (3), 445–471.

Ross, D.L., 2000. Emerging trends in police failure to train liability. Policing 23 (2), 169–193.

Ross, D., 2018. Civil Liability in Criminal Justice, seventh ed. Routledge, New York, NY.

Rossmo, D.K., 2008. Criminal Investigative Failures. CRC Press, Boca Raton, FL.

Rossmo, D.K., 2016. Case rethinking: a protocol for reviewing criminal investigations. Police Pract. Res. 17 (3), 212–228.

Roszkowski, M.E., Roszkowski, C.L., 2005. Making sense of respondeat superior: an integrated approach for both negligent and intentional conduct. South. Calif. Rev. Law Wom. Stud. 14 (2), 235–285.

Rothlein, S., 2007. Brady v Maryland: Do You Understand Your Obligations? Legal & Liability Risk Management Institute a Division of the Public Agency Training Council. Available from: www.llrmi.com (web archive link, 09 July 2018) | www.patc.com (Accessed 9 July 2018).

Rottenstein Law Group LLP, 2018. What Is Respondeat at Superior? Available from: http://www.rotlaw.com/legal-library/what-is-respondeat-superior/ (Accessed 27 March 2018).

Rountree, P.W., Land, K.C., Miethe, T.D., 1994. Macro-micro integration in the study of victimization: a hierarchical logistic model analysis across Seattle neighborhoods. Criminology 32 (3), 387–414.

Rublin, A., 2011. The role of social science in judicial decision making: how gay rights advocates can learn from integration and capital punishment case law. Duke J. Gend. Law Policy 19, 179–222.

Rudd, M.D., Berman, A.L., Joiner Jr., T.E., Nock, M.K., Silverman, M.M., Mandrusiak, M., Van Orden, K., Witte, T., 2006. Warning signs for suicide: theory, research, and clinical applications. Suicide Life Threat. Behav. 36 (3), 255–262.

Ryan, J., 2007. The Law and Best Practices of Successful Police Operations. Legal and Liability Risk Management Institute, Indianapolis, IN.

Ryan, J., 2009. The Law and Best Practices of Successful Jail/Corrections Operations. Legal and Liability Risk Management Institute, Indianapolis, IN.

Saferstein, R., 2001. Criminalistics: An Introduction to Forensic Science, seventh ed. Prentice-Hall, Upper Saddle River, NJ.

Saitz, R., Naimi, T.S., 2010. Adolescent alcohol use and violence: are brief interventions the answer? JAMA 304 (5), 575–577.

Sakis, J.R., Kennedy, D.B., 2002. Violence at work. Trial 38 (13), 32–37.

Saks, M.J., Faigman, D.L., 2005. Expert evidence after Daubert. Ann. Rev. Law Soc. Sci. 1, 105–130.

Saks, M.J., Faigman, D.L., 2008. Failed forensics: how forensic science lost its way and how it might yet find it. Ann. Rev. Law Soc. Sci. 4, 149–171.

Salfati, C.G., Canter, D.V., 1999. Differentiating stranger murders: profiling offender characteristics from behavioral styles. Behav. Sci. Law 17 (3), 391–406.

Sampson, R.J., 1985. Race and criminal violence: a demographically disaggregated analysis of urban homicide. Crime Delinq. 31 (1), 47–82.

Sampson, R.J., 1987. Urban black violence: the effect of male joblessness and family disruption. Am. J. Sociol. 93 (2), 348–382.

Sampson, R., 2001. Drug Dealing in Privately Owned Apartment Complexes. U.S. Department of Justice, Office of Community Oriented Policing Services. U.S. Department of Justice, Washington, DC. Available from: https://popcenter.asu.edu/content/drug-dealing-privately-owned-apartment-complexes (Accessed 12 March 2019).

Sampson, R., 2004. Misuse and Abuse of 911. U.S. Department of Justice, Office of Community Oriented Policing Services, Washington, DC.

Sampson, R.J., 2012. Great American City: Chicago and the Enduring Neighborhood Effect. University of Chicago Press, Chicago, IL.

Sampson, R.J., Wooldredge, J.D., 1987. Linking the micro- and macro-level dimensions of lifestyle-routine activities and opportunity models of predatory victimization. J. Quant. Criminol. 3, 371–393.

Sampson, R.J., Raudenbush, S.W., Earls, F., 1997. Neighborhoods and violent crime: a multilevel study of collective efficacy. Science 277 (5328), 918–924.

Santiago, A.M., Galster, G.C., Tatian, P., 2001. Assessing the property value impacts of the dispersed subsidy housing program in Denver. J. Policy Anal. Manage. 20 (1), 65–88.

Savard, D.M., Kennedy, D.B., 2014. Crime and security liability concerns at shopping centers. In: Walby, K., Lippert, R.K. (Eds.), Corporate Security in the 21st Century: Theory and Practice in International Perspective. Palgrave Macmillan, London, UK, pp. 254–275.

Savard, D.M., Kennedy, D.B., 2017. On the applications of forensic criminology. J. Phys. Sec. 10 (1), 8–29.

Schell, B., Lanteigne, N., 2000. Stalking, Harassment and Murder in the Workplace. Quorum Books, New York, NY.

Schlesinger, L.B., 1996. The catathymic crisis, 1912-present: a review and clinical study. Aggress. Violent Behav. 1 (4), 307–316.

Schmerler, K., 2005. Disorder at Budget Motels. U.S. Department of Justice, Washington, DC.

Schneider, R., Kitchen, T., 2007. Crime Prevention and the Built Environment. Routledge, New York, NY.

Schonten, R., Brennan, D., 2016. Targeted violence against law enforcement officers. Behav. Sci. Law 34 (5), 608–621.

Schopp, R.F., Quattrocchi, M.R., 1995. Predicting the present: expert testimony and civil commitment. Behav. Sci. Law 13 (2), 159–181.

Schug, R.A., Fradella, H.F., 2015. Mental Illness and Crime. Sage Publications, Thousand Oaks, CA.

Schulman, T., 2005. Biting the Hand That Feeds: The Employee Theft Epidemic. Infinity Publishing, West Conshohocken, PA.

Schwartz, G.T., 1996. The hidden and fundamental issue of employer vicarious liability. South. Calif. L. Rev. 69.

Schwartz, M.D., Pitts, V.L., 1995. Exploring a feminist routine activities approach to explaining sexual assault. Justice Q. 12 (1), 9–31.

Schwarz, E.D., Kowalski, J.M., McNally, R.J., 1993. Malignant memories: post-traumatic changes in memory in adults after a school shooting. J. Trauma. Stress. 6 (4), 545–553.

Scott, R.C., 1987. Negligent hiring: guilt by association. Pers. Admin., 32–34.

Scott, M., 2001. Street Prostitution. U.S. Department of Justice, Washington, DC.

Scott, L., 2010. It never, ever ends: the psychological impact of wrongful conviction. Am. U. Crim. L. Brief 5 (2), 10–22.

Scott, M., Dedel, K., 2006. Assaults in and Around Bars, second ed. U.S. Department of Justice, Washington, DC.

Scott-Brown, K.C., Cronin, P.D., 2008. Detect the unexpected: a science for surveillance. Policing 31 (3), 395–414.

Seaman, B., 2006. Binge: Campus Life in an Age of Disconnection and Excess. Wiley, New York, NY.

Security Executive Council (SEC), 2018. SEC Security State of the Industry: Could Your Security Program Fall Below Industry Standard of Care Resulting in a Finding of Negligence? Briefing of the SEC Security State of the Industry, December 18, 2018. Available from: https://www.securityexecutivecouncil.com/spotlight/?sid=31112 (Accessed 7 May 2018).

Sennewald, C.A., 2014. From the Files of a Security Expert Witness. Butterworth-Heinemann, Waltham, MA.

Shaw, C.R., Mckay, H.D., 1942. Juvenile Delinquency and Urban Areas. University of Chicago Press, Chicago, IL.

Shearing, C.D., Stenning, P.C., 1983. Private security: implications for social control. Social Problems 30 (5), 493–506.

Sherman, L.W., 1993. Defiance, deterrence, and irrelevance: a theory of the criminal sanction. J. Res. Crime Delinq. 30 (4), 445–473.

Sherman, L.W., 1995. Hot spots of crime and criminal careers of places. Crime and Place 4, 35–52.

Sherman, L.W., Gartin, P.R., Buerger, M.E., 1989. Hot spots of predatory crime: routine activities and the criminology of place. Criminology 27 (1), 27–56.

Shipp, K., 2012. Employment Background Check Guidelines. Business Management Daily, A Division of Capitol Information Group, Inc., McLean, VA.

Sickel, J., 2015. U.S. Hotel Supply Breaks 5 Million-Room Mark. August 13, 2015. Business Traveler News BTN. Available form: http://www.businesstravelnews.com/Strategic-Sourcing/U-S-Hotel-Supply-Breaks-5-Million-Room-Mark (Accessed 10 February 2018).

Sidebottom, A., Wortley, R., 2016. Environmental criminology. In: Piquero, A.R. (Ed.), The Handbook of Criminological Theory. Wiley-Blackwell, New York, NY, pp. 156–181.

Siegel, L., 2004. Criminology, eighth ed. Wadsworth, Belmont, CA.

Silver, J., Simons, A., Craun, S., 2018. A Study of the Pre-Attack Behaviors of Active Shooters in the United States Between 2000–2013. Federal Bureau of Investigation, U.S. Department of Justice, Washington, DC.

Simon, R., 2003. The law and psychiatry. Focus 1 (4), 349–372.

Simon, D., 2012. In Doubt: The Psychology of the Criminal Justice Process. Harvard University Press, Cambridge, MA.

Simpson, S.S., 2010. Making sense of white-collar crime: theory and research. Ohio State J. Crim. Law 8, 481–502.

Skogan, W., 1990. Disorder and Decline: Crime and the Spiral of Decay in American Neighborhoods. University of California Press, Berkeley, CA.

Slobogin, C., 2014. Lessons from inquisitorialism. South. Calif. Law Rev. 87 (3), 699–732.

Smith, M.S., 1996. Crime Prevention through Environmental Design in Parking Facilities. US Department of Justice, Office of Justice Programs, National Institute of Justice, Washington, DC.

Smith, A., 2004. Law, Social Science, and the Criminal Courts. Carolina Academic Press, Durham, NC.

Smith, M.J., Clarke, R.V., 2012. Situational crime prevention: classifying techniques using good enough theory. In: Welsh, B.C., Farrington, D.P. (Eds.), The Oxford Handbook of Crime Prevention. Oxford University Press, New York, NY, pp. 291–315.

Smith, E.G., Kim, H.M., Ganoczy, D., Stano, C., Pfeiffer, P.N., Valenstein, M., 2013. Suicide risk assessment received prior to suicide death by Veterans Health Administration patients with a history of depression. J. Clin. Psychiatry 74 (3), 226–232.

Snook, B., 2004. Individual differences in distance traveled by serial burglars. J. Investig. Psychol. Offender Profiling 1 (1), 53–66.

Snook, B., Cullen, R., 2009. Bounded rationality and criminal investigations: has tunnel vision been wrongfully convicted? In: Rossmo, D. (Ed.), Criminal Investigative Failures. CRC Press, Boca Raton, FL.

Solomon, S.M., Hackett, E.J., 1996. Setting boundaries between science and law: lessons from Daubert v. Merrell Dow Pharmaceuticals, Inc. Sci. Technol. Hum. Values 21 (2), 131–156.

Sorrells, E., 2016. Security Litigation: Best Practices for Managing and Preventing Security-Related Lawsuits. Butterworth-Heinemann, Wadsworth, MA.

Southerland, M., Collins, P., Scarborough, K., 1997. Workplace Violence. Anderson Publishing Company, Cincinnati, OH.

Spalek, B., 2016. Crime Victims: Theory, Policy and Practice. Palgrave Macmillan, London, UK.

Stafford, K.P., Sellbom, M., 2013. Assessment of competence to stand trial. In: Otto, R.K., Weiner, I.B. (Eds.), Handbook of Psychology: Forensic Psychology, second ed. John Wiley and Sons, Hoboken, NJ, pp. 412–439.

Stark, R., 1987. Deviant places: a theory of the ecology of crime. Criminology 25 (4), 893–910.

Stefan, S., 2006. Emergency Department Treatment of the Psychiatric Patient: Policy Issues and Legal Requirements. Oxford University Press, New York, NY.

Steiner, R.L., 2006. Policy oscillation in California's law of premises liability. McGeorge L. Rev. 39, 131–191.

Stephan, C., Stephan, W., 1990. Two Social Psychologies, second ed. Wadsworth, New York, NY.

Stevenson, P., Katz, C., Decker, S., 2013. The foundation of an evidence-based justice system: the need for meaningful academic and applied researcher partnerships. Trans. Criminol. 5, 22–25.

Strauchs, J., 2008. CCTV Panacea or Problem, Security Management. ASIS International, Alexandria, VA.

Stuart, H., 2003. Violence and mental illness: an overview. World Psychiatry 2 (2), 121–124.

Sugahara, T., Sugahara, K., 2014. Preventing workplace violence and litigation through preemployment screening and enforcement of workplace conduct expectations. In: Morewitz, S.J., Goldstein, M. (Eds.), Handbook of Forensic Sociology and Psychology. Springer, New York, NY, pp. 185–199.

Suresh, G., Vito, G.F., 2009. Homicide patterns and public housing: the case of Louisville, KY 1980–2007. Homicide Stud. 13 (4), 411–433.

Sutherland, E.H., 1945. Is "white collar crime" crime? Am. Sociol. Rev. 10 (2), 132–139.

Swanson, J.W., 2011. Explaining rare acts of violence: the limits of evidence from population research. Psychiatr. Serv. 62 (11), 1369–1371.

Sweeney, M.A., 2017. Reasonable response: the Achilles' heel of the seventh circuit's deliberate indifference analysis. Seventh Circuit Rev. 12 (1), 62–91.

Sykes, G., 1966. The Society of Captives. Atheneum, New York, NY.

Talley, L., 2000. Using experts in premises cases. 36-Apr Trial 46. April, 2000.

Tanay, E., 2007. Virginia tech mass murder: a forensic psychiatrist's perspective. J. Am. Acad. Psychiatry Law 35 (2), 152–153.

Tartaro, C., 2015. What is obvious? Federal courts' interpretation of the knowledge requirement in post-*Farmer v. Brennan* Custodial Suicide Cases. Prison J. 95 (1), 23–42.

Taylor, M., Nee, C., 1988. The role of cues in simulated residential burglary. Br. J. Criminol. 28, 396–401.

Taylor-Austin, L., 2014. The role of a gang expert in court. In: Morewitz, S.J., Goldstein, M.L. (Eds.), Handbook of Forensic Sociology and Psychology. Springer, New York, NY, pp. 109–113.

Tenopyr, M., 1999. A scientist-practitioner's viewpoint on the admissibility of behavioral and social scientific information. Psychol. Public Pol. Law 5, 194–202.

Teplin, L., 2000. Keeping the peace: police discretion and mentally ill persons. Nat. Inst. Jus. J. 244 (July), 8–15.

Terr, L.C., 1983. Time sense following psychic trauma: a clinical study of ten adults and twenty children. Am. J. Orthopsychiatry 53 (2), 244–261.

Terrill, W., Reisig, M.D., 2003. Neighborhood context and police use of force. J. Res. Crime Delinq. 40 (3), 291–321.

Texas Apartment Association, 1995. Bluebook: A Crime Awareness Guide for Apartment Owners and Managers. Texas Apartment Association, Austin, TX.

Thacher, D., 2008. The rise of criminal background screening in rental housing. Law Social Inquiry 33 (1), 5–30.

Thornberry, T.P., Christenson, R.L., 1984. Unemployment and criminal involvement. Am. Sociol. Rev. 49 (3), 398–411.

Thornton, J., Peterson, J., 2008. The general assumptions and rationale of forensic identification. In: Faigman, D.L., Kaye, D.H., Saks, M.J., Sanders, J. (Eds.), Modern Scientific Evidence: The Law and Science of Expert Testimony, vol. 4. West/Thomson, St. Paul, MN.

Thornton Jr., W.E., Voigt, L., 1988. Roles and ethics of the practicing criminologist. Clin. Sociol. Rev. 6 (1), 113–133.

Tilley, N., 2013. Handbook of Crime Prevention and Community Safety. Routledge, New York, NY.

Tillman, R., 2009. Making the rules and breaking the rules: the political origins of corporate corruption in the new economy. Crime Law Soc. Chang. 51 (1), 73–86.

Tillyer, M.S., Eck, J.E., 2011. Getting a handle on crime: a further extension of routine activities theory. Secur. J. 24 (2), 179–193.

Toch, H., 1975. Men in Crisis: Human Breakdowns in Prison. Aldine, Chicago, IL.

Topalli, V., Wright, R., 2004. Dubs, dees, beats, and rims: carjacking and urban violence. In: Dabney, D. (Ed.), Criminal Behaviors: A Text Reader. Wadsworth Publishing, Belmont, CA, pp. 149–169.

Torrey, E., 2008. The Insanity Offense: How America's Failure to Treat the Seriously Mentally Ill Endangers Its Citizens. W.W. Norton, New York, NY.

Toseland, R.W., 1982. Fear of crime: who is most vulnerable? J. Crim. Just. 10 (3), 199–209.

Turvey, B., 2008. Criminal Profiling: An Introduction to Behavioral Evidence Analysis, third ed. Elsevier, Boston, MA.

Turvey, B.E., 2013. Forensic Fraud: Evaluating Law Enforcement and Forensic Science Cultures in The Context of Examiner Misconduct. Academic Press, Cambridge, MA.

Turvey, B.E., 2014. Forensic victimology and civil remedy in premises liability cases. In: Turvey, B.E. (Ed.), Forensic Victimology: Examining Violent Crime Victims in Investigative and Legal Contexts, Academic Press, Waltham, MA.

Turvey, B.E., Cooley, C.M., 2014. Miscarriages of Justice: Actual Innocence, Forensic Evidence, and the Law. Academic Press, Cambridge, MA.

Turvey, B.E., Petherick, W.A., 2010. An introduction to forensic criminology. In: Petherick, W., Turvey, B.E., Ferguson, C.E. (Eds.), Forensic Criminology. Elsevier Press, Burlington, MA, pp. 3–49.

Turvey, B.E., Torres, A.N., 2010. Forensic criminology in correctional settings. In: Petherick, W., Turvey, B.E., Ferguson, C.E. (Eds.), Forensic Criminology. Academic Press, New York, NY (Chapter 8).

Twerski, S.J., 2018. Bringing the science of policing to liability for third-party crime at shopping malls. Brooklyn Law School, Legal Studies Paper No. 514, Marquette L. Rev. 101.

Twinam, T., 2017. Danger zone: land use and the geography of neighborhood crime. J. Urban Econ. 100, 104–119.

U.S. Census Bureau, 2017. Geographic Terms and Concepts—Census Tract. U.S. Census Bureau, Washington, DC. https://www.census.gov/geo/reference/gtc/gtc_ct.html (Accessed 5 April 2018).

U.S. Department of Labor, 2011. OSHA issues compliance directive to address workplace violence. Occupational Safety and Health Administration, Office of Communications, September 8, 2011. News Release. Available from: https://www.osha.gov/news/newsreleases/trade/09082011 (Accessed 4 May 2018).

U.S. Department of Labor, 2018. Workplace violence. Occupational Safety and Health Administration (OSHA). Available from: https://www.osha.gov/SLTC/workplaceviolence/ (Accessed 4 May 2018).

U.S. Postal Service Commission on a Safe Secure Workplace, 2000. Report of the United States Postal Service Commission on a Safe and Secure Workplace. National Center on Addiction and Substance Abuse, Columbia University, New York, NY.

Van Soomeren, P., 1989. The physical environment and the reduction of urban insecurity: a general introduction. In: Local Strategies for the Reduction of Urban Insecurity in Europe. Standing Committee of Local and Regional Authorities of Europe, Council of Europe, Brussels, Belgium.

Vellani, K.H., 2001. Applied Crime Analysis. Butterworth-Heinemann, Wadsworth, MA.

Vellani, K.H. (Ed.), 2007. Strategic security management: a risk assessment guide for decision makers. Butterworth-Heinemann, New York, NY.

Vellani, K., 2010. Crime analysis for problem solving security professionals in 25 small steps. Available from: http://www.popcenter.org/library/reading/pdfs/crimeanalysis25steps.pdf (Accessed 12 January 2018).

Vellani, K., Nahoun, J., 2001. Applied Crime Analysis. Butterworth-Heinemann, Boston, MA.

Venkatesh, S.A., 2000. American Project: The Rise and Fall of a Modern Ghetto. Harvard University Press, Cambridge, MA.

Victor, D., 2018. Woman who was raped as a teenager is awarded $1 billion in damages. New York Times. May 23, 2018.

Vizzard, W.J., 2014. The current and future state of gun policy in the United States. J. Crim. L. Criminol. 104, 879.

Voigt, L., Thornton, W., 1996. Sociology and negligent security: premises liability and crime prediction. In: Jenkins, P., Kroll-mith, S. (Eds.), Witnessing for Sociology: Sociology in Court, Praeger, Westport, CT, pp. 167–193.

Vrij, A., 2000. Detecting Lies and Deceits: The Psychology of Lying and the Implications for Professional Practice. John Wiley and Sons, New York, NY.

Wakefield, K., Wann, D., 2006. An examination of dysfunctional sport fans: method, classification and relationships with problem behaviors. J. Leis. Res. 38 (2), 168–186.

Walby, K. (Ed.), 2014. Corporate Security in the 21st Century: Theory and Practice in International Perspective. Springer, New York, NY.

Walker, L., Monahan, J., 1988. Social facts: scientific methodology as legal precedent. Calif. L. Rev. 76, 877–896.

Wallace, E., Diffley, C., 1998. CCTV: Making It Work. Police Scientific Development Branch, Hertfordshire, UK.

Wallace, H., Roberson, C., 1998. Victimology: Legal, Psychological, and Social Perspectives. Allyn and Bacon, Boston, MA.

Walters, G.D., DeLisi, M., 2013. Antisocial cognition and crime continuity: cognitive mediation of the past crime-future crime relationship. J. Crim. Just. 412, 135–140.

Warner, B.G., 1991. Premises liability in Florida after *Holiday Inns, Inc. v, Shelburne-Will Florida* extend a landowner's duty of care beyond the physical boundaries of his property. Nova L. Rev. 16 (1), 597–615.

Warr, M., 1990. Dangerous situations: social context and fear of victimization. Soc. Forces 68 (3), 891–907.

Wassell, J., 2009. Workplace violence intervention effectiveness: a systematic literature review. Saf. Sci. 47, 1049–1055.

Watson, A.C., Corrigan, P.W., Ottati, V., 2004. Police responses to persons with mental illness: does the label matter? J. Am. Acad. Psychiatry Law 32 (4), 378–385.

Wayne, P.B., DeHart, N., 1998. Apartments bait for litigation. J. Prop. Manag. 63 (4), 22–27.

Weber, R.R., 1991. Scope of employment redefined: holding employers vicariously liable for sexual assaults committed by their employees. Minnesota L. Rev. 76, 1513–1514.

Webster, B., Connors, E.F., 1992. The Police, Drugs, and Public Housing. US Department of Justice, Office of Justice Programs, National Institute of Justice, Washington, DC.

Weinstein, J.B., 1999. Expert witness testimony: a trial judge's perspective. Neurol. Clin. 17 (2), 355–362.

Weisburd, D., Bushway, S., Lum, C., Yang, S.M., 2004. Trajectories of crime at places: a longitudinal study of street segments in the city of Seattle. Criminology 42 (2), 283–322.

Weisburd, D., Groff, E.R., Yang, S.M., 2014. Understanding and controlling hot spots of crime: the importance of formal and informal social controls. Prev. Sci. 15 (1), 31–43.

Weisburd, D., Eck, J.E., Braga, A.A., Telep, C.W., Cave, B. (Eds.), 2016. Place Matters: Criminology for the Twenty-First Century. Cambridge University Press, Cambridge, MA.

Wells, G.L., 2014. Eyewitness identification: probative value, criterion shifts, and policy regarding the sequential lineup. Curr. Dir. Psychol. Sci. 23 (1), 11–16.

Wells, G.L., Quinlivan, D.S., 2009. Suggestive eyewitness identification procedures and the Supreme Court's reliability test in light of eyewitness science: 30 years later. Law Hum. Behav. 33 (1), 1–24.

Wells, G.L., Steblay, N.K., Dysart, J.E., 2011. A Test of the Simultaneous vs. Sequential Lineup Methods. American Judicature Society, Des Moines, IA.

Wells, G.L., Steblay, N.K., Dysart, J.E., 2015. Double-blind photo lineups using actual eyewitnesses: an experimental test of a sequential versus simultaneous lineup procedure. Law Hum. Behav. 39 (1), 1–14.

Welsh, B., Farrington, D., 2003. Effects of closed-circuit television on crime. Ann. Am. Acad. Polit. Soc. Sci. 587 (2003), 110–135.

Welsh, B.C., Farrington, D.P., 2009. Public area CCTV and crime prevention: an updated systematic review and meta-analysis. Justice Q 26, 716–745.

Welsh, B.C., Farrington, D.P., 2014. CCTV and crime prevention. In: Bruinsma, G.J.N., Weisburd, D. (Eds.), Encyclopedia of Criminology and Criminal Justice. Springer, New York, NY, pp. 310–319.

Welsh, B.C., Mudge, M.E., Farrington, D.P., 2010. Reconceptualizing public area surveillance and crime prevention: security guards, place managers and defensible space. Sec. J. 23, 299–319.

Welsh, B.C., Farrington, D.P., Taheri, S.A., 2015. Effectiveness and social costs of public area surveillance for crime prevention. Annu. Rev. Law Soc. Sci. 11, 111–130.

Welsh, B.C., Zimmerman, G.M., Zane, S.N., 2018. The centrality of theory in modern day crime prevention: developments, challenges, and opportunities. Justice Q. 35 (1), 139–161.

Westervelt, S.D., Humphrey, J.A. (Eds.), 2001. Wrongly Convicted: Perspectives on Failed Justice. Rutgers University Press, New Brunswick, NJ.

White, G.F., 1990. Neighborhood permeability and burglary rates. Justice Q. 7 (1), 57–67.

White, G.F., Muldoon, C.V., 2015. Convenience stores and routine activities in a summer tourist destination. Crim. Justice Stud. 28 (3), 280–296.

Whitmer, G., 1980. From hospitals to jails: the fate of California's deinstitutionalized mentally ill. Am. J. Orthopsych. 50 (1), 65–75.

Whitten, A.D., Mosley, D.M., 2000. Caught in the crossfire: employers' liability for workplace violence. Mississippi L. J. 70, 505–555.

Wiesel, D., 1990. Tackling Drug Problems in Low-Income Housing. Police Executive Research Forum, Washington, DC.

Wikstrom, P.O.H., 1985. Everyday Violence in Contemporary Sweden: Situational and Ecological Aspects. The National Council for Crime Prevention, Stockholm, Sweden.

Wilber, K., Reynolds, S., 1996. Introducing a framework for defining financial abuse of the elderly. J. Elder Abuse Neglect 8 (1996), 61–81.

Wilcox, P., Cullen, F.T., 2018. Situational opportunity theories of crime. Annu. Rev. Criminol. 1, 123–148.

Wilcox, P., Eck, J.E., 2011. Criminology of the unpopular. Criminol. Public Pol. 102, 473–482.

Wilcox, P., Land, K.C., Hunt, S., 2003a. Criminal Circumstance: A Dynamic Multi-Contextual Criminal Opportunity Theory. Walter de Gruyter, New York, NY.

Wilcox, P., Quisenberry, N., Jones, S., 2003b. The built environment and community crime risk interpretation. J. Res. Crime Delinq. 40 (3), 322–345.

Wilcox, P., Madensen, T.D., Tillyer, M.S., 2007. Guardianship in context: implications for burglary victimization risk and prevention. Criminology 45 (4), 771–803.

Wilcox, P., Tillyer, M.S., Fisher, B.S., 2009. Gendered opportunity? School-based adolescent victimization. J. Res. Crime Delinq. 46 (2), 245–269.

Wiles, P., Costello, A., 2000. The Road to Nowhere: The Evidence for Travelling Criminals. Home Office Research Study 207. Home Office, London. Available from: www.homeoffice.gov.uk.

Wilkins, R., Latimer, C., 2014. Advocacy in an atmosphere of violence. In: The Mississippi Bar Litigation Section E-Newsletter. Summer 2014, https://www.msbar.org/media/2454/litigation-newsletter-summer-2014.pdf.

Williams, A., 2014. Forensic Criminology. Routledge, New York, NY.

Wilson, W.J., 1987. The Truly Disadvantaged: The Inner City, the Underclass and Public Policy. University of Chicago Press, Chicago, IL.

Wilson, J.Q., Kelling, G.L., 1982. Broken windows. Atlantic Monthly 249 (3), 29–38.

Winick, B., 1997. The Right to Refuse Mental Health Treatment. American Psychological Association, Washington, DC.

Wise, R.M., 2005. From Price Waterhouse to Dukes and beyond: bridging the gap between law and social science by improving the admissibility standard for expert testimony. Berkeley J. Emp. Lab. L. 26, 546–581.

Witt, P.H., Conroy, M.A., 2013. Evaluation of sex offenders. In: Roesch, R., Zapf, P.A. (Eds.), Forensic Assessments in Criminal and Civil Law: A Handbook for Lawyers. Oxford University Press, New York, NY, pp. 60–73.

Wivell, M., 2003. Deliver a Daubert-proof expert report. Trial 39 (13), 38–40.

Wogalter, M., Malpass, R., McQuiston, D., 2004. A national survey of U.S. police on preparation and conduct of identification lineups. Psychol. Crime Law 10 (1), 69–82.

Wolfgang, M.E., 1957. Victim precipitated criminal homicide. J. Crim. L. Criminol. Police Sci. 48 (1), 1–11.

Wortley, R., 2001. A classification of techniques for controlling situational precipitators of crime. Secur. J. 14 (4), 63–82.

Wortley, R., 2008. Situational precipitators of crime. In: Wortley, R., Mazerolle, L. (Eds.), Environmental Criminology and Crime Analysis, first ed. Willan Publishing, Cullompton, UK, pp. 48–69.

Wortley, R., 2017. Situational precipitators of crime. In: Wortley, R., Townsley, M. (Eds.), Environmental Criminology and Crime Analysis, second ed. Routledge, New York, NY, pp. 62–86.

Wortley, R., Mazerolle, L., 2008. Environmental Criminology and Crime Analysis. Willan Publishing, New York, NY.

Wortley, R., Townsley, M., 2017. Environmental criminology and crime analysis: situating the theory, analytic approach and application. In: Wortley, R., Townsley, M. (Eds.), Environmental Criminology and Crime Analysis, second ed. Routledge, London, UK, pp. 1–25.

Wright, R., Decker, S., 1997. Armed Robbers in Action Boston. Northeastern University Press, Boston, MA.

Wrightsman, L.S., Fulero, S., 2005. Forensic Psychology, second ed. Thomson and Wadsworth, New York, NY.

Wrightsman, L.S., Kassin, S., 1993. Confessions in the Courtroom. Sage Publications, Newbury Park, CA.

Yearwood, D.L., Koinis, G., 2011. Revisiting property crime and economic conditions. Soc. Sci. J. 48 (1), 145–158.

Yelnosky, M.J., 1986. Comment, business inviters' duty to protect invitees from criminal acts. U. PA. Law Rev. 134 (4), 883–911.

Young, E., 2014. Cause of Action Against Tavern Owners, Restaurants, and Similar Businesses for Injuries Caused to Patrons by the Criminal Acts of Others. Shepard's/McGraw-Hill, West Group, New York, NY.

Zalman, M., 2006. Criminal justice system reform and wrongful conviction: a research agenda. Crim. Justice Policy Rev. 17 (4), 468–492.

Zalman, M., 2010/2011. An integrated justice model of wrongful convictions. Albany L. Rev. 74 (3), 1465–1524.

Zalman, M., 2012. Qualitatively estimating the incidence of wrongful convictions 2012. Crim. L. Bull. 48 (2), 221–279. Available from: https://ssrn.com/abstract=2913631 (Accessed 12 March 2019).

Zalman, M., 2017. Introduction: special issue, the innocence movement and wrongful convictions. J. Contemp. Crim. Justice 33 (1), 4–7.

Zalman, M., Carrano, J., 2013/2014. Sustainability of innocence reform. Albany L. Rev. 77 (3), 955–1003.

Zhang, V., 2011. Throwing the defendant into the snake pit: applying a state-created danger analysis to prosecutorial fabrication of evidence. Boston U. L. Rev. 91 (6), 2131–2167.

Zinober, F.S., 2015. Litigating the negligent security case: who's in control here? Stetson Law Rev 44 (2), 289–333.

Zipf, G.K., 1949. Human Behavior and the Principle of Least Effort. An Introduction to Human Ecology. Addison-Wesley, Cambridge, MA.

Index

Note: Page numbers followed by *f* indicate figures, *t* indicate tables, *b* indicate boxes, and *np* indicate footnotes.